JAMES ROOD ROBERTSON, M.A. Ph.D.
Member of the Filson Club.

FILSON CLUB PUBLICATIONS No. 27

PETITIONS OF THE EARLY INHABITANTS OF KENTUCKY

TO THE

General Assembly of Virginia

1769 to 1792

BY

JAMES ROOD ROBERTSON, M.A.Ph.D.

Member of the American Historical Association, the Filson Club,
the Ohio Valley Historical Society, and the Oregon
Historical Society; Professor of History and
Political Science in Berea College.

Southern Historical Press, Inc.
Greenville, South Carolina

This volume was reproduced from
Personal copies located in the
Publisher's private Library

All rights reserved. No part of this publication may be reproduced,
stored in a retrieval system, transmitted in any form, posted
on to the web in any form or by any means without
the prior written permission of the publisher.

Please direct all correspondence and orders to:

www.southernhistoricalpress.com
or
SOUTHERN HISTORICAL PRESS, Inc.
PO Box 1267
375 West Broad Street
Greenville, SC   29601
southernhistoricalpress@gmail.com

Originally published: Frankfort, KY 1914
New Material Copyright 1981
By: The Rev. Silas Emmett Lucas, Jr.
ISBN #0-89308-228-7
All rights Reserved.
Printed in the United States of America

DEDICATED TO

THE PIONEERS OF KENTUCKY

Men and women whose courage, endurance, and integrity
laid well the foundations of our first commonwealth west of the Alleghany Mountains.

PREFACE

THE petitions here printed are offered as a contribution to the early period of Kentucky history. During a visit of the editor to Richmond, Virginia, in the summer of 1910, they were found in the archives of that State. The archivist had recently segregated them from a large mass of other material and an examination of the contents showed their value as a source of information on the beginnings of Kentucky.

The petitions are printed verbatim, with the thought that they will be more useful and interesting to the student of history in the language of the pioneer inhabitants of our first Commonwealth west of the Alleghany Mountains. The editor has added foot-notes which may help to explain the purpose, the subject-matter, and the effect of the various petitions.

The names attached to the petitions have been separated from them and arranged in alphabetical order, with numbers referring to the petitions on which they appear. This saves considerable space, as many of the names are signed to two or more petitions. It also makes reference to them more easy.

The appearance of the original material from which these petitions were copied may be seen in the facsimile

Preface

of a petition from the settlers of Lincoln County. This is, however, better than the average in form and state of preservation. Many of the petitions are worn, the writing faded, and the style not so good as the illustration given.

The wording of the petitions, though formal, is full of life and spirit, and in some cases reflects quaintness of expression. There is always a respectful deference for the authority of the Commonwealth of Virginia at the same time that freedom of speech is indulged.

The petitions are printed in chronological order rather than topical, with the thought that the development of community life can best be seen in that way. The first petition is dated 1769 and the last 1831. Only two are earlier than 1776 and six later than 1792. Thus they are seen to pertain to the period when Kentucky was a County of Virginia and those of earlier and later date are logically connected with that period. Thus the collection presents a unity that is valuable.

The collection does not include petitions which were sent to the National Government at Philadelphia or New York which have been used extensively in the printed histories of Kentucky, as they have been more accessible than the ones here printed. Nor is the collection entirely complete, as there are some laws, passed by the Assembly of Virginia, evidently based on petitions which have not been found. The collection, however, is essentially complete, and is fully representative of the activities of the pioneer population.

Preface

I desire to express appreciation to the following for assistance rendered me in the preparation of this book: To William G. Frost, President of Berea College, for encouragement and financial aid in gathering the material; to the late Colonel Reuben T. Durrett, formerly President of the Filson Club, for use of his extensive library; to R. C. Ballard Thruston, President of the Sons of the American Revolution, for his cordial interest and support; to the Filson Club and its officers for publication; to Doctor H. R. McIlwain, Librarian of the State Library of Virginia, and Doctor H. J. Eckenrode, Archivist of State Library of Virginia, for courtesies in use of source material in the Virginia archives.

JAMES ROOD ROBERTSON.

Berea College,
   Berea, Kentucky.

CONTENTS

	PAGE
INTRODUCTION	1

PETITION No. 1. Request of the inhabitants east of the Alleghany Mountains for sixty thousand acres of land in the upper valley of the Cumberland River... 35

PETITION No. 2. Request of the inhabitants of Kentucky at Harrodsburg to be taken under the jurisdiction of Virginia..................... 36

PETITION No. 3. Request of the Committee at Harrodsburg to be taken under the jurisdiction of Virginia................................. 38

PETITION No. 4. Request of Thomas Slaughter and other inhabitants of Kentucky for a method of defense................................ 41

PETITION No. 5. Request of Hugh McGary for compensation for services rendered as a messenger to Fort Pitt............................. 42

PETITION No. 6. Request of the inhabitants of Kentucky for salt manufactories.. 43

PETITION No. 7. Request of Nathaniel Henderson for compensation for a negro slave killed at Fort Boone.................................. 44

PETITION No. 8. Statement of grievances by inhabitants of Kentucky in regard to land laws and request for a remedy...................... 45

PETITION No. 9. Statement of grievances by the inhabitants of Boone's Fort and request for a grant of six hundred and forty acres for town site and a board of trustees... 48

PETITION No. 10. Request of Richard Calloway for the right to establish a ferry across the Kentucky River at Boonesborough................ 53

PETITION No. 11. Request of the inhabitants at the Falls of the Ohio River for an act to establish a town at that place.................. 53

PETITION No. 12. Request of the inhabitants north of the Kentucky River for a division of the County of Kentucky........................... 55

PETITION No. 13. Request of George Rogers Clark for confirmation of a grant of thirty-six thousand acres of land northwest of the Ohio River, given to him by the Indians....................................... 57

PETITION No. 14. Request of the inhabitants of Lexington for a grant of land for a town site... 60

PETITION No. 15. Statement of grievances by the inhabitants of Kentucky and a request either for a better government or independence from Virginia... 62

Contents

	PAGE
Petition No. 16. Request of the inhabitants of the three counties of Kentucky for the old land law which required cultivation; also for the creation of a Superior Court.	66
Petition No. 17. Request of inhabitants of Lincoln County for laws to secure better military protection, care of orphans, civil marriage, and stray stock.	68
Petition No. 18. Request of the trustees appointed to hold forfeited land, used for school purposes, for an extension of powers.	69
Petition No. 19. Request of John Campbell that the act creating the town of Louisville be repealed.	72
Petition No. 20. Request of John Morton for aid in securing a title to land pre-empted in Fayette County.	73
Petition No. 21. Request of Patrick Doran for a warrant on a tract of land pre-empted in Lincoln County.	74
Petition No. 22. Request of William Lytle for aid in securing the title to a tract of land at a place called Dry Run.	74
Petition No. 23. Request of the inhabitants of the District of Kentucky for the establishment of Circuit Courts.	76
Petition No. 24. Request of the inhabitants of Kentucky either for a better government by Virginia or a statement of the intentions of that Commonwealth.	78
Petition No. 25. Request of the inhabitants of Jefferson, Fayette, Lincoln, and Nelson Counties for an act acknowledging the independence of Kentucky from Virginia.	79
Petition No. 26. Request of the inhabitants of Lincoln County for a grant of land for a town site.	82
Petition No. 27. Request of the inhabitants of Lincoln County for a division of the county.	84
Petition No. 28. Request of the inhabitants of the County of Fayette for a division of the county.	85
Petition No. 29. Request of James Hogan for the right to establish a public ferry across the Kentucky River near Hickman's Creek.	87
Petition No. 30. Request of David Crews for the right to establish a public ferry across the Kentucky River near Jack's Creek.	88
Petition No. 31. Request of William Steele for the right to establish a public ferry across the Kentucky River at Stone Lick.	89
Petition No. 32. Request of the inhabitants of part of Bourbon County at Limestone Settlement for division of the county.	89
Petition No. 33. Protest of the inhabitants of Bourbon County against a division of the county.	91

Contents

	PAGE
PETITION No. 34. Request of the inhabitants of Washington, in Limestone Settlement of Bourbon County, for the grant of land for a town site..	91
PETITION No. 35. Request of James Holloway for land in payment of services in the Revolutionary War.	92
PETITION No. 36. Request of the inhabitants of Lincoln County for the establishment of the town of Stanford.	93
PETITION No. 37. Request of Jane Todd for the appointment of trustees for an estate left by John Todd of Fayette County.	95
PETITION No. 38. Request of Mary Ervin to be allowed to inherit the land of John Askins.	96
PETITION No. 39. Request of Christopher Greenup, Clerk of Supreme Court of Kentucky, for change of procedure in regard to taxes arising from legal processes.	97
PETITION No. 40. Request of the inhabitants of Fayette County for the inspection of tobacco at the mouth of Hickman's Creek, on the north side of the Kentucky River.	98
PETITION No. 41. Request of Ignatius Mitchell for the establishment of a town to be called Charlestown, on his land on the Ohio River near Lawrence's Creek.	100
PETITION No. 42. Request of the inhabitants of the District of Kentucky for establishment of a Commission to settle pay rations and other claims under expeditions of Clark and Logan.	100
PETITION No. 43. Request of the inhabitants of Fayette County for the establishment of tobacco inspection on the Kentucky River near the mouth of Stone Lick.	102
PETITION No. 44. Request of James Buchanan of Bourbon County that a public ferry be established on his lands across Licking Creek.	103
PETITION No. 45. Request of sundry inhabitants of Fayette County for the establishment of tobacco inspection on the land of General Scott on the Kentucky River near Craig's Creek.	105
PETITION No. 46. Request of the inhabitants of Lexington for an act incorporating the town.	106
PETITION No. 47. Request of sundry inhabitants of Fayette, Bourbon, and Madison Counties for a new county to be created from them, with courthouse at Boonesborough.	107
PETITION No. 48. Request of the inhabitants of Limestone Settlement and other parts of Bourbon County for a division of Bourbon County.	108
PETITION No. 49. Protest of the inhabitants of Bourbon County against a division of the county.	110
PETITION No. 50. Request of the Trustees of Transylvania Seminary for one-sixth of Surveyors' legal fees, for support of the Seminary.	112

Contents

PAGE

PETITION No. 51. Request of inhabitants of Fayette County for tobacco inspection on Kentucky River near the mouth of Stone Lick Creek.... 113

PETITION No. 52. Request of the inhabitants of Fayette County for a division of the county... 114

PETITION No. 53. Protest of the inhabitants of Fayette County against a division of the county... 116

PETITION No. 54. Request of the inhabitants of the Limestone Settlement of Bourbon County for a division of the county..................... 117

PETITION No. 55. Protest of the inhabitants of Bourbon County against a division of the county... 119

PETITION No. 56. Request of the inhabitants of Bourbon County for tobacco inspection on Licking Creek 120

PETITION No. 57. Request of the inhabitants of Bourbon County for the establishment of a town at Bourbon Courthouse..................... 121

PETITION No. 58. Request of the inhabitants of the District of Kentucky for a repeal of the Act of Separation.............................. 121

PETITION No. 59. Request of George Muter, Samuel McDowell, Caleb Wallace, and Harry Innes that taxes be made payable in specie...... 122

PETITION No. 60. Request of the inhabitants of the District of Kentucky that Lexington and Bardstown be appointed as places for sittings of the Supreme Court... 124

PETITION No. 61. Request of Benjamin Stevenson, that he be relieved from the penalty of the law against bringing slaves into Kentucky without notice 125

PETITION No. 62. Request of the inhabitants of Bourbon County for the establishment of the town of Hopewell............................. 127

PETITION No. 63. Request of the inhabitants north of the Kentucky River for tobacco inspection on the Kentucky River near Tate's Creek..... 128

PETITION No. 64. Request of the inhabitants of Kentucky for appointment of Commissioners by Supreme or County Courts for locating places for tobacco inspection... 129

PETITION No. 65. Request of the inhabitants of Fayette and Bourbon Counties that a new county be created from parts of the same........ 130

PETITION No. 66. Protest of sundry inhabitants of Bourbon County against a division of the county... 131

PETITION No. 67. Request of the inhabitants of Fayette County for the establishment of tobacco inspection on lands of Eli Cleveland on the Kentucky River... 132

PETITION No. 68. Request of the inhabitants of the town of Louisville for the appointment of trustees who live in the town..................... 133

Contents

PAGE

PETITION No. 69. Request of the inhabitants of Kentucky that the Supreme Court be not removed.. 134

PETITION No. 70. Request of William McKenzie for value of forfeited lands of Robert McKenzie which were taken for a public school............ 137

PETITION No. 71. Request of Anne Craig that the right of escheat of lands of James Douglass may be set aside in the interests of a debt to her.... 138

PETITION No. 72. Request of some inhabitants of Fayette County for tobacco inspection opposite Boonesborough and on Howards Creek.. 139

PETITION No. 73. Memorial of the Convention of the District of Kentucky which asks for an amendment to the act separating Kentucky from Virginia.. 140

PETITION No. 74. Request of the inhabitants of Lincoln County living on lands reserved for officers and soldiers, for a division of the county.... 141

PETITION No. 75. Request of Jane and Robert Todd, executors, for powers in regard to sale and conveyance of estate of John Todd.............. 142

PETITION No. 76. Request of the inhabitants of Lexington for certain powers and authorities.. 143

PETITION No. 77. Request of the inhabitants of Bourbon County for the right to erect grist mills on the Stoner and Hinkson's forks of the Licking River.. 144

PETITION No. 78. Request of the inhabitants of Bourbon County to establish the navigation of the Licking River and that grist mills be not erected.. 145

PETITION No. 79. Request of sundry inhabitants of Bourbon County that the navigation of the Licking River and its forks be not impeded by grist mills.. 146

PETITION No. 80. Request of the trustees of the town of Hopewell that the land on which the town is located be condemned and vested in the trustees, and that the name be changed to Paris..................... 147

PETITION No. 81. Request of Laban Shipp that no act be passed in favor of navigation on the Licking River and its forks that will cause the removal of his mill.. 148

PETITION No. 82. Request of the inhabitants of Bourbon County for act to allow the erection of grist mills on the Licking River and its forks.. 150

PETITION No. 83. Request of claimants to tracts of land in the Illinois grant and others, for an extension of time to give proof before Commissioners... 151

PETITION No. 84. Request of sundry inhabitants of Bourbon County for the establishment of tobacco inspection on land of Lawrence Protzman. 152

PETITION No. 85. Request of William Bruce and John Linn for compensation as scouts in 1789.. 153

Contents

PAGE

PETITION No. 86. Request of James Smith that he be granted the right to prove his pre-emption claim to land improved in 1773............ 154

PETITION No. 87. Request of the inhabitants of the town of Maysville for an extension of time, to fulfill the requirements for title to their lots.. 155

PETITION No. 88. Request of some inhabitants of Bourbon County for an extension of time for recording deeds, on account of death of the sheriff.. 156

PETITION No. 89. Request of William Shannon for the adjustment and settlement of his accounts as Commissary and Quartermaster to the Illinois Department...................................... 157

PETITION No. 90. Request of the Trustees of Transylvania Seminary for the right to raise money by a lottery............................. 160

PETITION No. 91. Request of the Trustees of Transylvania Seminary for a reduction of the number of trustees............................. 161

PETITION No. 92. Request of Henry Banks that the register of land office be authorized to accept land warrants on a claim................... 162

PETITION No. 93. Request of the inhabitants of the District of Kentucky for an extension of time for recording surveys, as required by a new land law of 1791... 164

PETITION No. 94. Request of John Crow for compensation for keeping Indian prisoners... 165

PETITION No. 95. Request of Isaac Ruddle for payment of claims for service and horses furnished, thus far unsettled because of charges of disloyalty... 168

PETITION No. 96. Request of Levi Todd, Clerk of Fayette County, for the refunding of money paid as tax on clerks......................... 169

PETITION No. 97. Request of Joseph Martin for the establishment of a ferry across the Cumberland River............................... 170

PETITION No. 98. Request of James McAfee for compensation for supplies furnished the troops at the Falls of the Ohio in 1780 and 1781........171

PETITION No. 99. Request of James Wilkinson for the establishment of tobacco inspection at Frankfort..................................... 171

PETITION No. 100. Request of George Rogers Clark for the payment of his general statement of claims, debts, and arrearages, due for services and for advances to the State... 172

PETITION No. 101. Request of John Campbell for payment of wages as inspector of tobacco at the Falls of the Ohio........................ 174

PETITION No. 102. Request of John Stewart for the right to enter and survey a tract of land on the Licking River, improved by Henry Stewart in 1775... 176

Contents

                                        PAGE

PETITION No. 103. Request of James Gilmore and Stephen Huston, for compensation for service as scouts.................................. 177

PETITION No. 104. Request for delay in the establishment of a ferry across Patterson's Creek... 177

PETITION No. 105. Request of George Rogers Clark for half pay for life or full pay for five years.. 178

PETITION No. 106. Request of Daniel Boone for a land-office treasury warrant for six hundred and twenty-eight acres of land.............. 178

PETITION No. 107. Request of James Bullock for duplicate certificate issued for a horse impressed into the service of the State............. 179

PETITION No. 108. Request of William Bledsoe for a warrant on the treasury in payment for a beast taken into service in 1782................ 179

PETITION No. 109. Request of Edmond Southard and his wife Sarah, for a land-office treasury warrant for land unlocated thus far because of the separation of Kentucky from Virginia and other causes.............. 180

PETITION No. 110. Request of Berry Cawood of Harlan County for a grant of land in lieu of land to which he was entitled in the tract set apart for Clark and his soldiers.. 186

INTRODUCTION

The value of this collection of legislative petitions of early Kentucky is general as well as local. Since Kentucky was the first Commonwealth to be established west of the Alleghany Mountains, anything which illustrates the formative growth of society is significant of the subsequent growth of the nation westward. It is believed that these petitions will prove of interest and value for three main reasons: First, as an illustration of the process of petitioning; second, for the subject-matter contained in them, and third, for the list of names attached to the petitions which is a large one and representative of the pioneer population.

The right and the practice of petitioning is an old one, much prized by our English ancestors. It has occupied an important place in the development of liberty and government by the people. It was in use in the Colonies and their records all show to what a large extent it figured. Hence, it may be said that the early settlers of Kentucky, in petitioning, were only doing that which they were accustomed to do east of the mountains.

The petitions here presented are the basis of almost all the legislation of Virginia for her western settlers. The editor has followed them through the various steps of legislation as recorded in the Journal of the House of Burgesses, the Journal of the Convention, the Journal

Introduction

of the House of Delegates, the Calendar of State papers, and the Statutes as edited by Hening. In many cases the preamble of the bill enacted repeats the substance and in some cases the very phrases of the petition, thus linking the two together in a most interesting and unique manner.

A regular process was followed in the matter of petition. The law required posting for a certain length of time that all might have an opportunity to be acquainted with the contents. Certifications of such posting may be seen to accompany several of the petitions as printed. Then the petition was taken to Williamsburg or Richmond, either by Kentucky's representative to the Virginia Assembly or by a special messenger. Before the outbreak of the Revolution the petition was addressed to the colonial Governor, and after that to the legislative body. Only one of our petitions was thus addressed to the Governor and a second referred to in the Calendar of State Papers. All the others are addressed to the Convention, the General Assembly, or the House of Delegates.

If a western community was not organized it sent its petitions to the most westerly county by which it was forwarded to the capital. Thus the settlers of Kentucky gained access to the ear of the legislative body through Fincastle County. The organization of a body of settlers into a committee to petition was the first step in the formation of civic life in the westward expansion of population.

The petitions presented to the legislative body must, by the law of Virginia, be deposited with the Clerk of the

Introduction

House of Delegates. The Clerk read the petition and it was then referred to one of the standing committees, of which there were five—on religion, on propositions and grievances, on claims, on courts of justice, and at times on the state of the country. Special committees were sometimes appointed, and often petitions were considered by committee of the whole. These committees were appointed at the beginning of the session and often were composed of the most prominent men of the Commonwealth. Thus the affairs of the distant western settlers were sometimes discussed by such men as Henry Lee, Patrick Henry, James Madison, and Thomas Jefferson.

The House ordered the committees to which the matters were referred to take them under consideration and make a recommendation. In the original documents the course through which the petitions passed is endorsed on the back as they were filed away. These endorsements are given in the notes to the text of the petitions. If the judgment of the committee was favorable the word "reasonable" was written across the back and a bill was generally drawn to conform to the request. If the judgment was not favorable the word "rejected" was written across the back, and no bill was enacted. Sometimes the petitions, if important, passed through quite a long and devious course, as may be seen. In some cases the requests were divided and part were granted and part rejected. The reasons for this action are not on record, though it may often be inferred from the action or the language in the Journals.

Introduction

The statutes which match these petitions are well known and embody, in general, the substance of the petitions. They consist of a preamble, an enacting clause, and the provisions of the law. The petitions, however, add considerable to our knowledge as they give us the settler's point of view in his own language. Taking the two together it is possible to have as perfect a picture as may be of the relations of the old Commonwealth and her remote inhabitants. That these distant settlers suffered is certainly true; that they were dissatisfied with their parent State is evidenced by the petitions they sent to the Government at Philadelphia; but one can not make a study of the petitions and the laws based upon them without being impressed with the fact that Virginia attended to the affairs of her "good people" on the "western waters." The impression is left of a population self-assertive and resourceful but withal respectful toward constituted authority.

In the second place the petitions are of value because of the light which their subject-matter throws on the early history of Kentucky and the West. It would be difficult to find a more graphic picture of the life of a pioneer population in all its lines of activity, in the expression of difficulties, hopes, and desires. We have too often been content to select some typical hero of frontier life and record his exploits. In these petitions we have set before us the associated life of the community. Allowance must be made, it is true, for extravagance of statement, but even

Introduction

such phrases are a vivid reminder of the strenuous life of those early state-builders whose sacrifices and efforts made possible the conditions that exist to-day.

The petitions are not all of equal importance. Some deal only with personal affairs or with matters of small account. Others throw light on matters that belong to the field of serious history and are significant. The greatest good can be derived by taking them as a whole, illustrative of the beginnings of a community.

The topics that make up the subject-matter of the petitions may be summed up as follows: The system of landholding, the establishment of courts, the organization of a militia for protection from Indians, the organization of the community into counties and towns, the establishment of communication by ferries and roads, the inspection of tobacco, the building of gristmills, the perfecting of a medium of exchange, the foundation of an educational system, the status of slavery in the western country, the effort to secure better social conditions in the care of orphans and in the performance of marriage rites, and finally the movement of the population toward separation from Virginia.

The question of land naturally occupies a large place in the petitions. The settlers came to the country west of the mountains with certain ideas regarding land which had been worked out through many years of controversy in the colonial period of Virginia. The Journals of the House of Burgesses reflect this struggle. In general it may be

Introduction

said that the representatives of the people stood for westward expansion, for small grants of land to bona fide settlers, for titles free from quit rents, and for legislative management of land conditions rather than executive.

A resolution of the House of Burgesses of December, 1766, urged upon the administration that settlers who had taken up lands on the waters of the West could not be deprived of their land or compelled to move without a violation of public faith and of law. It showed that the encouragement of settlement to the west would be conducive to the King's service and Colony's interest and the King was urged to rescind his restrictive proclamation and give orders to grant land to "all adventurers" in the accustomed manner. Many of the lands were shown to be unoccupied by Indians and others could be readily secured by purchase.

In 1768 the treaty of Fort Stanwix with the Indians was in line with the wishes of the settlers and seemed to prepare the way for settlement. Our first petition of 1769 is a request for land in the valley of the Cumberland River, to the west of the mountains, and in the same year the House of Burgesses discussed expansion again, urging that the country be opened as far as the confluence of the Ohio with the Mississippi, and a purchase be made from the Cherokees which would add to the King's revenue and the trade and navigation of the western country.

The desire for small holdings is seen in the memorial which asks that the King in his "royal wisdom" be graciously pleased to "discourage all monopolies of those lands" by

Introduction

granting them "in small or moderate quantities to such adventurers as might incline to seek and settle the same."

The feeling against quit rents may be seen in the opposition to the grants of Lord Dunmore in 1775, when the surveyor of Fincastle County refused to return a survey until it had received the approval of the House of Burgesses and that body inquired, whether "his majesty may of right advance the terms of granting lands in the colony."

The few settlers in Kentucky had not been able to secure from Virginia a title to their lands until the Revolutionary War came on. Petitions Numbers 2 and 3 are requests for such recognition. It was the War which brought the western settlers and the government of Virginia together, through mutual need of one another, the former for money and riflemen and the latter for settled titles to land. Thus the first land act in behalf of the trans-Alleghany settlers was passed by Virginia in response to those petitions, in the latter part of 1776, and curiously enough, is entitled "An act for raising a supply of money for public exigencies."

This law referred to the fact that "great numbers of people had settled in the waste and ungranted lands on the western waters to which they have not been able to secure titles." It resolved that all such settlers upon unappropriated lands, to which there was no just prior claim, should have the "preemption or preference to the grant of such lands" and it gave to all bona fide settlers, previous to June 24, 1776, a right to "four hundred acres for each family." The land thus located was to bear a tax to the colony of Virginia according to the "pound rate."

Introduction

The Transylvania Company, under the lead of Richard Henderson and by the aid of Daniel Boone, had anticipated Virginia by the purchase of the land between the Cumberland and Kentucky Rivers from the Cherokees and had started a colony of a proprietary type with quit rents to the land and features not in accordance with the ideas which had been shaping in Virginia during the period between the close of the French Wars in 1763 and the opening of the Revolution. The petitions are wonderful exhibitions of the tact and skill with which the settlers induced the Commonwealth of Virginia to extend jurisdiction over Kentucky, and thus change the subsequent course of events.

The Land Act of 1776 was in accord with the popular views on the subject and had it remained the law there would not have been the grounds for complaint which many of the petitions so strongly voice. An act of the Assembly in 1779 confirmed the grants as given in the previous law and extended it to all settlers before January 1, 1778. It departed, however, from the first in granting the right to preempt one thousand acres on the condition of erecting a cabin. Another act of the same year established a land office and gave to any person the right "to acquire title to so much waste and unappropriated land as he or she shall desire on paying the consideration of forty pounds for every hundred acres."

These two acts were due to the emergencies of the War and the pressure to secure funds for it. They became,

Introduction

however, a source of great annoyance to the actual settlers of the West who were bearing the burdens of the day. Petition No. 8 is a pitiful wail by the "distressed inhabitants" of the county of Kentucky, who saw men surveying the thousand-acre tracts, when they had not so much as a hundred and in some cases none at all—"too rough a medicine ever to be dejested by any set of people that have suffered as we have." Petition No. 15 protests against the second act by which every person is "at liberty to purchase without cultivating as much Land as He or She shall think proper." Petition No. 16, though pertaining to the same grievance, is more restrained, and recognizes the acts as emergency acts in the time of war.

To the settler west of the Alleghanies the period just following the War was one of great perplexity. He did not know to whom he should look for security in the title to his land. Petition No. 24 contains an expression of this feeling of uncertainty. Referring to a refusal of Congress to accept the cession of land offered by Virginia and a report of the committee to the effect that Virginia had no just claim to any of the land northwest of the Alleghanies, they assert their right "for it is through them and those they claim as citizens that the greatest part of the western waters is not now in the possession of our most inveterate enimies."

The changes made from time to time by the Virginia laws for perfecting a title to land gave rise to a great deal of trouble and discontent. Some of the settlers did not

Introduction

conform to the necessary steps by reason of ignorance, some were prevented by absence from the section in service of the country in the War or against the Indians. The death of a sheriff would prevent the perfecting of a title; fraud is sometimes charged, through concealment of the law by "knavish" men who expected to profit thereby; legal processes were forced on settlers who could not stand the expense and would thus lose their land, and finally the separation of Kentucky from Virginia left titles incomplete. These and other complaints are found in Petitions Nos. 22, 23, 88, 93, 102, 106, 109, and 110. With the complaints there is to be found a very graphic and complete revelation of the land question of the early period.

Closely connected with the land question and second, perhaps, in importance in the petitions, was the establishment of courts for the securing of order and for the regulation of the various relations of community life. The county courts were the first to be created and they began with the act by which the Kentucky County was separated from Fincastle in 1776. By this act justices were to meet at Harrodsburg on the first Tuesday of April to establish a court. They were instructed to appoint a clerk and arrange for a permanent place of meeting. The Assembly manifested its appreciation of the difficulties of getting things started in the remote region beyond the mountains by providing that the meetings might be postponed where a majority may have been detained "by bad weather or accidental rise of the water courses."

Introduction

County courts were established in each of the counties as they came into existence, previous to separation from Virginia. In fact the desire for more courts to facilitate the matters of record, land titles, and secure order in the community was the main motive in creating new counties. For example, in Petition No. 12, which is the basis of the first division, we read: "the settled parts of the county of Kentucky is of late growing so extensive that in a Time of peace it would be extremely inconvenient for your petitioners to attend at Court House much more so at present when an inveterate war rages with unremitted violence."

The increase in land troubles was responsible, largely, for a request for a superior court, as shown in Petition No. 16. This was established in 1782, and in Petition No. 17 the settlers of Lincoln County thank the Assembly for the establishment of this court, "the good effects of which we begin already to feel by the discouragement of vice and fraud which was too prevalent among us." That there was opposition may be inferred from the statement of the petition which alludes to a set of inhabitants "who were never friendly to the government of Virginia nor would be pleased with any laws its Legislature can pass."

The act which established the superior court created the District of Kentucky, after August 1, 1782, and it was generally referred to henceforth as a District rather than a County. This court was a supreme court of judicature, separate and independent of all other courts except the Court of Appeals. It had jurisdiction in cases of treason,

Introduction

murder, felony, crimes, and misdemeanors, except those reserved for the General Court in Virginia. It also had jurisdiction of matters at common law and cases in chancery arising therefrom. There was to be one judge and three assistants, and four sessions of eighteen days duration were provided for each year. It was also to be a court of record, to take cognizance of matters such as probating of wills, deeds, and the granting of letters of administration and cases of escheat and forfeiture. The rates for suits at law were set somewhat lower than in the courts of Virginia and did not always provide sufficient funds to make the court efficient. Several subsequent acts of the Assembly sought to strengthen the court by raising the rates, by using the receipts of custom on the Ohio, and by appointment of "naval officers" for that purpose. Petition No. 59 requests that taxes from which the salaries of court officials were to be met must be paid in specie, and Petition No. 39 requests that the money collected from taxes, so far as it is to be used for officials' salaries, may be kept out from the funds sent to Virginia. This request led to the appointment of a receiver in Kentucky and measures which constantly strengthened his hands.

Requests soon came for the establishment of assize or circuit courts and for the establishment of different places for the sitting of the Supreme Court. These are found in Petitions Nos. 23, 24, and 60. The objections are stated in Petition No. 69, which asserts the principle that "those governments are best who employ fewer officers." Accom-

Introduction

panying Petition No. 60 is an interesting statement of the business of the Supreme Court with number of cases pending.

The establishment of the local units of government occupies a large place in the petitions. Each county and town required a separate act of the Assembly for its creation. Petitions Nos. 2 and 3 are the basis for the establishment of the county of Kentucky, independent from Fincastle. In the organization of this western county they profess to be following the example of West Augusta County in Virginia, which thus becomes a model in county development. There is a great deal of shrewdness wrapped up in the insinuation of these westerners that "it would be impolitical to suffer such a Respectable body of prime Riflemen to remain even in a state of Neutrality." The act was passed by the Convention granting their request and the boundary is thus described: "all that part therof which lies to the south and westward of a line beginning on the Ohio at the mouth of Sandy Creek and running up the same and the main or northeasterly branch thereof to the Great Laurel Ridge or Cumberland Mountains thence southwesterly along the said mountain to the line of North Carolina."*

The county, thus created, was entitled to representation in the legislative body of Virginia by two delegates elected by free white men, possessing "twenty five acres of land with house and plantation thereon." The first election was delayed and had to be validated by a special act which

---
* This written description does not correspond exactly with its physical features, as later surveyed.

Introduction

referred to the election as "fair and open" with "most of the landholders in the county present and voting." Petition No. 12 is a request for a division of Kentucky County in 1780. The details of county administration as provided by the act were essentially similar to those of the first county. By 1785 the three counties thus created were again subdivided. Petitions Nos. 27, 28, 32, 33, 47, 48, 49, 53, 54, 55, 65, 66, and 74 are requests for and against such division. The opponents of division thought such act would weaken the military force, increase expense, and derange public business. They do not seem disposed to make an attempt to "bring the Courthouse and church to every man's door," and they think that "some individuals in such cases ought to give up their private case for the good of the people at large." Division was held to be unnecessary since "their numbers are too inconsiderable to enable them to accumulate expense, without adding either to their convenience or general welfare."

The first request for a town came from Boonesborough. Petition No. 9 gives an interesting summary of the troubles and suspicions of the settlers under the proprietors who first began this settlement, as the capital of the Transylvania colony. They complain of the distribution of lots and selection of trustees. They desire that every settler be allowed to draw a free lot, and that the town be laid out on the south side of the river, as the land at this township "lies much incommoded by hills." The act establishing this town became the model for all that followed. A

Introduction

board of trustees was provided and lots were to be granted to settlers on condition that they built "a dwelling house, sixteen feet square at least, with a brick, stone, or dirt chimney to be finished fit for habitation within three years from the date of their respective deeds."

Petitions Nos. 11, 14, 19, 26, 34, 36, 41, 46, 57, 62, 76, 80, and 87 bear upon this subject, and provide for towns at Louisville in 1780, Lexington in 1781, Harrodsburg, in 1785, Washington, Charlestown, Hopewell, Maysville, Stanford and Milford. The petitioners for a town at Louisville think it will render them secure from any "hostile intention of the Indians and will induce merchants to bring articles of commerce that the merchants of this western part of the state stands much in need of." When this town was established it was supposed to be on forfeited land but it was later found that part of this land was held by John Campbell, as security for a debt, and this situation gave rise to considerable petitioning before it was straightened out.

The settlers asking for a town at Lexington had at "considerable risque and expence" located there, laid off a town, and selected trustees, depending on an act of the Assembly allowing settlers six hundred and forty acres for such a purpose. They desired to be assured of their right to do this. This place is elsewhere referred to as "most flourishing and best peopled place of any at this time in the District of Kentucky." They wish to encourage "well disposed persons, artisans and mechanicks" to come, "who from motives of convenience do prefer a Town life."

Introduction

The settlers of Lincoln County had "taken into serious consideration of a Proper place for Trade and Domestic Business and for the more ready procuring of those articles in our precincts that are much wanted in the new country." Their site for a town is described as "sufficiently level, very fertile, and well watered by never failing springs and a large Stream running quite through the same." The town of Hopewell, in Bourbon County, was later changed to Paris by request of the settlers. Maysville was established on a site "intirely exposed to the depredations of hostile Indians." Several petitions ask an extension of time for fulfilling the conditions of building to secure their lots because of their constant struggles with Indians.

The statutes of Virginia show towns established also at Campbellstown, in Jefferson County, New Market in Mercer County, Danville in Mercer County, Warwick in Lincoln County, Beallsborough in Nelson County, Bardstown in Nelson County, Milford in Madison County, and Georgetown in Woodford County, although no petitions for the same were found.

Many of the petitions pertain to the industrial development of Kentucky. More space is given to the provisions for inspection of tobacco than anything else. The statutes of Virginia regarding this product are many and long, thus showing the important place it held in the industrial life. Previous to 1775 the provisions concerning inspection seem to have lapsed and in that year an act was passed reviving several warehouses for the reception of tobacco. This bill

Introduction

is interesting as illustrative of the legislation on the subject. Subsequent bills provided more detail but along essentially the same lines. Inspection was to be had "at and near the heads of creeks and rivers." The inspectors, after examining and recording the quality of the tobacco, were to issue warehouse receipts and these could be used as currency in certain cases. By an act of 1786 the value of tobacco was fixed at twenty shillings per hundred pounds for Kentucky. The first act for inspection "on the western waters" was passed in 1783. Petitions Nos. 40, 43, 45, 63, 64, 67, 72, 84, and 99 pertain to this subject. Because of the important part that James Wilkinson occupies in the development of the tobacco industry in Kentucky, his petition, No. 99, asking for inspection at Frankfort is significant.

The rise of gristmills suggests the increase in wheat and corn. Petition No. 77 in 1790 is the first request that refers to that subject. The inhabitants of Bourbon County complain that they are obliged "to go from eighteen to twenty five miles to mill," that they are subjected "to grate loss of time," and they wish a mill established on Stoner and Hinkson's Forks of the Licking River. They think that if "either locks or slopes sufficient for boats to pass by the dams with safety" were constructed, "the Stoner and Hinkson would be above ten times the value to Bourbon than what it is at present with only them navagations alone."

In the petitions regarding the mills there is a sharp controversy between the construction of mills and the pres-

Introduction

ervation of the stream open for navigation. In opposition to the view expressed above is that of Petition No. 78 which strenuously objects to dams and mills. The stream is said to flow "through a fertile soil thickly Inhabited, abounding with a variety of Fish" and "it is the only stream by which the greater part of the county can be relieved from a Difficult Land carriage of many miles." The petitioner in No. 81 has "nearly spent his little fortune" on a mill and its removal would bring himself and family ruin. At any rate the navigation is not so all important a matter as "only one boat has had a safe passage in two years" and several boats "have been obliged to unlode and waggon their loades to other landings more safe and certain"; "some have been overset and their loads lost, some have been drowned and many more have been exposed to the Greatest hardship." Petitioners in No. 82 think their opponents "puffed up with the most romantic expectations of the utility acruing from the free and open navigation of the Stoner and Hinkson."

Intercommunication by land and water was a matter of much importance to the early settlers. In 1779 an act of the Assembly was passed to mark and open a road over the Cumberland Mountains. In the preamble the purpose is thus set forth: "To afford mutual aid and support to one another and cement in one common interest all the citizens of the state a good wagon road through the great mountains into the settlements will greatly contribute." A commission was appointed to examine a route and a guard of fifty

Introduction

men was provided to protect them from Indians, if necessary. In 1786 another commission was appointed to receive subscriptions for a road from the falls of the Great Kanawha to Lexington. In 1792 an act for better communication expresses the sentiment that "This Assembly are at all times willing to contribute every encouragement to such designs as are represented to be of general utility so far as is consistent with prudence and good economy."

There are many references throughout the petitions to the difficulties of communication by land and requests are made for the improvement of waterways. In Petition No. 78 the inhabitants of Bourbon County request that the navigation of the Licking River be established, "beginning at its junction with the Ohio thence up the south fork to the Junction of Hinkston and Stoner, thence up Stoners Fork to Bramblets Lick."

Ferries were established at an early date. Petition No. 10 is the first request, and was made by Richard Calloway in 1779, for a ferry across the Kentucky at Boonesborough. It states that from the "first seating of This Town both the inhabitants and travilers has Found it very inconvenient to get across the Kentucky River only in dry seasons in the summer time." Because "this Town and country is become very popular and much Resorted to by travilers," he asks the privilege of keeping a public ferry. The right was granted by the Assembly. Calloway later lost his life while working on the ferry which is still in existence and in use. Petitions Nos. 29, 31, 44, 97, and

Introduction

104 are requests to establish ferries at different points. One across the Cumberland River was especially desired where the "Kentuckey road crosses the same."

In many cases individuals had been carrying people across the water ways and a private service was turned into a public one. One man says that "by request of his neighbors" he had provided a boat and had at "his own Expence set over passengers in the time of high water."

The petitions give occasional hints at other matters of an industrial nature. Petition No. 6 is a request regarding salt. The petitioners had not for some time been able to make salt because of the incursions of Indians and they were feeling the lack of that article of importance to frontier life. Salt springs abounded in the country and could be worked at small expense. They had not been worked by their owners, however, and the request is made that unless works are erected at once the springs be made "publick Property and [salt] be manufactured by Government" to the profit of Virginia as well as the settlers. The request is not so peculiar as it appears at first sight, for the statutes of Virginia show that the Commonwealth had at various times taken an active part in the production of salt. An act of 1775 provided for the erection of salt works in the colony; a later act allowed a bounty for the manufacture of salt, and still another act placed an embargo on the export of salt.

Slavery, of course, is referred to in the petitions. Petition No. 7 asks compensation for a negro killed at the

Introduction

siege of Boonesborough in 1778, in the famous attack by Indians in September. He was described as very "likely" and his value was estimated as six hundred pounds. The charge is made that he was put in an exposed place purposely. Petition No. 37 requests that the administrator of an estate be allowed to dispose of part of it and purchase a couple of "likely fellows" for the young heiress of the estate.

Petition No. 61 is the request of a slaveholder in 1787, who had come from Maryland, bringing with him his slaves. Through ignorance of the law—passed by Virginia, requiring notice from those bringing in slaves—he had forfeited his property. The Assembly was lenient to his petition, asking relief for "those who have neither education nor leisure to enable them to be acquainted with the Laws of their country." He asks for such relief as "will secure to him the possession of the hard earnings of many years industry."

The law referred to required that those coming into Virginia should give oath within ten days that no slaves were brought from Africa or the West Indies since November, 1778, and that none were brought with the "intention of selling them." The petitioner in this case was allowed extra time to conform to the law, "as such failure hath been chiefly, if not altogether, owing to the impracticability of complying with the said act."

The social relations and development of the pioneer community are suggested in several of the petitions. The

Introduction

early population was awake to the advantage of schools, and the parent Commonwealth seems also to have had that interest at heart. By an act of 1780 the Assembly had vested some eight thousand acres of lands, forfeited from loyalists in the Revolutionary War, in a board for the cause of "public education." The preamble of the act refers to "the interest of the commonwealth always to promote and encourage every design which may tend to the improvement of the mind and the diffusion of useful knowledge, even among its remote citizens, whose situation a barbarous neighborhood and a savage intercourse might otherwise render unfriendly to science." The land was placed in trust of a body of thirteen trustees "as free donation from the commonwealth for the purpose of a public school, or seminary of learning, to be created within the said county as soon as the circumstances of the county and the state of its funds will admit and for no other purpose whatever." At a future time it was thought these lands might "be a valuable fund for the maintenance and education of youth."

Several petitions pertain to the incorporation of the Board of Trustees for the Transylvania Seminary and the vesting in them of the forfeited land, defining their powers, fixing the number, and increasing their facilities for getting funds. The attitude of the pioneer population toward education may be seen in the words of Petition No. 18: "The solicitous anxiety which discovers itself in the principal inhabitants of this country for having Schools or Semi-

Introduction

naries of Learning among them that their children may be educated as becomes a civilized people, encourages your Petitioners to hope that the Liberality of Individuals will be extended in aid of the public Donations were Trustees incorporated by Law &c." They are confident that the "Assembly will listen with pleasure to every proposition that has a Tendency to banish Ignorance and Error and to introduce in their room what may polish the manners, encourage the improvement of the mind promote liberality of sentiment and by refining give additional Incentives to virtue."

By Petition No. 50 a request is made for an allotment of one-sixth of the land surveyors' fees to the funds of the institution. This had previously been assigned to William and Mary College, "a Seminary which we greatly respect but from which the Inhabitants of Kentucky are too remote to derive any immediate advantage." This was granted, as also the request that escheated lands should revert to the benefit of education. Petition No. 90 asks the privilege of conducting a lottery to raise five hundred pounds for the erection of an academy, a request which was granted in an act allowing the same privilege to a church and a school east of the mountains. Petition No. 91 also pertains to the educational matters. Petition No. 70 is a request from a descendant of the owner of one of the confiscated estates which had been donated to the cause of education. He had been informed that the Assembly "have always shewn a readiness to give the value

Introduction

of all confiscated property to the next in succession" and he requests the value of the property. The request is marked as reasonable but no act seems to have been passed.

Social conditions and needs are illustrated, along other than educational lines, by requests made in various petitions. In Petition No. 17 the settlers of Lincoln County ask for the passage of a "few more laws indispensibly necessary for this District." Among these is one seeking "some civil power to solemnize the Rites of matrimony as we have no clergy either of the church of England or Presbyterians, who compose the Greater part of our inhabitants."

This request was granted in 1783 and provision was made that "Where it shall appear to the court of any county on the western waters that there is not a sufficient number of clergymen authorized to celebrate marriages therein, such court is empowered to nominate so many sober and discreet laymen as will supply the deficiency." Those so nominated were to receive a license and could perform the ceremony according to the church of which they were members. Parties to the ceremony were obliged to have a license or a certificate of the publication of the banns made for three successive times.

In the same petition was a request for a law to provide for the "orphans of poor people as we have no church wardens to bind them out." The law of Virginia required that orphans should be bound out to a master or mistress under certain conditions. An act of 1785 provides that they must "be taught some trade, art or business;" also reading,

Introduction

writing, and if a boy, arithmetic, including the rule of three. Monthly reports had to be made by the overseers who had the authority to bind out the orphans.

A large number of the petitions are claims of various kinds. Such are Petitions Nos. 5, 13, 35, 83, 85, 89, 92, 94, 95, 100, 103, 105, 106, 107, 108, and 110. Three of these requests are from George Rogers Clark. In No. 13 he refers to his services in Illinois in the War, speaks of a grant of land adjoining the Falls on the northwest side of the Ohio River, of an extent of thirty-six thousand acres "which he could not refuse without giving umbrage," given by the Indians with the request that he live among them. Though claiming no title by virtue of this gift he asks the Commonwealth to confirm the title, as it would save the State the expense of purchase and would reimburse him for what he had lost through his service to the country.

In Petition No. 100 Clark asks half pay for life or full pay for five years for debts "arising from past Military services or from advances of the better part of his Fortune for the credit of the state"; for debts incurred in "the necessary maintenance of your Troops under my Command in the Western country, troops (it behooves me to say) who with a fortitude, fidelity and martial hardihood, perhaps unexampled, have braved heroically and with successful effect every kind of want and every Species of peril to preserve the very fairest portion of your State and indeed of the whole Union"; debts for "having, from my own funds,

Introduction

supplied your Garrisons and those heroic Troops with bread to feed on."

There are many personal claims presented of various kinds. Petition No. 5 is a request from the impulsive Hugh McGary, who figured so prominently later in the defeat of the settlers at the battle of Blue Lick. He asks pay for his services as a messenger to Pittsburgh, as bearer of a list of horses stolen by the Indians that they may be recovered by an expedition about to start for the recovery of stolen property. Petition No. 35 is a request for bounty as a reward for three years in the service. Petition No. 83 is a request for extension of time to present claims to the commission appointed to hear them. Petition No. 110 is the request of a member of the regiment of Clark, in the Illinois campaign, for land. The petitioner gives account of the difficulties of the campaign; says he was at the taking of Lieutenant Governor Hamilton and acted as his guard part of the way to Kentucky, and the rest of the way he served as spy. He had received a discharge from the army but had lost it. He could have shared in the lands allotted to the followers of Clark but he had lived in isolation "in the hills and mountains detached from almost every community or opportunity for information."

Petitions Nos. 85 and 103 are requests from scouts for consideration. Petition No. 89 is the request of a quartermaster in control of supplies for the Illinois division of the army under Clark for three years. The memorialist had drawn bills of exchange on the State for some of the bills,

Introduction

they had been protested, and he was in "a very disagreeable situation not only on account of these bills but by being charged with monies paid him during the time he was in the office and no credit allowed him." Petition No. 92 refers to a suit brought in the High Court of Chancery for payment of salt purchased by a public agent of Virginia. Petition No. 94 is the claim for payment as compensation for the keeping of Indian prisoners. Part of the bill had been paid but the amount had been reduced in the later months and petitioner could not get rid of the Indians. Petition No. 95 is a claim for service in raising a company on the Holston, supplying them with arms, provisions, bags, pack horses, and marching them to the Falls of the Ohio in 1779, for the reduction of Illinois under Colonel Clark. The amount had once been allowed by the commissioners, but some person had been making trouble by stating that the petitioner was "enimical to the United States" when he was a captive at Detroit where he was taken in 1780. Petitions Nos. 107 and 108 are requests for payment for horses impressed into the public service.

The petitions, lastly, are valuable as a means of determining the feeling which the settlers west of the mountains had for the parent State and the gradual movement toward separation. We have already seen that there was a population unfriendly to the jurisdiction of Virginia, even from the beginning. The Revolutionary War, however, had led them to prefer her jurisdiction to any alternative. There were many causes for dissatisfaction which were due to

Introduction

the necessities of the case rather than intentional neglect. As the War drew to a close and the new system of Federal Government was established, expectation turned toward a separate existence as a State.

Petition No. 15, May, 1782, contains the first expression of that feeling in this collection of petitions. It grew out of the discontent of the settlers with the land policy of Virginia, especially the grants to absentee purchasers. The petitioners had proposed the setting aside of tracts of land for actual settlers; they referred to considerable dissention among them as the result of a pamphlet in circulation on the "Public Good" and asked the Assembly to create them "a power sufficient for the Controul and Management of all Civil and Military affairs in this Country" or else to grant them "a Separation with your Intercession with the Honourable the Continental Congress for their incorporation with them." The request is respectfully worded and they speak of "a proper deference to your wise Determinations, Reposing special Trust and Confidence in you." Part of their request was rejected, but "so much thereof as prays for the establishment of some kind of controuling power for the better management of their civil and military affairs is reasonable."

Petition No. 16, June, 1782, renews the same complaints and asks in definite terms for the passage of an act for cultivating and improving the lands and the creation of a superior court which will "carry us towards that stage of maturity when with the tenderness of a kind parent to a

Introduction

departing child, you will direct us to form a constitution and act for ourselves." They refer, in Petition No. 24, to the unsatisfactory conditions, mention a resolution of Congress denying Virginia's title to lands northwest of the mountains, but express loyalty in the words: "When your memorialists through your Honble. house make a request to Congress for a new state and are received into the Union, They are then and not before subject as another state"; and again they say, "your memorialists have ever considered themselves and country as part of Virginia and were happy in being so. Her laws suited them and do yet suppose it to be their interest to be Governed by Her, untill it shall appear for their mutual advantage to separate at which period it is expected there will be no objection." The creation of a superior court in the same year seems for a time to have satisfied the requests of previous petitions.

Petition No. 25, October, 1785, is the request of a convention for separation. It was called "to take into consideration the General State of the District and especially to decide the expediency of making application to your Honorable Body, for an Act of Seperation." They give various reasons for their request; they say they have waited patiently "the hour of Address nor ever ventured to raise their voices in their own cause, Untill Youth quickening into manhood hath given them vigor and Stability." If their application is granted they count it "a new spectacle in the History and Politicks of Mankind. A Sovereign Power, solely intent to bless its People, agreeing to a dis-

Introduction

memberment of its parts, in order to secure the Happiness of the Whole," the beginning of a movement which "we persuade ourselves is to diffuse throughout the World the inestimable blessings which mankind may derive from the American Revolution." Their request was considered in committee of the whole by the Assembly, referred then to a special committee, and a bill was passed which provided for the calling of a convention at Danville, to consider the matter of separation. Three bills were passed before the separation actually took place.

The opposition to separation is seen in Petition No. 58, which says: "An augmentation of states under the general government, by the erection of a new government here which will be clothed with no new national power" will only serve "as one of Pharos lean kine to devour our liberty whilst it can be of no security to our property." They ask for a repeal of the act of separation lest it "injure us until time shall be no more."

The general tone and tenor of the petitions here printed is considerably different from that of the petitions sent to Philadelphia or New York, now in the Library of Congress and which have been referred to and quoted in the printed histories of Kentucky.

The list of names attached to the petitions is the third and last source of value to be mentioned in this introduction. The signatures of the larger part are autograph which adds to their worth. Many of the lists of early pioneer populations have been gathered secondhand and often

Introduction

from the sound of the name. Thus the army rolls of the Virginia soldiers found on pay-rolls or official papers are often incorrect. In some cases it is evident that the list of names attached to a petition was copied in one handwriting and in some cases names have been written for the petitioner, but in most cases the autograph signature appears on one of the petitions if not more. The editor spent over a month on the names, examining them with a magnifying glass and copying them. In this way it was possible to gain a familiarity with them. Where the name appeared several times, as most of them do, it was possible to check and come to a judgment as to the proper form. Variations of spelling have been preserved in order to make the list of as much value as possible. The same name occurring on different petitions does not necessarily indicate the same person. No effort has been made to go beyond the preservation of the name in this work.

Facsimile reproductions have been made of some of the signatures by way of illustration. Not all the autographs are so good as these. Many are barely legible, but there were very few that could not be made out after some study. Surely this list of names is abundant proof that the pioneer population of Kentucky was not illiterate.

The list of names is important for two main reasons, first, it throws light on the racial composition of the early population of Kentucky, and second, it is of use for the study of genealogy.

The earlier petitions show a decided preponderance of Scotch and Scotch-Irish names with a large number of

Introduction

English and a few German, Dutch, and French. The number of English names increases in the later petitions. The large number of religious names indicates the nonconformist character of much of the population.

While the list will not give much detail to aid the genealogist, it fixes the existence of a certain name in a locality at an early period and thus gives a clue that may be followed further.

Text of the Petitions

Verbatim transcript with editor's emendations in brackets only when meaning requires the same.

TEXT OF THE PETITIONS

NUMBER 1.

To the Right Honble. Norborne Baron de Botetourt His Majesty's Lieut. and Governor General of Virginia and Vice Admiral of the Same and the Honble. Council Thereof:—

The Petition of Joseph Cabell, Junr., Nicholas Cabell, William Megginson, William Horsley, Robert Horsley, John Horsley, Wm. Hopkins, Jas. Hopkins, Saml. Burks, Cornelius Thomas, John Thomas, Jas. Thomas Junr., Henry Hopson, Samuel Hopson, John Hughs, Joseph Hornsby, Edward Harris, John Harris, Thos. Harris, John Davis, John Warberton, Benj. Warberton, Gary Wilkinson, Emanl. Taylor, Joseph Turner, Wm. Cabell Junr., Sanders Cabell, Hector Cabell, Frederick Cabell, John Cabell Junr., George Cabell, Frederick Cabell, Hugh Innes, Robert Innes, Harry Innes, Jas. Innes, James Buchanan, Tavener Beal, Abraham Hite, Isaac Hite, the Younger, Abraham Hite Junr., Joseph Hite, Thos. Harmon, Benj. Hains, Joseph Hains, Ebenezer Severn, Philip Ross, Felix Seymour, Isaac Hite, Isaac Hite, Junr., John Mc. Donel, Abel Randle, Garret VanMeter, humbly sheweth that his Majesty's Title to the Lands situate on the east side of the Ohio having lately been recognized by the six nations of Indians, your Petitioners humbly pray that they may have leave to take up and survey sixty thousand acres of Land to begin at the Falls of the Cumberland River and extend down the said River for compliment in one or more surveys and your Petitioners will pray.

(December, 1769. According to Calendar of State Papers.)

In the Calendar of State Papers reference is made to a Petition of April 25, 1772, asking for a large grant of land in the valley of the Louisa River; in the Journal of the House of Burgesses for May 25, 1774, reference is made to a Petition from several persons on the Western Waters; in the Journal of the Convention reference is made to several Petitions: on May 21, 1776, to a Petition from settlers in West Fincastle; on May 30, to a Petition from John Craig, a settler in Transylvania; on June 15, 1776, to a Petition from Richard Henderson and his associates of the Transylvania Company; and on June 10, 1776, to two Petitions from settlers in the western part of Fincastle beyond the mountains.

In the sources there are quite full summaries of the above mentioned Petitions but the text itself has not been found. The Petitions or copies of them may be in existence. Together with Petitions Nos. 2 and 3, of this collection, they led to the act separating Kentucky County from Fincastle, confirming the land titles of the settlers and ensuring the jurisdiction of Virginia over the country west of the Alleghanies.

NUMBER 2.

To THE HONORABLE THE CONVENTION OF VIRGINIA.

The Humble Petition of the Inhabitants of Kentucke (or Louisa) River on the Western parts of Fincastle County. Humbly Sheweth that many of your Petitioners became Adventurers in this part of the Colony in the year 1774, in order to provide a subsistance for themselves and their Posterity; but were soon obliged by our Savage Enemy to abandon their Enterprise and in the year Following, after the Country had been discovered and explored, many more became Adventurers, some of whom claimed Land by Virtue of Warrant by Lord Dunmore agreeable to the Royal Proclamation in the year 1763 and other by Preoccupancy, agreeable to the Entry Laws of Virginia. And in the meantime a Company of men from North Carolina *purchased* or pretended to Purchase from the Cherokee Indians all that track of Land from the southernmost waters of the Cumberland River to the Banks of the Louisa or Kentucke River including also the Lands on the which inhabitants live in Powells Valley, By Virtue of which Purchase they stile themselves the true and absolute Proprietors of the new Independent Province, (as they call Transylvania) they are indeavoring to Erect and in consequence of their Usurped authority officers both Civil and Military are appointed, Writs of Election issued Assemblys convened, a Land Office opened, Conveyances made, Lands sold at an Exorbitant Price and a System of Policy introduced which does not at all Harmonize with that lately adopted by the United Colonies, But on the Contrary for ought yet appears this Fertile Country will afford a safe Asylum to those whose principles are Inimical to American

To the General Assembly of Virginia

Freedom. But your Petitioners have the greatest Reason to question the Validity of those mens purchase being well informed that the Cherokees never extended their claims north of the Cumberland River, nor would warrant any Lands on the other side. Besides its well known, that the Indians of the Six Nations Claimed and ceded those very Lands to the Crown of Great Britain at a Treaty held at Fort Stanwix in November 1768. We therefore are not willing to obey those men, or the Authority they have assumed or indeed to acknowledge any power or prerogative, which is not derived from the Convention of Virginia whose subjects we desire to be considered.

Virginia, we conceive, can claim this country with the greatest justice and propriety, its within the Limits of their Charter, They Fought and bled for it. And had it not been for the memorable Battle at the Great Kanaway, these vast Regions had yet continued inaccessable. Nor can we conceive how it is practicable for those men who stile themselves Absolute proprietors, to settle this Country at so great a Distance from all the Colonies and in a Neighborhood of some Enemy Indians.

But should our Infant Settlement become the object of your deliberations, and be taken under your protection and Direction unto whom we justly conceive to Belong, Every obstacle would be Removed, Population increase and of consequence a Barrier to the interior parts of Virginia from the Indians. A new source of wealth would then be opened, as Trade and Navigation under the auspices of Virginia would Flourish, in the Western world, And therefore willing to acquit our conscience and not entail *Slavery* upon our posterity by submitting to the pretensions and impositions of the pretended proprietors, We the Inhabitants of the North and South Sides of Kentucke River having assembled togather after preparatory notice on the Eighth day of June 1776 and continued to poll till the 15th. of said Instantin . . . [illegible] a majority has chosen Captain John Gabriel Jones and Captain George

Petitions of the Early Inhabitants of Kentucky

Rodgers Clark, and hope ye Honorable the Convention will receive them as our Delegates from this the Western parts of Fincastle County. And as we sincerely concur in the measures established by the Continental Congress and Colony of Virginia, And willing to the utmost of our abilities to support the present laudable cause, by raising our Quoto of men and bear a proportionable share of Expense that will necessarily accrue in the support of our common Liberty. And that good order may be observed we proceeded to Elect a Committee consisting of Twenty one members, already some in West Augusta and which precedent we rely upon to justify our Procedings to the world, for without Law or authority, Vice here could take its full scope having no Laws to Restrain or Power to Controul. Upon the whole we Cheerfully submit to the Authorities and Jurisdiction of this House, not doubting but you will take us under your protection, and give us such direction by our Representatives, as you, in your great Wisdom may think Best, and your petitioners as in duty Bound &c.

Herrodsburg, June 7—15th. 1776
Signed by order of the Inhabitants

Abraham Hite Jr.
Clerk.

This was sent first to the committee of Fincastle County and by them to the Convention.

NUMBER 3.

To the Honourable the Convention of Virginia:

The Humble Petition of the Committee of West Fincastle of the Colony of Virginia, Being on the North and South sides of the River Kentucke (or Louisa) Present John Gabriel Jones Esqr. Chairman, John Bowman, John Cowen, William Bennett, Joseph Bowman, John Crittendon, Isaac Hite, George Rodgers Clark, Silas Harland, Hugh Mc. Gary, Andrew Mc, Connel, James Herrod, William Mc. Connel, and John Maxwell, Gent'n.

To the General Assembly of Virginia

The Inhabitants of this Frontier part of Virginia who are equally desirous of contributing to the utmost of their power to the support of the present laudable cause of American Freedom, and willing to convince and prove to the world that tho they live so remote from the seat of Government that they Feel in the most sensible manner for their suffering Brethern; and that they most ardently desire to be looked upon as a part of this Colony, notwithstanding the Base proceedings of a Detestible, Wicked and Corrupt Ministry to prevent any more counties to be laid off, without the Inhabitant would be so pusilanimous as to give up their right of appointing proper persons to represent them (in Assembly or) in Convention; And as we Further conceive that as the Proclamation of his Majesty for not settling on the Western parts of this Colony, is not founded upon Law, it cannot have any Force, and if we submit to that Proclamation and continue not to lay off new Counties on the Frontiers that they may send Representatives to the Convention, its leaving an opening to the wicked and Diabolical designs of the Ministry, as then this immense and Fertile Country would afford a safe Asylum to those whose Principles are inimical to American Liberty. And if new Counties are not laid off, as Fincastle County now Reaches and already settled upwards of Three Hundred Miles from East to West it is impossible that two delegates can be sufficient to Represent any such a Respectable Body of People, or that such a number of Inhabitants should be bound to obey without being heard. And as those very people would most cheerfully cooperate in every measure tending to the Publick Peace, and American Freedom, They have delegated two Gentlemen who was chosen by the Free voice of the People, and which Election was held Eight days at Harrodsburg (on the Western waters of Fincastle on Kentucke) after the preparatory notice of Five Weeks given to the Inhabitants and on the poll being closed Captain John Gabriel Jones and Captain George Rodgers Clark, having the majority were chosen and not doubting the acceptance of them as our Representative by the Honorable the Convention, to serve in that capacity; as we conceive the precedent Established in West Augusta will justify our Proceeding; and we cannot but observe how impolitical it would be to suffer such a Respectable body of prime Rifle men, to remain (even in a state of Neutrality) When at this time a Certain set of men from North Carolina, stiling themselves, proprietors and claiming an absolute right to these very Lands taking upon themselves the Legislative authority, Commissioning officers, both Civil and Military, having also opened a Land office, Surveyors General and Deputies appointed and act, Conveayances made and Land sold at an Exorbitant Price many other Unconstitutional practices, tending to disturb the minds of those, who are well disposed to the wholesome Government of Virginia, and creating Factions and Divisions amongst ourselves. As we have not hitherto been Represented in Convention; And as at this time of General danger we cannot take too much Precaution to prevent the Inroads of Savages, and prevent the Effusion of Innocent Blood. We the Committee after receiving a message from the Chiefs of the Delawares who are now settled near the mouth of the Waubash, informing us that a Treaty was to be held at Opost, by the English and Kiccapoos Indians, and that they would attend to know the purport of the same, and if their Brothers the Long Knives would send a man they could rely on, they would, on their return, inform him of the same, as they were apprehensive the Kiccapoos would strike their Brothers the Long Knives, therefore we thought it most prudent, and shall send immediately a certain James Herrod and Garret Pendergrass to converse with them on the same. And as its the request of the Inhabitants that we should point out a number of men capable and most acquainted with the Laws of this Colony to act as Civil Magistrates, a list of the same we have enclosed. And for other matters relative to the country we conceive that Captain Jones and Captain Clark our Delegates will be able to inform the Honourable the Con-

To the General Assembly of Virginia

vention, not doubting but they will listen to our just petition and take us under their Jurisdiction, And your petitioners as in Duty Bound &c.

Signed by order of the Committee, Herrodsburg, June 20th. 1776.

J. G. Jones Chairman
Abraham Hite Jnr. Clerk.

This was sent first to the committee of Fincastle County and by them to the convention.

The division requested was made and West Fincastle created into the Kentucky County by an act entitled, An act for dividing the county of Fincastle into three distinct counties and parishes of Botetourt into four distinct parishes. Henings Statutes, Vol. 9, 257.

"Whereas, from the great extent of the county of Fincastle many inconveniences attend the more distant inhabitants thereof on account of their remote situation from the courthouse of the said county and many of the said inhabitants have petitioned this present general assembly for a division of the same; Be it therefore enacted &c."

The division was to take effect after December 31, 1776, and the boundaries are thus described: "All that part thereof which lies to the south and westward of a line beginning on the Ohio at the mouth of the Great Sandy Creek and running up the same and the main or northeasterly branch thereof to the Great Laurel Ridge or Cumberland Mountain, then southwesterly along the said mountain to the line of North Carolina shall be one distinct county and called and known by the name of Kentucky."

A system of administration was provided for the county to consist of a court to meet the first Tuesday of every month. They were to give bond and could appoint a clerk and select a place of meeting. The court was to meet for the first time at Harrodsburg. Any appointment had to be by majority of the justices and could be postponed "where such majority shall have been prevented from attending by the bad weather or accidental rise of water courses."

The right of franchise was vested in "every white man possessing twenty-five acres of land with house and plantation thereon . . . and having right to an estate for life at least in the said land in his own right or in the right of his wife."

NUMBER 4.

To the Honorable the Speaker & Gentlemen of the House of Delegates of Virginia.

The Petition of Thomas Slaughter on behalf of himself & the other inhabitants situate near Kentukke humbly sheweth; That the said Inhabitants are exposed to the incursions & depredations of the Indians & from the small number are incapable of protecting themselves. & this inconvenience is greatly increased on Account of the melitia's not being imbodied. The Petitioner therefore humbly prays that some method may be fixed on to protect & defend the said inhabitants, & if in the meantime military Commissions were issued for training the militia of the place a smaller number of men to act in conjunction with the said militia would answer the end desir'd.

Your Petitioner humbly submits the Premises to the consideration of the honorable house & hopes such relief will be affoarded as the exigence of the Case requires.

Thos Slaughter.

Endorsement on the back of the petition: Thomas Slaughter October 11th. 1776. Ref'd to Com. on state of the country.

NUMBER 5.

TO THE HONBLE. THE SPEAKER & GENTLEMEN OF THE HOUSE OF DELEGATES:

Hugh McGary humbly sheweth, That in the months of March and April last the northern Indians invaded the County of Kentucky, killed many of the inhabitants, destroyed part of their stock & took off upwards of two Hundred horses. News arriving that Government had ordered an Expedition against the Towns of the Enemy Indians from Pittsburg The Commanding officer at Kentucky sent your petitioner thither as Express with a List of Horses lost & their descriptive marks in order that they might be recovered to the Owners. Your petitioner hath obeyed his Orders which are hereto subjoined with General Hand's Receipt & a Certificate of his return to Kentucky & the Distance he rode. Your petitioner only prays the customary allowance to Expresses if this honble House thinks proper & shall pray &c.

Fort Pitt 22th June 1777 reced of Hugh Mcgary Express from Kentucky, a List of the Horses, taken by the Northern Indians at or near Harrodsburg.

To the General Assembly of Virginia

This is to Certify that sd Hugh McGary was sent express by me to Pittsburg the Distance Seven Hundred & Fifty Miles Given under my hand Harrodsburgh 22d Augst. 1777.

     G R Clark, Cmd.
     Edwd Hand Brigadr Genl.

this is to Certify that Mr Hugh McGary is appointed by me as Express to Pittsburg I do request all persons to assist him as such
Given from under my hand at Harrodsburgh May 17. 1777

     G R Clark, Cmd.

  Endorsement on the back of the petition: Hugh Mc.Gary Pet.n. Decr.1. Ref'd to claims. reasonable . Alld. for 750 miles at lbs. 28- 2-6.

NUMBER 6.

To the Honourable House of Delegates for the Commonwealth of Virginia—

  The Petition of the Inhabitants of the County of Kentucky humbly sheweth, . . .

  That your Petitioners are and have for some time past been almost destitute of the necessary Article Salt. That by reason of the Incursions of the different Nations of Indians this year past we have been prevented from making what Quantities would be necessary for ourselves and Families as we formerly did, for small Parties would be in great Danger of being cut off and larger ones could not be spared from the defence of the Families.

  That as bountiful Nature hath plentifully furnished this Country with Salt Springs where at a small expence Salt might be made in abundance many of which are claimed by Persons resident in this State who have never been at any Pains or Expence to errect Manufactories at them which if done would be very Beneficial to not only adjacent Settlers but also interior Inhabitants of this Commonwealth—

Petitions of the Early Inhabitants of Kentucky

Now your Petitioners humbly pray that if the Claimants do not immediately errect Salt Manufactories at the different Springs claimed by them The honourable House would take it into their consideration and Order that the said Springs should be made publick Property and be Manufactored by Government by which Means Government would be profited & your Petitioners have speedy relief and your Petitioners in duty bound shall ever pray

[Names.]

Endorsement on the back of petition: Petition of Inhabitants of Kentucky. 1777, Nov. 25. Ref'd to Propns. ref'd to next session of Assembly. 1st (Rejected)

The importance of a conservation of salt and the encouragement of its production may be seen from the following acts bearing upon the subject and passed at different times by the Assembly:
An ordinance for erecting Salt works in the colony and for encouraging the making of Salt. Henings Statutes Vol. 9—122. An Act for encouraging the making of Salt. Henings Statutes Vol. 9 —310.
An Act authorizing the seizure of Salt in the same manner as provisions for the use of the army. Henings Statutes Vol.9. 381. An Act to supply the inhabitants of the commonwealth with salt upon reasonable terms. "Whereas divers ill disposed persons have possessed themselves of large quantities of Salt, which they have not only refused to sell at any reasonable price, but to enhance the value of their own salt&c." An embargo was placed on the shipment and the freeholders might seize salt upon warrant issued by a justice of the peace.

NUMBER 7.

To the Honorable the General Assembly of Virginia.

The Humble petition of Nathaniel Henderson Sheweth, that on or about the Eleventh day of Septer last, in defending fort Boon in the County of Kentucky against an attempt of the Indians, your Petitioner had a valuable negro fellow[ed] killed— That the said negro was ordered by the Commanding officer to take a gun, and place himself in a dangerous post and to keep watch & fire on the Indians, which he accordingly did and was killed—That if the said negroe had been suffered to remain within his Cabbin, he could not have been hurt, That the loss of so valuable a slave together with the many other losses sustained by your petitioner in that Country distress him very much—Therefore hopes, that the Assembly will order a recom-

To the General Assembly of Virginia

pense—and that the value of the said slave may be paid to your petitioners, who as in duty bound shall ever pray &c
Wmbg. Novr. 21. 1778.   Nathaniel Henderson

The Deposition of Captain William Buchanan of lawful age, being first sworn on the Holy Evangelist of Almighty God, deposes and says, that in the month of September last Fort Boon was attacked by a party of Indians, to the number of about three hundred and forty, at which time there was not more than sixty men in the Fort, including the Garrison Soldiers, & all the settlers; that arms & ammunition were given to the negroe men in the said Fort, and stationed by the commanding officer in such a manner, so as to make the best defence possible; that a certain negroe man the property of Nathaniel Henderson (who was then absent) had taken post on the outside of the Fort, as directed by the Commander, and in consequence thereof, the said negroe fellow was killed by the Indians; the Deponent further says, that the said Negroe was very likely, about twenty four years of age, and in his opinion worth upwards of Six hundred pounds—and further sayeth not—
Wmsburg. Novr. 28th 1778   W. Buchanan
   Sworn to before
     Edwd Charlton

   Endorsement on back of petition. Ref.d to Claims Nov.24 1778 rejected—to be reported especially—recommitted— rejected— reported Decr. 10th.

NUMBER 8.

TO THE HONOURABLE HOUSE, OF ASSEMBLY, FOR THE STATE OF VIRGINIA.

The petition of the Destressed Inhabitants of the county of Kentuckky, Humbly, shweth, That whereas we your distressed petitioners, situate in this remote part, exposed to all the Barberous ravages of inhuman savage, whose savage disposition, being animated by the rewards of Governour Hamilton has enabled, them to hold up a constant war this four years, which term has reduced many, of us so low that we have scarce cattle amongst us to supply, our small Family's and many of us that brought good stocks of both Horses and cows, now at this juncture have not left so much as one cow for the support of our familys, which to our great disadvantage may plainly appear to every spectator, we have thought proper to present you with a just estimation of our losses in settling and defending this extensive country, which we hope will contribute much to the benefit of the common charge, by virtue of the late act of Assembly, in opening and establishing a Land office. tho at the same time we your depressed petitioners many of us will be intirely deprived of the opportunity of geting so much as one hundred acres of land, notwithstanding the loss of our properties and so many of our lives which we have expended in Defence of this country, except we your petitioners get speedy redress by this our petition, (this must be the unhappy event) we must lie under the disagreeable necessity of going Down the Mississippi, to the Spanish protection, or becoming tennants to private gentlemen who have men employed at this junction in this country at one hundred pounds per Thousand for, running round the land, which is too rough a medicine ever to be dejested by any set of people that have suffered as we have, you the Honourable House of Assembly in whom rests our most sacred rights and priviledges, justice at this time loudly calls your attention we your petitioners hope that the extensive distance of our situation will not create a negligence of this nature, but rather a curious reflection, on our inabilities, we think it expedient to show you the reasons why some of us who first setled in the country will be deprived of geting amends for our losses and troubles first. that many, of our inhabitants both married and single, have been taken by the Indians and carried to Detroyt others killed and their wives and children left in this destitute situation not being able as yet even to support their indigent family's some of

To the General Assembly of Virginia

which never marked or even choose a piece of Land in the country, we your petitioners think four hundred acres two small a compensation, which will be all we have in our powers to procure. Secondly those who have setled since the year one thousand seven hundred and seventy seven who have suffered equally as much as they that first setled, who could only loose their all; is now deprived of the opportunity of securing any land except four hundred acres and that at the state price which is fair from many of our capacities to be able to comply with the terms proposed to us by act of Assembly, by our being reduced so in coming to the country and loosing what we had after we got to it by the Indians. Thirdly those who have been in the country before the year, one Thousand seven hundred and seventy eight and only raised a small cabbin perhaps never stayed, three weeks in the country never lost to the amount of one shillings worth yet they are intituled to their choice of one Thousand Acres at State price. If no alteration be made it had been well for us if we had all been such cultivators and never come to settle in the country untill there had been a peace. We have long united on the opening of a Land office hoping each sufferer to receve some compensation in Land for his loss trouble and risk, and we your petitioners are still in hopes that when this our petition comes under your consideration, and a mature reflexion is cast upon the whole, that you will find that our loss is at this juncture to the great advantage of this state. On a reflection of your justice & mercy we congratulate ourselves that a good cause never suffered in the hands of just men, we cheerfully refer the whole of our grievances to do as you in your wisdom may think right, and we your petitioners as in duty bound shall ever pray &c

[Names.]

Endorsement on back of petition: Octr.14th.1779—Referred to Propositions — Novr.5th to be heard— reasonable.

The first action recognizing the rights of settlers to titles in the land is found in an act entitled, An Act for raising a supply of money for public exigencies. Henings Statutes, Vol. 9, 349.

The grievances of the settlers led to the passage of an act entitled, An Act for adjusting and settling the titles of claimers to unpatented lands under the present and former governments previous to the establishment of the commonwealth's land office. Henings Statutes, Vol. 10, 38.

"And whereas great numbers of people have settled in the county upon the western waters, upon waste and unappropriated lands for which they have been hitherto prevented from suing out patents or obtaining legal titles by the king of Great Britain, proclamations or instructions of government, and the present war having delayed until now, the opening of a land office and the establishment of any certain terms for granting lands and it is just that those settling under such circumstances should have some reasonable allowance for the charge and risk they have incurred and that the property so acquired should be secured to them, Be it enacted," etc.

All bona fide settlers after January 1, 1778, were allowed to have four hundred acres even though they had laid off a less amount.

The right to buy an indefinite amount of land was granted by an act entitled, An Act for establishing a land office and ascertaining the terms and manner of granting waste and unappropriated lands. Henings Statutes, Vol. 10, 50.

"Be it therefore enacted that any person may acquire title to so much waste land as he or she shall desire to purchase, on paying the consideration of forty pounds for every hundred acres," etc.

NUMBER 9.

To the Honourable House of Assembly for the State of Virginia.

The petition of the Distressed Inhabitants of Boonsfort Humbly sheweth, that whereas the late act of Assembly has reserved in this county of Kentuckky six hundred and forty acres of Land for the use of a Town that is not to be entered or surveyed by any private individual untill a true representation of our case is laid before you the Honourable House of Assembly, the better to inable you the Honourable House of Assembly to be compitent judges of the cause, we your petitioners are now laying before you, we your petitioners think it expedient at this time to set forth to you the Honourable House of Assembly the plan and form that this fort and Township was first settled on, and also the methods that has been used by some of those gentlemen that first pretended a claim to this country by a purchase from the Cherukee Indians, and also the names of every person kill'd and taken belonging to this sd fort since the time of its being first settled, with the dates as near as can be calculated at this time, which we hope will enable you the Honourable House of Assembly to judge

To the General Assembly of Virginia

who has suffered in setling this place. In the first place after Richard Henderson & Company had made purchase from the Indians they applyed to Daniel Boon who was to be their pilot to this country they further desired to know the most convenient place for a Town on the Kentuckky river sd Boon Directed them to this place letting them know the length and breadth of the low grounds as near as he could, upon his information it was resolved that this was the spot. they would place the Town on, and in coming to the place the company agree'd to lay it off into two acre tending lotts which was to be given up the next year for the use of a Town and Town common's tho at the same time this would entitle every man to draw a free lott in Town and also, entitle him to his Bounty Land altho he had made corn on his own entry as the proprietors proclamation run thus that every man that made corn in this country in the year one Thousand seven hundred and seventy five should be entitled to five hundred acres of Land at this time of all the men raised corn here the first year there is now but three at this fort. after the people that has made corn the first year had gone into the Inhabitants and times began to grow somewhat difficult sd Colo. Richard Henderson had the fence that was made by the people broke and took the rails and fenced in betwixt twenty and thirty acres of the most convenient ground next the fort which has been held under sd Henderson ever since except the value of one or two acres that was taken for gardians for people in sd fort, we your petitioners think it a grand Imposition that sd Henderson should hold such a quantity of Ground whilst some of us your petitioners have been under the necessity of clearing ground at the risk of our lives and tending our crops round sd Hendersons slaves. In the second place John Luttrel one of the Gent, proprietors enterd on the S W. side of sd Township and improved on the Land, first allowed by sd proprietors for a Town. In the third place Nathaniel Heart another of the sd proprietors entered the upper half of the Town Land which was cleared and fenced by the people who tended corn the first year, there may perhaps be one hundred acres within the fence and the one half of that clear'd this sd Nathaniel Heart finding his entry under sd proprietors would not entitle him to the Land sd Heart came out last spring to this country and warmly recommended to the Inhabitants of this fort to lay off a Town which some of the Inhabitants agreed to in some measure, they thought it would be well for every man to know his own ground as the Land convenient was held by two or three men. without the least notice given for an election for trustees the Drum beat to arms and these names read over by one of these trustees to wit. Richard Callaway Nathaniel Heart George Madin, James Estill & Robert Cartright and these questions was ask'd, Gentlemen has any of you any objections to these gentlemen to be trustees for this Town. to which little or no, Answer was made our silence taken for conscent. they proceeded to Business. in the first place they reserved five hundred acres of Land for the use of a Town & Town commons two hundred acres on the south side of the Kentuckky and three hundred on the north side which three hundred acres on the North side is not of the least advantage to this Town by reason of a large steep hill that binds all that side of the river opposite to this town and the hill so steep that it will be with great difficulty to get timber down from any place on that side. what could be the motive of these men to reserve Land on that Inconvenient side we are at a loss to know except some private views incited this sd Nathaniel Heart in order to obtain the upper half of this Town Land which sd Heart unjustly claims as circumstances seem to make it appear, in the first place it could not be supposed had we been left to our choice that we would have choose men that were intire strangers to us as three of these men were and not even settlers in the country & especially men that was deeply interested as Capt. Heart was, the terms that the tolls were let upon was entirely out of the power of several of them that suffered most for them and Especially

To the General Assembly of Virginia

widowes who in justice ought to have the greatest indulgence there was not the least Distinction made, for they that had been here but two days had the same previledg to draw a lott as they that first settled so that they complyed with the terms which was, that, every lott holder should build upon his lott one House twenty by sixteen with hew'd or sawed loggs with a shingled or clapboard roof with a brick stone or mud chimney by the first day of February next, and they that did not comply with these terms was to forfeit their lott, which must certainly be the case with several of us your petitioners who have not left so much as one Horse even to Draw Timber. Upon information that the late Act of Assembly intituled the Inhabitants of this Township to six hundred and forty acres of Land, we your petitioners Assembled ourselves called upon Colo. Richard Callaway being one of the Trustees in the first appointment and Desired that a fair Election should be held and that he would still serve as a Trustee but he utterly refused to serve any other way, than by the first appointment and seemed much Disaffected at our proceedings however as it is impossible for some of us your petitioners to subsist with our Family's unless we have some convenient pice of ground allowed us at this Township we your petitioners pray that the sd six hundred and forty acres of Land be established for the use of this sd Township by the Name of Boonsborough and that you appoint James Estill Capt., David Gass Capt, Jno. Holder, John South Pemberton Rawlings Stephen Hencock & Jno Martin Trustees for the same being unanimously [Chosen] for that purpose we your petitioners further pray that every Actual settler at this Township may be entituled to Draw a free lott; and in the lemitation of three years make such improvement as before Directed, the lotts to consist of half acre in lott and five acre out lott as the Indians is so frequent amongst us that we cannot settle any other way than in Forts or Townships, at this time and whereas several single men from convincing circumstances have resided with us with no other motive than

Petitions of the Early Inhabitants of Kentucky

to give their assistance that we might not become a prey to our Enemies which was nearly the case with all the assistance we had in Septr seventy eight when the Indians laid close seige Eleven Days to our fort we your petitioners pray that every such single man be intituled to a lott upon the like terms upon applying to the trustees for the same we your petitions pray that the sd Six hundred and forty acres of land allowed to the Inhabitants of this sd Township be laid upon the south side of the Kentuckky river and that the lines may be Directed by the late Trustees Elected, as the land at this Township lies much incommoded by hills and that we your petitioners may have, the previledg of running the land as may be most convenient for the use and benefit of sd Township as there is no claim prior to the Township claim and we your petitioners as in Duty bound shall ever pray &c

[Names.]

Endorsement on back of petition: October 16th. 1779— referred to Propositions — reasonable.

Land for the purpose of settlers in towns was provided by the act in Henings Statutes, Vol. 10, 39. To those settling in towns for the purpose of protection six hundred and forty acres were to be set apart for such use until a true representation could be made to the Assembly.

The town of Boonsborough was created by the act entitled, An Act for establishing the town of Boonsborough in the county of Kentucky. Henings Statutes, Vol. 10, 134.

"Whereas it hath been represented to the present assembly that the inhabitants of the township called Boonsborough, lying on the Kentucky river, in the County of Kentucky, have laid off twenty acres of land into lots and streets and have petitioned the assembly that the said lots and streets together with fifty acres adjoining thereto may be laid off into lots and streets and established a town for the reception of traders and that six hundred and forty acres of land allowed by law to every such township for a common may also be laid off adjoining thereto, Be it enacted," etc.

The trusteeship was vested in Richard Callaway, Charles Thruston, Levin Powell, Edmund Taylor, James Estil, Edward Bradley, John Kennedy, David Gist (Gass?), Pemberton Rawlings, and Daniel Boone.

The plan of the town was to be recorded with the court of the county. Lots were to be conveyed to applicants "subject to building on each a dwelling house, sixteen feet square at least with a brick, stone or dirt chimney to be finished fit for habitation within three years from the date of their respective deeds."

The same general plan was followed in the creation of all towns while the Kentucky County lasted, and until separation was granted.

To the General Assembly of Virginia

NUMBER 10.

TO THE HONOURABLE THE SPEAKER AND GENTLEMEN OF THE HOUSE OF DELEGATES

The petition of Richard Calloway of Boonsborough Humbly sheweth that from the first seating of This Town both the inhabitants and travilers has Found it very inconvenient to get across the Kentucky River only in dry seasons in the summer time, and as both this Town and country is now become very popular and is much Resorted by travilers: I therefore pray that your Hone. House will pass an Act of Assembly That shall intitle me to keep a publick ferry across the Above said River from the Town Land to the land of this state and your petitioner as in duty bound will pray &c

Richard Calloway

Endorsement on back of petition: Octor.25.1779 — Ref'd to Propositions— reasonable—drawn.

This request was granted by an act entitled, An Act for establishing several new ferries and for other purposes.

"Whereas it is represented to this present general assembly, that publick ferries at the places hereafter named will be of great advantage to travellers and others, Be it therefore enacted, etc." ". . . at the town of Boonsborough, in the county of Kentucky across Kentucky river to the land on the opposite shore, the price for a man three shillings and for a horse the same; the keeping of which last named ferry and emolument arising therefrom are hereby given and granted to Richard Callaway, his heirs or assigns, so long as he or they shall well and faithfully keep the same according to the directions of this act. And for the transportation of wheel carriages tobacco, cattle and other beasts at the places aforesaid the ferry keeper may demand and take the following rates; that is to say, for every coach charriot or wagon, and the driver thereof the same as for six horses; for every cart or four wheeled chaise and the driver thereof the same as for four horses; for every two wheeled chaise or chair the same as for two horses; for every hogs head of tobacco as for one horse, for every head of neat cattle as for one horse; for every sheep goat or lamb one fifth part the ferriage of one horse; and for every hog one fourth part the ferriage of one horse and no more." Henings Statutes, Vol. 10, 196.

NUMBER 11.

TO THE HONOR. THE SPEAKER AND GENTLEMEN OF THE HOUSE OF DELEGATES.

The petition of the inhabitants of the County of Kentuckey living at the falls of the River Ohio Humbly sheweth, that your petitioners have at great risque and expence removed to this remote part of the state and from the advantageous situa-

Petitions of the Early Inhabitants of Kentucky

tion of the place, both for Trade and Safety was induced to settle here, and having laid out a Town under directions of persons appointed for that purpose by the Court of Kentuckey (a plan of which we have sent to be laid before you) and when laid out we cast lotts for the choice of the Lotts in the said Town, have improved & settled on some of the Lotts, and some have sold their houses & Lotts to persons that have come here since the Town was laid out who are still adding to our improvements, but the uncertainty of the title thereto prevents some from settling here that are inclined thereby making us less secure from any attack of the Indians, for we are informed the land that we have laid out for a Town above the mouth of a gutt that makes into the river opposite the falls was surveyed & patented for Connelly who we have understood have taken part with the Enemies of America, and agreable to a late act of Assembly the Land we expect will be escheated and sold; we are well assured that a Town established at this place will be of great advantage to the inhabitants of Kentuckey, and think the plan on which the Town is now laid out will conduce towards its being a populous Town and of great advantage to us, as many of us have built houses according thereto; and will render us secure from any hostile intention of the Indians & will induce Merchants to bring articles of commerce that the inhabitants of this Western part of the State stands much in need of, we therefore pray that an act may pass to establish a Town at the Falls of the Ohio river agreable to the plan sent, and that the present settlers & holders of the lotts in the said Town may have them confirmed to them on paying a compensation that may be thought reasonable to any one having a right thereto if thought requisite or to the Commonwealth; and not let us be turned out of houses we have built and from lotts we have improved & are about to build on & thereby loose the labour we have preformed at the risque of our lives,— all these several matters we your petitioners beg leave to lay before your Hone. House and hope, you will comply with our

To the General Assembly of Virginia

request in [a]dopting the prayer of our petition, or some other method that you in your wisdom may think proper, that will conduce to the Interest and Security of this exposed part of the State, and we as in duty bound shall ever pray &c. &c. &c. May 1, 1780.

[Names.]

Endorsement on back of petition: Reasonable—Propositions—May 1st. 1780.

This request was granted by an act entitled, An Act for establishing the town of Louisville at the falls of the Ohio. Henings Statutes, Vol. 10, 293.

"Whereas sundry inhabitants of the county of Kentucky have, at great expense and hazard settled themselves upon certain lands at the falls of the Ohio, said to be the property of John Connaly, have laid off a considerable part thereof into half acre lots for a town, and having settled thereon have preferred petitions to the general assembly to establish the said town Be it enacted," etc.

Following were trustees: John Todd, Jr., Stephen Trigg, George Slaughter, John Floyd, William Pope, George Meriwether, Andrew Hines, James Sullivan, and Marshen Brashiers.

The grant was one thousand acres of the forfeited land of John Connelly adjoining the land of John Campbell.

Lots were to be sold at auction and if they brought $30 the money was to be put into the treasury of the Commonwealth.

NUMBER 12.

To the Honble the Speaker, and Gent. of the House of Delegates,

Your petitioners Inhabitants of the north side of Kentucky humbly represent

That the setled part of the County of Kentuckey is of Late grown so Extensive that in a time of pace it would be extremly inconvanient for your petitioners to attend at the Courthouse mutch more so at present when an invetorate War rages with unremited violance.

That the Militia Inhabitants of the north side of Kaintucky Amount to about four hundred with Eleven fortified posts—That a place Central to Every post might be fixed upon Distant from the farthest not more than fifteen miles—That the nearest settlement to the Courthouse is at least forty miles and the farthest about Seventy miles at present That the River Kentuckey is rendered impasable half the year by

Petitions of the Early Inhabitants of Kentucky

high waters & is ever inconveniant and Dangarous by Reasons of its Craggy and precipitate Bancks Thus severed by nature from our felow Citizens of the Southside of the river and Compactly situated in a fertile Land where aditional adventurers bid fair for a farther population your petitioners conceive themselves ripe for a Separation and pray

That the said County be Divided by a Line begining at the mouth of Kaintuckey River runing up the same and its midle fork to the head thence South East to Washington Line —Your petitioners farther pray that Comissioners be apointed to colect the sentements of the people upon the properest place for holding a Court & invested with authoraty to purchase Lands for a town to be laid off under such regalations as your Honarable House shall please to derect & your petitioners as in Duty bound shall pray &c—Signed in behalf of Lexington Station Signed in behalf of McConnells station

[Names.]

The Inhabitants of Unity Station twenty in Number unanimously desired this Petition to be signed in their behalf by May 1st 1780. Levi Todd

To the Honble the Speaker and Gent. of the House of Delegates,

The Petition of the Inhabitants at and near the Falls of the Ohio Humbly sheweth that your Petitioners are situated generally near one hundred Miles from the Court house of this County in a compact, rich settlement. That so great a Distance from holding Court, General-Musters render all Civil & Military Regulation altogether ineffectual—that the Number of Setlers at present amount to (at least) eight Hundred & are daily increasing.

To remedy the Disorders ever attendant upon the Want of Law & render the Administration of Justice less Burdensome; Your Petitioners pray: that all that Part of the south side of Kentucky River which lieth below Hammonds Creek and the Beach-Knobs, may be erected into a seperate County, and that all the Priviledges & Advantages of other Counties within the

To the General Assembly of Virginia

Common-Wealth, may be granted to its Inhabitants, and your Petitioners.—

shall ever pray &c.—

[Names.]

Endorsement on back of petition: Reasonable—Propositions.

The division of the county of Kentucky is provided in an act entitled, An Act for establishing three new counties upon the western waters. Henings Statutes, Vol. 10, 315.

"Whereas the inhabitants of the county of Kentucky are subject to great inconveniences for the want of due administration of justice, arising principally from the great extent of the county and the dispersed situation of the settlements Be it enacted," etc.

The names of the new counties were Jefferson, Fayette, and Lincoln. Court was to be held in each alternately on the first, second, and third Tuesdays of the month. Fayette was to try all cases in equity not settled to date. County seats to be at Louisville, Lexington, and Harrodsburg. The surveyors of Kentucky could choose the county they preferred.

NUMBER 13.

To the Honourable the Speaker and Gentlemen of the House of Delegates,

HUMBLY SHEWETH.

THAT your petitioner, soon after the Discovery of the fine lands upon the Kentucky and the adjacent waters of the Ohio River, removed into that Country, where he determined to lay out and risk all his little Fortune, and accordingly was deeply engaged in settling, building on, and improving Lands there, according to the Custom of the Country; expecting thereby to secure considerable Quantities of Land; but finding, during his Residence there, that the Inhabitants in that Quarter, and other parts over the Alleghany Mountains, were constantly exposed to the Incursions and Depredations of the Indians on the North west side of the Ohio, instigated and aided by the British Garrisons at the Kaskaskies near the Mississippi, and at St. Vincents upon the Obache, and Experience having proved it extremely expensive and difficult, if not impracticable, to protect so extensive a frontier against the Savages by troops stationed among the Settlements, He formed the Design of surprising and reducing the before mentioned British Garrisons; thereby to prevent the evil Consequences of their Influence upon the Indians, and by establishing military posts of our own Troops in their Country, to deter them from distant Expeditions against our frontier Inhabitants on the South East of the Ohio, and by Degrees bring them over to the American interest. Deeply impressed with these Sentiments, he, at his own Expence, sent confidential persons, in the Character of Indian Traders, to reconnoitre and examine those places, and sound the Disposition of the French Inhabitants; and having made himself perfectly acquainted with the strength and situation of the said posts, and other material Circumstances, he was thoroughly convinced of the practicability and success of a secret Expedition against them, and of its great importance to the public, and therefore determined to lay his plan before the Governor and Council, and relinquishing all his undertakings and Improvements at Kentucky, to devote himself to the service of his Country, by engaging in the said Expedition (if it should be approved) either as an Officer, or a Voluntier; or in any other Character in which it should be thought he could do most Service.

That upon the said Expedition being approved, the Governor and Council, unsolicited by your Petitioner, were pleased to appoint him to command it; by the Blessing of divine providence, and the bravery of his fellow Soldiers, he has been able to carry it into effectual execution, and in the ample and honourable testimony he has received of the public Approbation, enjoys the most pleasing of all Reflections—of having discharged the Duty of a good Citizen, and thro' Scenes of uncommon Difficulty and Danger, rendered essential Service to his native Country. Your petitioner, in his Negotiations and Treaties with the numerous Indian Tribes settled in those parts, has spared no pains in endeavouring to alienate them from the British, and fix them in the American Interest, wherein he

To the General Assembly of Virginia

flatters himself he has in a great measure succeeded. In the Course of these Treaties, the Indians inhabiting the Country on the Obache, and the adjacent parts of the Ohio, express the most earnest Desire that your Petitioner should continue to reside among them, and as a proof of their Affection and Attachment, insisted upon giving him a Tract of Land, adjoining to the Falls, on the North West Side of the Ohio River, of seven miles and a half square, and containing about thirty-six thousand Acres, which he could not refuse without giving them umbrage and forfeiting the Influence he had acquired among them; they accordingly made him a Deed of Conveyance in the French Language, which being registered in the Records of the Court of St. Vincents, the Original is humbly submitted herewith to the Consideration of the General Assembly.

Your Petitioner is sensible, that the Commonwealth hath, and ought to have, the exclusive Right of pre-emption from the Indians of all Lands within its own Territory, and therefore presumes to claim no Title, under the said Deed to the Lands therein mentioned, unless the same shall be confirmed to him by the Legislature; but he begs leave to observe, that this Deed will save to the public the Expence of hereafter purchasing the same Land; and as his Fortune was at best small, the greater part of which he had expended in improving Lands at Kentucky, which by engaging in the service of the Public, at the time and under the circumstances before mentioned, he was obliged to abandon, and has been disabled from carrying into Execution the Improvements and Settlements he had begun, so as to entitle him to Certificates for anything considerable under the late Land Law, whereby he hath, in a manner, lost his All; Confiding therefore in the Liberality of his Country, he is induced to hope, and humbly prays, that the General Assembly will be pleased to grant him the Lands contained in the said Deed—according to the Bounds therein expressed, upon such Conditions and Terms, as they, in their Wisdom shall think fit—

And your Petitioner shall ever pray.

George Rogers Clark

Endorsement on back of petition: Petition of Colo. Geo. Rogs. Clarke— May 27 1780— Referred to Propositions—Reported.

There is no act showing that this was done, but the following is a resolution for a cession of the lands on the northwest side of the Ohio to Clark's regiment. Henings Statutes, Vol. 10, 564.

"As Col. Geo. Rogers Clarke planned and executed the secret expedition by which the British posts were reduced, and was promised if the enterprize succeeded a liberal gratuity in lands in that county for the officers and soldiers who first marched thither with him, that a quantity of land not exceeding one hundred and fifty thousand acres, be allowed and granted to the said officers and soldiers and other officers and soldiers that have since been incorporated with said regiment, to be laid off in one tract the length of which is not to exceed double the breadth, in such place on the northwest of the Ohio as the majority of the officers shall choose, and to be afterwards divided among the officers and soldiers in due proportion according to the laws of Virginia."

This reservation is preserved in an act entitled, An Act to authorize the delegates of this state in Congress to convey to the U. S. in Congress assembled all right of this commonwealth to the territory northwestward of the Ohio. Henings Statutes, Vol. 11, 326.

NUMBER 14.

TO THE HONORABLE THE SPEAKER OF THE HOUSE OF DELEGATES—

The Petition of the Subscribers, settlers at Lexington in the County of Fayette humbly sheweth—

That they at a considerable risque and expence settled themselves at this place which was then and still is unappropriated and unclaimed by any private person, That from an Act of Assembly passed in May 1779 intitled An Act for adjusting and settling the Titles of claimers to unpatented Lands, under the present and former Government, previous to the Establishment of the Commonwealth's Land Office. they were induced to expect a Grant of Six hundred & forty acres, in confidence of which they elected Trustees who proceeded to lay off a Town, including the said Quantity, a plot of which is hereto annexed, making condition at Lines with adjacent claimers, a suitable square is reserved for the publick Buildings

FACSIMILE OF MAP

To the General Assembly of Virginia

of the County and a Sum of money granted by the Trustees for said Buildings, a considerable part of the Land is divided among the present settlers, upon the most equitable and just Terms, a part reserved to be disposed of to future settlers to create a fund for making necessary Improvements in the Town and encourage Settlers in future. That they have purchased Seventy acres being part of a Survey made for John Floyd to augment the Quantity and add to the convenience and benefit of the Inhabitants a former Petition to the same purpose for reasons unknown to your Petitioners having been unanswered raises in us an anxiety to know the Determination of your honorable House, Your Petitioners therefore pray that the said 640 acres together with the adjoining purchase be vested in Trustees for a Town that the present Lot holders be confirmed in their Titles and subjected to such Reasonable requisitions towards settling and improving thereon as to your honourable House shall seem just & we in Duty bound shall ever pray

[Names.]

Fayette County Court

We do certify that we have no Objectson to the confirming to the Lexington Trustees the Survey of the Town Lands agreeable to the within plat & that no person hath any just claim to said Lands to our knowledge

J. N. Todd
Levi Todd
atty. for John Maxwell
R. Patterson

April 14—1782.

Map and the following:—

June 16th 17th 1782 Drew near 10 miles to the inch From the T Falls to Squire Boons 30 miles from thence to Leeston 20 miles from thence to Lexinton 25 miles, from Elkhorn to the mouth of Lickin 70 miles, from Elkhorn to the Salt Spring on Lickin 40 miles, from thence to Lime stone 20 miles

Petitions of the Early Inhabitants of Kentucky

From Elkhorn to Lime stone a level country except near the Salt Springs and from Elkhorn to the mouth of the Lickin great part of the way Hilley and poor

Robt. Johnson

Endorsed on back of petition: Dec. 7th 1781—Referred to Propositions—June 6th 1782—Reasonable—Repd.

The request is granted in the act entitled, An Act to establish a town at the courthouse in the county of Fayette.

"Whereas it is represented to the assembly that six hundred and forty acres of unappropriated lands in the county of Fayette whereon the courthouse of the county stands, have been by the settlers thereon laid out into lots and streets for a town and that the said settlers have purchased seventy acres of land contiguous to the said six hundred and forty acres, being part of a survey made for John Floyd. And whereas it would tend greatly to the improvement and settling the same if the titles of settlers on the lots were confirmed and a town established thereon, Be it enacted," etc.

The trustees were: John Todd, Robert Patterson, William Mitchell, Andrew Steel, William Henderson, William McCowwald, (?) and William Steel. Henings Statutes, Vol. 11, 100.

NUMBER 15.

TO THE HONOURABLE SPEAKER AND THE GENERAL ASSEMBLY OF VIRGINIA.

We your Petitioners Inhabitants of Kentuckey, Humbly beg leave to address you as their Legislative Body, imploring you to take into consideration our grievances; considering us as faithful subjects to the Republick and equally intitled to the Common Privileges with our fellow Citizens who pay a due reverence to the Constitution, and a proper regard for the preservation of it.

Your Memorialists thro' the Paternal Tenderness they have for their Infant Families, the obligation which Nature binds to provide for them, Removed from the Interior parts of the Country through a Wilderness infested with the most Savage and cruel Enemies, combating with the greatest Difficulties, and yet continue to be Invaded by the Merciless Banditty, continually Harrased, confin'd to stations, and even debarr'd from applying the necessary means for the support of their Families, and have thought proper first to have recourse to redress through your Honourable Body, as Duty calls us to pay all Imagenable

To the General Assembly of Virginia

Deference to your Paternal Authority and Guardianship over us which your Memorialists are bound to observe while you Act for their safety and defence.

Your Memorialists humbly beg you to have a Retrospect to the year Seventy nine, at which time your Honourable House thought proper to open a Land office for the Population of the Country & the megration of Foreigners, as Express'd in the Act of Assembly, at which time and ever since, every person was at Liberty to purchase without Cultivating as much Lands as He or She should think proper, which has been very injurious to the Indigent Inhabitants, and of but small advantage to the commonwealth, it has not only prevented sufficient Immigration, but has been Destructive to all Ages Sexes and Conditions of Existence, which has occasioned a continual Demegration, with those exterminated out of being by the Savage Barbarians that your Memorialists find their Number of Fighting Men considerably deminished since the year seventeen Hundred and Eighty, notwithstanding the small continued Immegrations since that Time.

Your Memorialists beg leave to point out a way for the Emolument and happiness of the Indigent Inhabitants, as also the most easy and Indubitable way of defending this Country, unless you can without an Infringment of the Rights of the People, Revive the antient Cultivation Law which seems very difficult to your Memorialists after such Lands has been appropriated with Reserve.

Your Memorialists beg leave to inform you that the Persons granted Land by the Act of May Session in Eighty one, in Consideration of their setling here since Seventy nine, and for other causes, have been prevented from acquiring such Lands by an Inundation of Warrants being in the County where the Land office continued open before the county courts issued certificates, but there being great Quantities of Waste and un-enter'd Lands yet in the other Counties in the District of Kentuckey which your Memorialists Conceives may be held in

Petitions of the Early Inhabitants of Kentucky

Reserve for the aforesaid setlers, as also for the Immediate Peopling of this Country, and such megrants to be allowed according to Antient Custom, who shall immediately cultivate such lands or become Inhabitants with your Memorialists, as all other means has hitherto been found inadequate to the happiness and Safety of this Country, your Memorialists conceives this Method to be the most easy and least injurious to the Publick weal, and as the Depretiation of Land Warrants being equal to that of the Paper Currency has become a Publick notority, and that the one Exchanges for the other without being in credit for scarcely any other Commodity. And your Memorialists must beg leave to add that the moneys in their hands died being in this Exterior part, they conceive this Mode if adopted, will quickly raise a Fund sufficient for the Redemption of such Warrants upon the same Terms they shall Receive for their Paper Currency. Your Memorialists wish to have their Locations secured to them who came early into this Country, and many of them through illetrisy, and unable to ascertain the true meaning of the Law with the Troubles of Indians, have not Enter'd their Lands so special and precise as the Law Requires—many of whose Entries have been Reenter'd by others, which without the kind interposition of your House, will produce Tedious Letigations.

Your Memorialists pray you to take into consideration their Scatter'd Situation, which is neither Eligible nor happy, and neither Aids nor any apparent Redress of their Grievances has appeared, which has produced Considerable Desentions amongst them, which an Inflamatary Pamphlet intitled publick Good has augmented which, we pray you to take into Consideration and Create them a power Sufficient for their Controul and better Government, as well as for the Controul and Management of all Civil and Military affairs in this Country which they only claim according to the Rights of Constitution, or otherwise that you will grant them a Separation with your Intercession with the Honourable the Continental Congress

To the General Assembly of Virginia

for their Incorporation with them, at the same time they pay a proper Deference to your wise Determinations, Reploring [Reposing?] special Trust and Confidence in you. And your Petitioners as in Duty bound shall ever pray &c.

[Names.]

The Committee of the Courts of Justice to whom the Petition of sundry Inhabitants from Kentucky was referr'd, has gone thro' the same and come to several Resolutions thereupon, as follow.

Resolved, That so much of the said Petition as relates to the revival of the ancient cultivation Law be rejected.

Resolv'd, That so much thereof as relates to the claims of poor persons under the act of May Session 1781 and prays for the Liberty of locating their Claims in other Counties, is reasonable; and that where other Entries on Warrants of a subsequent Date should be offer'd at the same time for the same Land, such claims shall have the preference.

Resolv'd, That so much thereof as prays for all other unappropriated Lands to be set apart for encouraging the Settlement of the Country be rejected.

Resolv'd, That that part which prays a confirmation of former Locations, tho' not made with that exact precision which the Law directs, provided they are so describ'd as that the Location can be known and that the Claimants shall not be at Liberty to lay off their Land in such a manner as to injure any one adjoining Claim in order to favor another or to make a vacancy adjoining thereto for themselves or others, is reasonable.

Resolv'd, That so much thereof as prays for the establishment of some kind of controuling power for the better management of their civil and military affairs, is reasonable.

Endorsement on back of petition: May 30th 1782—Ref'd to Courts of Justice—Security for their Entries—do. for poor persons—in having civil and military Govermt. ref'd to Propositions. June 13th 1782—Some parts Reasonable —Other parts rejected—Reported.

The request for some kind of controlling power was provided in an act entitled, An Act for establishing a District Court on the western waters. "Whereas the mode of administering justice has become exceedingly inconvenient and burdensome to suitors living westward of the Alleghany mountains, Be it enacted," etc. Henings Statutes, Vol. 11, 85.

The act provided that Jefferson, Fayette, and Lincoln counties should be united into one district after August 1st, for a supreme court of judicature of original jurisdiction separate of all other courts except the Court of Appeals. It was to have jurisdiction in cases of treason, felonies, misdemeanors and crimes, except those triable in the General Court according to the Constitution. Also all matters in common law and equity arising therefrom. There were to be three judges, four sessions of court to be held each year on the first Monday of March, June, September, and November, lasting eighteen days exclusive of Sunday. Three days were set for criminal matters, five for chancery and the remainder for other cases.

The court was to be a court of record, was to take cognizance of matters relating to probating of wills, deeds, and the granting of letters of administration, escheat, and forfeiture, and caveats.

A grand jury of twenty-four was to be chosen at the beginning of each term. The court appointed a clerk and gaoler and the attorney of the Commonwealth was selected by the Assembly.

A tax of twenty shillings was charged at the beginning of a suit and the judge at the close was to receive fifty pounds. Assistants received twenty shillings a day for attendance, the attorney for the Commonwealth received thirty-seven pounds and ten shillings a quarter and the remainder was to go toward buildings, etc.

The court was to be held at Harrodsburg and could adjourn to places thought proper.

NUMBER 16.

To the Honourable the Speaker of the House of Delegates—

We the Inhabitants of the three Counties of Kentuckey, beg leave with reverence & freedom to address your honorable house—

The former favours shewn by the Government of Virginia to the Inhabitants of this Country thro the various stages of its population, till now, call forth our warmest acknowledgements—When we were weak we were assisted with aids of men and money, until by the blessing of providence we have arrived to a considerable degree of strength, but just as we emerge from a state of obscurity & Indigence we find ourselves and our dear bought possessions to become a subject of noted controversy.—But we place our entire confidence in your honorable house, having no person or power on earth, in whome to rely, but under shelter of the Government of Virginia—

To the General Assembly of Virginia

When our parent state was engaged in an expensive war, and taxes on all the articles of luxury and husbandry proved insufficient to raise supplies, we never once murmured that the Lands around us, as well as those we possessed, should be seized as a sinking fund and offices opened for disposing of it, tho' we were aware that the Land System adopted would at first cause very unequal distribution of Land by giving enormous Quantities to those who could advance most money, yet we apprehended that the fertility of the soil, and the former acts of assembly enforcing a Cultivation proportionate to the Quantity, would induce the adventurer to become a settler.—But Mr. Speaker, Experience! sad Experience! proves that without further compulsory acts, the Engrosser will neither settle himself, nor dispose of it to those who will.—We are surrounded by numerous savage nations, Disjoined from every other settlement in the united states, and amounting to only fifteen hundred men here a tract of Country of five Million of acres of Tillable Land nearly secured under rights from Virginia to defend for those whome ease & Cowardice prevent settling—Usual supplies of men seem just expended, and the fury of war yet unabated.—Such is our melancholy situation—We fly to your house for redress, To whome else shall we apply? We know by experience that Kentuckey has friends in your house, and we now call on them with an Importunity that becomes distressed Citizens to espouse the use of justice for us—

We therefore humbly Petition

That the act of assembly for Cultivating & Improving Lands may be declared in force—

That all Lands as well those granted under the old Military and Treasury rights as the new, be subject to such regulations—

That a superior Court competent to the decision of these as well as all other Land disputes be established in this Country.—

These regulations we have, will carry us still towards that stage of maturity when with the tenderness of a kind parent to a departing child, you will direct us to form a constitution and act for ourselves.

[Names.]

Endorsement on the back of petition. June 1st. 1782—To lie on the table.

The act for establishment of a District Court is referred to in previous petition.

NUMBER 17.

To the Honble the General Assembly of Virginia.

The Petition of sundry inhabitants of the county of Lincoln humbly sheweth—

That your Petitioners have the highest sense of, and acknowledge with thankfulness the attention which your Honourable Body paid the Trustees of this remote corner of the State in the last May Session, in establishing a court of general Judicature in this District, the good effects of which we begin already to feel by the discouragement of Vice & fraud which was too prevalent among us—and we cannot help expressing our concern to understand that there are some people in Kentucky lost to virtue, honesty & good order as to wish for its repeal—We cannot but believe that those are a set of people who never were friendly to the Government of Virginia, nor would be pleased with any law that its Legislature can pass—We therefore hope your Honourable House will pay no regard to any Petitions which may be sent to you by a disaffected few whose wishes are rather to overturn, than support your Government.

Encouraged by our former success we now petition for the passage of a few more laws indispensibly necessary for this district. and first. That our militia may be put on a footing that may more effectually defend us against our savage Enemy.

2ndly—A Law to dispose of the orphans of poor people; which cannot be done at present, as we have no church Wardens to bind them out.

To the General Assembly of Virginia

3rdly—A particular law respecting Strays—it being impossible to put them in the Gazettes according to the present Law.

4thly—A Law authorising some Civil power to solemnize the Rites of matrimony—as we have no clergy either of the church of England or Presbyterians who compose the Greater part of our inhabitants

These requests we make no doubt you will grant, because it is the Interest of our whole District—But where we may be of different Interests, we wish no new laws to pass or amendments to be made until you know the sentiments of a majority of our District because frequent alterations in the Laws are very inconvenient to our remote corner of the State

[Names.]

Endorsement on the back of petition. May 21st. 1783—Referred to Courts of Justice—June 19th 1783—Referred to consideration of the next session of the Assembly.

The request for the right to perform civil marriage is provided in an act entitled, An Act to authorize and confirm marriages in certain cases. Henings Statutes, Vol. 11, 281.

"Whereas it hath been represented to the present General Assembly that many of the good people in the remote parts of the commonwealth are destitute of any persons, authorized by law to solemnize marriages amongst them, Be it enacted," etc., "That where it shall appear to the court of any county on the western waters, that there is not a sufficient number of clergymen authorized to celebrate marriages therein, such court is empowered to nominate so many sober and discreet laymen as will supply the deficiency."

Those so nominated were to receive a license to perform the act in accordance with the church of which they are members. Parties to be married must produce a certificate showing that the bans had been thrice published. Previous marriages might be confirmed in a similar manner.

NUMBER 18.

To the Honorable the General Assembly of Virginia.

The Petition of several of the Trustees in whom certain escheated Lands in the County of Kentucky were vested for a public School, humbly sheweth,

That the General Assembly, sensible of the Advantages resulting to Society from the general diffusion of Learning in the various parts of the community; at the May Session, 1780, vested certain escheated Lands amounting to eight thousand acres, late the property of Robert M'Kinsie, Henry Collins and

Alexr. M'Kee in Trustees as a free Donation from the Commonwealth for the purpose of a public School or Seminary of Learning to be erected within the County of Kentucky as soon as the circumstances of the Country and the state of its Funds will admit. That your Petitioners (a majority of the surviving Trustees) having convened for the purpose of carrying into execution the laudable design of the Legislature, and finding themselves greatly embarassed as to the manner of executing the Trust reposed in them, inasmuch as the Law does not declare whether a majority of the Trustees are sufficient to act, nor in case of the Death of any of the members, how vacancies are to be filled up, and as it does not appear that the Trustees have power under their present appointment to receive Donations from Individuals or in any respect to forward so desireable an Institution, without the Interposition of the Legislature; have unanimously come to the Resolution of petitioning the Assembly, for an amendment of the Law, & an enlargement of the Powers of the Trustees; not doubting but that the same benevolent disposition which actuated the Assembly when this Donation was made will influence the present Members of the Legislature chearfully to contribute as far as in them lies to the noble designs of diffusing useful knowledge and cultivating the unimproved minds of the South in every corner of the State. The sollicitous anxiety which discovers itself in the principal Inhabitants of this Country for having Schools or Seminaries of Learning among them that their Children may be educated as becomes a civilized people, encourages Your Petitioners to hope that the Liberality of private Individuals will be extended in aid of the public Donations, were Trustees incorporated by Law with power of perpetuating their Succession, and authorized to purchase Estates, to receive Donations, make sale and conveyances of Land and to legislate for the Seminary in such Cases as are customary and under such restrictions and limitations as may be prescribed by Law.

Impressed with this hope and the full persuasion that the Assembly will listen with pleasure to every proposition that

To the General Assembly of Virginia

has a Tendency to banish Ignorance and Error, and to introduce in their room what may polish the manners, encourage the improvement of the mind, promote liberality of sentiment and by refining give additional Incentives to Virtue. Your petitioners pray that the said Law may be amended in the several Cases herein before recited, and some fixt plan and Form adopted which may be most conducive to the welfare and success of the Institution, and your Petitioners as in duty bound will ever pray etc.

[Names.]

Endorsement on the back of petition: June 3rd. 1783.—Bill pursuant to Peto.—by Mr. Wallace; Avery; A. White; C. M. Thruston; Ct. Jones.

The process of forfeiture is provided for in a measure entitled, An ordinance for establishing a mode of punishment for the enemies to America in this colony. Henings Statutes, Vol. 9, 101.

"Whereas the most dangerous attempts have been made by some persons in the colony to subvert the rights and liberties of the inhabitants," etc., "Be it enacted," etc.

"All persons in arms within two months after the ordinance and all persons aiding the enemy by enlisting soldiers, giving intelligence, furnishing them with arms, provisions, or naval stores may be imprisoned, and their estates will be placed in the hands of persons chosen by the committee and subject to the determination of the Convention."

Escheated or forfeited lands were set apart for public education in an act entitled, An Act to vest certain escheated lands in the county of Kentucky in Trustees for a public school. 1780. Henings Statutes, Vol. 10, 287.

"Whereas it is represented to the General Assembly, that there are certain lands, within the county of Kentucky formerly belonging to British subjects, not yet sold under the law of escheats and forfeitures which might at a future day be a valuable fund for the maintenance and education of youth, and it being the interest of this commonwealth always to promote and encourage every design which may tend to the improvement of the mind and the diffusion of useful knowledge, even among the most remote citizens, whose situation a barbarous neighborhood and a savage intercourse might otherwise render unfriendly to science, Be it therefore enacted," etc.

"That eight thousand acres of land within the said county of Kentucky, late property of Robert Mc.Kenzie, Henry Collins and Alexander Mc.Kie, be and the same are hereby vested in William Fleming William Christian, John Todd, Stephen Trigg, Benjamin Logan, John Floyd, John May, Levi Todd, John Cowan, George Meriwether, John Cobbs, George Thompson, and Edmund Taylor, as a free donation from the commonwealth for the purpose of a public school or seminary of learning to be created within the said county as soon as the circumstances of the county and the state of its funds will admit and for no other use or purpose whatsoever."

The fund above referred to was made over to the trustees of Transylvania Seminary in an act entitled, An Act to amend an act entitled an act to vest certain escheated lands in the county of Kentucky in trustees for a public school.

The act refers to the forfeited land and says that representations had been made that private donations might be obtained were the trustees incorporated and such privileges granted as would enable them to carry into effect the intention of the Legislature.

Transylvania Seminary was incorporated with the following board of trustees: William Fleming, William Christian, Benjamin Logan, John May, Levi Todd, John Cowan, Edmund Taylor, Thomas Marshall, Samuel McDowell, John Bowman, George Rogers Clark, John Campbell, Isaac Shelby, David Rice, John Edwards, Caleb Wallace, Walker Davie, Isaac Cox, Robert Johnson, John Craig, John Mosby, James Speed, Christopher Greenup, John Crittenden, and Willis Green.

The escheated land was vested in the above board of trustees and was exempt from taxation. Future escheats were to revert to the trustees and professors and students were to be free from military duty.

Henings Statutes, Vol. 11, 282.

NUMBER 19.

To the Honorable the General Assembly of Virginia—

The Memorial of John Campbell Respectfully Sheweth—

That in your last session a Law was passed for suspending the Sale of Lotts in the Town of Louisville and also the Sale of Land adjoining which was Escheated as the property of John Connolly. That nevertheless the Trustees of the Town have proceeded to sell on Credit several Lotts within the same altho no single Lott heretofore disposed of is built upon and saved according to the Conditions of the Act of Assembly

That the Land laid out into a Town is Mortgaged to your Memorialist and his former partner in Trade Joseph Simon—

That half of the land Escheated is the property of your Memorialist and great Damage may accrue to him if the Appropriation made by the Assembly be confirmed—

That some of the Title Deeds of the same are Defaced and not recorded others tho duly executed and Intire have not yet been recorded owing to the Confusion of the Times to their being executed in another State and the long Captivity of your Memorialist

Your Memorialist therefore prays that the Act for Establishing the Town of Louisville be repealed—That the Lines of Division between his Lands and the Escheated Lands be run agreeable to the Deed of Partition between him and John

To the General Assembly of Virginia

Connolly That the Deficiencys of the Title Deeds may be remedyed as far as their authenticity deserves, Or any other Relief be granted to him which may seem meet and your Memorialist in Duty bound will ever pray &c.

   Endorsement on back of petition: December 1st, 1783—referred to the courts of Justice—December 8th, 1783—Reasonable and Reported, by Charles Hay.

   The request was met by an act entitled, An Act for repealing in part the act for establishing the town of Louisville. Henings Statutes, Vol. 11, 321.
   The act states that the line had not been run between the land of Connolly and Campbell; that money was not yet paid for which Connolly gave mortgage; that it was unjust to deprive Campbell of his security. The act was repealed so far as it effected the land of Campbell and Simon, and surveyors of the county were to run a line between the land of Connolly and Campbell.

NUMBER 20.

To the Honble. the Speaker & Genn. of the House of Delegates

The Petition of John Morton humbly representeth—

That your Petitioner was captur'd by the Indians at the battle of the Blue Licks whilst a soldier under Capt. Daniel Boon, was taken by them to their Towns, from there to Detroit where he remained sometime & from thence was carried to Canady where he was confin'd in close Gaol for upwards of Two years—That previous to your Petitioner's Captivity he had acquir'd a right of Preemption in the County of Fayette & that shortly after his releasment, went out to the Western Country laid his claim before the County Court of Fayatte & obtained a Preemption Certificate for One thousand Acres of Land which Certs. is hereunto annexed and that upon application for a preemption Warrant is inform'd, that your Honble House did at their last Session of Assembly pass a Resolution forbidding the issuing any Treasury Land Warrants untill the further order of the Genl. Assembly, Which has depriv'd your Petitioner of the Benefit of his Location. Your Petitioner therefore prays that your Honble House will take his Case under Consideration & grant him such relief as you in your Wisdom shall think just—And your Petitioner as in duty bound will ever pray &c.

Endorsement on back of petition: May 26th. 1784—Refd. to props. Moved to be discharged—June 10th 1784—propositions discharged and referred to a committee of the . . . on the state of the Commonwealth.

NUMBER 21.

To the Honourable the Speaker & Gentlemen of the House of Delegates—

The Petition of Patrick Doran Humbly sheweth that your Memorialist is entitled to a right of Preemtion to a tract of land in Lincoln County which will apear by a certificate issued November 1783. by the Court of the said County of Lyncoln—

Your Memorialist prays that your honourable house will so order that a warrant may Issue on his certificate & he as in duty bound will pray &c.—

Endorsement on back of petition: May 28, 1784—Refd. to props—(rejected) (repd.)

NUMBER 22.

To the Honourable Speaker and House of Delegates for the Commonwealth of Virginia.

The Petition of William Lytle of Kentuckey Settlement humbly Sheweth, That Your Petitioner in the year 1775 hired a Certain Ash Emerson to make an improvement for him in Kentuckey at a Certain place called the dry run, for which he made him full satisfaction as by his Certificate herewith sent will appear. Also that your Petitioner came by Water, and landed at the falls of Ohio with his family in the Spring of the Year 1780, a few days before the term of the Court of Commissioners Expired, then siting at Herodsburgh 70 or 80 miles Distant from the falls, shortly after Landing your Petitioners horses Strayed away, and having a wife and large family of small Children to provide for was compelled to stay till he could make some shelter to protect them from the weather and before

To the General Assembly of Virginia

he could find them to enable him to proceed to the Commissioners to lay in his claim, their powers Expired and he being unacquainted with the law and reduced to such Circumstances by Sickness & Misfortunes, as rendered him unable to apply to the general Court to make good his Claim within the time limited by law, Your Petitioner was therefore advised to apply to the County Court wherein his claim lay for redress, the Court was of opinion his case did not come under the Description prescribed in the law for their Cognizance, Whereby your Petitioner is deprived of his just right, & Claim, Your Petitioner therefore most humbly prays that you will be pleased to take his unfortunate case under your Serious Consideration, and Grant him Such redress by a law, or otherwise as you in your wisdom and Judgment may think just and reasonable and your Petitioner as in duty bound will ever pray.

William Lytle.

April 14th 1782—

We the undernamed Subscribers, Inhabitants of Fayette County, in Virginia, being made Duly sensible of the truth of every circumstance Your Petitioner has herein mentioned, do humbly pray your honourable House his behalf, to grant him his petition, and we your Petitioners as in duty bound shall pray—

Willim. M Connell
James McConnell
James January
William Steel
Levi Todd

This is to certify that I Ash Emerson made an improvement for the youse [use] of William Little in the year 75 in Cantucky on a run called the Dry Run above my owne improvement for which he made me full satisfaction   pr me Ash Emerson.

Endorsement on back of petition: June 4th 1784—referred to propositions—(rejected) (rept.)

Petitions of the Early Inhabitants of Kentucky

NUMBER 23.

TO THE HONOURABLE THE GENERAL ASSEMBLY OF VIRGINIA,

The petition of the Inhabitants of the District of Kentucky humbly sheweth, That your petitioners from a variety of Incidents which have accrued and will still accrue in acquiring property in Land in this Western Country, are like to be overwhelmed in Litigation; which will not only create discords amongst us, but ruin hundreds of poor Families, who being opprest and stript of almost their whole Substance by the Indians, have not the Means of defraying the Expences of a Law Suit upon the present Establishment. In this State of Indigence we have the additional mortification to find that not a few of those who have been more fortunate are taking possession of our just Claims knowing that we are not able to make Opposition. Such of your Honourable House as have not been Eye Witnesses can form no Idea of the Distresses which many of your petitioners have suffered for a Series of Years from the cruel and vindictive Hand of the Savages; and now on the back of these Distresses to be compelled into a Court of Judicature, by those who are endeavouring to avail themselves of our poverty and that Ignorance of the Law which was unavoidable in our remote Situation, will complete our Ruin: If we prosecute our Claim the last Cow and Horse must be sold to maintain the Suit; or if we decline the Contest, the Land upon which we had Hopes of supporting ourselves and Families in peace during the Remainder of our Lives will be wrested from us.

Your petitioners are therefore induced to pray that Circuit Courts may be established for the special purpose of trying Caveats, to be held by the Judges of our Supreme Court at such stated Times and places in each County as they shall think most convenient to the people, where they shall proceed in a summary Way to hear and determine according to Law and Equity all Caveats in the respective Counties where the Lands lie. These Courts to be attended by the Sheriff of the County

To the General Assembly of Virginia

and his Deputies, and by the Clerk of the Supreme Court who shall keep record of the Business relating to Caveats in each County in separate Books:

In all other Respects the Court and their officers shall exercise the same powers, observe the same Rules of procedure, and be entitled to the same Fees as are now prescribed by Law in the Case of Caveats; save only, that a Jury need not be summoned and empannelled unless the Nature of the Cause shall make it necessary, or either of the parties contending shall require it; and as the pleadings are not to be had in writing, if Counsel shall be thought necessary at all, we presume that the Fee heretofore allowed to Attorneys for conducting Land Causes in County Courts will be sufficiently adequate.

We are encouraged by the former Benevolence of the Legislature in appointing Circuit or District Commissioners in a Case nearly Similar, to submit this plan to the Consideration of the General Assembly, which if it can consistently be adopted, will curtail the greater part of the Expence of Litigation and at the same time render equal Justice to the Litigants; and we flatter ourselves that in Compassion to our many and complicated sufferings, this or some other Mode suited as far as possible to our Circumstances will be established for the Trial of Caveats, which at present are like to be the great Source of Contention amongst us.

And your petitioners shall ever pray &c.

[Names.]

Endorsement on back of petition: June 5th 1784—referred to propositions—(rejd.)

Relief was given to complainants in two acts entitled, An Act for giving further time to enter certificates for settlement rights and to locate warrants upon preemption rights and for other purposes. Henings Statutes, Vol. 11, 291.
An Act to give further time for the probation of deeds and other instruments of writing and for other purposes. Henings Statutes, Vol. 11, 294.

Petitions of the Early Inhabitants of Kentucky

NUMBER 24.

To the Honble the Speaker and the General Assembly of Virginia

That whereas a memorial was presented by the representatives and others on their behalf in December last to the Honble Assembly then sitting, praying for a court of assize &c for the better government of your memorialists. And they finding a matter of that very great importance to the reciprocal interest of the State in general, neglected, or at least not attended to agreeable to their wishes as part of the state, more particularly at this critical conjuncture of affairs, when the interest of the indigent inhabitants so loudly call for some ease or indulgence; Your memorialists would wish to observe that the very great distance from them to the seat of Government render it impracticable for those in poorer circumstances to maintain their Just rights to lands, and next to impossible for the civilist to punish offences of the most criminal nature, a number of other evils might be enumerated to prove the utility of the exersize of laws—under the authority alluded to, or some other similar thereto

Your memorialists must beg leave to observe that they have been lately alarm'd at finding that Congress has not only refused the Cession offer'd them by a former Assembly, But a committee of that August body appointed for the purpose of Enquiry have resolved, "That Virginia, has not any just right to land, Northwest of the Alleghany mountains, That with pamphlets we have seen and now conceive to have been written for the purpose of prejudicing the publick against the claim of Virginia, and to prepare your memorialists for paying twenty pounds sterling pr hundred for their own lands, Your memorialists do conceive from the very principal of the constitution of America, that if the country they possess does not in right belong to Virginia, the prosperity [property] of course must be vested in themselves, and that congress has no right to any part thereof, and when your memorialists through your Honble house make a request to Congress for a new state and are

To the General Assembly of Virginia

received into the union, They are then and not before subject as another state, Those are reasons they think necessary to offer to your Honble house, But your memorialists have ever considered themselves and country as part of Virginia and were happy in being so. Her laws suited them and do yet suppose it to be to their interest to be Governed by Her, untill it shall appear for their mutual advantage to separate, at which period it is expected their will be no objection, What your memorialists at present wish is Virginia protection to them as part of the State intitled to all its privileges or an information of what they may expect; Justice is what they claim, and that the Equity of their pretentions will allow them, they view themselves as Virginians, and as such they hope what is alluded to will not be given up without their consent—They allso know that it is through them and those they claim as citizens of their detached country that the greatest part of the western waters is not now in the possession of our most inveterate enimies, and could easily prove the importance they have been to the interest of the United States—Your memorialists therefore hope that your Honble house will take their case into consideration & grant them such relief as to you may seem Just & reasonable

[Names.]

NUMBER 25.

To the Honorable the General Assembly of Virginia.

The Subscribers resident, in the Counties of Jefferson, Fayette, Lincoln, and Nelson, composing the district of Kentucky, being chosen at free Elections, held in these Counties respectively, by the Freemen of the same, for the purpose of constituting a Convention to take into Consideration the General State of the District, and espressly to decide on the expediency of making application to your Honorable Body, for an Act of Seperation—: deeply impressed with the importance of the measure, and breathing the purest filial affection,—Beg leave to Address you on the momentous Occasion.—

The Settlers of this distant region, taught by the arrangements of Providence, and encouraged by the conditions of that Solemn Compact, for which they paid the price of Blood, to look forward to a Seperation, from the Eastern parts of the Commonwealth, have viewed the subject leisurely. at a distance and examined it with caution on its near approach; irreconcileable as has been their situation to a connexion with any Community beyond the Apulachian Mountains, other than the Federal Union Manifold as have been the grievances flowing therefrom, which have grown with their growth, and increased with their Population; They have patiently waited the hour of Address nor ever ventured to raise their voices in their own cause. Untill Youth quickening into manhood, had given them vigor and Stability.—

To recite minutely the causes and reasoning, which directed, and will justify this Address, would we conceive be a matter of impropriety at this Juncture; It would be preposterous for us, to enter upon the support of facts and consequences, which we presume are incontestible; our sequestered situation, from the seat of Government, with the intervention of a mountainous desart of two hundred miles, always dangerous, and passable only at particular seasons, precludes every Idea of a connexion, on Republican principles; The Patriots who framed our Constitution Sensible of the impracticability of connecting permanently, in a free Government, the extensive Limits of the Commonwealth, most wisely made provision for the Act which we now Solicit—. To that Sacred Record we Appeal.—

'Tis not the ill directed or inconsiderate Zeal of a few, 'tis not that impatience of Power to which ambitious minds are prone, nor yet the baser consideration of Personal Interest, which influence the people of Kentucky; directed by superior motives, they are incapable of cherishing a wish unfounded in justice, and are now impelled by expanding evils, and irremedi-

To the General Assembly of Virginia

able grievances, universally seen, felt and acknowledged, to obey the irresistible dictates of self preservation, and seek for Happiness, by means honourable to themselves, honourable to you, and injurious to neither.—

We therefore with the consent and by the authority of our Constituents, after the most Solemn deliberation being warned of every consequence, which can ensue, for them, for ourselves and for Posterity unborn—do Pray—That an act may pass at the ensuing session of Assembly, declaring and acknowledging the Sovereignty & Independence of this district.—

Having no object in view, but the acquisition of that Security and happiness, which may be attained by a Scrupulous adherence to principles of private justice and public Honor, we should most willingly at this time, enter into the adjustment of the concessions, which are to be the condition of our Seperation, did not our relative situation forbid such negotiation, anxious however to bring this interesting part of the transaction, to a Speedy Issue, we have appointed the Honble George Muter & Harry Innes Esquires to present this Address, and in our behalf to enter into & ratify such engagements, as may ascertain the general Principles, on which the final adjustment of the conditions of Seperation is to be established.—

Our application may exhibit a new spectacle, in the History & Politicks of Mankind—A Soverign Power; solely intent to bless its People agreeing to a dismemberment of its parts, in order to secure the Happiness of the whole—and we fondly flatter ourselves from motives not purely Local, it is to give Birth, to that catalogue of great events, which we pursuade ourselves, is to diffuse throughout the World. the inestimable blessings, which mankind may derive from the American Revolution.—

We firmly rely, that the undiminished Lustre of that Spark, which kindled the flame of Liberty, and guided the United States of America to Peace & Independence, will direct the Honourable Body, to whom we Appeal for redress of Manifest grievances, to embrace the Singular Occasion, reserved for them, by Devine Providence; to Originate a precedent, which may Liberalize the Policy of Nations and lead to the emancipation of enslaved millions.—

In this Address we have discarded the complimentary stile of adulation & insincerity—it becomes Freemen when speaking to Freemen, to imploy the plain, manly unadorned Language of Independence . . . .[?]
September 23d 1785.

[Names.]

Endorsement on back of petition. Octo. 1785—Refd. to Whole as Com.—November 14th 1785—Committee of Whole discharged and referred to Ths. Madison, Henry Lee, Bullit, Ronald, Carrington, Alexr. White, Corbin, Page, Th. Smith, and Prentis.

The first action looking toward the creating of Kentucky into a separate State is found in an act entitled, An Act concerning the erection of the district of Kentucky into an independent state. Henings Statutes, Vol. 12, 37.

"Whereas it is represented to be the desire of the good people inhabiting the district known by the name of the Kentucky District that the same should be separated from this Commonwealth whereof it is a part and be formed into an independent member of the American Confederacy and it is judged by the General Assembly that such a partition of the Commonwealth is rendered expedient by the remoteness of the more fertile which must be the more populous part of the said district and by the interjacent impediment to a convenient and regular communication therewith, Be it enacted," etc.

A convention was to be held at Danville on the fourth Monday of September made up of delegates from the seven counties, five from each. The call was to be posted twenty days and the election was to continue five days to give full opportunity for expression of opinion.

The boundary was to be unchanged, the new State was to assume its just proportion of the debt, the lands of non-residents were not to be taxed above those of residents, grants of land by the new State were not to interfere with grants made by Virginia, lands set apart for soldiers were subject to grant only by Virginia, up to 1788, the use of the Ohio River to be common, disputes between Virginia and Kentucky to be settled by a commission, and assent of United States Congress to the separation necessary.

NUMBER 26.

To the Honourable Representatives of the Citizens of the Commonwealth of Virginia, in General Assembly met—

The petition of the Inhabitants of Lincoln County— humbly sheweth—

That your petitioners beg leave to present their following Request to your Honble House, confiding in your Wisdom &

To the Honourable Representatives of the Citizens of the Commonwealth of Virginia, in General Assembly met,

The Petition of the Inhabitants of Lincoln County humbly Sheweth

That your Petitioners beg leave to present their following Request to your Honble House, confiding in your Wisdom & generous Encouragement of this Scheme, which they presume to lay before you.

That your Petitioners taking into their serious Consideration, of a proper Place for Trade and Domestic Business and for the more ready procuring those Articles in our Precincts that are much wanted in this new Country, Are of Opinion, that the Survey of Six hundred and forty Acres of Land, which your Honble House formerly reserved for the Use of the Garrison & Town of Harrodsburgh, is the most convenient and suitable in the County. It not only being commodious to any convenient Division of the county, but also central to the present Inhabitants of the Same: And we can assure your Honble House not only its relative, but its natural Situation, Conveniencies are almost in every Respect suitable for Domestic Trade; the Premises being sufficiently level, very fertile & are well watered, by many never failing Springs and a large Stream running quite through the Same; from which Circumstances we are of Opinion that no Survey of the Same Quantity can exceed it in the County.

And we would further beg leave to present to your Honble House, an exact Plot of the Premises, with the Plan of a Town adapted to the Same; Praying that your Honble House would take the Whole into Consideration, & pass an Act for Conveying the Same to Freeholders and other Citizens in a Manner most agreeable to your Wisdom and Determination.

For which your Petitioners are bound in Duty to Pray.

CUT OF FACSIMILE PETITION

...ograph of a petition from Lincoln County to the General Assembly. Illustrative of the source from which the book is made.

To the General Assembly of Virginia

generous Encouragement, of this Scheme; Which they persume to lay before You—

That your petitioners taking into their serious Consideration, of a proper place for Trade and Domestic Business, and for the more ready procuring those Articles in our precincts that are much wanted in the new Country; Are of opinion, that the Survey of Six hundred and forty acres of Land, which your Honble House formerly reserved for the Use of the Garrison & Town of Harrodsburgh, is the most convenient and suitable in the County, It not only being commodious to any convenient Division of the County, but also central to the present Inhabitants of the same; And we can assure your Honble House not only its relative; but its natural Situation & Conveniences, are almost in every Respect suitable for Domestic Trade; The Premises being sufficiently level very fertile and well watered, by many never failing Springs and a large Stream running quite through the same; from which Circumstances We are of opinion that no Survey of the same Quantity can excel it in the County—

And we would further beg leave to present to your Honble House, an exact plot of the premises, with the plan of a Town adapted to the same; praying that your Honble House would take the whole into Consideration, & pass an Act for Conveying the same to Freeholders, and other Citizens in a Manner most agreeable to your Wisdom and determination—

For which your petitioners are bound in duty to pray—
[Names.]

Endorsement on back of petition: Lincoln Pets. for a Town—(reasonable).

The request for a town in Lincoln was granted in an act entitled, An Act for establishing a town in the county of Lincoln. Henings Statutes, Vol. 12, 223.
"That six hundred and forty acres of land allowed by law, including the said village or township, shall be and the same is hereby vested in William Christian, John Brown, Robert Mosby, Samuel Lapsley, peter Casey, John Smith, Samuel Taylor, John Cowan, John Gilmore, James Harrod, Abraham Chaplaine, William Kennedy, and Benjamin Logan."

Petitions of the Early Inhabitants of Kentucky

NUMBER 27.

To the Honourable the Speaker and Gentlemen of the House of Delegates for the Commonwealth of Virginia—

The petition of sundry inhabitants of the county of Lincoln humbly sheweth—

That they labour under great inconveniences from the large extent of said county and number of inhabitants therein; and that the vast number of litigants whose causes must of necessity be determined in the court of said county renders it very tedious and expensive attending the same for the calling of their causes and oppressive to the justices who determine them—

Your petitioners beg leave to represent to your honourable house that the aforesaid Grievances may be redressed by laying off two distinct counties to be taken from the county of Lincoln to be bounded as follows, viz. The first county— By a line beginning at the confluence of sugar Creek and Kentucky river thence proceeding by a direct line to John Crows sinking spring, the mouth of Clark's Run, thence a straight line to Wilson's Station in the fork of Clark's run thence the same course continued to the line of Nelson County—Thence with said line to the line of Jefferson county, thence with that line to the Kentucky River, Thence up said river to the Beginning. For one distinct county—The second county—By a line beginning at the confluence of Kentucky river and sugar creek, thence up said creek to the fork James Thompson lives on, thence up said fork to the head thereof, thence a straight line to where an East course from John Ellis's will intersect the top of the ridge that divides the waters of Paint Lick from the waters of Dicks river, thence along the top of the said ridge southwardly opposite Harman's lick, thence 45° East to the main Rock Castle river, thence running up said river to the head thereof, thence with the ridge that divides the waters of Kentucky river from the waters of Cumberland river to the line of Washington county, thence along said line to the main

To the General Assembly of Virginia

fork of Kentucky river that divides Fayette from Lincoln county, thence down the said river to the Beginning for one distinct County.

We your petitioners in reliance upon the propriety and the Justice of your prayer, hope that you in your wisdom will duly consider the premises and that our request will be attended to—and your petitioners as in duty bound will ever pray &c.
[Names.]

Lincoln, to wit:

I hereby certify that it has been publickly advertized within the said county that a petition would be presented to the next session of Assembly for a division of the county of Lincoln by a line to run as proposed in the within petition. Given under this 26th day of September 1785.
(Copy)   Willis Green Clk. L. C.

Endorsement on back of petition: November 23rd. 1785—Refd. to Props.

The request was granted in an act entitled, An Act for dividing Lincoln into three distinct counties. Henings Statutes, Vol. 12, 118.
The division was to date from August, 1786. The counties were Mercer and Madison.

NUMBER 28.

To the Speaker and Gentlemen of the House of Delegates—

The petition of Sundry Inhabitants of the County of Fayette Humbly sheweth

That from the extensive Boundaries of this County it subjects many of its Inhabitants to great Inconveniences, In Transacting their necessary business at their County Court, Many of your Petitioners have at least Sixty five miles to Lexington their present Court House; and most of the way being uninhabited render it dangerous to your petitioners In going to and from Court, from the frequent Incursions of Hostile Savages, And as your petitioners conceive, that in all governments the obtaining of Justice should be made as safe

& easy as possible to all its Citizens, and as no persons can possibly receive any Injury from the Division of this County; And your Petitioners acquire an Imediate Benefit. Pray, that your Honorable House will at the next Session pass an act for the Division thereof In manner following—

Beginning at the mouth of Uper Howards Creek on Kentucky River runing up the Main fork thereof to the Head thence with the Dividing Ridge between Kentucky & Licking Creek untill it comes opposite the Head of Eagle Creek, from thence a Direct Line to the nearest part of Ravin Creek a Branch of Licking, Down Ravin Creek to the Mouth thereof, thence with Licking to the Ohio—thence with the Ohio to the mouth of Sandy Creek, Up Sandy to the Cumberland Mountain with sd Mountain to Lincoln Line thence with the Lincoln Line & Down Kentucky River to the Beginning, And all that part within the Lines above described, be Established into a seperate County. And your petitioners shall ever pray &c.

[Names.]

Fayette County to wit

I Levi Todd Clerk of the Court of the County aforesaid do certify That an advertisement setting forth (that a Petition praying for a division of the County aforesaid nearly (if not quite) agreeable to the plan mentioned in this Petition would be presented to the next Session of the General Assembly) On two different Court days at the Courthouse of the said County.

Test Levi Todd

Endorsement on back of petition: Nov. 25th. 1785—Refd. to Props.— (reasonable).

The request was granted in an act entitled, An Act for dividing the County of Fayette. Henings Statutes, Vol. 12, 89.
The division was to date from May, 1788. Bourbon Co.

To the General Assembly of Virginia

NUMBER 29.

To the Honourable the General Assembly for the Commonwealth of Virginia.

The Petition of James Hogan Humbly sheweth

That your Petitioner at the request and solicitations of a number of the Inhabitants in the Kentucky District has provided himself with a Boat, Hands &c for the purpose of keeping a Ferry across the Kentucky River from Lands of his own in Lincoln County to his Lands in Fayette County at the mouth of Hickmans Creek where the publick Warehouses are ordered to be erected. Your Petitioner therefore prays this Honorable House to pass an Act for establishing the same a publick Ferry and fixing the rates of Ferriage. And whereas the keeping of a Ferry across the Kentucky River will be attended with more trouble and inconvenience than is usual on Rivers of that size owing to its peculiar situation & its being fordable generally six or seven months of the year your petitioner is induced to ask your Honble House for such as Augmentation to the general rates of Ferriage as may enable him to attend and serve the publick faithfully—

And your Petitioner shall ever pray etc.

James Hogan
October 1st 1785—

Fayette County

I Levi Todd Clerk of the County aforesaid do certify that James Hogan did legally advertise that he intended presenting this Petition at the ensuing Session of Assembly. Given under my Hand this 13th day of September 1785—

Levi Todd Cl.

Lincoln to wit:—

I hereby certify that James Hogan did advertise at the Courthouse of said County on two several Court days that he intended to prefer a Petition to the next Session of Assembly for establishing a Ferry across the Kentucky at the mouth of Hickman. Given under my hand this 4th day of October 1785—

Willis Green

Endorsement on back of petition: Nov. 29th. 1785—(Refd. to Props) (reasonable)
This and subsequent requests were granted in an act entitled, An Act for establishing several new ferries. Henings Statutes, Vol. 12, 83.

NUMBER 30.

To the Honorable the General Assembly of the Commonwealth of Virginia.

The Petition of David Crews Humbly sheweth That at the request of sundry Inhabitants of the County of Lincoln & others Your Petitioner was induced to build a Boat for the purpose of Transporting passengers across the Kentucky River near the mouth of Jacks Creek from Lands of his own in Lincoln County to other Lands which he claims in the County of Fayette to which place Roads are now clearing and generally adjudged the most convenient crossing place on the Kentucky River above Hickmans Creek.

Your Petitioner prays that an Act may pass your Honorable House establishing the same as a publick Ferry and to ascertain the rates of Ferriage.

And your Petitioner shall ever pray &c

David Crews
Oct. 1st 1785—

Lincoln County Sct.

I do hereby certify that an Advertisement was set up at the Courthouse Door of this County at the July and August Courts last. notifying that an application would be made to the next General Assembly for the within purpose signed by David Crew.

Teste Willis Green Cl. L. C.
Oct. 7th 1785—

Endorsement on back of petition: Dec. 9th, 1785—(Refd. to Props) (Reasonable)

To the General Assembly of Virginia

NUMBER 31.

To the Honble the General Assembly of the Commonwealth of Virginia—

The Petition of William Steele Humbly sheweth

That your Petitioner has furnished himself with proper Boats for the purpose of keeping a Ferry across the Kentucky River at a place called the Stone lick from Lands of his own in Fayette to the Land supposed to belong to John Craig in Lincoln County, to which place a Road is now opening from Lexington. Your Petitioner prays that an Act may pass your Honble House for establishing the same a publick Ferry And shall pray &c.

Will Steele

Notice is hereby given to all whome it may concern that a petition will be presented to the next General Assembly to obtain an act for Establishing a publick ferry across the Kentucky River from the Lands of William Steele on the uper side of the mouth of the Stone Lick branch in Fayette County to the lands opposite in Lincoln County Oct. 11th 1785

This day came before me David Henderson and made oath that the within was set up on Fayette Court House two Courts. Given under my hand this 11th day of Oct. 1785—

Wm. McConnell.

Endorsement on back of petition: Dec. 10 1785—Refd. to Props—(Reasonable)

NUMBER 32.

To the Honorable the Speaker and Gentlemen of the House of Delegates

The petition of sundry inhabitants of the County of Bourbon humbly sheweth, That a Number of your petitioners are settled in that part of the said County of Bourbon which is commonly known by the name of Limestone Settlement about forty miles distant from the place agreed on for holding the Court of the said County, and which is not only a distinct settlement at present from the part of the said County but must remain so for many yea.s by the Intervention of a Mountainous tract of Barren Land running down on each side of the main branch of Licking Creek. that cannot be inhabited. And exposes your petitioners to be surprised & murdered by the savages who frequently infest such places. And the main branch of Licking being a considerable and Rapid Water course often obstructs a convenient communication with the other part of the County and renders it inconvenient and expencive to suitors and others to attend the present Courthouse. And altho it may be objected that the number of Inhabitants in the neighborhood of Limestone are too inconsiderable to be separated from the other part of the County at present. Yet when it is considered that one of the principal inlets for Emigrants into the Country is at this place, and from the Rapid Settlement that is now making. There is no doubt but a sufficiency of Inhabitants will soon be collected. Your Petitioners therefore pray that your Hon. House will take their situation into consideration, and Erect all that part of the said County of Bourbon, which lies North of the main branch of Licking, To begin at the mouth of the said Licking Creek, thence up the main branch thereof to the Head thence a direct line to the Junction of the Maddison & Russell County lines thence along the Russell line to Bigg Sandy, thence down the same to the mouth, thence down the Ohio River to the Beginning into a distinct County, and your petitioners as in duty bound will ever pray

August 25th 1786 [Names.]

I do hereby certify that advertisements have been exhibited according to Law for them shewing the Intention of the within petitioners In presenting the same to the next General Assembly

John Edward Cl

Endorsement on back of petition: Octo. 26. 1786—Refd. to Props.—Rejected—recommitted next session.

To the General Assembly of Virginia

NUMBER 33.

To the Honorable the Speaker and Gentlemen of the House of Delegates of Virginia.

The Petition of Sundry Inhabitants of the County of Bourbon humbly sheweth that advertisements have been exhibited at the door of their Court House ever since the May past at which time the Court of Bourbon took place for dividing the same into three Counties, and as your Petitioners conceive that such Division if granted will not only derange all the public business of the County which has been very much the Case by the late Division to the great injury of individuals, but must so weaken the militia of the present County as to render them incapable of defending themselves as well as of paying their County Levy; the County having now in all not more than four hundred effective militia, and your Petitioners further conceive that as the Erection of Kentuckey into a free independent state will most undoubtedly take place and that the good people of the said District may divide the same into Counties as they think proper: And as your Petitioners conceive that the Petition to be presented to your Honorable House for the Division of the County of Bourbon, if it takes place may be very oppressive to your Petitioners who pray that no such Divisions may take place, but that the same may be postponed until the next session of Assembly or until it is known whether the District is erected into an independent State and your Petitioners as in duty bound will ever pray

[Names.]

Endorsement on back of petition: Octo. 26th. 1786—Refd. to Props—reasonable—recommitted.

NUMBER 34.

To the Honourable the Speaker and Gentlemen of the House of Delegates

The petition of sundry inhabitants of the county of Bourbon humbly sheweth, that the most of them are settled in a new

Petitions of the Early Inhabitants of Kentucky

Village called Washington in the settlement of Limestone in the Cty aforesaid, where there are upwards of Seven hundred Acres Land laid off for in & out lots for the use of sd Village, and where there are now settled upwards of Fifty families among whom are Mechanicks of divers kinds, and the prospect of a rapid settlement being made to the great advantage of village & Country. The sd Village is also judged to be situated in the most central & convenient place to the adjacent County, and that it would be the most proper place for erecting publick buildings for the use of a County as soon as one is laid off. We therefore humbly pray that your honourable House will establish the said Village into a Town by the name of Washington and your petitioners as in duty bound will ever pray &c

August 22d 1786—

[Names.]

I do hereby certify that advertisements according to Law have been Exhibited shewing the Intention of the petitioners In presenting the same to the next General Assembly.

John Edward Cl. B. C.

Endorsement on back of petition: October 27th. 1787—Refd. to Props— (Reasonable)

The request was granted in an act entitled, An Act for establishing a town in the County of Bourbon. Henings Statutes, Vol. 12, 361.
The name was to be Washington. The trustees were Edmund Lyne, Edward Waller, Henry Lee, Miles W. Conway, Arthur Fox, Daniel Boone, Robert Rankins, John Gutridge, William Lamb.

NUMBER 35.

To the Honourable the Speaker and Gentlemen of the House of Delegates,

the petition of James Holloway humbly sheweth,

That he entered the Service in March 1776, in the fourth Virginia Regiment and continued as an officer in sd. Regiment untill the engagement at White Plains, Sept. 1778, at which time he became a Supernumerary. After returning home he raised a company of militia and fought in the battle of Guilford

To the General Assembly of Virginia

under command of Gen. Lawson, who had been Commander of sd 4th Regiment. During the service, your petitioner was in the following engagements, viz, at Trenton, Princeton, Brandewyne, German-Town and Monmouth.

As it has been allowed to several persons in similar circumstances to receive the bounty in lands which was stipulated for three years service; and as your Petitioner continued more than that time in the duties of a soldier on every opportunity of action, and still continues to act his part in defending the Western Frontiers in present expeditions against the Indian Tribes; it is the prayer of this petition that your Honourable House will take his case into consideration and indulge him with such recompence as his conduct may seem to merit, such as has been conferred in like cases, and such as may have been requested or obtained by several whose circumstances rendered them less proper objects of liberality to their Country: And your Petitioner, as in duty bound shall ever pray &c.
Fayette County, Sept. 21 1786

Endorsement on back of petition: Holloways Rep.—October 27th. 1786—Rejected.

NUMBER 36.

THE HONOURABLE THE SPEAKER & GENTLEMEN OF THE HOUSE OF DELEGATES

The petition of Sundry of the Inhabitants of Lincoln County humbly sheweth—That the Courthouse of the said County Now is and heretofore has been on the Land of a private Individual. In consequence of which no person could undertake to Build houses and provide proper accomodations for those whose business obliges them to attend the said Court of said county.—That Colo Benjamin Logan the proprietor of the Land whereon the courthouse now stands, has given up and conveyed twenty six acres of Land to the Court of said County for the purpose of laying off a Town and Building a courthouse and prison thereon for the Use of said County. In consequence of which conveyance, the Court of said County have proceeded to lay off the said 26 acres of Land into Lotts and streets, and have made sale of the Lotts some of which are considerably improved.

The said 26 acres of Land lies within one half mile of where the courthouse now stands, and as near the center of the County as any place can be had with Equal advantage, The Roads to and from the place where the Courthouse now stands being easyly turned in a Direction to any part of the 26 acres of Land,—

Your petitioners therefore humbly pray that a Law may pass for establishing a Town of the said 26 acres of Land, to be called Stanford and that John Logan, Benjamin Logan, Isaac Shelby, Henry Pauling, Walker Baylor, Wm. Morrison and Alexander Blair—Be appointed Trustees of said town that the Court of said County be empower'd to remove the Courthouse and prison of said County to the Town of Stanford; Or to Erect new ones as to them shall seem most expedient for the holding of Courts in said County for the future and your petitioners shall ever pray &c.

[Names.]

Lincoln to wit

I hereby certify that it has been publickly advertised at the Courthouse of said County on two several Court days, that the within Petition would be preferr'd to the next Session of Assembly Given under my hand this 28th day of September 1786.

Willis Green.

Endorsement on back of petition: Octo. 27. 1786—Refd. to Props. (reasonable)

The request was granted in an act entitled, An Act to establish a town on the lands of the late Benjamin Logan, in the county of Lincoln and to fix the place of holding court therein. Henings Statutes, Vol. 12, 396.

The following were to be the trustees: Benjamin Logan, John Logan, William Montgomery(?), Henry Pauling, Isaac Shelby, Walker Baylor, Alexander Blane.(?)

The amount of land was twenty-six acres and the name of the town was Stanford.

To the General Assembly of Virginia

NUMBER 37.

To the Honorable the General Assembly of Virginia—

The Petition of Jane Todd widow and relict of John Todd late of the County of Fayette deceased, and also Executrix of the said John Todd; and Robert Todd Excr. of the said John Todd Humbly sheweth

That their Testator upon the opening of the Land office in the year 1779 vested the greatest part of his personal property in Land Warrants and settlements & Preemption Claims, which were located in the District of Kentucky, but before titles could be obtained for the Lands to which he was intitled, he was killed by the Indians in an engagement with them, in the County of Fayette, as is supposed, he not having been heard of since—

That none of the said Lands were surveyed in the Lifetime of the Testator, and Since his decease your Petitioners have been obliged to pay the expence of surveying & obtaining Titles for the said Lands and to discharge Debts due from the Testator to a much greater amount than the Personal Estate

That there are a number of Debts still due from the Estate of the said John Todd and other claims upon the Estate for Lands sold by the Testator, for which Titles cannot be made and for the payment of which the few slaves belonging to the Estate consisting of two Women only, must be sold but which will not it is supposed be sufficient for that purpose.—

Your Petitioners beg leave further to observe that the Testator has only one Child Mary Owen Todd living, who is about five years old, and that the Estate would be very sufficient to support her genteely, & to pay all Taxes upon the Lands could a Sale of Part of the Lands be made, and after discharging the Debts a Sum not considerable be applied to the purpose of purchasing Slaves for her, as she has several very valuable Tracts of Land—That your Petitioner Jane who is entitled to Dower would chearfully join in a sale of any part thereof for the purpose aforesaid and would be satisfied to take her Dower in the slaves to be purchased, in lieu of her Dower in the Lands—

Your Petitioners therefore Humbly Pray that an act may pass, appointing Trustees to sell & convey as much of the Lands belonging to the Estate as will pay off the Demands thereupon and purchase two likely young negro fellows and one wench to be vested in the said Mary Owen Todd & your Petitioner Jane as aforesaid—

And they as in duty bound will ever pray &c.

Endorsement on back of petition: Octo. 28th. 1786.—Refd. to props.—(Reasonable)

The request was granted in an act entitled, An Act appointing trustees to sell part of the lands of John Todd, deceased, for the payment of his debts and for other purposes. Henings Statutes, Vol. 12, 369.

NUMBER 38.

To the Honble The House of Delegates

The petition of Mary Ervin most humbly sheweth That your petitioner's Son John Askins served as a soldier in the continental service for three years and afterwards as a captain of the militia in the District of Kentucky and always distinguished himself as a good and faithful citizen of the United States in general and of Virginia in particular. That he, in common with the rest of his fellow soldiers, received an opportionment of Land in the District afsd as a Reward for his services and to the great distress of your Petitioner lately died—leaving neither wife nor children nor any person so nearly related to him as your Petitioner—That during his life time he sold fifteen hundred Acres of the above mentioned Land to sundry persons whose titles have not been confirmed—Now your Petitioner most reluctantly sheweth to this Honble House That her afsd Son John Askins was not born in lawful wedlock and therefore by the laws of this Commonwealth his property escheats.

To the General Assembly of Virginia

But your petitioner most humbly prayeth that in consideration of her being the nearest and dearest Relation to the deceased, your Honble House will compassionate her situation and permit a Law to pass relinquishing the Right of the commonwealth to the Land afsd. and vesting the Title in her, reserving nevertheless the equitable Rights of the purchasers afsd. and your Petitioner as in duty bound will ever pray.

Monongalia County SS. Before Me one of the Justices of said County came Mary Ervin you worships [?] Petitioner & made oath that the above mentioned John Askins was her son and was illegetmate Born & is Dead and Died without Being Tested or having any Heirs at Law

her
Mary X Ervin
mark

Sworn & Subscribed this 11th Day of Oct 1786
   Dal McCollum

    Endorsement on back of petition: Octo. 30th. 1786—Refd to props—(Reasonable)

    The request was granted in an act entitled, An Act to vest the land whereof John Askins died seized in Mary Arvin, [Ervin] his mother. Henings Statutes, Vol. 12, 363.

NUMBER 39.

To the Honourable the General Assembly of the Commonwealth of Virginia—

The Petition of Christopher Greenup Humbly sheweth That your Petitioner being appointed Clerk to the Supreme Court for the District of Kentucky, is obliged by virtue of his office to transmit an Account, and pay into the publick Treasury, all Taxes arising on Process and other Law proceedings instituted, or admitted in the said Court, That the distance of his residence from the seat of Government is so great, he cannot possibly attend in person to make the Payments, but is under the necessity of applying to and trusting such Persons as he can procure to do that business for him, by which he is constantly exposed not only to considerable expence and inconvenience but the risk of incurring the Penalty inflicted by Law on Delinquent Clerks

Your Petitioner begs leave further to Represent to your Honourable House, that he is entitled to draw money from the Treasury annually for his Ex offico Services, which is also attended with inconvenience and Risk, and might in a great measure be remedied if he was authorized to retain in his hands so much of the money arising on Taxes as wou'd satisfy his demand, and also the Expence of procuring Record Books and other incidental charges of the said Court (the Same being first Liquidated and Certified by the Judges, to be just) and the Treasurer authorized to receive such claims in discharge of those Taxes—

Your Petitioner therefore prays that your Hon'ble House will so far indulge him as to settle his publick account of Taxes in the manner herein pointed out, or such other mode of indulgence as your Honors shall deem Just And your Petitioner will pray &c

Christr Greenup
September 26th 1786

Endorsement on back of petition: Novr. 6th. 1786—Refd. to Props.—(Reasonable)—(rept.)

The request was granted in an act entitled, An act for further amending an Act intitled, an Act for establishing a district court on the western waters. Henings Statutes, Vol. 12, 704.
Provision was made for a receiver to avoid the necessity of judges and other officials applying to counties for salaries.

NUMBER 40.

TO THE HONORABLE THE SPEAKER AND GENTLEMEN OF THE HOUSE OF DELEGATES

The petition of Sundry of the Inhabitants of the county of Fayette, humbly sheweth, that from the situation of your petitioners they think it highly convenient that an Inspection of Tobacco be established on the North side of the Kentucky

To the General Assembly of Virginia

River at the mouth of Hickman Creek, your Petitioners therefore prays this honorable house to take the same under their consideration and to pass a law for the purpose aforesaid. And your petitioners as in duty bound shall ever pray &c.
[Names.]

Fayette County Virginia to wit—

I Levi Todd Clerk of the Court of the County aforesaid do certify that an advertisement was set up at the door of the Court house of the said County on the Court days in the months of July and August notifying that a Petition would be presented the next Session of the General Assembly praying that a Warehouse may be established on the North side of Kentucky River at the mouth of Hickmans Creek. Given under my hand this Seventeenth day of September 1787.

Levi Todd

Endorsement on back of the petition: October 19th. 1787—Refd. to propositions—(reasonable) (repd)

The request was granted in an act entitled, An Act for establishing several new inspections of tobacco and reviving and establishing others. Henings Statutes, Vol. 12, 580.

This act provides inspection in Fayette, Mercer, Mason, Madison, and Bourbon counties.

An earlier act provided for inspection of tobacco, entitled, An Act for establishing inspections of tobacco on the western waters. Henings Statutes, Vol. 11, 345.

This was in October, 1783, and provided inspection in Fayette, Lincoln, and Jefferson counties.

The provisions generally included in the inspection acts may be seen in a general act entitled, An Act for reviving several public warehouses for the reception of Tobacco and other purposes. Henings Statutes, Vol. 9, 153.

Several acts previous to this had expired in 1775, and it was now "thought expedient that some temporary method should be provided for the reception and inspection of tobacco at or near the heads of the rivers and creeks."

Among the details of inspection it is provided that "if the inspectors, upon breaking open a hogshead, shall agree that the same is merchantable they shall weigh such tobacco and the cask, entering in their books and stamping on the cask the mark, number, gross, tare, and new weight thereof, and give to the owner a note or receipt for the same," etc.

These notes of the warehouse "shall pass in payment of levies, officers fees, and other tobacco debts payable in the counties," etc. Forging and counterfeiting tobacco notes renders liable "to suffer death without benefit of clergy."

Petitions of the Early Inhabitants of Kentucky

NUMBER 41.

To the Honorable the Assembly of the Commonwealth of Virginia—

The Petition of Ignatius Mitchell humbly Sheweth—

That your Petitioner is possessed of a Tract of Land lying on the River Ohio, at the mouth of Lawrence's Creek about Six miles below Limestone, a Spot remarkably advantageously situated for a Town, it is well known, to have an excellent Bank on the River, and from accurate Surveys a road far preferable to any other, may be obtained: Your Petitioner conceives it unnecessary to detail the advantages of this Spot, and begs leave to refer your Honbl House to the Representatives of Bourbon and Fayette Counties, for particulars.—

Your Petitioner prays that a Town by the name of Charles Town may be established by an Act of your Hona House at the aforesaid Spot, subject to such regulations as your wisdom may direct; And your Petitioner as in duty bound shall ever pray &c.

We the Subscribers are of opinion, that the Spot, before described, is well calculated for a Town; and a good road may be made thereto,

[Names.]

Endorsement on back of petition: 20th. October. 1787—Referred to propositions—(reasonable) (Repd.)

The request was granted in an act entitled, An Act to establish a Town on lands of Ignatius Mitchell, in Co of Bourbon. Henings Statutes, Vol. 12, 608.
The trustees were John Grant, Charles Smith, Jr., Thomas Warren, Miles Withers Conway, Henry Lee, John Machir, Robert Rankin.
The name of the town was to be Charlestown.

NUMBER 42.

To the Honourable the Speaker and Gentlemen of the House of Delegates.

The petition of the Subscribers Inhabitants of the District of Kentucky humbly sheweth That the Commissioners appointed to settle the pay rations and other claims accruing from two Expeditions carried on in the year 1786 under General Clark and Col. Logan have sat in different parts of the District

To the General Assembly of Virginia

and issued certificates for claims to them preferred for such Services & property as is enumerated in the Law under which they acted But it appears there are some Claims which have not been offered for settlement owing to the inattention of the claimers and their not having Knowledge of the Law and in some instances Certificates have issued for Property supposed to be lost which has since come to hand, and as there was Property necessary for the army which is not particularly mentioned in the Law such as Liquor, Vessels for the transportation of the Troops and stores, some Tents, & a few other articles which tho necessary for the army but not being enumerated in the Law. The Commissioners did not think themselves justifiable to issue Certificates therefor—Your Petitioners therefore pray that the Law may be amended authorizing and directing the County Courts upon due proof being made to grant Certificates for claims yet unsettled for all necessaries furnished or Impressed for the use of the said armies, and where it is made appear that the property for which a Certificate is issued is tendered or restored to the original owner that he may be called on and compelled to deliver to the commanding officer of the County or some other person such property or Certificate of the same value under such penalty and regulation as the Honorable Houses of Assembly may judge proper or that such other method may be desired that may render equal Justice to the Inhabitants of the District and we in Duty bound will ever Pray &c.

[Names.]

We are of opinion this Petition is just and reasonable witness our Hands this 19th day of Septr 1787.

Edmund Lyne
Isaac Shelby
Rich. Taylor

Endorsement on the back of petition: 22nd, October 1787. Referred to Propositions.—County Courts to finish business—not to extend allowances—(rejd.)

Petitions of the Early Inhabitants of Kentucky

The request was granted in an act entitled, An Act to amend the Act for appointing Commissioners to liquidate and settle the expenses incurred in two expeditions carried on from the Kentucky District against the neighboring Indians and for other purposes. Henings Statutes, Vol. 12, 521.

By the act the powers of the Commissioners were extended. They were authorized to settle claims, grant certificates to pay militia necessary to defense of frontier during 1786 and 1787 and for removing arms and ammunition from Limestone to Lexington, and from Blockhouse to Danville.

The act first creating the board of commissioners is an act entitled, An Act for appointing Commissioners to liquidate and settle the expenses incurred in two expeditions carried on from the Kentucky District against the neighboring Indians. Henings Statutes, Vol. 12, 231.

"Whereas the citizens of this Commonwealth in the District of Kentucky have lately carried on two expeditions against the neighboring tribes of Indians and it is reasonable that such services should be rewarded, Be it enacted," etc.

The commissioners were Edmund Lyne, Isaac Shelby, Richard Taylor.

The lands of officers and soldiers in the Kentucky District were to be exempt from taxation until further direction of the Legislature.

NUMBER 43.

To the Hon'ble the Speaker and Delegates of the General Assembly of Virginia—

The Petition of Sundry inhabitants of the County of Fayette and those contiguous to Steeles ferry, near the mouth of Stone Lick on the Kentucky River. Sheweth to your honors that your Petitioners are desirous of making Tobaco to pay their taxes and for other purposes and have not at this time any Convenient warehouse or Inspection to receive it when made, they therefore pray that your honors may pass an Act to establish Inspections on the Land of William Steele, who has already a convenient house erected for the purpose at his landing near his ferry on the said River, it being a very convenient place for the reception and shiping Tobaco, and convenient to a large number of the Inhabitants of the said County, and your Petitioners shall pray &c &c.

[Names.]

Fayette County Virginia to wit

I Levi Todd Clerk of the Court of the county aforesaid do certify that it was publickly advertised at the Door of the Courthouse of the County aforesaid at the Courts held in the months of July and August that a Petition would be presented to the next General Assembly for the Establishing a Warehouse

To the General Assembly of Virginia

for the reception of Tobacco at or near Steels landing near the mouth of Stone Lick

Given under my hand this 12th day of September 1787.
Levi Todd.

Endorsement on back of petition: 22 October 1787—Referred to Props.—reasonable—(rept.)

The request was granted in an act entitled, An Act to enable the citizens of this Commonwealth to discharge certain taxes, by the payment of tobacco. Henings Statutes, Vol. 12, 258.

Notes for inspected tobacco were to be used and rated at twenty shillings for one hundred pounds. They were good in payments to superior judges, and expenses of government due to public treasury in case of surplus.

NUMBER 44.

To the Honorable the General Assembly of Virginia

the petition of James Buchanan of the County of Bourbon humbly sheweth that your Petitioner having acquired at a great expence the claim of one half the lower blue Licks on Licking Creek of a certain James Parberry of Henry County & hath lately had the same divided and conveyed by Deeds in Fee Simple which were acknowledged and recorded according to Law: Your Petitioners part of the said Tract or parcel of Land includes the only good place for a Ferry across said Creek on the road leading from the mouth of Limestone to Lexington & your Petitioner at the request of many of his Neighbours hath provided a Boat & hands at his own Expence & set over passengers in time of high water from many of whom he has neither received Fee nor reward therefore your Petitioner prays that a Ferry may be established on his Lands on the one side of Licking Creek to his Lands on the opposite Shore. Your Petitioner lately alarmed by an advertisement set up at the door of the Court House of this County by said Parberry declaring his Intentions of applying to the next General Assembly for the establishment of a Ferry on what he calls his Lands on the said Creek running parallel with your Petitioner's which Place your Honorable House may be assured is a rapid and entirely unfit for a Ferry & therefore he can derive very little advantage to himself but would do much Injury to your Petitioner who hath for some Time lived with his Family on the Place much exposed to the Indians: Your Petitioner in support of the above allegations hath obtained a certificate of Colo James Garrard Surveyor of the said County who run the dividing Line by Consent of the Parties which Line stands as the Boundary mentioned in the Deed To which Certificate your Petitioner hopes your Honorable House will give the highest credit he being no way interested. Your Petitioner begs Leave further to inform your Honorable House that the said Parberry had prior to the Sale of the one Half sold to your Petitioner disposed of his other Half of the said Claim unto William Buchanan at the same time giving sufficient writings for the Conveyance of the Same and receiving full value in Lands lying on Holstan's river which obligations have since been assigned over and now become the claim of Mr. James French of the District of Kentuckey. And your petitioner for the better Information of your Honorable House hath inclosed a true copy of the Articles of agreement between William Buchanan and sd Parberry & your Petitioner humbly hopes that your Honorable House will take the same Into consideration & grant him the said Ferry & your Petitioner as in duty bound shall ever pray.

James Buchanan

This is to certify that being call'd on by Mr. James Parberry to Divide the Tract of Land that contains the lower Blue Licks and having run the Dividing Line through the two Licks, one on each side of Licking Creek and having View'd the situation of the Landings proper for a Ferry are of opinion that the Lands of Mr James Buchanan is by far the most proper for a ferry By reason of a short Break of the Hills which forms a perfect Eddy and secure Landing when the Creek is past fording which runs rapidly over Mr. Parberrys Landing, and I do further certify that I am not Interested any way in the Establishment of the ferry at the Lick, only as a Citizen Given under my hand this 15th day of Sept 1787.

James Garrard, Surveyor Bourbon C.

To the General Assembly of Virginia

I John Edmund Clerk of Bourbon County do Certify that the within Petition was advertised according to Law

John Edmund C B C
September the 20th 1787.

Endorsement on back of petition. 27th October 1787—Referred to Propositions—(rept.)

NUMBER 45.

To the Honble the Speaker and Delegates of the Genl Assembly of Virginia

The petition of Sundry inhabitants of the County of Fayette and those Contiguous to the Mouth of Craigs Creek on the River Kentuckey sheweth to your Honors that your petitioners are desirous of making Tobacco to pay their Taxes and for other purposes and have not at this time any Convenient Warehouses or Inspection to receive it when made they therefore pray that your Honors may pass an act to establish inspections on the Land of Genl Scott near the mouth of Craigs Creek on the said River it being the only place for a considerable distance on the River where the banks are acceptable we farther pray your Honours to establish a ferry upon said Scotts Land at the same place & your petitioners shall pray &c &c

[Names.]

Fayette County Virginia to wit

I Levi Todd clerk of the Court of the County aforesaid do certify that it was publickly advertised at the door of the Courthouse of the County aforesaid on two several Court days to wit in the months of June & July 1787 That a Petition would be presented to the next General Assembly for the Establishing a Ferry and also a Ware house for the Inspection of Tobacco on the Kentucky River on the Lands of Genl. Charles Scott near the mouth of Craigs Creek In witness whereof I have hereto set my Hand this Twelfth day of Septr 1787.

Levi Todd

Endorsement on back of petition. Nov. 6. 1787—Referred to Propositions—reasonable—reported.

Petitions of the Early Inhabitants of Kentucky

NUMBER 46.

To the Honble the General Assembly of Virginia

The petition of the Inhabitants of the Town of Lexington and County of Fayette most humbly sheweth

That whereas the said Town being well designed and commodiously, situated in the midst of a fertile country; and haveing met with the earliest attention and approbation of your Honorable body as will appear by the Act establishing the same, hath continued to increase in population and improvement, so that it is the most flourishing and best peopled of any at this time in the District of Kentucky.

And as we are persueded that a Strict attention to the internal police of the same, which like that of Similar bodies require perticular rules, for its regulation, would greatly contribute to the comfortable accommodation of its inhabitents; and consequently be an inducement to well disposed persons, artizans and mechanicks who from motives of convenience do prefer a Town life to come and settle among us. And believing that the true interest of our Country will be greatly promoted by such. Your Petitioners therefore Humbly pray that the Honorable the General Assembly will be pleased to take these matters into consideration, and if they should deem it expedient, pass an Act erecting the said Town into a body Corporate, with such rights and priviledges as other inland Towns which are Incorporated, within this Commonwealth have and possess, as the most effectual means of produceing those desirable ends above specefied. And your Petitioners as in duty bound shall ever pray &c. [Names.]

Endorsement on back of petition: Nov. 6th. 1787.—Referred to propositions—rejd.) (repd.)

The request was granted in an act entitled, An Act concerning certain regulations in the town of Lexington and county of Fayette. Henings Statutes, Vol. 13, 191.

Trustees were to be elected by all living within a mile, owning twenty-five pounds of property, and having lived there six months, except negroes and mulattoes.

Trustees could erect market house, appoint clerk of market, repair streets, impose taxes under one hundred pounds, and make ordinances.

To the General Assembly of Virginia

NUMBER 47.

To the Honourable the General Assembly of the Commonwealth of Virginia.

We your Petitioners Sundry of the Inhabitants of the counties of Fayette Bourbon & Madison humbly sheweth, that from the late Division of the counties of Fayette & Lincoln, the remote and detach'd, situation of a number of Inhabitants on the extreame parts of the new counties conceive ourselves greatly discommoded and a large number are excluded the advantage and benefit of an easy and convenient access to the place of publick Resort, therefore the good Intension of the Legislature is not fully extended to the community in general tho a much larger expense incur'd Pray a division of that part of the counties of Fayette & Bourbon & Madison (and the court house to be fix'd, in the Town of Boonsborough) to witt Beginning at the mouth of silver creek thence up the same to the mouth of Taylors fork thereof, thence a strait line to saltpetre cave near Capt. David Gases, thence a strait line to the uper Blue Lick, thence a southeast course to Russel county line, thence with said line so far as a Northwest course will strike Bramlets lick on Stoners fork of Licking creek, thence down the same so far as a southwest course will strike the head of the main branch of Boons Creek, thence down the same to the Kentuckey River thence Down said River to the mouth of Silver Creek the Beginning—

And your Petitioners as in duty bound shall ever pray &c
[Names.]

This is to inform the publick that there will be a petition presented to the next General Assembly of Virginia for a Division of part of the counties of Fayette, Bourbon & Madison to be added into one county as followeth viz—

Beginning at the mouth of Tates Creek, thence up the same to Taylors fork thereof thence a strait line to a salt petar cave near Capt. Gass's—Thence a strait line to the Blue Lick—, thence a southeast course to Russel county line thence with said line so far as a northwest course will strike Bramblet lick on Stoners fork of Licking creek. Thence down the same so far a south west cours will strike the head branch of Boons Creek, thence down said creek to the Kentucky River, then down said River to the mouth of Silver Creek the Beginning

This was advertised two Courts at Lexington.

Levi Todd Cl

Endorsement on back of petition: Nov. 6. 1787.—Referred to propositions —reasonable—reported. See note to Petition No. 54.

NUMBER 48.

To the Honourable the Genl. Assembly of the Commonwealth of Virginia

The Petition of the People of Limestone; and other Inhabitants of the County of Bourbon Humbly sheweth that your Petitioners on account of their detach'd situation; subject to much danger inconvenience and expence; in having to attend their transactions of their County Business at the distance of forty miles from their habitations (for the most part surrounded with all the horrows of a Savage Enemy.)

Petitioned your Honourable house at their last Session for a division of the sd County of Bourbon; which for reasons appearing to them, they thought proper to postpone the consideration of till the present Session. That your petitioners finding the inconveniences greatly increased; and that it is to your honorable house only they are to look up for relief. Beg leave to recall your attention to their disagreeable situation; and to crave the indulgence of your honorable house in laying before you a state of their grievances.

Your Petitioners humbly observe that Twelve or fifteen miles of the way they must travil to their Courthouse is thro a Barren Country unfit for Cultivation that this aggrevates their danger as it is and may remain a secure Asylum to the Savages who infest the road, that for the most part it is unsafe to travil

To the General Assembly of Virginia

it in the Summer time unless in Companies of armed men, and that in the Winter time, the journey to or from Court cannot be perform'd in much less time than two daies, And that there are several considerable & rapid water courses, which often obstructs a convenient communication with the other part of the sd County. Which renders their attendance at Court extremely expensive & inconvenient, that they are often under the indispensible obligations of attending Court being subject as they become freeholders to attend on Grand Juries & other necessary duties which as Citizens they are liable to. That from being so much expos'd to the inroads of the Savages they have not a horse left for every tenth man. Neither can they on these accounts attend their Elections, which will ever be oppressive; as it will be in the power of the Inhabitants, South of Main Licking, to send members to the Genl. Assembly; opposed to a division who may be unwilling to become advocates for our distress, or not feeling the inconvenience we labour under unable to represent them;

That your Petitioners while attending Court are obliged to leave their dearest connexions exposed to the Merciless attack of a Cruel enemy, and that the division of Fayette hath afforded them little or no relief in any of these cases, And that the Clerks office being kept almost at the extremity of the sd County. Subjects them to additional inconveniences as recourse thereat is absolutely necessary in many Cases.

Your Petitioners are duly sensible of the Inconsistancy of dividing Counties where the numbers are so few as there is at present but humbly conceive their situation to be peculiarly distressing; And that a division might be a means of speedy strengthing their frontiers whereas few will ever risk their lives & property under the present disadvantages; Your Petitioners also expect that the Erection of the district of Kentucky into an Independent State will soon take place; and that they must continue to groan under their present Burden, till a Legislative body is formed here; unless relieved by your honorable house,

Petitions of the Early Inhabitants of Kentucky

this they humbly conceive to be another cause of remonstrance, and for reasons already appearing they will not have a representation in forming the Constitution, to which their property, their lives and happiness will be subject.

Your Petitioners therefore pray your honorable house to take their case into consideration, and grant them a division of the sd County of Bourbon as follows, Beginning at the mouth of Licking, runing up the main branch thereof to the head, thence a direct line to the nearest part of Russell County line, along the Russell line to Bigg Sandy, & down the same to the mouth, thence down the Ohio River to the Beginning into a distinct County. And your Petitioners as in duty Bound will ever Pray &c.

[Names.]

September the 19th 1787.

I do hereby certify that an advertisement of the within Petition was set up at the door of Bourbon Court House.

John Edward C. B. C.

NUMBER 49.

To the Honorable the General Assembly of Virginia

The petition of sundry Inhabitants of the County of Bourbon, humbly sheweth that your petitioners warned by two advertisements one from the neighborhood of Limestone, and the other from the County of Madison proposing to petition your honorable house for the devision of Bourbon County. The first to divide the County by a line running up the main fork of Licking, The other to run from the head of Boon's creek near the Kentucky river a North East course untill it strikes Stoner's fork the south branch of Licking and up the same until a south east course shall strike the Russell line. Your Petitioners beg leave to observe the division proposed from Limestone will leave this County very weak and will render both Counties (should a division take place) very deficient both as to the judiciary as well as to the military departments. They further shew that

To the General Assembly of Virginia

the settlements of Limestone do not contain more than one hundred and thirty militia, nor more than one hundred and fifty Tithables, Their taxable property under the revenue law does not amount by the last return to 100 £ as strength and wealth altogether inadequate to the expences of a new County, but as inconsiderable as it is, it will greatly distress the remaining part should a division take place, we beg leave to observe the division proposed from Madison to include a part of this county will run within four miles of Bourbon courthouse, and take fifty settlers, and drag them across the Kentuckey river through clifts and hills almost impasible to the proposed courthouse at Boonsborough amoungst whome are many of your petitioners who are living near twenty miles from the proposed courthouse and within six miles of the present, Your petitioners beg leave further to observe that the good people of the present County of Bourbon is sufficiently distressed already with the payment of their County and the whole military strength of the County as it now stands doth not exceed four hundred, Therefore your petitioners hope that your honourable house sensible of the detached small Bodies of settlers in all new frontier Counties, and that it is impossible to bring the Courthouse and church to every mans door and that some individuals in all such cases ought to give up their private case for the good of the people at large untill such time as the county may populate and such division become necessary, Your petitioners therefore pray that no such division may take place at present.—And as in duty bound shall ever pray &c

[Names,]

Endorsement on back of petition: 1st. November-1787—Referred to Props—Rejected—(reasonable in House) (bill drawn)

Petitions of the Early Inhabitants of Kentucky

NUMBER 50.

To the honorable the General Assembly of Virginia

The Petition of the Trustees of the Transylvania Seminary humbly sheweth.

That the one sixth part of all legal Fees received by Surveyors, are by the Law appropriated to the University of William & Mary, a Seminary which We greatly respect but from which the Inhabitants of Kentucky are too remote to derive any immediate Advantage; And as the Legislature have repeatedly manifested their benevolent Disposition of providing the Means of Education within this district, We are induced to pray that you would be pleased to direct that the One Sixth part of the said Fees hereafter arising within the said District may be paid by the several principal surveyors therein to the Trustees of the Transylvania Seminary for the Use and Support thereof

We also beg leave to represent that many Entries and Surveys of Land have been made in the district which may become justly liable to be escheated thro' the default of Heirs or otherwise; But as it is supposed that such Lands cannot be regularly escheated before Grants have been obtained, for which no Person is authorized to apply, such Lands will lapse or become forfeited in such a way as that other private adventurers may reenter and obtain Grants for the same to the great Injury of the Transylvania Seminary, the Trustees of which are empowered to appropriate to its use twelve thousand Acres of escheatable Lands. We therefore pray that an act may pass declaring, That Claims to unpatented Lands may be escheated in the same manner and for the same Reasons as are prescribed by Law in the Case of Lands for which the Titles have been compleated, and that it may be particularly directed, how & by whom such escheatable Lands may be surveyed, or the surveys returned to the Register's office so that a proper Grant may issue.

To the General Assembly of Virginia

And your Petitioners shall ever pray &c
Signed by order & in Presence of the Board—
Test: Harry Innes Ck.
Ebenezer Brooks, Clk.

Endorsement on back of petition: 22d. November 1787.—Referred to Propositions—Survey's fees rejected—escheatable survey's rejd.—(repd.)

NUMBER 51.

To the Honorable the Speaker and Members of the House of Delegates,

the petition of Sundry inhabitants of the County of Fayette and District of Kentucky humbly sheweth,

That from their local situation, they find it very inconvenient, and attended with considerable expence, to send their Tobacco to any of the warehouses for the reception of Tobacco, now by Law established, and that there is a place on the Lands of William Steele near the mouth of the Stone Lick Creek, where a warehouse might be established, which would be very advantagious to them and to many of their neighbours, and where there is one of the most convenient landing places on the river Kentucky.—

Your petitioners therefore humbly pray that an act may pass by the Assembly, establishing a warehouse for the reception of Tobacco, on the lands of William Steele near where the Stone Lick Creek emptys into the Kentucky: And your petitioners as in Duty bound shall pray—

[Names.]

Fayette County Virginia to wit

I do certify that it was advertised at two different Court days at the Door of the Courthouse in the County aforesaid that a petition would be presented to the next General Assembly agreeable to the purport of the within Witness my hand this 10th Sept. 1788—

Levi Todd Cl

Endorsement on back of petition: 23 October—Referred to propositions—(reasonable) (repd.)

Petitions of the Early Inhabitants of Kentucky

NUMBER 52.

To the honourable the General Assembly of Virginia

The petition of the subscribers Inhabitants of Fayette County humbly sheweth that we conceive a Division of our County would be highly condusive to the convenience, safety & public Interest of a great Number of its Inhabitants.

Many of our Magistrates as well as litigants live so remote from Lexington where our Courts are held that they cannot attend without Incurring a greater expense than they can sustain & from the great Number of Inhabitants in the . . . County our Docket which is already crouded must shortly be so far in arrears as greatly to Delay the due administration of Justice.

Our Militia have been formed into three Batalions and before the Division we wish for can take place there will probably be more than four which in our scattered situation prevents us from exerting our strength against the savages with the same unanimity & vigour as if the extent of the County was less and our Commanding officers more contiguous to each other

We beg leave also to present that our County contains three times the Number of Inhabitants as any other County within the District and unless it is Divided it will destroy every idea of equality in representation.

For these Reasons we humbly pray that the County of Fayette may be Divided by a line to begin on the Kentuckey River at Todds Ferry to run a direct course to the south Fork of Elkhorn opposite Abraham Bowmans house thence down the Creek to the old Road from Lexington to the surveyers office thence a Direct line to the five mile tree on the Leestown Road thence a straight line to Run one mile below Wm. Russells to the line of Bourbon.

N B since our advertisement we are inform'd the Division line propos'd is disagreeable to some of the Inhabitants of our County unless the following alteration is made (viz) From Todds

To the General Assembly of Virginia

Ferry to run a straight line to the six mile marked tree on the Leestown Road thence a direct course to cross North Elkhorn three miles below Wm. Russells to the line of Bourbon which alteration we have no objection to if the Honourable Assembly think proper to redress our grievances

And your petitioners shall ever pray—
[Names.]

We the Subscribers do certify that the proposd alteration in regard to the Division of Fayette viz. From Todds Ferry to run a straight line to the six mile markt Tree on the Lees Town Road thence a Direct course to cross North Elkhorn three miles below William Russells to the Bourbon Line, that we think the Division reasonable and necessary and that we wish our Delegates to use their endeavours to carry the same into Execution.

Septr 17th 1788—

Robt Todd
Robt. Johnson
Wm. McConnell
Richd Young
Andrew Gatewood
Lewis Craig
Wm. Henry
Benjn Craig
Jn. Clark
Richd W Shippy
Laban Shippy
Colby Shippy

This is to certify that I was aganst the first proposed division of Fayatte & had signd a petetion against the proposed plan but I am now willing that the county may be devd agreeable to the above direction, which I think reasonable & wish the above Devision to be granted as witness my Hand this 18th of Sepr 1788—

Edwd. Payne.

Petitions of the Early Inhabitants of Kentucky

Fayette Sct.

Coleby Ship of this County made oath before me one of the Justices of said County that he saw publickly advertized at the Court house of the aforesaid County at August Court the Division of Fayatte as set forth in the petition for that purpose and that he personally applyd to Levi Todd Clerk of sd county Court for a certificate of the same and that he refused to give one, application was made this day

Sworn to before me this 22d day of Sepr 1788

Richd Young

Endorsement on back of petition. 24 October, 1788.—Referred to props—(rejected) (reasonable).

Request was granted in an act entitled, An Act for dividing the county of Fayette into two distinct counties. Henings Statutes, Vol. 12, 663. Woodford County.

NUMBER 53.

To the General Assembly of the Commonwealth of Virginia—

The petition of Sundry Inhabitants of the County of Fayette, humbly sheweth—

That your petitioners deeply interested in the welfare of their County, cannot but express their disapprobation of the artifices made use of by Individuals, to bring about a division of their County, and would suggest the impropriety of entering upon this business circumstanced as our District is with respect to the State of Virginia—

They conceive the proposed division highly improper at this period, as the infancy of their County, renders it entirely unecessary and as their numbers are too inconsiderable to enable them, to accumulate expense, without adding either to their convenience or general welfare—

They would therefore hope, that your Honble. House would not assent to the division of their County at this period—And as they conceive it unecessary to detail the reasons in opposition

To the General Assembly of Virginia

to the division beg leave to refer your Honb. House to the Delegates from their County—

[Names.]

Endorsement on back of petition. 24th October 1788—Referred to Propositions—reasonable—rejected.

NUMBER 54.

TO THE HONOURABLE THE SPEAKER AND GENTLEMEN OF THE HOUSE OF DELEGATES.

The petition of Sundry inhabitants of the County of Bourbon; humbly sheweth. That your Petitioners heard with great concern the rejectment of their petition to your last session for a Division of their County. Your petitioners are induced again from the hardships and disadvantages they labour under to approach your honourable house; and to lay before you the grievances they labour under; by being connected with the County of Bourbon. (viz) your petitioners live in the Limestone settlements near the Ohio River and are detached from every other Inhabitant of said County—at least thirty miles, except a small settlement at the Blue Licks, they have forty miles to Court, thirty of which is thro, a verry dangerous Wilderness exposed in every part to the attacks of the savages and there are four large Creeks to Cross; which in all rainey Seasons are not fordable.

These things it is hoped will be sufficient inducements to your honourable house to Grant to your petitioners a division of their County; especially also; When your honourable house is informed that the settlements near Limestone are lately greatly increased by a number of respectable Inhabitants; so that there are now Two hundred and six Families & three hundred and fifty Tithables; and as Limestone is the inlet for Emigration by Water to this Western Country; there is a prospect of the settlements being rapidly increased and largely extended which will be greatly promoted by your honourable house granting to your petitioners the priviledges and authority of a County. We your petitioners therefore pray that a division of sd County of Bourbon may be made in the following manner—Beginning at the Junction of Licking with the Ohio runing up the main branch of Licking to the head, then a direct course to strike the nearest part of Russell County line, thence along said line to Bigg Sandy, and down the same to the Ohio River, thence down the Ohio River to the Beginning—all which part of said County lying on the North side of the main branch of Licking—to be a New and distinct County—

In full confidence that your honourable House will do us every act of Justice; We as in duty bound shall ever pray &c.
[Names.]

Bourbon County
  I do hereby certify that I have the above petition for the Division of Bourbon was advertised according to Law
Test John Edwards Clerk of Bourbon.

This will notify the publick that a petition will be presented to the next general assembly for the purpose of forming a New County out of the Counties of Bourbon, Fayette and Madison, Viz, Begining at the mouth of Silver Creek, thence up the same to the mouth of Taylors Fork thereof, thence a direct line, to a saltpeter Cave, near Capt. David Gasses thence a strait line to the Blue Licks, thence a South East Course to Russell County line, thence with said line so far as North West Course, will strike Bramlets lick, on Stoners forks of licking Creek, thence a strait line to the head of the main Branch of Boons Creek thence down the same to the Kentuckey River thence down the River to the Beginning:—

August the 25th 1787 I do hereby Certify that this advertisement have been set up according to Law at Bourbon [Court] House.

John Edward Clerk Bourbon Co.

To the General Assembly of Virginia

August the 28th 1787 I do certify that the within has been advertised as the Law directs.

Will Irvine Clk, M C

Endorsement on back of petition: 25 Octo. 1788.—Refd. to Props.—For a Division—repd.

The request was granted in an act entitled, An Act for dividing Bourbon. Henings Statutes, Vol. 12, 658. Mason County.

The last two paragraphs were filed with this petition but belong to No. 47.

NUMBER 55.

TO THE HONOURABLE THE SPEAKER AND GENTLEMEN OF THE HOUSE OF DELEGATES

The petition of Sundry Inhabitants of Bourbon County South of Main Licking Humbly sheweth—That your petitioners being notified by an advertisement at the Court House Door that a petition would be presented to your Honourable House praying for a Division of Bourbon County by Main Licking beg leave to observe that a petition of this Kind was rejected at your Last Session as your petitioners are informed for the want of a sufficient number in that part of the County praying a Division your petitioners can affirm with confidance that the number of Titles North of Main Licking does not by the Last return amount to more than One Hundred and Seventy a number altogether inadequate to the Expence of a County and your petitioners cannot but express their astonishment when they find a clause in their petition praying that the monies paid by them for erecting the Public Buildings in the County should be repaid by your Petitioners this part of their petitions is as unreasonable as the other part is designing the whole calculated to gratify the ambition & averice of a few Individuals; Your Petitioners therefore pray that no such Devision may be granted. but should a Division be thought reasonable that your petitioners may not be obliged to refund any money paid toward erecting the public buildings & Your petitioners shall ever pray &c.

[Names.]

Endorsement on back of petition: 25th Octo. 1788—Referred to props.—rejected.

Petitions of the Early Inhabitants of Kentucky

NUMBER 56.

To the Honorable the General Assembly of Virginia—

The Petition of Sundry Inhabitants of the county of Bourbon Humbly sheweth that Every other county in the District of Kentucky have been indulged with the advantages of Publick warehouses for the reception of Tobacco and that your Petitioners living near the Courthouse & on Licking Creek in the most populous part of said County—too far remote from either of the other—Inspections to remove their Tobacco by Land without much labour and Expence. and your petitioners fully sensible of the disposition of your Honorable House to do Justice & upon all occasions to afford relief to such of the community as you conceive is intitled to your patronage we your petitioners therefore pray that an inspection for the reception of Tobacco may be established on the South fork of Licking Creek at the Confluence of Stoner and Hinksons forks of said Creek and in the fork near Isaac Ruddles Mill which your petitioners conceive will be of great publick utility and of singular advantage to them provided the article of Tobacco should continue to be of value and your petitioners as in duty bound will ever pray

[Names.]

July 1788 I do hereby certify that the within Petition has been legally advertised at the Door of the Courthouse the several days required by Law given under my hand.—

John Edwards Clerk Bourbon County

Endorsement on back of petition: 25th Octo. 1788. Referred to propositions—reasonable—on Isaac Ruddles land—(repd.)

The request was granted in an act entitled, An Act for establishing an inspection of tobacco on the lands of Isaac Ruddle, in the county of Bourbon. Henings Statutes, Vol. 12, 677.
According to this act it was not lawful to build houses within fifty yards, in which fire was to be used.

To the General Assembly of Virginia

NUMBER 57.

To the Honourable the General Assembly

A petition for Establishment of the Town of Bourbon Courthouse [One of several papers circulated.]

[Names.]

I do hereby certify that a petition for the Establishment of a Town at Bourbon Courthouse was advertised at said courthouse according to Law

    Test John Edwards Clerk Bourbon County Court
September 2d 1789   John Edwards

NUMBER 58.

To the Honourable the General Assembly of Virginia.—

The petition of sundry inhabitants of the District of Kentucky Humbly sheweth.—That whereas in consequence of an act of the legislature in their session of Octr 1788 intitled an act concerning the erection of the District of Kentucky into an independant State: a convention met at Danville under the strongest conviction as your petitioners conceive that it was not the will of the good people of said District that the same should be erected into an independant state: and we are pursuaded that to have voted the same in the affirmitive would have been too glareing a violation of the trust reposed in them when brought into contrast with their avowed sentiments previous to their election; Notwithstanding which they have petitioned your Honourable body to make certain amendments to the terms proposed in the late act of separation. Your petitioners therefore beg leave to suggest that although the objects complained of, might greatly injure a fiew of the sons of liberty yet their amendments can be of no importance to an independant sovereignty. Your petitioners further beg leave to express their apprehentions (which is) that the smallest alteration may be thought sufficient to santify the prosecution of a separation after cloaking their designs with a ficticious zeal for the public good, should the present convention be continued, to consider the same: Your petitioners beg leave further to observe that as no special powers were given the convention to sue for terms; but only to determine on the expediency of said separation on the terms in said act contained therefore the evasion of said determination has tacitly confirmed that truth, which your petitioners and the good people in General both wished, and expected to have been declared, in positive terms.—Your petitioners therefore conceiving that an augmentation of states under the general Government, by the erection of a new Government here, which will be clothed with no national power and which will only serve as one of Pharos lean kine to devour our liberty, whilst it can be of no security to our property, Therefore your petitioners in full faith, hope and confidence request that the general Government will secure everything which the most sanguine can desire: and that a separation may injoure us until time shall be no more do pray that the tacit acknowledgement of said convention be confirmed and the will of the people be established by a repeal of the separation Act: and your petitioners as in duty bound shall ever pray &c.—

[Names.]

No endorsement appears on the back, but the request is based on an act entitled, An Act concerning the erection of the district of Kentucky into an independent state. Henings Statutes, Vol. 12, 788.

The Convention provided for previously had been hindered from meeting and another had been provided for in August of 1787, according to an act entitled, An Act making further provision for the erection of the district into an independent State. Henings Statutes, Vol. 12, 240.

NUMBER 59.

To the honourable the General Assembly of Virginia,

The Memorial of the Subscribers respectfully represents, That notwithstanding the attention of the two last Assemblies to the support of the Supreme Court for the District of Kentucky, their favourable designs are like to be frustrated.

To the General Assembly of Virginia

By the late Laws appointing Commissioners to settle and adjust certain Claims in that District, the Certificates granted by them are made receivable in discharge of any of the Taxes which should afterwards become due therein: and this privilege is supposed by many still to extend to all or to most of the Taxes which since have been appropriated to the payment of the Salaries of the officers of the said Court. This will probably give rise to tedious litigations between the Collector of these Taxes and those from whom they are due; and in the meantime the officers of the Court will be obliged to sell their Certificates at a large discount, or at still greater loss and delay apply to the Treasury at Richmond for payment. Therefore we hope, that on this representation, the intention of the Legislature in the Case will be more explicitly declared; and that all the Taxes for which the several Clerks in the District are accountable may be either made payable in Specie only, or that some other fund may be established for defraying the Expences of the said Court.

And your Memorialists shall ever pray &c.

George Muter.
Saml. McDowell
Caleb Wallace
Harry Innes

Endorsement on back of petition: Petition referred to Courts of Justice—22d. October 1789—Reasonable—Law of 1786 to be amended—Reported.

The request was granted in an act entitled, An Act to amend the Acts for appointing Commissioners to liquidate and settle the expenses incurred in two expeditions, carried on from Kentucky district against the neighboring Indians and for other purposes. "Be it enacted," etc. Henings Statutes, Vol. 13, 2. "That from and after the passing of this act the tax on law process and alienations and also the tax on tobacco receivable within the district of Kentucky, shall be paid and accounted for in specie only, any law to the contrary notwithstanding."

This was to take the place of certificates issued by the Commissioners.

Petitions of the Early Inhabitants of Kentucky

NUMBER 60.

To the Honorable the General Assembly of Virginia.

The Petition of a number of Inhabitants of the District of Kentucky, humbly sheweth;

That whereas a very great expence and inconvenience attends the sitting of the Supreme Court only at one place in this District, the greater part of which expences and inconveniences may be obviated by appointing additional places for holding the said Court: We therefore pray your Honorable body to take the same into your serious consideration, and should you in your wisdom think our prayer reasonable, that you appoint the two following places in addition to the former (to wit,) the one at Lexington, in the County of Fayette, and the other at Baird's Town, in the County of Nelson; and we as in duty bound shall ever pray &c.

[Names.]

[There are about fifteen or twenty printed sheets with the above paragraph on them, and each one of them has a number of names on it—over eight hundred in all.]

Endorsement on back of petition: Referred to Props.

Danville Augt

Sirs

Agreeable to your request I herewith give you a Statemt. of the business in the Supreme Court as it will stand at the ensuing September Term.—together with some past statemts concerning Wits attendance

State of the Docket to Septr

Caveats now on the Court Dock (of which 82 have been upwards of 4 yrs depending)_____ Amt 96

N B near one half of these depend on the priority of Location. Specialty of Entry or written agreements which will require few or no Witnesses.—

To the General Assembly of Virginia

Chancery causes for hearing............................ 23
Chancery References & apprs. on the Rule Dockett...... 132
Common Law Issues..................................... 146
New Issues & References &c on Rules................... 140

NB. of the above 286—there's about 139 for Debt which do not require Witnesses 90 in Case of which 11 are for Slander— 21 for Batteries & the residue are for breach of Covt Detinues, Trespaser & Ejectmts—

Pleas of the Commonwealth................................ 13

An Acct. of Witnesses attendance for 1789—

March Term 18 days No of Wits............... 90   1300   50
June Term 24 days...........................109   400   50
NB   More Witnesses Attende entered these Courts [than] were entered in any two courts before

State of the office

There is lodged in the present office of the Supreme Court, Books containing the copies of all the Entries for Settlements & preemptions granted by the commissioners of the Kentucky District and that promiscously as they were entered without regard to County

There is lodged in the same office 5637 entries from the county surveyors pursuant to a late law—Also I am well informed that the surveyor of Jefferson has copied all the old Kentucky entries to be lodged as the said Act directs

Four large blank Books lately procured by the clerk for the use of the sd Court & not immediately wanted

NUMBER 61.

To the Honorable the General Assembly of Virginia.

The Petition of the Subscriber humbly sheweth, That in the year 1787 Your petitioner removed from the State of

Petitions of the Early Inhabitants of Kentucky

Maryland into the District of Kentucky and brought with him a few Negro Slaves; but doth most solemnly aver that he never was informed, or heard that it behooved him to take any oath concerning the importation of his Negroes into the State of Virginia until sometime in May in the present year 1789, when he was informed that by neglecting to take the Oath prescribed by law his Negroes were entitled to freedom, and himself liable to heavy penalties; and that then it was too late even to avail himself of the indulgences granted by an Act of the last Session of Assembly to persons in his situation: He was also informed that the Plea of Ignorance would be of no Avail in a Court of Justice: and that his only prospect of relief was from the Legislature. For those who have neither education nor leisure to enable them to be acquainted with the Laws of their Country, their only prospect for impunity is an honest inoffensive deportment; and in the prospect of absolute ruin, it is some Consolations that their misfortune does not arise from any wilful fault or neglect. But your petitioner conceives his case to be peculiarly hard, as the ruin with which he is threatened will be produced by Laws which it cannot be supposed he was acquainted with before he became a Citizen; and during the short period he has been in the State, it has required his most vigorous exertions to procure Shelter and Sustenance for a numerous Family, and in the meantime he has been necessarily secluded from the opportunities of information. Therefore your petitioner hopes and prays that the peculiarity of his situation may be taken into Consideration, and such relief granted as will secure to him the possession of the hard earnings of many Years industry, and deliver his beloved Wife and Children from that povorty which otherwise will be unavoidable.

And as in duty bound he will ever pray &c.

Benjamin Stevenson.

To the General Assembly of Virginia

District of Kentucky, August 1789—
At the request of Mr Benjamin Stevenson, the Subscriber to the within Petition, We certify—That since he came into this Country we are well assured he has supported Character of a good Citizen;—That he has applied himself with great diligence in building, clearing, and farming on a small tract of Land on which he has settled:—And that from his established veracity, as well as from the circumstances of the case, we verily believe the Allegations of his Petition to be strictly true.
[Names.]

Endorsement on back of petition: October 28th. 1789—Refd. to Courts of Justice.

The procedure regarding slaves referred to in the petition is found in an act entitled, An Act concerning the importation of slaves into the District of Kentucky. Henings Statutes, Vol. 12, 713.
"Whereas many persons who have removed from some other parts of the U. S. into the District of Kentucky and have become citizens of this Commonwealth, have failed within ten days after their removal into the same to take the oath or oaths, prescribed by two acts of assembly, the one intituled 'An act for preventing the further importation of slaves,' the other intituled, 'an Act concerning slaves to be taken on the importation of the same,' Although they might with great truth have taken the oaths; and whereas such failure hath been chiefly if not altogether, owing to the impracticability of complying with the said acts, Be it enacted," etc. Henings Statutes, Vol. 12, 713.
The act provides that those already removed may take the oath on or before May 1st. and those going to Kentucky after the act shall take the oath within sixty days. The act is not to affect the right of a slave to freedom when so entitled.

NUMBER 62.

To the Honourable the Virginia Assembly

the petition of the Inhabitants of Bourbon County Humbly Sheweth that the Land whereon our present Courthouse now stands to the amount of two hundred & fifty acres is laid off in Lotts by the Proprietor, for the purpose of selling a Town which Lotts are principly bought up by those who are now living on & improving them and have erected a number of very convenient buildings—on sd Lotts we your petitioners conceiving it realy necessary that sd Town be established by Law pray your Honorable body that a Law pass for the establishment of a Town agreeable to the manner the Lotts are now laid off and that Trustee be appointed for the purpose of suprintending & Regulating of the Building of sd Town and in duty Bound we pray—

[Names.]

Endorsement on back of petition. Octo. 28th. 1789.—Refd. to props. (reasonable) (repd.)

The request was granted in an act entitled, An Act to establish a town in each of the counties of Madison, Albemarle, and Bourbon. Henings Statutes, Vol. 13, 87.

The town for Madison was Milford, and for Bourbon it was Hopewell.

The trustees were Notley Conn, Charles Smith, Jr., John Edwards, James Garrard, Edward Waller, Thomas West, James Lanier, James Little, and James Duncan.

NUMBER 63.

To the Honorable the Speaker and Gentlemen of the House of Delegates

The Petition of sundry of the Inhabitants on the North side of the River in the district of Kentucky Humbly begs leave to Represent; that they experience many dificulties in carrying their Tobacco to the Warehouses already establish'd by Law at Jacks Creek on the South side of the River Kentucky and at the mouth of Hickmans Creek, owing to the danger of discending the cliffs, the badness of the Roads and the Risque of crossing the River. That there is a Comodious and conveniant place for an Inspection below the mouth of Tate Creek on the Lands of Michael [Bedinger] & nearly where the Main Road leads by an easy, and safe discent down the Hill to the said River of Kentucky

We your Petitioners therefore pray, that you would be pleased in consideration of the Premisses to pass a Law, establishing a Warehouse on the Lands of the said Michl Bedinger about three fourths of a mile below the mouth of the aforesaid Tates Creek, under such Regulations and Restrictions, as you, in your Wisdom may deem fit and Proper.

And your Petitioners as in duty bound, will ever pray &c

[Names.]

Endorsement on back of petition: 2nd. Novr. 1789.—Refd, to Props—Nov. 4th. 1789—Props discharged.

To the General Assembly of Virginia

NUMBER 64.

To the Honorable the General Assembly of the Commonwealth of Virginia

The petition of Sundry Inhabitants of the District of Kentucky humbly sheweth that your petitioners are much surprised to find many petitions in circulation and which we apprehend will be presented to your Honorable house prayg the Establishment of a number of Inspections of Tobacco on the Kentucky River Exclusive of those already Established and we conceive the principles of said petitions is founded on neither Justices or good policy; but wholy Calculated for the Interest & Convenience of a few Individuals because the Kentucky River is so inclosed with Hills & pricepeces [precipices] that it is in very few places that any kind of access can be had to said River or situations for public buildings your petitioners humbly pray that the said petitions may be rejected and that your Honorable house will vest a power in the Supreme or County Courts within the said District to Establish Inspection of Tobacco by appointing Disinterested free holders as Commissioners to view the different places proposed, and that not more than two shall be established in any one County & those where it is most Conveniant for the people in General as your petitioners humbly conceive that more than two will be injurious and . . . [torn off] because we are not able to build the necessary houses and furnish weights and scails for a greater number and a greater number will Certainly devid [divide] the attention of the people so that they must fall and your petitioners will ever pray &c.

[Names.]

Endorsement on back of petition: 3d. Novr. 1789—Refd. to Props. (reasl.) (repd.)

Petitions of the Early Inhabitants of Kentucky

NUMBER 65.

To the Honourable General Assembly of the Commonwealth of Virginia—

The Petition of us the subscribers of the Counties of Fayette and Bourbon whom it doth concern humbly sheweth, That your petitioners conceive it to be expedient and necessary that the upper parts of Fayette and Bourbon Counties be struck off, for the purpose of forming a new County, in the following manner (to wit) Beginning at the mouth of Boones Creek, and running up said Creek to the mouth of Bogg's fork, thence a Direct line to the Junction of Welch's fork, with the main fork, known also by the name of Robinson's fork of said Creek; thence up said Welch's fork and the longest branch thereof to the head; thence a direct line to strike Mason County line one mile below the upper Blue licks on main Licking Creek; thence with said Mason County line to Madison County line; thence with said Madison County line to the beginning which Division we conceive wou'd be very advantageous to the Inhabitants of the proposed new County, and not disadvantageous to the Counties of Fayette and Bourbon, we therefore Request that you will grant the prayer of our Petition, and your petitioners as in duty bound shall ever pray &c

[Names.]

I do certify that notice of the same purport of the within was publickly set up at two different Courts previous to September Court in the present year at the Court house in Bourbon County Given under my hand this 8th day of Septr. 1789.

John Edwards C B C

I do certify that Notice of the same purport of the within was publickly set up at two different Courts previous to September Court in the present year at the Courthouse in Fayette County Given under my hand this 8th day of Sept. 1789.

Levi Todd Cl. Co. F.

Daniel Boone

John Niblack · Squire Boone
Isaac Shelby · James Wilkinson
W Bartley · Charles Heezelyy
Patterson · E. Girault
Joseph Crockett · A Venable
Benj" Logan · Richard Durrett
Gabriel Madison · Levi Todd
James Garrard · George Jameson
Michael Goodrich · Daniel Trabue
Willis Green · Simon Kenton
· George Muter
Sam¹ W Powell · David Thathaway
M° Lacassagne

To the General Assembly of Virginia

Notice is hereby given that a Petition will be presented to the next General Assembly, praying that the upper parts of the Counties of Fayette and Bourbon be struck off, for the purpose of forming a new County in the following manner (to wit) Beginning at the mouth of Boones Creek and running up the same to the mouth of Boggs fork thence a direct line to the Junction of Welch's fork with the main fork, known by the name of the middle fork of said Creek; thence up said Welch's fork and the longest branch thereof to the head, thence a direct line to strike Mason County line one mile below the upper blue Licks on main Licking Creek, thence with said Mason County line to Madison County line, thence with said Madison County line to the beginning.

Endorsement on back of petition: 6th Novr. 1789—Refd. to Props.—Rejected.

There are five copies of this petition circulated in different places.

NUMBER 66.

To the Honorable the Speaker and General Assembly of Virginia

the petition of Sundry inhabitants of the County of Bourbon humbly sheweth that a petition for the Division of said county is to be presented to the General Assembly at their next setting contrary to the wishes of the majority of the inhabitants of said County, but being earnestly pressed by a few settlers in the upper end of Fayatte whose views can be no other than pecuniary ones which is proved by naming themselves for certain offices. They have prevailed upon a few scattered setlers in the upper end of this County who is amused with having the Courthouse among them; The amount of whom does not exceed one Militia Company amongst whom together with the inhabitants of said intended County in the upper end of Fayatte few or none have been found qualified for the office of civil or other department. The Line intended by said petition will destroy the very center of the now county of Bourbon and cause a removal of the Court house, as it will not run more than six Miles from the same and on that side which the body and extent of Good Land lies, the Two other sides is barred by the line of Fayatte and Hills unfit for cultivation, The setlers in this county so much injured by their detached situation is not almost above Sixteen or Seventeen Miles from the Courthouse and those who are so amazingly anxious for a County in Fayatte are from about twelve to Eighteen Miles from that Court house—Now your petitioners would inform your honorable house that the only thing they can urge in favour of the Division is that Mr Jacob Moyers is forming a setlement on State Creek twenty four miles from the upper settlement where it is said he intends erecting Iron works and there is still an extent of country above that place after the population of which your honorable house may decide with propriety with respect to the bounds of said Counties and leave each in possession of a number of men sufficient to administer Justice to the Citizens thereof—and your Petitioners as in duty bound will ever pray &c.

[Names.]

Endorsement on back of petition: 6th. Novr. 1789—Refd to Props.

NUMBER 67.

The petition of Sundry Inhabitants of The County of Fayette in the district of Kentucky humbly beg leave to Represent, that from their remote situation they experience many Inconveniences on getting their Tobacco to the Different Warehouses Established by Law, Oweing to the Badness of the roads and the difficulty in descending the Clifts down to the river Kentucky on which the said Warehouses are already established; that there is a commodious and convenient Place for an Inspection on the Land of Eli Cleaveland Gentleman on the said river Kentucky, to which an Exceeding good road may

To the General Assembly of Virginia

be made and an easy and safe descent down the Clifts to the river.

Your Petitioners therefore pray that you would be pleased in consideration of the premisses to pass a Law Establishing a Warehouse on the Lands of the aforesaid Eli Cleaveland gentn. on the said river . . . and in your Wisdom may deem fit and proper.

And your Petitioners as in Duty bound will ever pray &c.
[Names.]

NUMBER 68.

To the Honorable the Speaker & House of Delegates of Virginia.

The petition of the Inhabitants of the Town of Louisville, humbly sheweth.

That your petitioners, from the Number of Difficulties which the Settling of a new Country must unavoidably expose people to, from the savage Incursions, from the Want of materials and more particularly from the very great scarcity of Species, have hitherto been prevented from making the Improvements, as required by an act of your Honble House, on their several lots in the said Town of Louisville; your petitioners cannot but acknowledge your kind Indulgence in giving them Time still to make the necessary Improvements; which Time will expire on Jany next, we therefore humbly pray That you will farther extend your kindness to us and give us the farther Time of three years from the Expiration of the former act, to make such Improvements.

Your petitioners also beg leave to observe, that they are very much aggrieved by the appointment of new Trustees instead of the former ones in Louisville. That the present Trustees are Gent, who reside some distance from the Town and that very few of them have any Interest in lots therein. Which in the opinion of yr petrs occasions a very great Inattention in them to the Business of the Town. That there are numbers who are in want of Deeds for their lots, which they cant obtain by Reason of the present Trustees not attending,— Your petrs also think that the Town & its Interests wou'd be much better regulated by men who live in it.—We therefore humbly pray that an act may pass appointing such men as you in your wisdom shall approve, (who reside in Louisville) to be and act as Trustees to said Town, to all Intents & purposes instead of the Gent last appointed.—

[Names.]

Jefferson County Sct.

I William Johnston clerk of said county do hereby certify, that notice hath been twice publickly set up at the Court House Door of said County, on two several Court days, previous to this date, of the within petition's being to be presented to next Genl. Assembly of Virginia. Given under my Hand & seal August 25 1789.

Will. Johnston (seal)

Endorsement on back of petition: Nov. 12th. 1789—Refd. to Props.—further time to improve—reasonable—Present Trustees to be displaced—Rejected—Additional Trustees to be added—any to act.

The request was granted in an act entitled, An Act for appointing trustees to the town of Romney and for adding trustees to the town of Louisville in the county of Jefferson. Henings Statutes, Vol. 13, 90.

Trustees: Buckner Thruston, James Wilkinson, Michael Lacassange, Alexander Scott Bullitt, Benjamin Sebastian, James Felty, Jacob Reager, James Patten, Samuel Kirby, Benjamin Erickson, and Benjamin Johnson.

NUMBER 69.

To the Honourable the General Assembly of Virginia.

The petition of Sundry inhabitants of Kentucky Humbly sheweth that whereas petitions are handed about for Subscribers, seting forth their desire to have the Seat of the Supreme Court for the District of Kentucky removed, from the place where it is now held, to some other part of the said District & also others to have the business carried on by District Courts—

To the General Assembly of Virginia

your petitioners conceive it their duty to lay before your Honourable body the Reason upon which they found their dislike of both measures—being convinced that if they have any weight, you will not Grant such a removal or such division of the business of this District,

Your petitioners will observe that Kentucky is settled now *Generally speaking* in two lines one from North to South about ninty miles, & another from the Extremity of that Line west about the same Distance, that the point of that angle, is the place where the Court is now held—That Removing it either to Lexington or Bairds [Bards] Town as proposed, a distance from Danville between thirty and forty miles, will subject the setlers of one of those corners, to travil that distance in order to favour with the same distance the setlers of the other Extremity, which partiality your petitioners, hope you will not countenance—

Your petitioners will further add that they do not think it at present a proper time to remove the Seat of the Court, as it would force us to Expences for the new buildings, & that a most Rigid plan of Economy suits best our present circumstances.—

This last mentioned Reason for not allowing the removal of the Supreme Court to any other place will stand still better for not allowing three buildings in lieu of one, in case District Courts should be granted—

it is thought that those Governments are best who employ fewer officers, but the Creating District Courts will necessarily increase that number—

there is another Evil attending any alteration of that kind, which your petitioners beg leave to mention—the books of commissioners for settlement & previous Rights, those of Entries with the diferent surveyors are lodged with the present court—in case you Grant District Courts, copies of those books, must be had at a very great Expence & loss of time & business must Stagnate & have an End

Petitions of the Early Inhabitants of Kentucky

Your petitioners know full well the ostensible pretence of those other petitioners is to make it more convenient to the parties concerned, & their Witnesses, but that pretence are far from being founded on truth, as the Constant Removals [of] our Setlers make it to them one day more Disadvantageous & the next more convenient.—

We see with pain that the . . . of those petitions Grumble at the Distance which they must travil, when several of the Districts of this Commonwealth contain no more square miles than the settled parts of Kentucky do at present with more anxiety we observe that the consequence of District Courts, in lieu of expediting business will effectually retard it by double the time which is now required to obtain redress and what will humanity feel when it is considered that in Criminal Causes it Lengthens doubly the dreadfull punishment of a . . . in a country where the Laws show indulgence to the very Culprit who has infringed them—as your Honble body is to take a full view of the community at large & promote the greatest good possible to the greatest number,

Your petitioners hope, that you will not Grant those petitions, which tend only to favour a very small portion of this District, at the Expence of the far greater number & they shall ever pray &c.

Endorsement on back of petition: Novr. 14th 1789—Refd to Props.

The request was granted in an act entitled, An Act for further amending the act establishing a Supreme Court in Kentucky District. Henings Statutes, Vol. 13, 66.
By this act the power of the receiver was increased. He had joint authority with the auditor and treasurer to settle with sheriffs. Taxes were to be payable in any article receivable in other parts of the Commonwealth, and also in certificates granted by the Commissioners for service against the Indians. There were to be three sessions of the Supreme Court.

To the General Assembly of Virginia

NUMBER 70.

To the Honorable the General Assembly

The petition of William McKenzie humbly sheweth: that by an act of the legislature of this commonwealth, certain lands in the district of Kentucky belonging to Robert McKenzie were confiscated and granted to a public school: That your petitioner is the nearest in blood to the said Robert; and being informed that your honorable body have always shewn a readiness to give the value of all confiscated property to the next in succession, your petitioner prays, that such value may be allowed to him.

And as in duty bound he will ever pray &c. &c.

Extract of Law—

Whereas it is represented to the General Assembly, that there are certain lands, within the County of Kentucky formerly belonging to british subjects, not yet sold under the law of escheats and forfeitures, which might at a future day be a valuable fund for the maintenance and education of youth; and it being the interest of this common wealth always to promote and encourage every design which may tend to the improvement of the mind and the diffusion of useful knowledge, even among its most remote citizens, whose situation a barbarous neighborhood and a savage intercourse might otherwise render unfriendly to science: Be it therefore enacted that eight thousand acres of land within the said county of Kentucky, late the property of Robt. McKensie, Henry Collins, and Alexd McKie, be, and the same are hereby vested in Wm. Fleming, Wm. Christian, John Todd, Stephen Trigg, Benjamin Logan, John Floyd, John May, Levi Todd, John Cowan, Geo. Meriwether, John Cobbs, Geo. Thompson, and Edmund Taylor, trustees as a free donation from this Commonwealth for the purpose of a publick school, or seminary of learning, to be erected within the said county as soon as the circumstances of the County and the state of its funds will admit, and for no other use or purpose what so ever: Saving and reserving to the said Robert McKensie, Henry Collins, and Alexd. McKie, and of every of them, and all and every person or persons claiming under them, or either of them all right and interest to the above mentioned lands, or any part thereof to which they may be by law entitled and of which they shall in due time avail themselves, any thing herein contained to the Contrary notwithstanding. . . .

The Land Bounded as followeth—On the South side of the Ohio 8 miles above the Falls, on the upper side of the mouth of Harrods Creek—3000 acres.

Endorsement on back of petition: 16 Novr. 1789.—Refd. to Courts of Justiec—Reasonable.

NUMBER 71.

To the honorable the general Assembly of Virginia.

The petition of Anne Craig humbly sheweth:

That a certain James Douglass, now deceased, put his only daughter, Jessy Douglass, to board with your petitioner, and promised to make her ample compensation for the same: that she continued with your petitioner for several years; the board for which amounted to more than one hundred and thirty pounds: that your petitioner trusted the said James Douglass in contemplation of certain lands, which he held in Kentucky and other parts of Virginia: that the said James Douglass and the said Jessy Douglass are now dead intestate and without an heir: whereby the said lands are escheatable to the commonwealth.

Your petitioner therefore prays, that the right of escheat, now vested in this commonwealth, may be so far released, as to permit the said lands to be sold for the payment of the just debts of the said James and Jessy Douglass.

And your petitioner, as in duty bound will ever pray &c, &c.

Endorsement on back of petition: 16 Novr. 1789.—Refd. to Courts of Justice—Rejected.

To the General Assembly of Virginia

NUMBER 72.

TO THE HONOURABLE THE GENERAL ASSEMBLY OF VIRGINIA

The Petition of a number of Inhabitants of the County of Fayette Humbly sheweth—

That whereas a very Great Expence and Inconvenience attends the Ferriage of Tobacco over the River Kentucky to the Town of Boonsborough the greater part of which Expences and Inconveniances might be obviated by appointing Inspections on the North side of the said River at Two Distinct places to be attended by one appointment of Inspectors, as the Precipices of Howards will not admit of a waggon Road, we therefore pray your Honorable Body to take the same into serious consideration and should your Wisdom think our prayer reasonable that you appoint the Two following places, the one nearly opposite Boonsborough on William Bushes Land and the other on the west side of Howards Creek on John Holders Land and we as in Duty Bound shall ever pray &c

[Names.]

Notice is hereby given, that a Petition will be presented to the next General Assembly, praying that an Inspection be established for the Reception of Tobacco, on Colo John Holder's land on the Kentucky River, below the mouth of lower Howard's Creek, at the place called Holder's landing, also another Inspection on the land of Capt. William Bush, on the Kentucky River, above lower Howard's Creek, and nearly opposite to the Town of Boonsborough, to be included under one Inspection.

Fayette County

William Bush before me upon oath says that the within notice was publickly set up at the door of the court house of said county on two several Court days within the present year Sept. 9, 1789.

Robt. Todd

Endorsement on back of petition: 30 Novr. 1789—Rejected.

Petitions of the Early Inhabitants of Kentucky

NUMBER 73.

To the Honorable the Speaker and Members of the Genl. Assembly

The Memorial of the Convention for the District of Kentucky Sheweth, that by an Act of the last Session of the Assembly, the terms on which the sd District of Kentucky, may be erected into a seperate and independant State, are materially different from those heretofore offered by Virginia, and agreed to by a former Convention on the part of the sd District; and that the alteration in one of the terms is more particularly injurious to your Memorialists as it forever precludes them, tho declared an Independent and sovereign state from excessing [exercising] this right of sovereignty over part of the Lands contained within their own boundaries without the consent of the legislature of Virginia, a situation degrading to your Memorialists, as they would thereby not lie on equal footing with the other States in the Union and injurious, as it would prevent them from making the advantage of the surplus Lands within their boundaries, which in Equity they are intitled to.

From which circumstances your Memorialists find that they cannot at present determine whether it is expedient for and the will of the people that the District shall be erected into a seperate & independent State.

Your Memorialists reflect with gratitude on the generous and disinterested conduct pursued by the Legislature with respect to the wishes of the People of this District for a seperation and relying with the fullest confidence on the Justice and generosity of the present Assembly, they now request that the Act concerning the erection of this District into a seperate and independent State may be so amended that the terms offered by the Legislature of Virginia to the people of this District, respecting the Seperation of the District from Virginia, and its being erected into a seperate State may be made equal to those offered by former Acts of Assembly (except such part of the seventh Article of the Act of 1785 as relates to the concur-

To the General Assembly of Virginia

rent Jurisdiction of the Ohio with the States that may possess the opposite shores of the sd River) and agreed to on the part of the District by a former Convention. And your Memorialists as in duty bound shall ever pray—
A copy. Saml. McDowell Prest

Endorsement on back of petition: Novr. 1789.—Refd. to Whole on Co.—For Govr. Moreland of Kentucky.

The request was granted in an act entitled, An Act concerning the erection of the district of Kentucky into an independent state. Henings Statutes, Vol. 13, 17.
"Whereas it is represented to the present General Assembly the act of the last session intituled 'An Act concerning the erection of the district of Kentucky into an independent state' which contains terms materially different from those of the act of October session 1785, are found incompatible with the real views of the Commonwealth as well as injurious to the good people of the said district, Be it enacted," etc.
The act provides for a convention at Danville July 26th, selected as in previous acts. The seven conditions are similar to those of the act of 1785. The authority of Virginia over Kentucky was to end at date posterior to November 1, 1791. The objectionable features were omitted.

NUMBER 74.

To the Honourable the General Assembly of the State of Virginia.

The Petition of the Inhabitants of Lincoln County residing on the reserved Lands for the officers and Soldiers of the State aforesaid on the Waters of Cumberland River and Parts adjacent doth Respectfully shew.—

That your Petitioners find themselves sensibly aggrieved by their distance from Courts of Justice, it being near two hundred miles from this Settlement to Lincoln Court House, by which, when Business renders our attendance indispensably necessary, we are frequently exposed to much Danger in Travelling, through an uninhabited Country; being subjected to Fines, and other Inconveniances, when from High Waters, Enemies near our Frontiers; or other Causes it is Impossible to attend.—

We therefore most humbly Pray the General Assembly, to grant a County to be laid off including these settlements in the reserved Land for the officers and soldiers, on the south of Green River, and to the Coloney Line, thence to the Ohio, and your Petitioners as in Duty bound will ever Pray &c.—

[Names.]

Endorsement on back of petition: 21st. Oct. 1790.—Refd. to Props.—Reasonable—(repd.)

NUMBER 75.

TO THE HONORABLE THE GENERAL ASSEMBLY OF VIRGINIA.

The petition of Jane Todd and Robert Todd Executors of the Estate of John Todd deceased humbly sheweth—

That whereas an Act of Assembly passed in the year of our Lord 1786 appointing Trustees to sell a part of the Land of John Todd deceased for the payment of his Debts and for other purposes, vested power in four Trustees therein named to carry the same into execution reserving the Tract of Land in the County of Fayette where on the said John Todd resided at the time of his death, That the said Trustees found it difficult to act under the said Law as the decedent at the Time of his death resided on a lot in Lexington, that on the North West side of the Town he had a military claim of 130 acres and on the South East lands claimed by Settlement and preemption—

To remove which uncertainty, and to give the Trustees power to sell a part of the said military survey, one other act of Assembly was passed in the year 1787 reserving the Tract whereon his widow Jane Todd then resided, which was in the bounds of that part of the Land which was obtained by Virtue of the Decedents Settlement and adjoining to which there was 2400 acres procured by other Rights, which reservation strictly construc'd prevents the Sale of any of the said Tract and frustrates the good intent of the Legislature as we conceive the whole of the 130 acres ought not to be sold or if sold would prove insufficient to answer the purpose, and excepting this

To the General Assembly of Virginia

and the Tract before mentioned there is no land that belonged to the decedant that would sell unless to great [advantage.]

Your petitioners therefore pray that the said Trustees may be authorized to sell and convey any Lands of the Estate of the said decedant, for the purposes mentioned in the said recited acts, and to carry the same into full execution, excepting and reserving the four Hundred Acres obtained by virtue of the said decedants actual settlement and none other, and provided that the part sold shall not exceed one fourth of what the sd decedant died possessed of.

And as one of the Trustees before appointed is dead and other removed from the County so that it will be difficult to procure his attendance we pray that two additional Trustees may be appointed vested with the same powers as those first appointed and that any three may be authorized to act and we in duty bound will ever pray &c—

Jane Todd
Robt. Todd

Endorsement on back of petition: 21st. Oct 1790—Refd. to Courts of Justice—Reasonable—Bill drawn.

The request was granted in an act entitled, An Act to amend two acts of the assembly appointing trustees to sell part of the lands of John Todd, deceased, and other purposes. Henings Statutes, Vol. 13, 231.

The added trustees were Percival Butler and Robert Barr.

NUMBER 76.

To the Honble. The General Assembly of the State of Virginia—

The Petition of Sundry Inhabitants of the Town of Lexington (in the County of Fayette) and its vicinity; humbly sheweth That your Petitioners anxious for the welfare of the Town afsd and feeling sensibly a variety of inconveniences under which they labor, beg leave to request the interference of your Honble Body in their behalf.

They would pray that the Legislature would invest a certain number of Inhabitants of said Town and its vicinity, with the following powers & authorities—the appointment of officers by your Honble Body or by Election of the Inhabitants of said Town as your Wisdom sees fitt.

1st—To levy, collect, and appropriate such sums of money as the persons appointed for that purpose, may conceive necessary for the following uses—

2.—To regulate and improve the Market, the streets & Highways of the Said Town and its vicinity—

3.—To establish and preserve the peace and good order of the Town afsd & its vicinity—

4.—A power to remove & prevent Nusances—

In fine your Petitioners humbly pray that your Honble Body would invest the persons before referred to, with such powers & authorities as your wisdom may direct, for the more effectually promoting & preserving the hapiness of said Town &c.

Your Petitioners would beg leave to suggest to your Honble House, their wish, that the limits within which the said powers may be exercised shall be extended to one mile in each direction from the Court House in said Town.—

And your Petitioners as in duty bound shall ever pray &c
[Names.]

Endorsement on back of petition: Octo. 23d 1790.—Refd. to Props.

The request was granted in an act entitled, An Act concerning certain regulations in the town of Lexington and county of Fayette. Henings Statutes, Vol. 13, 191.

Trustees were to be elected by all within one mile possessed of twenty-five pounds in property, except negroes and mulattoes. Trustees could erect market houses, appoint clerk of market, repair streets, and impose taxes not exceeding one hundred pounds.

NUMBER 77.

To the Honble the Speaker and Gentlemen of the House of Delegates—

The Petitioners of Sundry Inhabitants of the County of Bourbone Humbly sheweth that your petitioner & resident on the waters of Stoner and Hinksons forks of Licking are desti-

To the General Assembly of Virginia

tute of Every advantage resulting from water Grist mills except what must be erected on branches of said Stoner and Hinkson which does not afford water sufficient to grind longer than the middle of April your petitioners therefore are necessiated to go from eighteen to twenty five miles to mill and even then under the disadvantage of frequantly being disappointed which subject your petitioners to grate loss of time and your petitioners are very confident that if mills was suffered to be built on stoner and Hinksons forks of Licking with ither good locks or slopes sufficient for boats to pass by the dams with safety that the said Stoner and Hinkson would be above ten times the value to Bourbone than what it is at present with only them navogations alone we therefore pray that Stoners fork and Hinksons may have mills on every Convenient place for erecting them but for all mills that is built on said Stoner and Hinkson to have a good lock or slope fixed for boats to pass and we in duty bound will pray

[Names.]

Bourbon County
I do hereby certify that the within Petition has been advertised at the Door of the Court house agreeable to Law, Given under my hand this 27th day of Aug. 1790

John Edwards Clk.

Endorsement on back of petition: Octo. 22d. 1790.—Refd to props—(in opposition)—(repd.)—Rejected H.L.

NUMBER 78.

TO THE HONOURABLE THE SPEAKER AND GENTLEMEN OF THE HOUSE OF DELEGATES

the Petition of Sundry Inhabitants of the County of Bourbon Humbly sheweth That in the year one thousand Seven Hundred and eighty eight there was an inspection of Tobacco established at the Junction of Hinkson & Stoner fork of Licking and that Stoners fork has been found by trial made as navigable a very considerable Distance above the Junction and for as large Boats, as it is below; and as long in the year and that it makes its way throug the center of the County, through a fertile soil thickly Inhabited, abounding with a variety of Fish, and that it is the only stream by which the greater part of the County can be relieved from a Difficult Land carriage of many miles, in exporting of their produce, and that an attempt is made for obstructing the same by the Court of sd County granting an order for a mill without any restricktions whatever, when granting two others the one prior & the other posterior to the former, obliging the owners to keep a passage for boats forty feet by twelve; the validity of which will evidently appear by the certificates attending this Petition from the Clerk of the County; Now being convinced that the obstructing the navigation of sd River would be highly injurious, and contrary to the Interest of the County; and also that your Honourable House are fully possessed of the advantages from a water carriage. We therefore pray that your Honorable House will take the same into consideration and remove all obstructions that shall be made across Sd River; and establish the navigation of Licking Beginning at its Junction with the Ohio thence up to the mainfork, thence up the South fork, to the Junction of Hinkston & Stoner thence up Stoners fork to Bramblets Lick in such manner as in your wisdom you may think best and we your Petitioners shall ever pray

[Names.]

Endorsement on back of petition. Octo. 22d. 1790.—Refd to props.

NUMBER 79.

To the Honourable the Speaker and Gentlemen of the House of Delegates.—

The Petition of Sundry Inhabitants of the County of Bourbon Humbly sheweth &c—That in the year 1788 There was an Inspection of Tobacco established at the Confluance of Stoner

To the General Assembly of Virginia

and Hinkstons fork of Licking; And that the south fork, which is called Stoners fork, is found by Experiance navigable a very considerable Distance above the Junction; even up to Bramlets Lick; for large Boats, and that it is the only Stream by which the greater part of the Inhabitants may be relieved from a Land Carriage of Many Miles in the Exportation of their produce, We therefore pray that the Navigation of said River may not be obstructed by Mill Dams or Fish Dams or the like &c and we your Petitioners shall ever pray

March 28th, 1790. [Names.]

NUMBER 80.

To the Honble the General Assembly of Virginia.

We the Trustees of the Town of Hopewell in the County of Bourbon Humbly sheweth that doubts have arisen with the purchers. of the Lots in said Town, whether Lawrance Protzmon may be found the real proprietor at a future day of the Lands laid of for said Town, your petitioners together with said purchasers having been notified of claims to the said Lands obtained from the Court of said County under an Act of Assembly authorizing and vesting said Court with powers of Commrs to hear and determine all disputes between claimants for Land, by right of settlement and for lands by right of Preemption on Improvement &c for granting certificates to all those who had been detained in the Service of this Commonwealth and also that a part of the Lots or lands laid of for said Town is yet unsold. Therefore your petitioners conceive they have not a power vested in them to sell or make conveyance of said lots or any part thereof, and that the Good people of said Town may be secured from future claimants And that every encouragement may be given to the population of said Town, which will be of Public utility, by reason of its situation on navigable water and the only stream by which the Inhabitants of said County could Export their produce. We your petitioners therefore pray your honble house will take the same in consideration and condemn said Land, vesting the same in trustees so as to give Security to the holders and purchasers of said Lots, as also the Laying of and making conveyance of such Lots as yet remains unsold and that you will devise such ways and means for the good of said holders as in your wisdom you may think best reserving to the real Proprietor the Value of said Lands as unimproved and your Petitioners further prays that said Town may no Longer retain the name of Hopewell, but may be called and known by the Name of Paris and your Petitioners shall ever pray &c.

[Names.]

Resolved that the petition of the Trustees of the town of Hopewell in the county of Bourbon, setting forth, that many doubts have lately arisen who is the real proprietor of the Lands on which the said town is established, in consequence whereof the present holders of the same are much disquieted, & the trustees cannot proceed in the sale thereof, And praying that they may be authorized to sell the said Lands—reserving the money arising from such sale, for the person who shall hereafter appear to be the real proprietor, and that the name of the said town may be altered, is reasonable.—

Endorsement on back of petition: 25th. Oct. 1790.—Refd. to Courts of Justice.—Reasonable—Bill.

The request was granted in an act entitled, An Act to amend the act establishing the town of Hopewell in the county of Bourbon and for altering the name of the said town. Henings Statutes, Vol. 13, 176.
The name was changed from Hopewell to Paris.

NUMBER 81.

To the Honorable the Speaker and Gentlemen of the House of Delegates.

The Memorial of Laban Shipp of the County of Bourbon, District of Kentucky, Humbly sheweth,

That your Memorialists Resident on Stoners Fork of Licking being impressed with the Great inconvenience of himself,

To the General Assembly of Virginia

and others for the want of water Grist mills was induced to apply to the county court of Bourbon for an order to Build a water Grist mill on the said fork; which was granted your memorialist without any other restrictions than to pay the Damage any person might sustain from the building of said mill; your memorialist immediately proceeded to and at the Expence of his little fortune which is nearly exhausted has got the mill nearly compleated: Your memorialist notwithstanding he has nearly spent his fortune in erecting this usefull Building felt himself happy in a prospect of being Usefull to his country and family; having proceeded under the sanction of the laws of his country thought himself safe and his property secure. It is with concern that your Memorialist finds a number of Persons have prepared a Petition to your Honorable House praying that the navigation of Stoners fork of Licking may not be obstructed but the subject of the navigation of this little stream has called the attention of most of the Inhabitants of this County; and many of them fully convinced of the Impropriety of attempting such a navigation have petition'd your Honorable House to permit the erection of Water Grist Mills on the said fork; However this subject may be agitated by the differant parties no other Inconvenience can arise to either of them than the mortification of being outdone by the other; but the case is materially differant with your Memorialist; his fortune has been laid out on this usefull building and if your Honorable House should oblige him to remove her for the precarias & Dangerous navigation; certain ruin must possess him and his family that the navigation is precarias apears from hence, near two years has elapsed since the Navigation was first attempted and but one boat has had a safe passage several Boats has been obliged to unlode and waggon their loads to other landings more safe & certain; that it is dangerous, is equally clear; several vessels have been overset & their loads lost, some men have been drowned and many more have been exposed to the Greatest hardship; from these facts your Memorialist trust your Honorable House will make no law to affect his property in the premises & Yr. Memorialist as in Duty Bound shall ever &c—

Laban Shipp—

Endorsement on back of petition. Octo. 27th. 1790.—Refd. to props—Reasonable—(repd.)

NUMBER 82.

To the Speaker & Gent of the House of Delegates

The Petition of Sundry Inhabitants of the County of Bourbon Humbly sheweth, that your Petitioners resident on the waters of Stoner and Hinksons forks of Licking are destitute of every advantage accruing from Water Grist Mills except what must be erected on said streams, every other stream failing to furnish a sufficiency of water to grind longer than to the middle of Aprl. Your Petitioners therefore are necessitated to go from eighteen to thirty miles to mill and even then under the disadvantage of frequent disappointment, which subjects us to great loss inconvenience, and labour. Your Petitioners are very confident if mills were suffered to be built without restricting the builders thereof to erect Locks &c for the passage of Boats numbers wou'd be encouraged to build mills sufficient to grind all the Grain of the Citizens of the County. But some of our fellow citizens puffed up with the most romantick expectations of the utility accruing from the free and open navigation of Stoner and Hinkson have prepar'd a Petition to your Hon House praying that the navigation of Stoner may be kept open and that no mills may be erected thereon; Your Petitioners beg leave to lay before you the following statement of facts, the distance of Strodes fork a branch of Stoners fork (the head of the propos'd navigation) to the junction of Hinksons and Stoners forks is not more than ten miles of Land and on the meanders of the Creek not less than thirty five or forty miles This stream being confind within narrow banks rises and

To the General Assembly of Virginia

falls so quick in the Winter Season (for in no other season is it navigable) that the water is generally exhausted before it can reach the confluence of the said Streams and what boats have attempted to navigate the fork of Stoner have been either wrecked injur'd or obliged to unlode for want of a water to continue Their passage These are facts so well authenticated that they cannot be contested. By an Act of Your Hon. House passed in October Session An Inspection of Tobo. was established at Ruddles at the junction of Hinkson and Stoners forks, from thence your Petitioners believe after a considerable expence to open the navigation that boats of small burden may navigate to the mouth of Licking perhaps as many as five or six times a year provided they manage with care and attention. Your Petitioners conceive that the erection of Water Grist Mills on said Streams will be of far greater benefit than the casual uncertainties of navigation can possibly be. We therefore pray that a Law may pass at the ensuing Session appropriating the afore mentioned Streams for the Building of Grist Mills &c to any person who may build according to Law. And that the navigation be open'd from the confluence of the forks to Main Licking by such ways and means as the Hon. the Legislature may [think] expedient and your Petitioners in Duty Bound will ever Pray &c

[Names.]

Endorsement on back of petition. Octo. 27th 1790. Refd. to props.

NUMBER 83.

To the Honorable the Speaker & members of the General Assembly of the State of Virginia.

The Petition of Sundry Claimants to portions of Land, contained in the Illinois Grant & others—Inhabitants of the District of Kentucky, humbly complaining sheweth.

That the Time limited for the Claimants to exhibit their Claims before the Commissioners appointed to settle and determine the claims of Persons entitled to portions of Land in the Illinois Grant was so short, that a number of Claimants &

Petitions of the Early Inhabitants of Kentucky

Infants Heirs at Law to deceased Claimants from their distant and dispersed situations in different parts of the United States have been prevented from having their several Claims, settled and determined according to the Act of October Session 1786 Your Petitioners further shew unto your Honorable Body that the Commissioners appointed under the aforesaid Law conceive that they have no power to grant Deeds for Claims that have already been settled & determined after the first day of September 1789 by which means a number of Claims already settled which have been assigned to innocent purchasers, & which are held by Infant Heirs at Law of deceased Claimants, who are dispersed in different parts of the United States & from a want of knowledge of the aforesaid Law are intirely prevented from receiving the benefit of their respective Claims or completing their Titles thereto, which your petitioners conceive is contrary to every principle of Equity and Justice. Your Petitioners therefore pray that you will pass an Act at the ensuing Session directing them to grant Deeds for all Claims that have heretofore been settled and determined when application shall be made therefor by the respective Claimants Assignees of Claimants or Infant Heirs at Law to deceased Claimants. And your Petitioners shall ever pray &c.

[Names.]

Endorsement on back of petition: 28th Oct. 1790.—Refd. to C. of Justice.—Reasonable.

The request was granted in an act entitled, An Act giving further time to the Commissioners for surveying and apportioning the lands granted to the Illinois regiment, to execute deeds for the same. Henings Statutes, Vol. 13, 178.

NUMBER 84.

To the Honorable the Speaker and Gentlemen of the House of Delegates.

The Petition of Sundry Inhabitants of the County of Bourbon Humbly sheweth—

That we your petitioners labour under much inconvenience for the want of an inspection of Tobacco in our County town—

To the General Assembly of Virginia

The town is situate upon Stoners fork of Licking which has been found navigable by large Boats loaded, navigating the same from the sd town—Now this being the most convenient for the County in general and the navigation is as good as tis risky Miles below we are convinced it will be of Publick utility and tend much to the Ease and Convenience of the good people of sd County We therefore [request] that an Inspection may be established upon the lots of Land set aside by the proprietor Laurance Protsman for that purpose and we your petitioners shall ever pray

[Names.]

Endorsement on back of petition: To land inspection—Reasonable H. L. —repd.

NUMBER 85.

THE HONOURABLE THE SPEAKER AND GENTLEMEN OF THE HOUSE OF GENERAL ASSEMBLY OF VIRGINIA,

the petition of William Bruce and John Lin Humbly sheweth that your petitioners served as scouts in the county of Bourbon for the year 1789 and was discharged legally and had their accounts setled with the auditors of publick accts & by certificates from the county Lieutenant of said county for particulars your petitioners must refer you to Mr Conn a member of your Honorable House—some time in the latter part of November in the same year Col John Edward Lieutenant of said county was seting out for Richmond by whome your petitioners hoped their money would be sent, and applyed to him to fetch the whole or any part he could get, and do the Best he could for them as they were in Great want, having made no crops the ensuing season on account of their being in the service of the State—the aforesaid Lieutenant recd 45 pound of the money and on his return to the District of Kentucky was attacked by a number of Indians well armed in two Boats prepaired for the capturing of the vessels of Emigrants on the Ohio river, and was obliged to dessert his Boat and make his Escape leaving considerable amount of his own property, his saddle bags and the money of your petitioners, which fell into the hands of the Enemy to the great Distress of your petitioners, who being well informed of the Justice & humanity that has hitherto marked the conduct of your Honorable House are Induced to ask a restoration of that money taken by the Enemy before it came to their hand which money they think in Justice they ought to receive in the country where they did the service—therefore your petitioners prays that your Honours would take the same into consideration and make such provision for them as in your wisdom may seem best and your Petitioners shall ever pray.

William Bruce
John Linn.

Endorsement on back of petition: 28th Oct. 1790.—Refd. to Claims—rejected —reported 3rd November '90.

NUMBER 86.

TO THE HONOURABLE THE REPRESENTATIVES OF THE STATE OF VIRGINIA IN GENERAL ASSEMBLY MET

the petition of James Smith Humbly Sheweth, that your petitioner spent Eleven months in Exploring the Kentuckey Country as Early as the year 1767 and in the year 1773 made an improvement on the Waters of Licking River, and sold the Chief of the land he then possessed in pennsylvania in order to move his family to Kentuckey, But as the War with Brittain at that Post Commenced your petitioner was Called upon to Serve his Country, and Continued in publick Business During the whole of Said War either as a Deligate in the House of Assembly or as a militia officer in the Jersey State or against the Indiens on our fronteers or on Expeditions against the Indien towns; During this time your petitioner was obliged by the legal tender act to take Depreciated Congress money as pay for his land—in the year 1786 he came to Kentucky and aplied for his Right of preemtion but the Court would not

To the General Assembly of Virginia

admit of his proving his Right of preimtion as he had not been in the Regular Service immediately under Congress—in the year 1787 your petitioner moved his family to Kentuckey and being much reduced by the Depreciation of the Congress paper money could only purchas one hundred acres of land which is the only land he now possesseth (as an Evidance of what he has said he sends the following papers), and as the land he improved in the year 1773. is not yet occupied, your petitioner Humbley prays that he may be yet admitted to prove his Right of preimtion, your petitioner would not at this time trouble the House with this Singular petition were it not that he looks on his Case altogether Singular, and he makes no Doubt but the Honourable Hous will Do what is Just and Right and your petitioner as in Duty Bound shall ever pray—

James Smith.

Bourbon County July the 15th 1790.

Jas. Smith setting forth—that in the year 1773 he acquired a preemption right to a Tract of Land on Licking River in the Ky-district—That he afterwards removed into the state of Pennsylvania in the year 1786 returned into this State: That upon application to the Court of the County in which the Land lieth they for reasons unknown to the Petitioners refused to admit his claim and praying that it may be permitted to prove his preemption Right to the sd Land

---

Endorsement on back of petition. Octo. 30th. 1790. Refd. to Ct. of Justice —Rejected.

NUMBER 87.

To the Honorable the Speaker and Members of the House Delegates of the Commonwealth of Virginia.

The Petition of Sundry Inhabitants of the Town of Maysville, Humbly sheweth; that your petitioners being settled in the said town of Maysville, which is situated on the Ohio River at the mouth of Limestone Creek and is a Frontier intirely exposed to the depredations of the Hostile Indians, which reasons alone has put it [out] of the power of your petitioners; to Compleat the necessary buildings for Securing their lotts within the time limited by an Act of Assembly Intitled an Act for establishing a town in the County of Bourbon;—Your petitioners therefore pray that your Honorable House will grant them such further time for Compleating their building as to you shall appear just & reasonable & your [petitioners] will ever pray &c

[Names.]

Endorsement on back of petition: 1st. Nov. 1790. Refd. to props.—Reasonable—(Repd.)

The act establishing the town referred to is entitled, An Act to establish a town in the county of Bourbon. Henings Statutes, Vol. 12, 633.

The name of the town was Maysville and the trustees were Daniel Boone, Henry Lee, Arthur Fox, Jacob Boone, Thomas Brooks, George Milford.

The town was on Mays land.

NUMBER 88.

To the Honorable the Speaker and General Assembly of Virginia—

The petition of a number of the inhabitants of the County of Bourbon In behalf of themselves and others most humbly sheweth that there is a number of Deeds in the County for Land that is not recorded there being no Court in said County from July until January in consequence of the Death of the high Sheriff of said County in which time deeds run out of date and the persons who made those deeds are some of them mov'd out of Kentuckey others of them dead and their heirs under age so that new deeds cannot be obtained, your petitioners therefore prays your honorable House to take their care into consideration and pass a Law to give a Longer time for Recording those deeds that was lawfully obtained in the year 1789 and your petitioners as in duty bound shall pray

[Names.]

To the General Assembly of Virginia

Bourbon County

I do hereby certify that the within Petition was advertised at the door of the Court house according to Law Given under my hand this 25th day of Aug. 1790.

                                    John Edwards Clk B. C.

    Endorsement on back of petition: 1st Novr. 1790—Refd. to Cts of Justice—reasonable—Bill drawn.

    The request was granted in an act entitled, An Act authorizing the Court of Bourbon Co. to admit the recording of Deeds in certain cases. Henings Statutes, Vol. 13, 150.

NUMBER 89.

To the Honorable the Speaker and Members of the General Assembly of Virginia—

The Petition of William Shannon.

Sheweth.

That in the month of March 1779, your petitioner was appointed Commissary and Quarter Master to the Illinois a Western department under the Command of General Clark, and continued to transact the duties of his office for upwards of three years, had employed several deputies to assist him, and during that period purchased and issued Sundry supplies to the troops in that department, which purchases and issues are accurately entered on his books of Accounts, for which books and Accounts he has receipts, (by order of the board of Commissioners appointed to settle the business relating to that department) ready to be produced.

That your Petr. in order to obtain a settlement of his Accounts, laid them before the said Commissioners, at their meeting at the Dutch-station—near Louisville, but the Commissioners conceiving them necessary for the purpose of settling other claims in the same department, kept them in their possession, without coming to any decision thereon, and appointed a meeting at Colo. Bowman's in Lincoln County, where your Petrs. attended, hoping the said accounts wou'd then be finally settled, but the said Commissioners hearing of your Petrs intention to travel thro' the Wilderness they declined to take up the said accounts, and appointed another meeting at Botetourt Court house or Richmond, at which places your Petr also intended to be present, but unfortunately for him, he had his Leg broke on his way to Botetourt, which prevented his carrying his intention into execution, (as will appear by sundry papers in his possession) whereby he has not been able to have his accounts settled, or to receive any Compensation for his services or the services of his deputies.

Your petr further shews, that in procuring the necessary supplies for the said troops, he became indebted to Sundry persons, and in order to discharge the same, drew bills of Exchange on the Treasurer of this State, several of which are protested, and others not paid, so that your petr remains in a very disagreeable situation, not only on account of those bills, but by being charged with monies paid him during the time he was in office, and no credit allowed him, either by the supplies furnished or his pay for his services or those of his deputies.

Your Petr therefore requests, you will be pleased to pass a Law appointing some person or persons to adjust and settle his Accounts, and to authorise the auditor to issue warrants for the amount of what shall appear due to your Petr. for his pay and depreciation as Commissary and Quarter Master in the said department, and also for what may appear to be due to his deputies, and he will Pray.

Jefferson County Sct.

This day Docter Samuel Culbertson personally came before me (James F. Moore) one of the Justices of the Commonwealth for the County aforesaid, and made oath on the Holy Evangelists of Almighty God that in the month of April 1783 Capt. William Shannon of Lewisville, passed by Field's Station (where the Deponant then lived) on his way to the settlement

To the General Assembly of Virginia

as he said to meet the commissioners appointed to settle the accounts of the Illinois Department and that he the said Shannon unfortunately broke his leg at Crows Station that this Deponant was sent for to set the bone which he did and attended him during his illness, but the bone was so fractured that he was not able to proceed on his journey that season and further this deponant sayeth not—Sworn to before me this 21st Sept. 1790.

James F. Moore

We certify that when the Commissioners for Western accounts sat in the neighbourhood of Louisville in the year 1783 Capt William Shannon who by appointment from Genl. Clark had for some time acted as Commissary General to the Illinois Regiment presented his accounts to have them settled; But the Board finding that his Books which appeared to be regularly kept would be helpful in adjusting the accounts of the other officers of that department detained Capt Shanon from about the middle of January to the last of February when it was found that more accounts had been presented and would be presented than could possibly be adjusted before the time it would be necessary for the Commissioners to return through the wilderness, and in the investigation of which Capt Shannons books would also be needed and finding that Capt Shannon intended to travel to the eastward about the same time, his books were detained and he directed to attend the Board when it should set in Botetourt County or at Richmond to have his accounts finally classed. But Capt Shannon by having his Leg bone broken before he set off was rendered incapable of the Journey; so that his accounts were never settled by the Commissioners and he informs us that the Auditors have hitherto declined a settlement by which he is suffering great loss. Therefore we take the liberty of making this representation of facts and beg lieve further to observe that as far as we can recollect, his Books appeared to be accurate & just, only in some instances paper money contracts were not distinguished from specie, which he assured the Board he did not know to be necessary when the entries were made, but that he should be able to make the distinction when it would be requisite. We further beg leave to represent that We understood that complaints had been made against Capt Shannon in the execution of his office. In order to examine into that matter the Board of Commissioners notifyed their Intentions to the publick of hearing all the charges that could be brought against him relative to his conduct as Commissary and appointed a time for exhibiting them—But that no charges were brought forward and supported nor anything made appear to his prejudice in the execution of his office given under our hands this 26th day of June 1790—

Saml McDowell
Caleb Wallace.

Endorsed on back of petition: Novr. 2d. 1790.—refd to Claims—reasonable—1st Reso: refd. to Executive—2nd Reso: that the Auditor of Public accts deliver him his papers—reported 8th Nov. 90.—19h pasd.

The request was granted in an act entitled, An Act granting a sum of money to William Shannon and others. Henings Statutes, Vol. 13, 211.

The Auditor of Public Accounts was instructed to issue certificates to those holding Shannon's drafts and to Shannon two thousand and twenty-six pounds, six shillings and one penny.

NUMBER 90.

To the Honorable the General Assembly of the Commonwealth of Virginia.

The Petition of the Trustees of the Transylvania Seminary humbly sheweth

That notwithstanding the Indulgence and encouragement they have hitherto experienced from the Legislature with the laudable design of propogating Science in this District they find the funds still so low as to be unable to errect any suitable Buildings

Encouraged by the favourable disposition to promote Education that has ever marked the proceedings of your

To the General Assembly of Virginia

honorable house we are Induced to pray that a Law may be passed authorizing the Board of Trustees for the Transylvania Seminary to raise by Lottery the Sum of five hundred pounds for the purpose of errecting an Academy Under such regulations and restrictions as the Legislature may judge proper and we in duty bound shall ever pray

[Names.]

Endorsement on back of petition: Nov. 6 1790.—Refd to Props—Reasonable —Repd.

The request was granted in an act entitled, An Act authorizing several lotteries and the sale of certain lots in the town of Portsmouth. Henings Statutes, Vol. 13, 173.

"Be it enacted by the General Assembly, That it shall be lawful for the trustees of Transylvania Seminary, or a majority of them, to raise by one or more lotteries, a sum not exceeding five hundred pounds, for the purpose of erecting an Academy."

The same bill allows a lottery to build a church, roads, and other academies in other places east of the mountains.

NUMBER 91.

To the Hble the General Assembly of the Commonwealth of Virginia

The Petition of the Members composing the Board of Trustees of the Transylvania Seminary humbly sheweth

Your Petitioners feeling sensebly an inconvenience under which they labor as a body constituted by Act of Assembly for conducting the business of the said Seminary, beg leave to request the interferrence of your Hble House in order the more effectually to enable them to carry into effect the Trust reposed in them.

They would suggest to your Hble House that one essential inconvenience to which they are subjected arises from the great number of members which by Law are required to constitute a board for the transaction of business as they are so widely scattered thro the district: And would pray that the number necessary to conduct the business of said Seminary

Petitions of the Early Inhabitants of Kentucky

should be reduced to seven or such number as the wisdom of the House may direct and your petitioners in duty bound shall ever pray.

[Names.]

Endorsement on back of petition: Nov. 6 1790.—refd. to props—Reasonable —Repd.

The request was granted in an act entitled, An Act concerning the Trustees of Transylvania Seminary. Henings Statutes, Vol. 13, 147.

Seven trustees were henceforth sufficient to do business at the two annual meetings provided by law.

NUMBER 92.

To the Honble the Speaker and Members of the General Assembly

The Petition of Henry Banks humbly sheweth

That during the latter period of the War your Petitioner was engaged in very considerable mercantile Transactions, as is well known to many honble members of the House, when it became absolutely necessary for him either to appropriate a large capital in the purchase of Land Warrants, otherwise a large sum would perish in his hands, being paper money

That your Petitioner was appointed the Sole agent of the House of Hunter Banks & Co. who had had very considerable Transactions with different public agents, and found that they had a demand for 800 Bus Salt, for which payment had never been made or a Certificate granted by which payment could be required, and that after attempting in various Instances to obtain payment without success your Petitioner was at length advised to bring a Suit in the High Court of Chancery against the Honble the Atty General, which suit has in due Course been referd to William Hay esqr. master Comr to the Honble High Court of Chancery, and he has reported and certified a Balance of One Thousand Sixty Six pounds 13-4 to be due to your Petitioner but the final decree for the same is suspended until March next

That in Consideration of the necessary purchase of Lands as aforesaid your Petitioner has created a large demand ag.

To the General Assembly of Virginia

himself for fees, without the Payment of which in advance, he is not permitted to enter the surveys in the Registers office, that in Consequence of some Misfortunes your Petitioner is not prepared with certain funds to pay those expences, and is therefore in great fear that he will loose some of them

Your Petitioner is well aware of the impropriety of asking a payment of the aforesaid money until it is established by a final decree, and therefore only prays that this Honble House will pass a resolution requiring the Register of the Land office and the Depy Register of Kentuckey be directed to receive the warrants which may be issued for the aforesaid claim, when finally ascertained or that this Honble House will grant to your Petitioner any other relief respecting the Premises which may be reasonable, and your Petitioner in duty bound will pray &c

Henry Banks.

that the petition of the said Henry Banks praying that any warrants which he may receive from the Aud. of public Accounts by virtue of the said Decree may be received by the Register of the Land office & Depy Register of Kentuckey in discharge of fees due for entering surveys & be reasonable the petitioner for grants [?]

Commissioners Office November 15 1790

Hunter Banks and Company_____Plfts.
         against
Turner Christian Richard Morris, James Innes Attorney General, and John Pendleton Auditor of public accounts_Defts_

Pursuant to the Direction of James Innes on Behalf of the Commonwealth in these Words, to wit. Sir, whereas there is a Suit now depending, in the honourable the high Court of Chancery, Hunter Banks and Company against myself as Attorney for the Commonwealth and others, it was my Intention to have consented that it should be sent to you for settlement at the last Term, but my Indisposition prevented, I do now consent on Behalf of the Commonwealth, that you do examine state and Report thereon, & that you ascertain what is due to the Complainants as soon as possible. Witness my Hand and Seal at Richmond the ninth Day of November one thousand seven hundred and ninety.

James Innes

To William Hay, Esq.

Your Commissioner, having examined the Papers and considered the claim of the Plaintiffs, is of opinion that they are intitled to one thousand and sixty six Pounds thirteen shillings and four pence for the eight hundred Bushels of Salt mentioned in the papers which is at the Rate of one hundred Pounds paper money pr Bushel, reduced by seventy five the scale in 1780, and he submits it to the Court whether they should be allowed Interest from Decbr 1780.

Wm. Hay, M. C.

Commissioners fee	0.7.6	a copy
Copy	1.6	Wm. Hay, M. C.
	0.9.0	

Endorsement on back of petition. 20 Nov. 1790—refd. to props. Reasonable—Repd.

The request was granted in an act entitled, An Act giving further time to owners of entries on western waters to survey the same. Henings Statutes, Vol. 13, 120.

NUMBER 93.

To the Honourable The General Assembly for the Commonwealth of Virginia.

Gentlemen—

We your Petitioners of the District of Kaintucky, do humbly petition for further time to fulfil, an Act passed last Session; obliging every person, to return their Plots of Surveys to the register's Office before the — day of August 1791—Our Delegates brought no account of such an Act having passed,

To the General Assembly of Virginia

And the Acts of Last Session coming late to this District fell into the hands of a few individuals; who either from Design or inattention never communicated to the publick, that such an Act was in being, Till the time of complying with it, was past, Therefore your Petitioners knew nothing of the Act till after the time was expired. And as advantages will now be taken by designing men; not only against your Petitioners, but against many of the good and industrious Citizens of this District. And Schemes entered into by persons, who support themselves, by fradulent and knavish practices, not only to the great damage of your Petitioners, but to the immense loss of many of the good people of this District. Therefore we petition for longer time to comply with the Act. And look up to you as the Guardians and Supporters of our lives liberty and property. Firmly relying on the justice and Equity of your honourable house so often experienced and which we are ever bound to acknowledge and your Petitioners will ever pray. September the 9th day 1791.—

[Names.]

Endorsement on back of petition: Oct. 22 1791—Refd. to Props—Reasonable —Repd.

The request was granted in an act entitled, An Act for the relief of persons owning surveys returned to the registers office, on which no patents can issue in consequence of the erection of Kentucky into an independent state. Henings Statutes, Vol. 13, 526.

Warrants were to be issued in cases of certificates of survey sent to the land office of Virginia previous to separation.

NUMBER 94.

To the Honorable The General Assembly of Virginia

The Petition of John Crow humbly Sheweth

That your Petitioner did keep in victuals & . . . . the Indian prisoners from the time they were put into his possession untill the tenth of May 1788, for which expenses of his, he has been paid in full according to his account.

That from the tenth of May 1788 untill the twelfth of September following your Petitioner still continued to keep those prisoners, & presented his account which was allowed likewise, but curtailed. Still he had his pay, according to the Curtailment.

That your Petitioner finding himself a considerable loser by this Curtail of his account resolved to get rid of the said prisoners as soon as possible; but it was the fifteenth of January 1789 before he could write to Colonel Benjamin Logan to take them away; that his account has been since stated before the Executive who thought it convenient to reject it.

That by the answer of Col. Logan Your Petitioner was obliged to take care of said prisoners from the 15th of January to sometime early in April, when at last they were taken away, which expence your petitioner hath not charged to Government.

That your Petitioner conceives he has as much right to be reimbursed his expences for Nine Indian Prisoners from the thirteenth of September 1788 untill the fourteenth of January 1789 as he had for the two former accounts, and That whatever compensation he may have received from the beginning to the twelfth of September 1788 does not invalidate his claim for his expences posterior to that last date, as he would still have had the same compensation, in case the Indians had been taken away at that time.

That your Petitioner refers your Honorable House to the letter of John Brown Esqr & the order of Council to shew that his just claim has been rejected; & to the letter of Col. Benjamin Logan to prove that your petitioner was still forced to keep the prisoners at his own expence from January till April when they were taken away from him.

That on considering the whole, your Petitioner begs of your Honorab Body that an order may pass ordering the payment of his expenditures from the thirteenth of September 1788 till the fourteenth of January 1789, as he is Justly intitled to; and as to your Wisdom shall seem meet.

And your Petitioner shall ever pray &c.

John Crow

To the General Assembly of Virginia

In Council October 15, 1789
On consideration of the Claim of John Crow for maintenance of Nine Indian prisoners & for Barracks hire—He is advised that the same be rejected—
The Gov. orders accordingly.
Extract from the minutes.

A Blair C. C.

The Commonwealth of Virginia to John Crow Dr
To the keeping of nine Indian Prisoners from the thirteenth Day of Septr 1788 till the fourteenth Day of January 1789— at 1 S pr Ration also Barracks at the Rate of £10 pr year—

John Crow.

State of acct according to the prayer of the Petitions
To 1007 Rations for 9 prisoners 123 days—9
    Rations pr day _____ £50--7--0.
Barrack hire_____4 mo £10 pr an_____ 3--6--8.

                                                  £53--15--8

Dear Sir
I have considered the situation of the Indians in your posession I have just Reason to think when you received them People you intended to have the profits arising from suporting them then you must know every person would supose any Deficences in Government ought to fall on you before it should be fixed on any other indeviduel as you have been liberaly paid for suporting them part of there time but I think you had better set them over the Ohio or leve them under the eye of those in the service of the United States I think this will be making the best of a bad bargain
    I am yours   Benjamin Logan
February 16 1787

                         Staunton Novr. 3d 1789
Sir
    Some Business which I did not expect when I left Kentucke made it indispensably necessary for me to pass through Win-

chester on my way to New York & consequently put it out of my power to call at Richmond to obtain a settlement of your Acct But on my arrival at N. York I inclosed your Acct. Colo. Logans Certificate & a power of Atty to Mr. Saml. McCraw requesting him to make application for a settlement on your behalf He did so but the Executive rejected your Claim supposing you had already recd. a Compensation adequate to your trouble & expence I inclose you a Copy of the Order of Council upon this application—I am sorry the determination was not more favorable—Had the Claim been my own I should not have done otherwise with it than I did—

I am Sir
   Your Mo. Hble Sevt.
                                            J. Brown.
Mr. John Crow.

   Endorsement on back of petition: Oct. 22. 1791—Refd to Claims—Mr. Todd (of Nelson) rejected—reported 2d qre. 1792.

NUMBER 95.

TO THE HONOURABLE THE SPEAKER AND GENTLEMEN OF THE HOUSE OF DELEGATES

The petition of Isaac Ruddle Humbly sheweth, that your petitioner In the year 1779 was appointed to the Command of a Compy for the Reduction of the Illinois under the then Colo. Clark, that He raisd a Company on Holstain and supplied them with the necessary arms Provision Bags and pack Horses, for the falls of Ohio to which place he Marchd them; that in the Beginning of March 1780 your petitioner with His Company was ordered on Duty to a frontier station on Licking By John Bowman the then County Lieutenant of Kentucky County, that your petitioner with His Company was on the 24th of June 1780 Captured by a party of British and Indians under the Command of Capt Bird from Detroit, to which place they were taken and their remaind in Captivity till the 3d Nov. 1782. when He returnd—to the District of Kenty where

To the General Assembly of Virginia

He Has since Resided, that after the return of your petitioner to the District of Kentucky He made out a pay role for the time of His last Services and Captivity for which He recd £497..0..0 as will more fully appear Referance thereto being Had, that your petitioner on His return also made application to the Commissioners for setling The western Claims for the Liquidation of His Accounts for His first Services, that they Did settle His account and that their appeard to be Due to your Petitioner the sum of £442..10..03-5 which will more fully appear by the Inclosd Copy of their proceedings that your petitioner also furnishd for the service of the District two Horses which were Valued at £65 which will more fully appear by the Inclosd affidivate of Colo Bowman that at the time of settlement some Evil Disposd person informd the Commissioners that your petitioner while a prisoner was Enimical to the united States they then gave it as their Oppinion that no Certificate should Issue without Orders from Govornment that prior to those proceeding your petitioner on His way from Detroit stood a trial in the County Court of Fredrick for the above Crime where all His accusers were, and was accquited, which will appear by the Inclosd. proceedings and Certificate which your petitioner could not procure till the Commissioners had rose and there Powers Had Expird your petitioner therefore prays that His accounts may be fully and fairly Settled and that your Honourable body will Direct your Auditors of public accounts to Issue warrants for the principal and Interest due thereon in such manner as you in your wisdom shall think fit and your petitioner as in Duty bound shall ever pray

Isaac Ruddle.

Endorsement on back of petition: October 26th 1791—Refd. to Claims—rejected—repd. 9th. qre. 1791 (?) Voucher delivered to Mr. Waller.

NUMBER 96.

TO THE HONOURABLE THE SPEAKER AND MEMBERS OF THE HOUSE OF DELEGATES—

The Petition of Levi Todd Clerk of Fayette County, on behalf of himself and the other clerks of Courts within the

District of Kentucky, Humbly sheweth, That by reason of your Petitioners remote situation from the seat of Government, The acts of the last Session of Assembly did not come to his hands untill a very late period—

That your Petitioner being entirely ignorant that Laws had passed to repeal those Laws which imposed a Tax on the Clerks of Courts, and to repeal in part the act imposing new taxes— did on the 9th day of last March pay to Thomas Marshall Treasurer of the District of Kentucky for taxes which he supposed to have become due under the said Repealed laws, but which were in fact abolished by the said Repealing laws, £23.7-7 That your Petitioner has great reason to believe that many other clerks within the said District, have for want of information made similar payments He therefore Humbly prays that a Law may pass authorising and directing the said Treasurer to repay any monies which may have been so paid to him by mistake as aforesaid—

Levi Todd

Endorsement on back of petition: 1st Nov. 1791—Refd to Props—Reasonable—rept.

The request was granted in an act entitled, An Act concerning the clerks within the District of Kentucky. Henings Statutes, Vol. 13, 313.
The receiver was authorized to pay Todd twenty-three pounds, seven shillings, and seven pence, which he paid on account of tax imposed on clerks subsequent to law repealing such tax.

NUMBER 97.

To the Honble the Speaker and members of the House of Delegates of the Commonwealth of Virginia now setting

The petition of Joseph Martin humbly sheweth that there is a very great necessity for a ferry across the Cumberland River where the Kentuckey road crosses the same from the land of your petitioner on the South side to the land—on the opposite shore claimed by William Hord Your petitioner therefore prays that this Honble House will take the same into consideration & prays an act may pass for establishing a ferry

To the General Assembly of Virginia

at the said place to be called & known by the name of Martins ferry & your petitioner as in duty bound will ever pray &c.

Endorsement on back of petition: 7th Nov. 1791—refd. to Props—Reasonable—reported.

NUMBER 98.

To the honorable the Speaker & House of Delegates.

The Petition of James McAfee humbly sheweth

That he did in the years 1780 & 1781 furnish the Troops at the falls of Ohio with money Provisions and whisky for which he received Bills drawn on the Executive for the several supplies.

That in the year 1782 he sent these papers to be laid before the Commissioners in the District of Kentucky and then went to New Orleans, from thence to the West Indies, from whence he did not return to America before the expiration of the Law for settling such Claims. That since his return the original papers have been delivered to him, with the information that no settlement with the State had been made. Your Petitioner therefore prays your honorable House to take his case under consideration and make him such compensation as shall be just

The bills No. 1, 2, 3 being drawn by persons not authorized by Government and not having been Reported on by the Western Commrs the Auditor cant act on them—The other Vouchers being in the latter situation the Auditor cant admit them

Audrs Office   I Pendleton
15 Nov. 1791.

Endorsement on back of petition: 7th Novr. 1791.—Refd to Claims—rejected —reported 18 qre. 91.

NUMBER 99.

To The Hon'ble The Speaker & Members of the Virginia Assembly.—

The petition of James Wilkinson sheweth

That the Lands now called Frankfort were some years ago called and known by the name of Lees Town bottom. That in the Year 1783 an Act passed for establishing an Inspection of Tobacco at the said Lees Town. That your Petitioner in the confidence and belief that the distance of half a mile or three quarters would make little or no difference in the site of the said inspection proceeded to erect a Ware House at Frankfort. That the County Court of Fayette being also of the opinion of your petitioner proceeded to appoint inspectors who were duly commissioned by the Executive & proceeded to Act. Large quantities of Tobacco have been inspected thereat but doubts have arisen whether the Tobacco there inspected are Legal Tenders in Contracts or for officers fees. Your petitioner therefore prays that an Act may pass for the Inspection at Frankfort to be established by the name of the Frankfort Inspection & your Petitioner &c.

Endorsement on back of petition. 11th. Novr. 1791—Refd. to Props—Reasonable, H. L.—Reported.

The request was granted in an act entitled, An Act to establish an inspection of tobacco in the county of Woodford, on lands of James Wilkinson, at Frankfort. Henings Statutes, Vol. 13, 272.

NUMBER 100.

TO THE HONORABLE THE LEGISLATURE OF THE STATE OF VIRGINIA—

The Memorial of George Rogers Clark, late a Brigadier General in the Troops of the State, and Commandant throughout the Western Jurisdiction of that Commonwealth—

Sheweth:

That your Memorialist, relying on the Justice, Magnimity & Indulgance of your venerable Body, experienced at all times by himself, and ever bountifully extended, in every instance, to those of your officers & Privates of the late war who, to say no more, as advantageously to the public weal as they could, have faithfully complied with their duty—now presumes as one among them, by this Instrument, to lay before your House, as well through devotional deference, as with modest confidence, his General Statement of claims, Debts, or Arrearages, with authenticated Vouchers substantiating the same,

To the General Assembly of Virginia

due to him from your State—, debts of long standing, and vitally detrimental to your Memorialist's affairs, from their having been thus long pending & unliquidated—, debts arising from his past Military Services, or from advances of the better part of his Fortune for the credit of the State, when that of the State itself (in the instance, at least, in which these advances were made) had been prostrate—, debts insured by a free Gift of your own to the officers of your Establishment for the necessary maintenance of your Troops under my command, in this Western country, troops (it behoves me to say) who with a fortitude, fidelity & martial hardihood, perhaps unexampled, had braved heroically, and with successful effect every kind of want, and every Species of peril, to preserve the very fairest portion of your State, and indeed of the whole Union—, debts of commutation for my half-pay, and debts for having, from my own funds, supplied your Garrisons & those heroic Troops with Bread, to feed on.

To say more on a topic so tissued with every incident that can have a rightful claim to the Equity & Humanity, not to talk of the Gratitude of any Government—, on a theme so well known to the existing Generation of our Countrymen—, on a subject so advantageously to be felt, in its consequences, not only by those who inhabit the various settlements now checquering the face of that wide-extended portion of our Empire, those redeemed from the Foe, but by the many Millions who, in the progression of not very many years, must cover it—; to say more, I say, on a Subject so teaming with past, present, and future benefits to the citizens of this Commonwealth itself, as well as to those of the Confederacy in general, would (in your Memorialist's humble opinion) derogate from his own, as well as the universal Sense of men, on a *Legislature of the State of Virginia*.

Your Memorialist, therefore, thinks it sufficient, at this Juncture, to have humbly requested, as he does, the attention of your venerable House to his *General Acct*, and to every

Petitions of the Early Inhabitants of Kentucky

Document vouching for or relating to the same as herewith transmitted in detached Papers, Nos 1, 2, 3, 4, 5, 6, 7, and 8—; and only to add: that the difficulty of collecting the aforesaid enumerated Papers of document from the different & remotely resident Persons who had held them, was the sole cause of your Memorialist's not having made an earlier application, for his claims, to the Legislature of Virginia.—

Signed   G R Clark

Gloster Town 28th Dec 1796

My friend

I reached this place on the 27th Inst. I found those for whom I felt the tenderest respect and affection well; but found myself impressed with that kind of Gloom which arises on returning to a country once the seat of grandeur and munificence but, now alas, exhibiting the most striking proofs of poverty. But my spirits were revived on seeing the refined buties of my fair relation. Indeed King I sincerely lament that fortune has so frowned on relation so dear to me. Come down my friend & lament with me that worth and beauty are now become a secondary object with the male sex. Will, you do me the favour to leave the enclosed letter with Boyd & Carr and will encrease my load of obligation by applying to Mr Hay for Genl Clarks papers

Adieu John Thurston

I have no wafr seal the enclosed   J T

Endorsement on back of petition: 11th Novr. 1791—p. 111. Refd to Claims—rejected 70,000 Flour—Reasonable—Bill Exche.—repd 24th qre 1791. 1 Decr. 1791—p 225-6.

NUMBER 101.

To The Honorable the General Assembly of Virginia

The Petition of John Campbell in behalf of himself & the Inspectors of Campbells Warehouse Sheweth:

That in the Year 1783 an Act passed for establishing an Inspection of Tobacco at the Falls of Ohio on the Lands of the

To the General Assembly of Virginia

said John Campbell without any condition restriction or exception. That in consequence thereof the said Campbell hath built a Ware House and Inspectors have been legally appointed thereto that in the last Year the Quantity of Tobacco shipped falls short £23. 15 that the said Campbell hath applied to the Auditor for settlement thereof which he refuses alledging that if the Inspection doth not support itself it is therefore discontinued your petitioner thinks and is certain the Inspectors believed they were to receive their Wages as no orders from the County Court had issued to suppress or discontinue the said Inspection which is the only one in Jefferson County and the only one on Ohio River within the Kentucky District and one that is essentially necessary as it often happens boats are wrecked on the Falls and the Tobaccoes cannot be transported to any other inspection without great expence and decrease in the Value which will readily appear by considering that an Inland carriage of many miles & a carriage back again to the river must be very expensive & distressing to the unfortunate sufferers Your Petitioner therefore prays the Honorable the Assembly to take the same into consideration & direct the Auditor of Publick Accounts to settle & certify the said accounts in the usual manner or to grant any other relief which to you may seem just & your Petitioner &c.—

The Auditor thinks that as the Inspection has never produced any surplus the Act under wch it is established will not suffer him to give a warrant on the public treasury for the deficiency and See Revisal Page 217. Chap. XXVIII—Sect 3d.

I. Pendleton.

Audrs office
11 Nov. 1791.

Endorsement on back of petition: 12 Novr. Refd to Props—(rejected.) (repd)

Petitions of the Early Inhabitants of Kentucky

NUMBER 102

THE HONOURABLE THE SPEAKER AND GENTLEMEN OF THE HOUSE OF DELEGATES

the petition of John Stuart Heir at Law to Henry Stuart Decd Humbly sheweth that the Decedent did in the year 1775 go down the river Ohio in the Company of Joseph Irwin James Cornahan James Campbell and others in order to improve lands in the District of Kentucky that the Decedent did make an Improvement on the waters of Hinksons fork of Licking after which he returned to the Monongahala Country that in Jany 1776 He Inlisted in the 13th Virginia regiment under the Command of Colo Wm Russell for During the war and that the Decedant Died in Service—

That in the year 1785 your petitioner then an Infant made application to Joseph Irwin who was going to Kentuckey to procure His right to the said land as Heir to the Decedant that the said Irwin did in April or May 1785 make application to the County Court of Fayette, in behalf of your petitioner that the said Court did grant your petitioner a right of settlement for 400 acres and a pre-emption of 1000 acres of Land adjoining that after this the said Irwin made application to the register of the land office who granted your petitioner a warrant for the land above mentioned. that the said Irwin Engagd to locate the same that on His way to Kentucky a difrance arose in which the said Irwin Killd His antagonist and fled Down the Misisipia river, that on His flight he left the Warrant and other necessary papers in Kentucky in the Hands of Major Moroson that Before your petitioner arrivd at the age of 21 years the time for Entering Certificates for settlement rights and locating Warrants on preemption rights had Expired your petitioner therefore prays that a Law may pass Impowering Him to Enter & Survey the same & your petitioner as in Duty Bound shall ever pray   John Stewart.

Endorsement on back of petition: 12th Nov. 1791. Refd. to Cts of Justice—15th Nov. 1791—Reasonable—provided not to interfere with rights of any other person, or persons—Reported—

The request was granted in an act entitled, An Act for giving further time to John Stewart to locate and survey certain lands.
Henings Statutes, Vol 13—304.

To the General Assembly of Virginia

NUMBER 103

To the Hone. the Speaker & House of Delegates—

The petition of James Gilmore and Stephen Huston, Humbly sheweth—

That your petitioners was employed in Lincoln County By Capt. John Martin and Capt. Samuel Kirkham as scouts to Discover the approach of the Indian Enemy That they served as such from the 25th Day of April untill the 2d day of July in the year 1781 and that they never Received any Compensation for their services—and prays that your Honorable Body may take their case into Consideration and grant them such Relief as you may think Just and Right

And your petitioners in Duty Bound shall ever pray

The Auditors office does not afford any check on these claims the Vouchers being in the hands of the State by Commr for setling the continental Account . . . [illegible].

Endorsement on back of petition: Gilmour & Huston Pets. 12 Nov. 1791. Ref. to Claims. Reasonable Vouchers to Col. Logan repd 25th Ex 91 Lincoln.

NUMBER 104

To the Speaker of the Honorable House of Representatives met in General Assembly

Whereas I am inform'd that a Petition will be presented, praying the Establishment of a Ferry upon the Lands of John Kimburlin, with liberty to Land on the oposite shore, across Pattersons Creek at the Town of Frankfort on the main ford leading from Winchester to Fort pitt, now your Petitioner Humbly sheweth that the Land calld in the aforesaid Petition the Land of John Kimburlin is the real Property of your Petitioner, and that your Petitioner hath never given, or is under any obligation to give the sd Kimburlin any title to sd Land, any further that sd Kimburlin is in possession thereof by virtue of a Verbial Contract; and your Petitioner further sheweth that he is very desirous to have a Ferry Established over the sd Creek in his own name and is always ready to comply with the sd Virtual Contract with sd Kimburlin; But your Petitioner Humbly prayeth that the General Assembly may at this time delay the establishment of sd Ferry, if they cannot consistantly establish the same in the name of your Petitioner who is the real owner of the Land on both sides of the Creek, and as in duty bound shall ever pray—

Frankfort Sep. 22d 1792. [Name.]

Endorsement on back of petition: 4 Oct. 1792.—to Props.—(next Session)

NUMBER 105

To the Honorable the Speaker & House of Delegates

The Petition of George Rogers Clarke humbly sheweth that he entered the service of this State the second day of January 1778 and commanded the Troops raised for the defence of the Western frontier from that period until the end of the War, in the rank of Brigadier General.

Your Petitioner therefore prays the consideration of the House and that they will allow him half pay for life or a commutation of five years full pay in lieu thereof.

The Commutation has not been paid to the Petitioner.

I. Pendleton

4 Nov. 1793.

Endorsement on back of petition: 4 Novr. 1793—Claims—Reasonable—Special—22d qre. 93.

NUMBER 106

To the Honorable the Speaker and Members of Both Houses of Assembly

The Petition [of] Daniel Boone Humbly sheweth, that your petitioner paid into the Treasury of this Commonwealth the sum of One thousand and five pounds, & was thereby entitled to a Land office Treasury Warrant, to amount of Six Hundred and Twenty Eight Acres of Land, as by Certificate obtained from the auditors of Publick accounts Dated on the 21st Day

To the General Assembly of Virginia

of February 1783 will fully appear,—your petitioner begs leave to represent that this certificate was obtained for him by a certain Samuel Pattison, who shortly after the Date thereof Departed this life, and lay amongst the said Pattisons papers untill some short time ago, when your petitioner applied therewith to the Register for a Land Warrant, who refused to Issue the Same, Your Petitioner therefore prays this General Assembly to pass an act Directing that the Register Issue to your Petitioner a Land office treasury Warrant for the quantity stated in the said certificate—and your petitioner will pray &c

Endorsement on back of petition: Novr. 24th 1794—Refd. to Props—(reasonable) (repd)

NUMBER 107

To the Honble the Speaker and Members of the Legislature of the Commonwealth of Virginia

the Petition of James Bullock of the State of Kentucky Humbly sheweth that your Petitioner sometime in the year 1781 obtained from the Auditor of Public Accounts two certificates of twenty five pounds each for a Horse impressed into the public service: that some time in or about April 1788 the said certificates were lost or destroyed: your Petitioner therefore prays that an act may pass directing the Auditor of Public Accounts to issue to him Duplicates of the said certificates on his complying with the necessary requisites—And your Petitioner as in duty bound will pray &c—

Endorsement on back of petition: Dec 7, 98—Claims—Reasonable Reported

NUMBER 108.

The Honorable the General Assembly of the State of Virginia.

Your Petitioner William Bledsoe in the year 1782 had a beast taken into the service in an expedition against the Indians as by Reference to a certificate granted at St. Asaphs the 11th of April 1783 by the Bord of Comisioners will appear Your

[179]

petitioner was Intitled to twenty pounds as a satisfaction for sd Beast that furthermore your petitioner was informed that an auditered certificate issued in favour of your petitioner By the name of William Bledsoe which certificate never came to the hands of your petitioner; Your petitioner caused due proof to be made to the court of Lincoln county then a district of the State of Virginia that sd certificate was the property of your petitioner and that the same was casually lost or mislayed upon which your petitioner entered into bond and Christopher Greenup esqr. Security to Indemnify the commonwealth of Virginia from the payment of sd Certificate in case a duplicate should issue that a duplicate has been applied for and your petitioner is informed that no Law exists in favour of issuing sd duplicate: forasmuch as your petitioner had sd Beast arrested from him and lost in the service of the State of Virginia to the hardship and detriment of your petitioner and not yet payed for your petitioner prays that a Law may pass authorising your petitioner to call on the auditor for his warrant on the Treasurer for the aforesaid sum of twenty pounds or grant such other Relieff as may appear Just and Right and Your petitioner as in duty Bound will pray &c.

William Bledsoe

February 1st 1799—

Your petitioner not having a safe oppertunity to forward this petition in time hopes this his petition will be received and acted upon on its Receipt with the voucher and bond certified.

William Bledsoe.

NUMBER 109.

To the Honorable the General Assembly of Virginia

The petition of Edmond Southard and Sarah his wife, formerly Sarah Thornton respectfully sheweth:

That on the 19th of April 1783 there issued from the Land office of this commonwealth, a Land office Treasury Warrant

To the General Assembly of Virginia

(No 15. 524) to the Revd Thomas Thornton the father of your petitioner Sarah for 1462 acres which warrant, was lodged at the time of the death of the said Thornton, and had been previous thereto, in the Land office of the Western District for location.

That the said Thomas Thornton died early in the year 1792 having first made a will by which he left the said warrant to your petitioner Sarah as will appear by a copy of that will herewith presented: That the **Erection of the State of Kentucky into an independent government, and its** consequent division from this state, and other causes, which are set forth in the letter of Major Charles Ewell also herewith presented, prevented the location of the said Warrant, and it remains unappropriated to this day, as will be seen by the accompanying certificate from the Registers office, and your petitioners consequently deprived of the most material and important part of their patrimony. Your petitioners have had no agency in bringing upon themselves this lamentable state of things: Their parent has paid his money to the state for a land right which the State by its own act has prevented the execution of, and which act leaves your petitioners "poor indeed"—An affectionate parent on his death had comforted himself with the belief that he had made provision for an infant **daughter**; but the operation of the Laws of the Commonwealth has deprived that daughter of the hope of ever enjoying a parents bounty—She throws herself upon the justice and magnammity of the Legislature of her Country, and asks at its hands some compensation for the loss she has sustained—She begs the Legislature will remember that money laid out in 1462 acres of Land in Kentucky in the year 1783 would now produce no small fortune—She asks that it will remember that lands have greatly appreciated, and money greatly depreciated since that period; and although she will not ask full price for her land, she asks a reasonable compensation either in money or other lands—She **asks the** Legislature to redeem her in some measure from the gaping jaws of poverty—to relieve her from the situation which her dying father had never anticipated she would be in, and she thinks she asks all this not without some reason. Your petitioners have now a numerous offspring to provide for, or they might not so strenuously press their claim, and they do not exagerate when they declare they are "poor indeed"—They hope therefore that the Legislature will hear their prayer, and grant them such relief as the nature of their case demands and they will ever pray &c.

Edmund Southard.

Land office Treasury warrant No 15,524 issued to The Revd Thomas Thornton for 1462 acs Apl. 19th 1783—no appropriation stands charged on the Register of said warrant. That is no survey is founded on said warrant. Searched from the year 1783 to the year 1793 and find no survey or grant in said Thorntons name.

On further examination no survey appears to have been returned to this office in his name.

In Case Mr Thornton in his lifetime should have made a location on said Warrant in Kentuckey and nothing further down therein, which might have escaped his recollection: By writing to some person who is acquainted with the nature of such things perhaps information might be obtained. If the warrant can be produced an Exchange warrant can issue for whatever appears due on same.—No location can be made on a Land office Treasury warrant or Exchange warrant & that bears date on or before Feby. 2nd 1804—"such warrants exchangeable." "By act of 1815 ch: 30. Entries *after 31 December* 1816 on such warrants were inhibited."

Land office
May 5th 1824.

John Davenport clk.

In the name of God amen I. Thomas Thornton of Fredericksburg [clerk] being weak of body but of sound and perfect mind and memory, do make and ordain in this my last will and testa-

To the General Assembly of Virginia

ment hereby revoking all former wills by me made, first I recommend my soul to God who gave it in hopes of a Joyful resurrection to eternal life though Jesus Christ our Lord and the worldly Goods and estate wherewith it hath pleased a gracious God to bless me I give and devise as follows. Imprimis I give and devise to my loving and well beloved wife Mary Ann Bertrand Thornton two tracts of land lying situate and being in the County of Prince William given unto me by her father Colo Bertrand Ewell containing by estimation four hundred and three acres be the same more or less to have and to hold to her during her natural life she making no waste or destruction thereupon and after her decease I give and devise the same to my Son Thomas Thornton Jun. to have and to hold to my said Son his heirs & assigns as an absolute estate of inheritance in fee simple forever. I further give and devise unto my said wife all that tract of land lying situate and being in the county of Prince William aforesaid which I bought of David Reno to have hold occupy and enjoy the said tract with the building thereon until my said Son Thomas shall attain unto the full age of twenty-one years she making no waste or destruction thereon and after the end and expiration of the said Term, that is to say when my Son Thomas shall attain unto the Said full age of twenty one years I give and devise the said tract of land unto him my said Son Thomas his heirs and assigns as an absolute estate of inheritance in fee simple forever. It is my will and desire that all my stock of horses, cattle, sheep, Hogs, &c and all my household furniture and planatation utensils be kept together for the joint use of my wife & children until my said Son Thomas shall attain unto the full age of twenty one years and then I give and bequeath the same unto my said wife and my said Son Thomas to be equally divided between them to their own use & behoof forever. I further give unto my said wife the following negro slaves viz: Lotto Senr. Winny Senr. Vernon Squire Tom the Son of Winny Senr. and Maryann the daughter of Ralph and Mary to her own use & behoof forever. Item. I give and bequeath unto my said Son Thomas four negro slaves, viz: Ralph, Mary, Lotto Jun. & Billy the Son of Ralph & Mary. all the books I shalt die possessed of one enameled gold ring in memory of Colo. William Goldsborough, also all my plate viz: one silver watch one large two handed cup and cover, two pint cans, two large sauce boats, one soup ladle, one soup spoon, one silver cup, or lamp four salts with their glasses and shovels, eleven Table spoons, twelve tea spoons, one spoon strainer and one pair of sugar tongs. Item. I give and bequeath to my daughter Ann Thornton the following negro slaves, viz: Ben Johnston Sarah and her other two children, Sam and Harry, which she had by Ben Johnson and her two children Lucy and Jack which she had by Col Taliaferro Randall to her own use and behoof forever. Item I give & bequeath to my daughter Sarah Thornton three negro slaves viz: Abraham, Davy and Winny to her own use and behoof forever and I further give and devise to my said Daughter Sarah Thornton a land office Treasury warrant No. 15.524 drawn in my favor by the Register of the land office for fourteen hundred and sixty two acres now lodged in the land office of the Western District for location hereby assigning unto my said Daughter all the right title or interest which I have in the same or which may accrue therefrom and to hold to her her heirs and assigns forever. Item. I give and bequeath unto my said wife my said Son Thomas and my said two daughters Ann & Sarah three loan office certificates, issued from the land office of the United States, in the State of Maryland the twentieth of October seventeen hundred and ninety viz: No 8 for the sum of nine hundred and ten dollars and fifty cents bearing interest of six per cent per annum from the first day of January seventeen hundred and ninety one. Also No 8 for the Sum of four hundred and fifty five dollars twenty five cents bearing interest at six per cent per annum from the first day of January One thousand eight hundred and one, also No 9 for the Sum of nine hundred and sixty two & eighty four cents

To the General Assembly of Virginia

bearing interest at three per cent per annum from the first day of January Seventeen hundred and ninety one also two other certificates issued December the thirtieth from the loan office of the State of Virginia Seventeen hundred and ninety both numbered One hundred and four One for the Sum of Sixteen dollars & eighty four cents bearing interest at six per cent per annum from the first day of January seventeen hundred and ninety one, the other for the Sum of eight dollars and forty three cents bearing interest at six per cent per annum from the first day of January Eighteen hundred and one to be equally divided between them together with the interest that has or may arise from the same to their own use & behoof forever, and I do hereby constitute & appoint my said wife to be Executrix and my worthy and esteemed friend Doctor Robert Wellford to be Executor of this my will & testament & joint Guardians to my said children. In witness whereof I the said Thomas Thornton have hereunto set my hand and seal this twenty fourth day of March in the year of our Lord One thousand seven hundred and ninety one.

         Thomas Thornton (seal)
           March 24th 1791.

Fixed and sealed and declared by the said Thomas Thornton to be his last will and Testament in presence of
Chilton Randell
W S Stone
Thomas Garnett

At a District court held at Dumfries the 17th day of May 1792 This will was proved by the oath of Thomas Garnett a witness thereto at a District Court held at Dumfries the 19th day of May 1792 the same was further proved by William Stone another witness thereto and ordered to be recorded. And at a District Court held at Dumfries the 21st day of May 1792 On the motion of Mary ann Thornton the Executrix herein named who made oath & executed & acknowledged bond as the law directs certificate is granted her for obtaining a probate thereof in due form

Teste G. Brooke C. C.

A copy teste
M. P. Sinclair C. P. W. S. C.

Endorsement on back of petition. Decr. 4th 1824—Refd to Claims—1825 Jany 1 Rejected—Jany. 3 Reported

NUMBER 110.

To the Honorable the General Assembly of the Commonwealth of Virginia at Richmond Assembled

The petition of Berry Cawood a citizen of Harlan County State of Kentucky and former resident of Washington County & State of Virginia

He represents and Humbly sheweth to your Honorable body that in fall of 1778 your petitioner enlisted with a Captain John Williams who was commanded by Col George Clark and marched on a campaign of seven months servitude and was at the taking of Lt. Governor Hamilton at the Opost also garded him to Herods station Kentucky part of the way as a gard & the residue of the way as a Spie and at which place sometime in the month of April 1779 your petitioner obtained a Discharge from his officer and afterwards lost or mislaid the same and returned to the aforesaid Washington county Virginia and lived in an Extream of the said County in the hills and mountains detached from almost Evry community or oportunity of information and has ultimately been kept out of his wages and Land bounty.

Your petitioner begs leave further to state that his former occupation was that of a hunter and being a man of little or no information but made repeted enquiry how to come at his rite his directions that he got were from such vague sources and such a contrast of opinions that he has hitherto been kept in the dark We presume there has been lands laid off near the

To the General Assembly of Virginia

falls of Ohio in the now Indiana state for Colo Clark and his soldiers & by refferance to the Acts of Congress you will discover the same but supposes your petitioners lott of Land has been otherwise appropriated and finely lost.

Your petitioner begs leave further to state it is given up by both officers and soldiers of the revolutionary war who was acquainted with that section of Country that Clarks campaign was amongst the hardest that was been performed enduring the revolutionary war as they had to travel a number of miles through inundated Lands and water cold.

Your Petitioner begs leave further to state that he is far advanced in years which the dates of the aforesaid campaign will justify the same and from the result of that Expedition together with divers other hardships through life has rendered him infirm & is left without the necessary means of support.

Your petitioner will further state that he would be willing that your Honourable body would contribute land in some section of country not far distant from this place otherwise its value thereof. We the undersigned subscribers do trust that the magnanimity of your Honorable body will hear your petitioners prayer and Extend your benevolance and in duty bound your petitioners will ever pray &c

[Names.]

State of Kentucky
    County of Harlan

I Berry Caywood aged sixty eight years do upon oath testify and declare that in the year 1778 I enlisted for the term of seven months in Captain John Williams Company in the regiment Commanded by Colonel George Clarke of the Virginia and that I continued in the service aforesaid during the term of seven months afsaid was at the taking of Lieut Governor Hamilton and guarded the said Hamilton to Herod station in Kentucky at which place I was discharged regularly and said discharge is lost or mislaid and that I have not received any compensation for said services nor has any person been authorised by me to receive the same.

Berry Cawood

Sworn to and subscribed before the undersigned a justice of the peace for the County afsd this 7th day of November 1831.

John Noe J. P.

Harlan County State af Kentucky January 9th 1830

    This day personally came before me Luke Noe One of the commonwealths justices of the peace for the County aforesaid William Hudson of the county of Clay & state aforesd and made oath that in the year of 1779 he saw Berry Cawood on an Expedition under the command of Colo George Clark & perhaps in the company of Capt John Williams and the said Cawood was at the taking of Lt Governor Hamilton & further the said Cawood held an Indian scalp in his hand and it was said that the said Cawood killed the Indian sworn to & subscribed this date above written

William Hudson
Luke Noe J P

    Endorsement on back of petition. Decr. 21st 1831.—Refd. to Revy. Claims.

Jacob Sadowsky
John M. L. Swan(?)
In Floyd
Clark
John Adams
Hugh McGarry

James Estill
Ben Sebastian
P. Tardwray
G. Nicholas
J. H. M. (?)
Harry Innes
Nimrod Glascock

Samuel Lamar
Marstan Clay
John Craig
Zachary Taylor
Hananiah Lincoln
Rich'd Callaway
George Slaughter
Tho's Dinwiddie
Jaspeed
John Crisenberry
John Crittenden
Edward Nelson
Jubirr Rupinn(?)
Zeter Schmoltzer(?)
Edward Harrod

FACSIMILE SIGNATURES

Tracings made from characteristic signatures found on the petitions herein printed

List of Names attached to the Petitions

(Figures indicate the number of the Petition on which the name occurs)

Adams, Alexander (Alexr.) (Adans.)..............46, 53, 76
Adams, George.................. 17
Adams, James.............27, 60, 64
Adams, John (Edams).....27, 28, 33, 48, 52, 64
Adams, Peter................... 12
Adams, Robert.................. 27
Adams, William................. 33
Admire, George (admire)........ 52
Ahearn, Edmund (Edmd.)..60, 65, 72
Aiken, John (Acken)............ 54
Akers, Joseph 40
Akers, Simon (Achors) 40
Akers, Thomas (Thos.)......... 40
Aldridge, William.............17, 84
Alester, James.................. 27
Alester, Samuel................. 27
Alexander, James.....23, 26, 55, 56, 58
Alexander, John (Jno.) (Elexander)....................47, 63
Alexander, Randall (Randol)...60, 65
Alexander, Samuel (Saml.)....... 63
Alexander, Thomas (Thomas) (Ellisander.) (Alixander)...60, 65
Alexander, William (Wm.)....... 58
Alford, Ancel (Ansel)............ 58
Alford, Charles................. 58
Algire, Adam................... 78
Alkire, John....................78, 84
Alkire, William (Alkier).......78, 84
Allen, Archibald (Allan)......... 48
Allen, Daniel................... 48
Allen, David.................... 60
Allen, Elijah.................... 74
Allen, John (Allin) (Allan).....43, 53, 63, 65, 66, 77, 78
Allen, John W. (Jno.)........... 49
Allen, Joseph (Jos.).....48, 51, 52, 54
Allen, Richard (Richd.).......... 40
Allen, Silvanus................. 52
Allen, Thomas (Thos.).........49, 57
Allen, Zachariah................ 58
Allen, William (Wm.).43, 58, 60, 65, 77
Allerson, John [Allison?]........ 60
Allerson, Peter................. 60
Allerson, Thomas............... 60
Allerton, David (Allarton).....78, 84

Allerton, Jacob.................. 84
Allerton, Jonathan (Allarton)..78, 84
Allison, John (Jno.) (Alleson) 45, 52, 53, 58, 60, 63, 78
Allison, Peter................... 40
Allison, Robert (Robt.) (Alison) 60, 78
Allison, Thomas...............27, 58
Alsop, George (Geo.)..........60, 67
Alsop, Joseph (Jos.) (Allsup).... 60
Alston, John McCoy............ 74
Alston, Phillip................. 74
Alvey, Robert.................. 60
Ames (Alender)................. 27
Anderson, Asher...............47, 65
Anderson, George.............. 60
Anderson, Henry............... 52
Anderson, James..........27, 46, 58
Anderson, John.........15, 27, 64, 78
Anderson, Joseph (Jos.)......... 52
Anderson, Nicholas............27, 65
Anderson, Presley (presley)24, 47, 60, 65, 78
Anderson, Reuben.............. 66
Anderson, William (Wm.)..15, 27, 28, 33, 48, 49, 58, 62, 63, 64, 78, 84
Anderson, William, Jr 48
Andrews, Alexander............ 58
Andrews, Isaac...............54, 56
Archer, Stephen................ 60
Archer, William (Wilm.)........ 55
Archer, Zacharias (Zach.)........ 52
Ardery, James.................. 56
Ardery, John (Jno.)............. 56
Ardery, William (Wm.).......... 56
Armstrong, James.............. 27
Armstrong, John............... 26
Armstrong, Joseph (Jos.)...66, 84, 88
Armstrong, Joshua............. 55
Armstrong, Thomas............ 27
Armstrong, William (Wm.)..27, 46, 58
Armstrong, William, Jr.......... 27
Arnett, David.................. 58
Arnett, James.................. 43
Arnold, James.............24, 27, 52
Arnold, John...16, 24, 43, 52, 58, 69, 82
Arnold, Nicholas................ 52
Arnold, Reuben................. 69
Arnold, Thomas (Thos.)....53, 60, 93

[189]

List of Names

Arnold, Stephen............... 16
Arnold, William (Wm.)....48, 49,
    52, 55, 56, 58, 62, 66, 84
Arrowsmith, Richard
    (Arrasmith)...........49, 78, 84
Arrowsmith, Samuel............ 54
Ashbrooke, Aaron
    (Ashbroke)............49, 54, 84
Ashbrooke, Felix............... 77
Ashby, Daniel (Asbey)......9 (List)
Ashby, David.................. 68
Ashby, Fielding................ 27
Ashby, John................... 23
Ashby, Stephen................ 58
Ashford, Thomas (Thos.)....... 58
Ashley, William..............60, 65
Ashurst, Robert............... 43
Aske, David................... 78
Askey, Zacharias [Ashby?]...... 74
Asturgus, James............... 26
Atchley, James................ 56
Atchison, James............... 63
Atkin, Robert (Robard)........ 78
Atkins, William............... 69
Atkinson, Jesse (Adkinson)..... 74
Ayres, Richard (Riard)......... 54
Ayres, Samuel (Saml.)......46, 51, 53

Baber, Stanley................65, 72
Bacum, Henry................. 54
Badger, Alexander............. 77
Bailey, Groombride (Baley)..... 54
Bailey, John (Jno.)............. 58
Bailey, Rezon (Baley).......... 54
Baird, James.................. 60
Baird, Thomas................ 78
Baker, David.................60, 63
Baker, Frederick.............. 78
Baker, H...................... 54
Baker, James.................. 58
Baker, John (Jno.).........16, 63, 74
Baker, Joseph................. 60
Baker, Joshua (Jasha).32, 34, 48, 60, 63
Baker, Moses................60, 63, 65
Baker, Nathan................. 63
Baker, Richard................ 36
Baker, Thomas (Thos.)........27, 77
Baker, Umphrey............... 69
Baker, William (W.)..........54, 83
Baldock, Reuben.............36, 58
Baldwin, John................. 68
Ball, James................... 63
Ball, William (Wm.)...........58, 69
Ballard, Fielden............... 52
Ballard, George............... 60
Ballard, Proctor............... 60

Banks, Henry................. 92
Banks, Reuben (Reubin)....... 58
Banks, Thomas................ 69
Banks, William................ 58
Barbee, Andrew............... 93
Barbee, Joshua................ 83
Barbee, Thomas (Thos.)....... 83
Barber, Elias (Elijah).........23, 36
Barber, John................23, 36
Barker, Joseph (Jos.) (J.).....48, 84
Barker, William............... 74
Barkley, John................. 93
Barkley, Matthew.............. 52
Barksbery, Samuel, Sr......... 58
Barkshire, Dickey.............. 63
Barlow, Ambrose (Ambrous).... 60
Barlow, Cornelius (Barlow).... 60
Barlow, Flanery............... 60
Barlow, Henry, Jr.............. 60
Barlow, William............... 56
Barnard, Jonathan............. 78
Barnes, Elijah...............60, 65
Barnes, Francis............... 60
Barnes, Joshua................ 54
Barnett, Alexander (Alexr.)....62, 78
Barnett, Edward (Barnet) (Eddy) 58
Barnett, George (Geo.)..27, 47, 60, 78
Barnett, Humphrey............ 74
Barnett, James (Jas.).......... 64
Barnett, John (Jno.).......27, 36, 54
Barnett, Robert............... 17
Barr, Isaac..................46, 53, 93
Barr, John.................... 49
Barr, Robert (Robt.)........45, 46,
    53, 63, 76, 90, 91, 93
Bartlett, Anthony (Bartlet)
    (Anth.)..................... 60
Bartlett, Edmund.............. 60
Bartlett, Henry (Bartlet)......67, 78
Bartlett, Richard.............. 45
Bartlett, Matthias (Bartlet)
    (Mathias)................... 27
Bartlett, Thomas.....45, 60, 67, 78, 83
Bartlett, W................... 17
Barton, Andrew............... 77
Barton, Joab................9 (List)
Barton, Joshua...........9 (List), 27
Baseman, John................ 84
Basil, John (Bazel)............. 27
Baskett, John (Jno.)............ 65
Basnett, Isaac................47, 72
Basnett, Robert............... 47
Bassett, William (Baset)
    (Wm.)..................27, 52, 58
Bastinett, John (Jno.).......... 60
Bates, Ephraim (Baits)......... 60
Battersell, Freeman (freeman)... 78

List of Names

Baugh, John................9 (List)
Baughman, Jacob...........9 (List)
Baxter, James................... 60
Baxter, Samuel.................. 46
Bay, David [Ray?]............... 82
Baylor, Walter (Wallner)........ 60
Bayne, Thomas................... 60
Beale, Leonard.................. 63
Beale, Richard Eustace.......... 16
Beall, Archibald (Beell) (Archd.)
  (Archble)..................27, 69
Beall, Edward................... 63
Beall, William (Willm.)......... 63
Bear, William (Bare)............ 28
Beard, John..................... 53
Beard, Joseph................... 74
Bearns, Will.................... 58
Beaseman, John.................. 78
Beasley, John (Beasly).....32, 48, 54
Beatty, Daniel (Beaty).......60, 65
Beatty, James................... 60
Beatty, John (Beaty).33, 49, 66, 77, 84
Beatty, Thomas (Thos.).......... 65
Beck, Daniel.................... 60
Beck, Jeremiah (Becks).......48, 54
Beck, Samuel (Saml.)............ 52
Bedford, Benjamin (Benj.)....62, 78
Bedinger, Michael (G).......... 8, 9
Beesley, William (Majr.)....9 (List)
Bell, David..................... 78
Bell, Hugh...................... 78
Bell, John...............43, 52, 84, 93
Bell, James..................52, 78
Bell, Joseph.................... 78
Bell, Richard................... 63
Bell, Samuel.................... 78
Bell, Thomas (Thos.).........24, 53
Bell, William (Wm.).......57, 58, 78
Benedict, John.................. 36
Benefil, John (Benefiel).....60, 63, 93
Bennett, Benjamin............... 60
Bennett, Daniel................. 58
Bennett, George................. 51
Bennett, Josephus (Bennit)...... 17
Bennett, Joshua................. 24
Bennett, Thomas................. 47
Bennett, William................ 3
Bennington, William............. 82
Benson, James (Coln.) (Jas.).... 82
Benson, Joshua.................. 84
Bentley, James...............60, 65
Benton, John.................... 54
Benton, Simon................... 54
Berson, William (Wm.)........... 55
Berry, Benjamin (Benj.).......43, 52
Berry, Edmund (Edmond) (Bery) 72
Berry, Edward................... 65

Berry, Elijah...........32, 34, 48, 84
Berry, George...............57, 78, 84
Berry, George Jr.............32, 34
Berry, Henry...........32, 34, 48
Berry, James...........8, 9, 26, 27
Berry, Joel..............32, 34, 48
Berry, Joseph.....27, 32, 34, 48, 54, 60
Berry, Joseph, Jr............32, 34
Berry, Robert................... 43
Berry, Reuben (Berry) (Reubin) 51, 52
Berry, Samuel (Bery).........43, 52
Berry, Themley.................. 54
Berry, Thomas (Tho.)............ 58
Berry, Thomas, Jr............... 58
Berry, William...........40, 48, 58
Berry, Withers.................. 54
Best, Humphrey.................. 27
Best, Stephen................... 27
Bethel, George.................. 56
Bett, Josiah.................... 68
Bever, Matthias (Mathias)
  (Mattheas)..............60, 78, 84
Bever, Obadiah (Bavor)
  (Obediah).................47, 72
Bibelin, William.............60, 65
Bickerstaff, Benjamin (Benj.)... 74
Bickley, James (Bickey)......... 51
Bickley, William (Beckley)...6, 32, 34
Biddle, Daniel.................. 78
Biggs, Daniel................60, 65
Bird, John, Sr.................. 67
Bird, John...................... 46
Bishong, John................... 63
Black, Hugh..................... 15
Black, James.................... 27
Black, John.................27, 58, 64
Black, Samuel................58, 93
Black, William (Wm.)............ 58
Blackburn, David (blackburn
  david)........................ 60
Blackburn, George (Geo.)...43, 51, 52
Blackburn, James................ 54
Blackburn, Isaac (blackburn).... 60
Blackburn, Joseph (Jos.).....54, 60
Blackwell, Armstead............. 46
Blackwell, James (blackwell).... 47
Blackwell, Robert (Robt.)...51, 52, 60
Blair, Alexander.............66, 78
Blair, Alexander, Jr............ 49
Blair, I....................49, 56, 66
Blair, John (Blare)........48, 56, 78
Blair, Samuel (Saml.)......45, 46,
                        53, 60, 78, 84
Blair, William...............49, 56
Blanchard, David.............46, 52
Blank, Joseph (Jos.)............ 52
Blanton, Carter................. 27

[191]

List of Names

Blanton, James (Jas.)..........52, 58
Blanton, John................... 43
Blanton, Thomas (Thos.)......52, 58
Bledsoe, Abram................. 52
Bledsoe, Benjamin (bledsoe) ...51, 58
Bledsoe, Elijah................. 69
Bledsoe, I..................... 58
Bledsoe, James................. 52
Bledsoe, John................60, 65
Bledsoe, Joseph (Jos.)........... 52
Bledsoe, Moses................. 60
Bledsoe, William............17, 108
Blincoe, James (Blencoe)......60, 65
Boffman, Catherine.............. 8
Boggs, Andrew.................. 27
Boggs, Andrew, Jr.............. 27
Boggs, James................60, 65
Boggs, John.................60, 65
Boggs, Robert..........52, 12, 63, 65
Bogie, Andrew.................. 15
Bohannon, Richard.............. 60
Bohun, Benjamin (Bohon) (Benj.)26, 58
Boke, Thomas................... 15
Bolar, Richard.................. 58
Boling, Henry (Henery)......... 93
Bonar, Arthur.................. 52
Bonn, Andrew [Boone?]........ 24
Boone, Daniel (Boon)..6, 9 (List)
                     12, 24, 45, 48, 106
Boone, Edward.................. 12
Boone, Israel................... 12
Boone, Jacob.............48, 54, 87
Boone, Jonathan...............11, 58
Boone, Josiah (Boon)............ 47
Boone, Joseph (Bone)........... 60
Boone, Misny (Boon).......9 (List)
Boone, Ovid.................57, 84
Boone, Samuel (Saml.)24, 27, 60, 65, 83
Boone, Samuel, Jr.............. 24
Boone, Squire..............11, 24, 27
Boone, Thomas (Thos.)..24, 54, 74, 87
Borns, Basil (Bazal) [Burns?].... 54
Boshart, Jacob.................. 60
Boswell, George..............60, 67
Boudry, John................... 69
Bourn, William................. 40
Bourns, George [Burns?]......... 66
Bowles, Jesse................... 84
Bowman, Jesse (Bowmine) (Jesse) 27
Bowman, John...............2, 6, 17
Bowman, Joseph................. 3
Bowman, Robert (Robt.)......... 58
Boyd, John...........16, 52, 66, 84
Boyes, Joseph................... 60
Boyle, James................... 78
Boyle, John (Boyls).....32, 34, 54, 64
Boyle, Stephen (Boyl)..........60, 78

Bradford, Enoch................. 53
Bradford, Fielding (F.)...46, 60, 65
Bradford, John............46, 53, 76
Bradley, Dennis..............60, 65
Bradley, Dewand ....[—?]
Bradley, Edward..........60, 65, 84
Bradley, John..................52, 60
Bradley, Moses (Bredley)......32, 78
Bradley, Robert...............52, 60
Bradley, Samuel (S.) (Saml.) 40, 60, 74
Bradley, Thomas................ 52
Bradshaw, Benjamin............. 26
Bradshaw, James (Brashaw)..... 65
Bradshaw, Thomas (Brashaw).... 65
Bradshaw, William (Wm.) (Brashaw).....................58, 65
Brady, William................. 66
Bram, Andrew.................. 77
Braun, Joseph...........66, 77, 84
Branham, Benjamin (Branum) (Benj.)........................ 52
Branham, Thomas (Thos.)...23, 52, 60
Brank, Robert (Robt.)........27, 64
Brasfield, Wiley................. 58
Brashear, John (Brasher)......... 78
Brashear, Mashan............... 11
Bray, James...............26, 45, 46
Breet, Joseph................... 78
Brent, Innes B.................. 93
Brent, James................... 17
Brent, Thomas (Thos.).....45, 52, 60
Brenton, John.................. 58
Brice, James.................... 84
Brice, Samuel.................. 84
Bridges, John................... 58
Bridges, William................ 64
Bright, Henry.................. 69
Bright, John................... 69
Brice, Daniel (Brise)............ 27
Briggs, David.................. 28
Briggs, Samuel (Saml.)......... 17
Brimagen, Jervis................ 55
Brimagem, John (Brinnagem) (Jno.)....................... 78
Brink, Hibert................60, 65
Brink, Samuel.........24, 12, 60, 65
Brinn, John (Jno.).............. 58
Bristow, James...............56, 63
Brite, Albertus [Bright?]........ 45
Brite, Samuel (Bright).......... 66
Brock, Henry................... 40
Brockman, Thomas (Thos.)....60, 65
Bromfield, Joseph............... 28
Bronson, Zebulon (Bronsun)..... 58
Brookie, John.................. 60
Brooking, Samuel (Saml.)........ 58
Brooks, Ebenezer (Ebenr.)..17, 50, 63

List of Names

Brooks, Henry (H.)............53, 60
Brooks, Samuel..............9 (List)
Brooks, Thomas (Thos.)....6, 24, 40, 54, 87
Brooks, William.............9 (List)
Brothers, Thomas............... 84
Brouse, Henry.................. 52
Brow, Bartlett................. 69
Brown, Absolom......15, 23, 47, 58, 69
Brown, Alexander (Alexr.).....66, 84
Brown, Andrew.................. 66
Brown, Benjamin................ 60
Brown, Beverly..............58, 69
Brown, Daniel.................. 26
Brown, Frederick (Fred.)....... 47
Brown, James (Brown).....6, 17, 26, 27, 28, 58, 60, 65, 83
Brown, Jeremiah................ 6
Brown, John...........26, 27, 60, 65
Brown, Joseph.................. 69
Brown, Manly................... 33
Brown, McCagey................. 69
Brown, Patrick (Patrick)...26, 60, 65
Brown, Robert (Robt.) (brown).. 27
Brown, Samuel.................. 6
Brown, Thomas (Thos.).......23, 60
Brown, William (Willm.) (Wm.)........52, 54, 60, 63, 65
Browning, Caleb.............60, 65
Brownlee, John................. 36
Bruce, Benjamin................ 65
Bruce, John.................... 17
Bruce, William................. 85
Brumberry, Jacob............... 27
Brumfield, Joab................ 17
Brundidge, Bartlett............ 72
Brundidge, Solomon..........65, 72
Brunner, Timothy............... 69
Brush, James................... 84
Bryan, Edmund (Bryans) (Edmum).................... 60
Bryan, George.................. 60
Bryan, Samuel (Saml.).6, 58, 60, 63, 78
Bryan, William (Wm.)........6, 12
Bryant, Daniel................. 63
Bryant, James (Briant)......... 9
Bryant, John......17, 47, 58, 60, 63, 69
Bryant, Thomas (Briant) (Tomas) 8
Bryden, Robert (Robt.)....58, 64, 69
Bryson, George................. 93
Buchanan, George............... 26
Buchanan, James (J.) (Buhanan).................27, 48
Buchanan, John................. 26
Buck, Conrad (Coonrad)........ 63
Buck, Wilbey................... 69
Buckner, William (Wm.)......... 17

Buford, A...................... 45
Buford, John (Buferd).........63, 69
Buford, Simeon................. 93
Bulger, Edward..............11, 12
Bullen, Jedediah............... 49
Bullitt, Parmenas (Bullett).... 26
Bullock, Edmund (Edm.)...53, 60, 65
Bullock, Garland............60, 65
Bullock, James (Jas.).........63, 107
Bullock, John........8, 9, 53, 60, 65
Bullock, Lewis...........60, 67, 93
Bullock, Nathaniel (Bullock) (Nathanel) (Nathel).....8, 9, ...9 (List) 65
Bullock, Thomas (Thos.)......53, 78
Bunch, Callaway................ 58
Bunch, Charles................. 58
Bunch, Clark................... 58
Bunch, Joseph.................. 58
Bunch, Record.................. 58
Bunch, Zachariah............... 58
Bundan, David..............9 (List)
Bunnel, James.................. 93
Bunnel, Jonah (Jona)........... 93
Bunnel, Stephen................ 93
Burbridge, Rowland (Roweland). 63
Burch, John.................... 84
Burch, Joseph...............60, 67
Burdette, Frederick, Sr........ 58
Burdette, Frederick, Jr........ 58
Burdette, John (Burdett).....58, 60
Burdette, Joseph............... 58
Burdette, Joshua (Burdett)..... 58
Burgin, Charles................ 47
Burgin, Dennis................. 46
Burgin, Thomas................. 47
Burgur, Henry (burgur) (Henry). 33
Burgur, John (burgur).......... 33
Burk, Elihu (Burke)............ 60
Burk, John..................... 77
Burk, Jonathan (Birk).......... 52
Burk, R........................ 55
Burnett, William............... 60
Burns, Andrew.................. 78
Burns, Arthur..........66, 78, 84, 88
Burns, George...........77, 78, 84
Burns, James................28, 84
Burns, John.................57, 78
Burrows, Thomas (Burress) (Burows)..................65, 72
Burton, Ambrose................ 69
Burton, Gerred................. 56
Burton, Jesse.................. 84
Burton, John................... 63
Burton, Reuben (Reubin)........ 52
Bush, Ambrose (Bush).........52, 72
Bush, Charles.................. 47

List of Names

Bush, Francis.............47, 65, 72
Bush, Gilson (Gholson)........... 72
Bush, John...................47, 77
Bush, Philip..............47, 65, 72
Bush, Philip, Sr................ 47
Bush, William (Wm.)....6, 47, 52, 60, 63, 65, 72
Bush, William, Sr. (Wm.)........ 47
Butcher, Gasper................. 74
Butcher, James (Boocher)....... 52
Butcher, Joseph................. 64
Butler, James................... 58
Butler, John.................... 58
Butler, Joseph.................. 58
Butler, Peter................... 58
Butler, Samuel (S.).........15, 45, 60
Butler, Thomas (Butlor).......27, 82
Butler, William........52, 54, 55, 57, 78
Byers, David.................... 56
Byers, Jeremiah (Byars).......... 58
Byers, Joseph (Jos.)............46, 93
Byram, James................... 32
Byram, Peter (P.) (Petter) (Pet.)......32, 48, 56, 77, 78, 84, 88
Byram, William (Wm.)........62, 77
Byrd, Abraham.................. 56
Byrd, John..................49, 56, 62
Byrne, Patrick (Patrick) (Byrn) 32, 34
Byrne, William.................. 60

Cabel, Hugh (Cable)............. 27
Cade, Charles................... 47
Calaman, John.................. 60
Calbreath, John................. 78
Caldock, Levi................... 58
Caldwell, Andrew............... 66
Caldwell, David...........48, 54, 60
Caldwell, George (Geo.)......... 17
Caldwell, James................. 55
Caldwell, John.................. 27
Caldwell, Robert................ 84
Caldwell, Thomas............... 93
Caldwell, William (Wm.)...48, 54, 55, 56, 60, 87
Callaghan, Patrick............... 6
Callaway, Caleb................. 6
Callaway, Charles............... 6
Callaway, Chesley (Calloway).............6, 63, 78
Callaway, Eager.............9 (List)
Callaway, Edmund (Edmond) (Edmon) (Ed).......40, 46, 63
Callaway, Elizabeth.........9 (List)
Callaway, Flanders (Coloway) (Caloway) (Calloway).8, 9, 60, 63

Callaway, Francis...........9 (List)
Callaway, James.......6, 9 (List) 63
Callaway, John (Calloway)...... 8
Callaway, Richard (Calloway) 6, 10, 27
Calvert, Ralls.................. 53
Cameron, Angus................ 6
Cameron, John.................. 60
Cammack, Christopher (Xpher).. 60
Cammack, John.................. 60
Campbell, Alexander..........52, 54
Campbell, Allen................ 52
Campbell, Archibald (Archd.)...............52, 60, 93
Campbell, Charles (Chas.).17, 60, 63, 64, 65
Campbell, Daniel................ 52
Campbell, George (Campbel) ..26, 52
Campbell, Hugh............27, 52, 64
Campbell, James (Jas.)..36, 52, 54, 60
Campbell, John........19, 40, 52, 58, 64, 83, 93, 101
Campbell, Michael (Mich.).....60, 83
Campbell, Matthew.............. 54
Campbell, Morry (Cample)...... 69
Campbell, Robert....40, 51, 53, 58, 60
Campbell, Samuel (Saml.)......6, 52
Campbell, Thomas............... 64
Campbell, William (Wm.) (Camble)........32, 43, 45, 51, 52, 53, 54, 58, 63, 78, 87
Campbell, William, Jr......32, 52, 58
Cannit, Edward (Edwart)........ 69
Caperton, William............... 27
Carey, Holman, (Holn.)......... 54
Carigan, Edward................ 58
Carlin, Thomas (Thos.).......42, 58
Carlton, Isaac.................. 58
Carlyle, George................. 52
Carlyle, James.................. 60
Carmichael, Patrick (Carmikel).. 26
Carns, John.................... 49
Carneal, Thomas (Tho.) [Corneal?] 63
Carneal, William (Wm.)......... 52
Carpenter, Adam................ 36
Carpenter, Christopher.......... 74
Carpenter, Henry (Hennary)..... 74
Carpenter, James, Jr............ 54
Carpenter, John................. 74
Carpenter, Peter................ 74
Carr, Peter..................60, 93
Carr, Walter..........40, 43, 51, 63
Carrington, William (Wm.) (Carinton)................... 65
Carson, James (Jas.)............ 78
Carson, John................... 69
Carter, Braxton................. 8
Carter, John.................... 60

[194]

List of Names

Carter, Shadrach................ 60
Cartmill, Andrew................ 78
Cartmill, John..............56, 63, 78
Cartmill, Thomas (Thos.)........ 78
Cartright, Jacob (Cartwright)... 26
Cartright, Jesse (Cartwright).... 27
Cartright, Peter (Cartwright)..78, 84
Cartright, Richard, Sr........... 78
Cartright, Richard (Curtright).33, 84
Cartright, Robert (Cartwright).. 26
Cartright, Samuel (Cartwright)78, 84
Cartright, Thomas (Thos.) (Cartwright)...................... 26
Cary, Joseph.................... 84
Case, Goldsmith..............78, 84
Case, Joseph (Jos.)............. 84
Case, Separate................58, 84
Casey, Belias (Kecy) (Bealleas).. 24
Casey, John..................... 36
Casey, Peter.................... 58
Casey, Peter, Jr................. 26
Casey, William (Caysey) (Wm.).. 36
Cash, Thomas................... 77
Cash, Warren................... 52
Cashaner, Jacob (Ceshener)............40, 60, 65
Castleman, Lewis............43, 52, 63
Casto, Jonathan................. 65
Cather, Edward................. 58
Catlis, F [Gatlif?].............. 84
Catoline, Benjamin (Bengemen).. 65
Caughey, John.................. 84
Cave, George.................... 6
Cave, Henry..................52, 60
Cave, John...................... 52
Cave, Richard................... 60
Cave, William.................52, 60
Cave, William, Jr............... 52
Cavins, Edward................. 60
Cawood, Berry..................110
Chambers, Alexander (Allexander)......................60, 65
Chambers, John................. 49
Chambers, John Thompson...... 78
Champ, John.................... 77
Champ, William (Wm.).......... 27
Champers, George............... 67
Cheney, Richard (Chania)((Chany) 65
Chapman, Amos................. 27
Chapman, George............... 74
Chapman, Thomas.............. 74
Cheatham, Edward (Edwd.)................62, 84, 93
Cheatham, James..........66, 78, 84
Chenoweth, Arthur............. 54
Chenoweth, Thomas............ 54

Cherry, Moses.................. 52
Chester, Nixon................. 27
Childress, John................. 24
Childreth, Squire............... 78
Chiles, David................... 58
Chiles, Henry................... 58
Chiles, James................... 58
Chiles, John.................... 58
Chilton, Thomas................ 69
Chinn, Christopher (Christophr.)..............67, 93
Chinn, Elisah..............15, 60, 67
Chinn, John.................... 93
Chinn, Raleigh (Rawleigh).....60, 67
Chinn, William...............67, 93
Chisley, John................... 52
Chisom, Absalom............... 74
Chisom, Elisha................. 74
Chisom, John................... 74
Chivelier, Anthony [Chevalier?]. 46
Chrisman, Joseph.............15, 63
Christian, John..............53, 60
Christy, Ambrose............... 60
Christy, Julius................. 60
Christy, Thomas................ 11
Church, Thomas (Ths.)......... 52
Churchill, George............... 52
Churchill, John, Jr............. 68
Clare, William (Wm.).......... 33
Clark, Charles (Cs.)............ 55
Clark, Frances.................. 27
Clark, George Rogers (G.R.).3, 5, 13, 17, 100, 105
Clark, George..........6, 32, 34, 54
Clark, James............60, 65, 67, 78
Clark, Richard................. 56
Clark, Robert (Robt.).....32, 34, 55, 56, 78, 93
Clark, Shadrach (Shadrack)..... 60
Clark, Thomas (Thos.) (Clarke)....17, 55, 56, 60, 65, 74, 84
Clark, William (Wm.).33, 48, 55, 78, 88
Clarke, John (Jno.).14, 46, 52, 54, 63
Clarkson, David...............78, 84
Clarkson, Julius..............60, 78
Clarkson, William (Wm.)...40, 78, 84
Clary, Elisha 15, 74
Clary, William (Wm.).......... 15
Clay, Marstan (M.).........40, 58, 63
Clay, Samuel (Saml.).......27, 78, 84
Cleeland, Alexander............. 11
Clem, Phillip................... 67
Clements, Roger................ 24
Clernand, William.............. 27
Cleveland, Alexander (Clevelad). 12
Cleveland, Eli...............60, 65
Clifford, Michael (Mich.)........ 52

[195]

List of Names

Clift, Joseph.................... 58
Cliffton, Burditt................ 60
Clindining, Robert (Robt.)
  [Clendening?]................ 78
Cline, Peter (Clyen Petter)...... 78
Clinkenbeard, Isaac.........58, 78, 84
Clinkenbeard, William (Clinkenbeard)........................ 24
Clinton, Archibald (Archy)...... 69
Clock, Richard................... 60
Cloyd, James..................... 15
Club, William.................60, 65
Coachyan, Andrew [Cushan?]... 78
Coats, William................... 74
Coburn, John...........25, 45, 46, 53, 63, 76, 90, 91
Coburn, William..............84, 88
Coby, Thomas (Thos.) [Colby?].. 52
Cochran, Andrew................. 78
Cochran, Dennis (Cochrin)....27, 64
Cochran, Hugh................... 43
Cochran, John (Cochran)......27, 64
Cochran, William (Wm.) (Cochrian).................... 27
Coffee, Ambrose (Coffy) (Ambros)........8, 9, 27, 47, 65, 72
Cofman, Abraham (Kauffman?)78, 84
Coker, Jesse (Cokker)...8, 9, 9 (List)
Coker, Augustine (Augustin).... 78
Coker, Michael................... 40
Coin, Edward (Coen)..........77, 84
Coldwell, David (Caldwell?)..... 32
Coldwell, Matthew (Mathew) (Caldwell)............43, 51, 52
Coldwell, William (Wm.)...32, 48, 49
Cole, Richard (Richd)............ 52
Cole, Jesse...................... 52
Coleman, Francis................. 52
Coleman, Page.................... 52
Coleney, John.[?]................ 64
Colley, James (Colly)....33, 49, 57, 84
Colley, Joseph [Colby?].......... 67
Collier, Alexander (Alexr.)..17, 58, 69
Collier, Daniel.................. 78
Collier, James................58, 77
Collier, John.........43, 51, 52, 58, 64
Collier, Joseph (Colliear)....... 60
Collier, Moses................... 58
Collier, Robert.................. 58
Collins, Bartlett........17, 51, 12, 60
Collins, Edmund.................. 84
Collins, Edward.................. 63
Collins, Elisha..............24, 52
Collins, James (Jas.)............ 60
Collins, Joel................43, 52
Collins, Joseph (Collings)...43, 51, 52
Collins, Joshua.................. 24

Collins, Josiah.................. 43
Collins, Robert (Robt.).....48, 63, 84
Collins, Stephen (Colins) (Stephan)..............14, 60, 76
Colter, Thomas (Thos.).......... 58
Colville, Joseph................. 78
Colvin, Aaron (Aron)............. 78
Colvin, Luther (Colwin).32, 34, 48, 54
Combs, Benjamin (Benj.)...47, 60, 65
Combs, Cuthbert................. 12
Combs, William (Comb.)......27, 60
Conaway, John................... 11
Conaway, John, Jr. (Connaway). 45
Conaway, Jesse................... 8
Conaway, Joseph................. 26
Congleton, William (Wm.)........ 63
Conn, Jacob..................... 60
Conn, John...................... 62
Conn, Notley.................... 78
Conn, Raleigh (Rolly)........... 84
Conn, Thomas (Thos.) 56, 60, 62, 66, 84
Connell, James (M.) Connall...14, 60
Connell, William (Wm.).......... 93
Connelly, Arthur (Connely)....46, 52
Connelly, James (Connely)....... 52
Connelly, Robert (Robt.)........ 52
Conning, Daniel (Danel)......... 78
Conning, James.................. 78
Conning, John................... 78
Conner, Daniel.................. 60
Connor, John (Conner)..43, 52, 60, 65
Connor, William................. 60
Connors, Dennis (Connyers)..... 58
Conrad, Abraham (Coonrad)..... 60
Conrad [—?].................... 48
Conrey, Jonathan................ 54
Consenbary, John................ 84
Consawley, James................ 54
Consawley, John................. 54
Constant, Isaac................. 84
Constant, John.................. 24
Constant, Thomas................ 78
Conway, James (Jas.)............ 55
Conway, Jesse (Jesey).......7, 40, 55
Conway, John (Jno.)..32, 34, 42, 45, 55
Conway, John, Sr................ 40
Conway, John, Jr................ 40
Conway, Joseph............40, 45, 60
Conway, Miles (W.).....32, 34, 48, 54
Conway, Samuel.................. 40
Conwenhovn, Joseph.............. 60
Conyers, David[Connors?]60, 65, 78, 84
Conyers, James.................. 74
Conyers, Isaac.................. 78
Cook, Abel...................... 54
Cook, David.................12, 36
Cook, Hosea..................... 60

List of Names

Cook, James, Senior............. 74
Cook, James, Junior............. 74
Cook, John, Senior.............. 49
Cook, John........27, 32, 33, 56, 60, 78
Cook, Samuel (Saml.).33, 55, 66, 78, 84
Cook, Seth..................... 52
Cook, William, (cook).........52, 74
Cooley, Daniel.................. 69
Cooley, Ebenezer................ 38
Coone, John.................... 59
Cooper, Benjamin............... 60
Cooper, James.................. 74
Cooper, John (Coopper)......... 54
Cooper, Samuel................. 53
Coopstick, Samuel.............. 52
Copelin, William (Copelen)...... 69
Copher, Jesse.................. 63
Copige, Isaac.................. 52
Copige, John (Coppege).......... 84
Copige, Rhodus (Rhodes)........ 52
Copper, McCagy................ 69
Corneal, Thomas (Thos.)
  [Carneal?].................. 52
Cornelison, Michael (Kelnelison)
  (Cornalisson) (Mickel).....77, 84
Counts, William (Wm.).......... 52
Courtenay, Charnick (Cortney)32, 34
Courtenay, Charno R. (Courtney) 54
Courtenay, John (Courtney)..... 27
Courtenay, Nehemiah (Corteney)
  (Courtney) (Nemiah)......48, 54
Corn, Andrew................... 27
Corn, Edward................... 27
Corn, Ebenezer................. 27
Corn, George.................16, 52
Corn, Solomon.................. 58
Corning, Ebenezer.............. 27
Corwin, I. Chebud.............. 46
Corwin, Jesse................48, 57
Corwin, Joseph............57, 58, 78
Corwin, Matthias.............58, 84
Corwin, Michael................ 60
Corwine, Richard (Richd.)...... 54
Coryell, Cornelius.............. 77
Coryell, Joseph (Corell)........ 77
Coryell, Levi................... 84
Coryell, Lewis (l.).............. 77
Cosgrove, James..............27, 64
Cotner, Frederick............... 69
Cotton, Henry................60, 65
Cotton, Ralph.................. 60
Couch, Francis (fransses)....... 65
Couch, James................... 48
Couchman, Benedict (Benndict
  (and Benedick)...........49, 84
Couchman, Benjamin............ 24
Couchman, Frederick............ 24
Couchman, Malachi............. 84
Couchman, Michael (Mikal)..... 49
Coulson, John................33, 48
Cowan, Hugh (Cowen)...53, 66, 78, 84
Cowan, James (Jas.)............ 26
Cowan, John (Jno.)(Cowen)3,17,18, 42
Cowes, Jacob................... 57
Cowherd, James (Jas.).......60, 67
Cowley, William (Wm.).......17, 60
Cox, Andrew................... 93
Cox, Benjamin (Benjn.)......... 61
Cox, David..................... 60
Cox, Francis................... 58
Cox, Gabriel................... 60
Cox, Isaac..................... 42
Cox, John (Cocks).......60, 74.76, 93
Cox, Jonathan.................. 60
Cox, Samuel (Saml.)............ 60
Crabb, John.................... 54
Crabb, Vinson.................. 54
Crach, Joseph [Creech?]........ 27
Cracraft, Joseph............... 66
Cracraft, Reuben (Ruben)....... 84
Cradlepaugh, William (Wm.)
  (Criddlebough) (Cradle-
  bough)..................6, 8, 27
Craddock, Thomas (Tho.)........ 42
Craddock, W.................... 83
Cradle, Thomas (thomas)........ 69
Craig, Absalom...............48, 54
Craig, Anne.................... 71
Craig, Benjamin (Bingn.)
  (Benj.)....................17, 52
Craig, Elijah.............51, 52, 60
Craig, James.............15, 17, 52
Craig, Jeremiah.........24, 43, 52, 60
Craig, John..15, 24, 23, 43, 45, 52, 61, 65
Craig, John H..........24, 51, 52, 93
Craig, Joseph................17, 60
Craig, Joseph, Jr.............. 60
Craig, Lewis....17, 43, 45, 52, 60, 63, 67
Craig, Martin (Martan)......... 15
Craig, Reuben.................. 52
Craig, Robert................60, 78
Craig, Samuel (Crage).......... 15
Craig, Toliver, Sr..........43, 52, 60
Craig, Toliver, Jr.............. 60
Craig, William (Craige).....58, 78, 84
Crancher, George............... 69
Cranchfield, William (Cranchfeld)
  (Wm.)....................... 69
Crass, Michael (Crase)......... 58
Crass, John.................... 69
Crawford, Abel................. 58
Crawford, James......53, 58, 65, 90, 91
Crawford, Josiah (Crofford)....32, 34
Crawford, William...........60, 65
Creals, James (Creal).........56, 57
Creamer, Henry................. 6

List of Names

Creed, Elijah 52
Crenshaw, James 65
Cresswell, Hugh 53
Cresswell, Samuel (Saml.) 52
Crew, David (Crews) 27, 30, 64
Crew, Elijah (Crews) 27, 47
Crew, Jeremiah (Crews) 27
Crew, Thomas (Thos.) 47
Crimm, Jacob (Crim) 65, 78
Crimm, John (Crim) (Jno.) .58, 65, 78
Crimm, Joseph 65
Crimm, William 65
Cripedge, Rhodin 52
Crisel, Jeremiah 52
Crittenden, John (J.) 3, 11, 60, 61
Crockett, Anthony 27
Crockett, Joseph 40, 45
Crocy, William 17
Cromwell, Joshua 58, 60
Crook, Absalom 24, 27
Crook, Jeremiah (Cruck) 77
Crook, John (Crooks) 27, 51, 58
Crosley, John 54, 63
Cross, Henry (Crose) 78, 84
Cross, John .... 9 (List)
Cross, Phillip (Crose) 78, 84
Cross, William 93
Crosthwait, Reuben 47
Crosthwait, Samuel 47
Crouch, Joseph 47
Crouchman, Benjamin (Ben)
 [Couchman?] 78
Crow, Daniel 56
Crow, John 94
Cruikshanks, Joseph (Crook-
 shanks) 52
Crum, Daniel (Crume) 60
Crump, Richard 60, 65
Crutcher, John (J.) 58
Crutchfield, William 65
Cruzen, Benjamin 78
Culberson, William (Culbertson)
 (Wm.) 49, 55
Culberton, Samuel (Saml.) 16
Cullin, Charles 55
Cunningham, Hugh 27
Cunningham, John (Jno.) 52
Cunningham, R. (Cuningham) ... 60
Cunningham, W 58
Curd, Charles 8, 11
Curd, James 40
Curd, John 40
Curd, Price 58
Curl, Dudley 60, 65
Curry, James 58
Curry, Robert 28, 48
Curry, William (Currey) 27, 77, 78
Curtis, John 48

Cusenberry, Elijah 32, 34, 84
Cusenberry, James (Quisenbey)47, 72
Cusenberry, John (Crisenberry)
 (Cusenbury) (Quisen-
 berry) 32, 33, 65, 72
Cusenberry, Moses (Crusonberry)
 (Chrisenberry) 32, 34, 48, 84
Cusenberry, Vinson (Vincin)
 (Cusenbary) 32, 34, 84
Cusenberry, William (Cusenbary) 84
Cusley, William (Will.) [Owsley?] 47
Cutbearth, Benjamin 6
Cutts, Shadrach (Shadrich) 65, 72

Dale, Abraham 52
Dale, George 52
Dale, Ignatius 52
Dale, William 51, 52
Daly, John 58
Daniel, John 63
Daniel, Peter 72
Daniel, W 42
Daniels, Nathan (Dannals) 27
Darnaby, Edward 67
Darnaby, John (Donebey) ..40, 67, 78
Darnwood, Boston 58
Darot, David [Durrett?] 51, 52
Date, Robert 52
Davenport, Jonas (Davinport).45, 53
Davenport, William (Wm.) 60, 65
David, Charles 60
David, H 66
David, Zebediah (Zebadiah) 54
Davidson, Adonijah (Davidson)
 (ADonijah) 32, 34
Davidson, George (Geo.) 17
Davidson, James [Davison] ...77, 88
Davidson, John 58
Davie, Charles 54
Davies, Azariah 6, 32, 34
Davis, Alexander 47
Davis, Augustine 65
Davis, Benjamin 54, 60, 58, 65
Davis, David 54, 84, 88
Davis, Edward 52, 74
Davis, Elijah 52
Davis, Hananiah 51
Davis, Harrison 58
Davis, J 68
Davis, James 58, 74
Davis, John (Davis) ...8, 15, 60, 63, 65
Davis, Joseph 27, 52, 58, 65
Davis, Lamach (Lamack)
 (Davies) 49, 55, 77, 78, 88
Davis, Leonard (Lenard) 65
Davis, Patrick 60

[198]

List of Names

Davis, Reason.................... 78
Davis, Richard.........27, 40, 51, 63
Davis, Robert.................49, 54
Davis, Samuel (Saml.).........27, 33
Davis, Stephen.................... 51
Davis, Theodore (Theodorus).... 27
Davis, Thomas (Davice)...24, 28, 32, 33, 49, 55, 58, 60, 66, 84
Davis, Thomas, Jr................ 49
Davis, William..........14, 52, 58, 78
Davy, Thomas..................... 48
Dawes, William (Wm.)............ 54
Dawson (Christopher?).......... 52
Dawson, Henry................... 78
Dawson, James (Dason)......... 14
Dawson, John............28, 49, 55, 77
Dawson, Richard (Rich.)......... 52
Dawson, Thomas (Tho.) (Dosson) 62
Deadman, Samuel (Dedman)...51, 52
Dearangar, Jacob................. 52
Dearengar, John.................. 52
Deatherage, Hillis................ 60
Deford, Charles.................. 93
Delaney, Joseph (Jos.).........45, 52
Demint, Jared.................... 52
Denham, Obed.................... 52
Denison, David................... 78
Denison, Daniel (Danl.).......... 63
Denison, Thomas (Thos.)......... 78
Denison, William................. 63
Denman, Samuel.................. 54
Denney, Jeremiah (Deney)...... 68
Denney, Lewis (Denny).......... 43
Denney, William (Wm.).......... 77
Dennis, Moses.................... 27
Dennis, Samuel (Saml.) (Dinnis)
................................26, 27, 58
Dennis, Samuel, Jr............... 36
Denton, David................40, 63
Denton, James................... 58
Denton, John..................... 6
Denton, Silas.................... 32
Denton, Thomas (Thos.).....6, 26, 58
Detay, Henry.................... 84
Devine, John..................... 27
Deweese, John (Jno.) (Dweise)...52
Deweese, Lewis (Dewese)......27, 52
Deweese, Samuel (Saml.)(Dewees) 46
Deweese, William (Wm.).......... 52
Dewitt, Elisha (Elishua) (Dwitt) (Dewit).................32, 34, 48
Dewitt, Henry................55, 82
Dewitt, Peter................23, 43, 52
Dewitt, William.................. 84
Dexter, Silas (Silos) (Siles) (Dextor).................34, 48, 54
Diar, John....................... 74
Dibrell, Charles................. 27

Dicken, Joseph................... 23
Dicken, William (Wm.).......... 60
Dickerson, A..................... 43
Dickerson, Edward............... 74
Dickerson, Griffen............... 74
Dickerson, Josiah................ 48
Dickerson, Martin (Martain).... 43
Dickerson, Valentine (Valentine) (Vaul)...................24, 43, 60
Dickerson, William............24, 43
Dickey, David.................... 58
Dickey, James.................... 52
Dickey, John..................... 58
Dickey, Michael (Mich.)......... 52
Dickey, Samuel................... 51
Dickinson, William (Wm.)........ 52
Dickson, John.................... 78
Dickson, Josiah...............78, 84
Dickson, Thomas................. 84
Dike, William.................... 77
Diller, Samuel (Sam.)............ 40
Dillon, Isaac (Dillion)........... 56
Dillon, John..................... 48
Dillon, Michael.................. 68
Dillon, Samuel................... 63
Dinwiddie, James (Jas.) (Dunwoodie) (Dunwiddy).17, 43, 53, 93
Dinwiddie, Thomas (Thos.)...... 60
Dive, Martin..................... 60
Diver, Dean (Dienn)............. 27
Doak, James..................26, 27
Dobyns, Edward.....32, 34, 48, 54, 62
Dods, Finley..................... 48
Dodson, Joshua.................. 58
Dodsshuler, Benjamin (Benj.)
..............................60, 65
Doman, Bartholemew (Barth.)... 63
Dougester, James (Dogester)..... 6
Dougester, James, Jr............ 6
Dole, John (Dolls).............. 78
Dole, Josiah M.................. 49
Dole, William (Doll)............ 45
Dolome [—?]..................... 17
Donald, Thomas.................. 28
Donaldson, Israel (Donalson)... 87
Donaldson, Jacob (Donelson).... 74
Donaldson, James................ 78
Donaldson, John (Donnalson).... 65
Donaldson, Richard (Donelson).. 93
Donaldson, Thomas (Thos.) (Donnalson).................. 62
Donaldson, William (Wm.) (Donalson).................... 52
Doniphan, Joseph...............8, 9
Doogans, William................ 58
Dooley, Abner................... 58
Dooley, Jacob................... 72
Dooley, Moses................... 58

List of Names

Dooley, Thomas.................. 52
Doran, Patrick.................. 21
Dorsey, Laken................... 54
Doster, Elijah (Dostor).......... 65
Doster, James..................8, 9
Doty, John (Jno.)............... 27
Dougherty, Cornelius..........15, 64
Dougherty, David (Doaherty)... 27
Dougherty, James (Jas.) (Daugherty)........................ 52
Dougherty, John (Doherthy).... 78
Dougherty, Roger (Doughorty) (Rogar)....................... 54
Dougherty, Thomas (Thos.)..... 17
Dougherty, William............. 27
Douglass, George............... 58
Douglass, Hugh (Dougless)...... 78
Douglass, James..............71, 84
Douglass, John...............24, 58
Douglass, Nathaniel (Dugles) (Nathan) (Nathenel)......58, 78
Douglass, Samuel (Saml.) (Dugles)..............49, 57, 78
Douglass, William.............. 57
Dove, Augustine (Auguston)..... 47
Dove, Francis................... 15
Dowden, Michael (Michl.) (Dowden)..................... 52
Dowden, Nathaniel.............. 52
Dowell, Martin (Dowel)......... 51
Dowling, James................. 60
Downer, E...................... 54
Downing, Andrew................ 58
Downing, Ezekiel (Ezekel)...... 58
Downing, James................. 17
Downing, John................17, 58
Downing, Robert................ 48
Downing, Thomas (Tomas)...... 58
Downing, Timothy.....32, 34, 48, 54
Downs, Jonathan................ 65
Downs, Richard................. 65
Downs, William................. 58
Doyle, Martin (Martain)......52, 58
Doyle, Thomas (Doyal).......... 47
Drake, Abraham................. 54
Drake, Cornelius............... 54
Drake, Ephriam..............40, 60
Drake, Isaac................... 54
Drake, James................... 60
Drake, John.................... 60
Drake, Joseph...............6 (List)
Drake, Margaret (Margret)...... 8
Drake, Nathaniel (Nath.).....40, 60
Drake, Philip.........24, 32, 34, 48, 54
Drake, Samuel.................. 60
Drake, William................. 60

Driggars, Julius (Julis).......... 74
Drinkard, Francis (drinkard).... 58
Dromgoole, James............... 74
Dryden, David.................. 53
Dryden, [—?].................. 64
Dryden, William (Wm.)......... 58
Dudley, Ambrose..............40, 60
Dudley, William..............60, 67
Dukes, Samuel.................. 58
Dulan, James (Dulen) (Duling).........24, 27, 60, 65, 66
Dumpard, Daniel................ 47
Dumpard, John (Dumferd)..9 (List)
Dumpard, Michael (Domppart) (Dompard)(Dompor)(Michal) (Mikel)..........47, 51, 59, 60, 65
Dunaway, Benjamin (Dunniway).........8, 9, 47, 60, 65
Dunaway, Thomas (Thos.).....47, 65
Dunaway, William............... 47
Duncan, Benjamin............... 27
Duncan, Charles..............40, 60
Duncan, Gabriel (Dunkin) (Gabril)...................... 64
Duncan, James (Duncken)..6, 49, 55, 62, 66, 78, 79, 84, 88
Duncan, John................... 88
Duncan, Joseph...............84, 88
Duncan, Nimrod..............26, 27
Duncan, Samuel (Duncom)...... 69
Dunlap, William (Wm.)......... 63
Dunn, Jacob....................104
Dunn, James.................... 60
Dunn, Jeremiah...............32, 34
Dunn, John..................9 (List)
Dunn, Joseph................... 58
Dunn, Richard (Richd.) (Dun) 27, 64
Dunn, Samuel................17, 58
Dunn, Vincent...............26, 27
Dunn, William.................. 60
Dupuy, Bartholemew (Dupey) (Bartw.)...................... 52
Dupuy, James............40, 43, 52, 60
Dupuy, James, Sr............... 43
Dupuy, James, Jr............... 51
Dupuy, Joel (Dupey)............ 52
Dupuy, John (Dupey).....43, 52, 60
Dupuy, John, Jr.............43, 52
Dupuy, Joseph..............43, 51, 52
Durbin, Christopher............ 47
Durbin, Joseph................. 47
Durrett, Richard.............48, 56
Dusker, John [Doster?]......... 84
Dust, David.................... 43
Duval, William................. 60
Dykes, Henry................... 84

List of Names

Eades, Robert.................... 66
Eades, Thomas (Thos.).....62, 66, 88
Eakin, John...................... 93
Eartywine, George............... 82
Easley, Stephen................. [—?]
Easley, Thomas.................. [—?]
Eastin, Achilles....55, 56, 66, 78, 84, 88
Eastin, Richard (Rich.).......... 68
Eaton, George................... 52
Eaton, Jonathan...............60, 65
Eaton, Joseph (Jos.)............ 52
Eaton, Levi..................... 52
Eckles, Robert (Eckels)......... 53
Edgar, David.................... 54
Edgar, John..................... 63
Edington, John.................. 40
Edmiston, David..............49, 66
Edmiston, Robert................ 66
Edmiston, Thomas................ 93
Edmundson, David................ 55
Edmundson, James (Edmondson). 58
Edrington, John................. 43
Edson, George (Eidson).......... 60
Edwards, Alexander...........32, 34
Edwards, Benjamin............... 69
Edwards, David, Jr.............. 56
Edwards, Elipha (Elepha)....... 60
Edwards, Frederick.............. 68
Edwards, Haden...........49, 56, 66
Edwards, Jacob................48, 54
Edwards, James.................. 48
Edwards, John (Jno.) 12, 42, 56, 60,
  66, 79, 90, 91
Edwards, Sanford................ 12
Edwards, Simon.................. 52
Egbert, David................... 52
Egner, Isaac.................... 82
Egner, John..................... 82
Elam, John (Elim)............... 74
Elam, Josiah.................43, 52
Elder, Andrew................... 58
Elder, William.................. 51
Elgin, Samuel (Saml.)........... 49
Elkin, Robert (Robt.).........47, 65
Elkin, Zachariah (Zachriah) 50, 65, 72
Ellet, Thomas [Elliot?].......... 65
Ellet, William (Wm.)............ 51
Elley, Henry.................52, 60
Elley, Thomas (Thos.)........... 52
Elliott, John (Jno.)..........52, 55
Elliott, Martin...............43, 63
Elliott, Robert (Robt.)......... 52
Elliott, Samuel (Eliot).......... 6
Elliott, Thomas..............60, 65
Elliott, William (Eliot) (Wm.)
  14, 49, 53, 55, 60, 65, 66, 84
Ellis, John Jr.................. 60

Ellis, Jezreel............15, 33, 49, 56
Ellis, Thomas (Thos.) (Elliss)..53, 54
Ellis, William Jr............... 43
Ellison, Benjamin (Benj.)........ 52
Ellison, John.................52, 60
Ellison, Joseph................. 27
Ellison, Thomas (Thos.)......... 52
Ellmaker, Edward................ 63
Embree, Jacob................... 72
Embree, Jesse (Embrey).......... 27
Embree, Joel (Embry)............ 27
Embree, John (Embry).........27, 58
Embree, Joshua.................. 58
Embree, Joseph (Embrey)27, 60, 65, 72
Embree, Tarlton (Embry) (Talton.)....................27, 64
Embree, William..............47, 65
Emerson, Ash (Emison.).......... 50
Emerson, Hugh (Emison).....26, 52
Emerson, Reuben..............60, 65
Enbow, Joseph................... 60
Enbow, Robert................... 36
Endamond, John.................. 53
English, Charles................ 15
English, John................... 15
English, Stephen................ 15
Erickson, Benjamin (Earockson)
  (Benj.)....................... 68
Ervin, Mary (Arvin)............. 38
Erwin, James.................... 48
Essvey, John.................... 60
Estes, Elisha (Eastes)......23, 46, 52
Estill, Benjamin................. 6
Estill, James.................... 8
Estill, Samuel (Samel)..8, 9, 27, 60, 64
Eubank, Willis (Killis)..47, 60, 65, 72
Evans, Alexander (Evins)......60, 65
Evans, Jacob (Evens)............ 28
Evans, Nathaniel (Evins)
  (Nathl.)..................23, 60, 93
Evans, Peter.................60, 65
Evans, Thomas................... 51
Evans, William (Wm.)............ 93
Ewing, Baker.................... 17
Ewing, Charles.................. 60
Ewing, George (Geo.)............ 60
Ewing, William (Eiliom.)........ 84

Fagin, David (fagin)............ 77
Fagin, William (Fegines)........ 78
Fair, Edmund (fair).......8, 9, 58, 63
Farbett, James.................. 51
Farlow, John (Forlow.).....28, 33, 49
Farlow, Robert (Forlow)......28, 49
Farmer, Abner................... 43
Farrar, Joseph R................ 60

[201]

List of Names

Farrel, Michael (Mickel)......... 15
Farrow, George................. 23
Faulkner, John (Faukner)....... 65
Faulkner, Joseph (Faulconer)
   (Fauconer)............53, 60, 93
Faulkner, Thomas (Thos.)....... 27
Fay, Jacob..................... 57
Felty, John.................... 68
Fenton, Bartholemew..........6, 64
Fenwick, John.................. 93
Ferguson, Abraham (Farguson).51, 67
Ferguson, Bryant........40, 53, 63, 65
Ferguson, Hugh................. 60
Ferguson, Isaac (Forgason)..... 54
Ferguson, James (Jas.) (Fargeson)
                    52, 60
Ferguson, Joseph............... 60
Ferguson, Josias............60, 65
Ferguson, Larkin (Farguson).... 52
Ferguson, Robert............... 52
Ferguson, Thomas (Thos.)....... 52
Ferguson, Thomas, Jr. (Thos.)... 52
Ferry, Jes..................... 60
Ficklin, John............24, 43, 53, 63
Ficklin, Thomas.............24, 52
Ficklin, William............... 52
Field, Henry (Fields)........51, 52
Fidler, Francis................ 63
Fight, Isham................... 77
Fight, Jacob................... 56
Filson, John................... 53
Finch, Josiah.................. 49
Finet, John.................... 53
Finley, David...............17, 58
Finley, George (Findly)......28, 33, 64
Finley, Isaac.................. 58
Finley, James.................. 68
Finley, John (Fendly)...58, 60, 64, 77
Finley, Samuel..............26, 58
Finney John [Finnie?]........... 52
Finney, Robert [Finnie?]........ 53
Finney, William (Wm.) [Finnie?]. 52
Fishback, Jacob.............42, 65
Fisher, Adam................... 58
Fisher, Barnett................ 58
Fisher, Elias...............26, 58
Fisher, James...............52, 60
Fisher, John................... 27
Fisher, Stephen................ 17
Fisher, Zachariah.............. 52
Fitch, Salathiel............77, 84
Fitzgerald, Batn. (Fitzgarld.)..52, 60
Fitzgerald, Daniel (Fitzjarrell)
   (Danl.)..................... 52
Fitzgerald, William (Wm.).....32, 34
Fitzwater, Thomas...........56, 60
Flanery, Elisha................ 74

Flannigan, Dominick............ 16
Flannigan, Lewis (Flanighan)..12, 24
Fleming, John (J) (Jo.)......11, 24, 48
Fleming, Ralph................. 17
Fleming, William (Willm.)...... 18
Fletcher, Thomas (Thos.) 48, 49, 77, 84
Fletcher, William...........27, 65
Flinn, Thomas (Thos.).......... 54
Flinn, William (Fline) (Flin) 49, 54, 56
Flournoy, David........43, 51, 52, 60
Flournoy, John (Jno.) (Flournia)
                  52, 54, 62
Flower, Thomas................. 58
Floyd, Benjamin................ 58
Floyd, Charles................. 48
Floyd, David................... 58
Floyd, George.................. 58
Floyd, John (Jn.)............18, 58
Floyd, Robert (Robt.) (Floid)... 54
Fluetey, John.................. 47
Foley, Henry................... 60
Foot, Thomas...............9 (List)
Forbis, George................. 60
Forbis, James................6, 36
Forbis, Joseph.............11, 60
Forbis, Robert (Forbas) (Robart). 69
Ford, John (Jno.).............. 62
Ford, Peter.................... 58
Ford, William (Willm.).......60, 65
Foreman, John.................. 74
Forker, Robert [Forbis?].......26, 27
Forkner, Alexander [Faulkner?].. 78
Forkner, John [Faulkner?]....... 78
Forkner, Thomas [Faulkner?].... 77
Forsythe, Phillip.............. 95
Forsythe, Robert............... 65
Forsythe, William.............. 78
Fort, Christopher............52, 60
Foster, Asa (A.).............60, 65
Foster, Henry.................. 60
Foster, Ichabod................ 54
Foster, Isaac.................. 16
Foster, Isaac, Jr.............. 68
Foster, Isaih.................. 27
Foster, James...............60, 65
Fowler, Benjamin............... 60
Fowler, John..............45, 61, 63
Fowler, Joseph................. 47
Fox, Arthur.................32, 33, 48
Fox, Richard (Richd.)......52, 54, 67
Frakes, Joseph................. 58
Frakes, Robert................. 66
Frame, John.................... 60
Francis, Evan.................. 46
Francis, William (Wm.)......... 46
Frankfort, William.............104
Franklin, Benjamin (Benj.)..... 47

[202]

List of Names

Franklin, James (franklin)..40, 43, 60
Franklin, John (franklin)......40, 60
Franklin, Stephen (franklin).....78
Franks, John M................46, 53
Frazel, Phillip....................15
Frazer, George (Geo.)..........51, 54
Frazer, James C. (Freser)...60, 78, 84
Frazer, Joseph (Jos.)...........43, 60
Frazer, Levi......................54
Frazer, Martin....................58
Frazer, Ralph.....................74
Frazer, William.............43, 46, 54
Freman, Samuel...................27
French, Henry....................16
French, James (Jas.).......47, 48, 64
French, Mo.......................72
French, Thomas...................11
French, William..................65
Frier, David (Fryer)...........60, 65
Frier, Donald (Donal)............26
Frier, James...................60, 65
Frier, Robert, (Robt.)............60
Friend, John.....................43
Froman, Jacob....................27
Frush, Francis [Brush?]..........58
Fry, Jacob.......................60
Frye, John.......................60
Fulton, Hugh.....................43
Fulton, James....................46
Fulton, Joseph...................53
Fulton, William..................60
Funk, Adam, Sr............26, 78, 84
Funk, Adam, Jr...................26
Furnish, James (Firnish).....28, 49
Furtad, Anthony (Anthy)......78, 84

Gaddy, Elijah....................27
Gaines, B........................45
Galbraith, Hugh..................27
Gale, Joseph...................45, 52
Gale, Josiah.....................60
Gale, Matthew.................24, 60
Gale, Robert (Robt.).............52
Galloway, James........52, 55, 66, 84
Galloway, John.............49, 54, 84
Galloway, William (Wm.) (Gelloway) (Gallway)49, 55, 56, 62, 66, 84
Gamble, David....................84
Gamble, William..................65
Gamblin, Andrew..................58
Gano, Daniel (Dan.)...........54, 60
Gano, Isaac E....................62
Gano, John S.....................54
Gardiner, J.......................6
Gardiner, Thomas.................68

Garnett, John..................52, 60
Garrard, James........42, 55, 56, 62
Garrard, William......28, 33, 49, 56
Garrett, William (Wm.)...........52
Garry, Henry.....................46
Gaskins, John..................66, 78
Gass, David.....................8, 27
Gass, John (Gess)......27, 60, 64, 65
Gates, David.....................58
Gates, Elijah....................58
Gates, William.................56, 74
Gatewood, Andrew.....43, 52, 60, 93
Gatewood, Augustine..............43
Gatewood, Hugh...................43
Gatewood, James................43, 60
Gatewood, John...................43
Gatewood, Peter................43, 60
Gatliff, Charles..................8
Gay, James.......................52
Gay, James, Jr...................77
Gay, Joseph......................56
Gayley, Benjamin.................58
Gayley, James (Galey)............58
Gayley, Samuel (Galey)...........58
Gayley, William (Galey)..........58
Geddis, James (Jas.).............43
Geklege, John....................69
George, Gabriel..........78, 84, 88
George, Nicholas (Nichs.)..27, 65, 72
George, Whitson................27, 72
George, William (Wm.)............54
Gerhart, Henry (Gherhart, Hennary)...........................74
Ghursin, Garret [?]..............88
Gibbs, Ezekiel...................69
Gibbs, Hugh....................27, 33
Gibbs, Jeremiah..................69
Gibbs, John......................27
Gibbs, Julius..................52, 60
Gibbs, Peter.....................74
Gibbs, Samuel....................27
Gibson, Francis..................52
Gibson, George (Geo.).........26, 27
Gibson, John...............26, 45, 52
Gibson, Paul...................26, 52
Gilbert, John....................74
Gilderess, Samuel................54
Gilkey, David....................60
Gilkison, William (Wm.)..........93
Gill, George.....................36
Gill, James M....................58
Gill, Samuel.....................69
Gilles, Thomas (Thos.)...........51
Gillet, Jonathan (Jona.).........88
Gilmore, James..........27, 58, 103
Gilmore, John....................63
Gilmore, Samuel (Saml.)........17, 93

List of Names

Gilpin, Israel..............66, 77, 84
Gilpin, James......................88
Gilpin, Joseph..................62, 88
Ginkins, John [Jenkins?].........77
Giraud, Andrew..................54
Girdle, James (Girdles).......32, 48
Girey, Richard.............9 (List)
Gist, Thomas (Thos.)............26
Gist, William (Wm.).............53
Glascock, James (Glasscock)32, 48, 49
Glascock, Nimrod................32
Glass, Thomas (Thos.)...........45
Glen, David......................6
Glencock, William................6
Gleson, David...................32
Gloove, Matthew (Mathew).......46
Glover, John....................60
Glover, Richard (glover)...16, 17, 74
Goff, Thomas.................78, 84
Goff, William...................60
Goforth, William................54
Goggin, John...............17, 23, 64
Golden, William...............27, 65
Goocy, John.....................65
Goocy, Thomas (Thos.)...........65
Gooden, Lewis...................52
Goodey, William (Wm.)..........54
Goodloe, Thomas..............60, 67
Goodloe, Vivion..............60, 65
Goodman, Ancel..........9 (List)
Goodman, Daniel..........9 (List)
Goodnight, David.............32, 34
Goodnight, John..............32, 34
Goodnight, Michael........32, 34, 60
Goodnight, Peter..........32, 34, 60
Goodwin, Jonas C................60
Goodwin, Patrick.............60, 78
Gordon, Ambrose.................58
Gordon, Evander (Evender).......6
Gordon, George (Geo.)..46, 60, 63, 76
Gordon, James................17, 23
Gordon, John (Gorden).....16, 60, 65
Gordon, Patrick (Gorden.)......58
Gordon, Robert (Gordan)........27
Gordon, Samuel (Gordane)
  (Saml.).................15, 27, 64
Gordon, William.................58
Gorham, Sandford................84
Gorham, Thomas (Goram).........93
Gorin, John..................43, 51
Gorten, Uriah (Garton).......24, 46
Goudy, Hugh..............62, 66, 77
Goudy, John.....................46
Goudy, Robert......62, 66, 77, 78, 84
Grace, Jeremiah (Jaremiah).....58
Grady, Jesse....................52
Graham, Arthur..................60

Graham, Benjamin................26
Graham, David (Grihem Daved)..54
Graham, Forgis...............60, 78
Graham, H.......................36
Graham, George..................53
Graham, James.........46, 58, 60, 65
Graham, John....................58
Graham, Joseph..................26
Grant, Adam.....................58
Grant, G........................66
Grant, Israel................52, 78
Grant, John(Jno.)45, 55, 56, 62, 66, 78, 84
Grant, Michael...............55, 78
Grant, Moses.................52, 57
Grant, William Sr. (Willm.).....52
Grant, William, Jr..............52
Graves, Benjamin (Benj.).......52
Graves, Bartlett.............52, 60
Graves, David...................40
Graves, George..................49
Graves, John..........45, 51, 60, 65
Graves, Leonard..............27, 58
Graves, Richard (Richd.).....40, 63
Graves, Thomas (Thos.).......52, 60
Graves, William..............40, 60
Gray, Archibald (Arcabold)......54
Gray, David...............40, 60, 63
Gray, Drakeford.................60
Gray, George..............52, 60, 65
Gray, James..........45, 47, 60, 65, 84
Gray, Jonathan..................52
Gray, John...............53, 54, 63, 93
Gray, Patrick (Patt.)........63, 93
Gray, Presley...................60
Gray, Richard...................53
Gray, Robert.................54, 60
Gray, Samuel.............63, 65, 72
Grayson, John (Jno.)...........46
Grayson, Richard (Grayston)....54
Grayson, William................66
Greathouse, John................40
Greathouse, William.............40
Green, Benjamin.................58
Green, George...................74
Green, Henry.................24, 58
Green, James....................74
Green, Jesse....................74
Green, John...........49, 58, 77, 78
Green, Robert...................58
Green, Samuel (Sammuel)........27
Green, Stephen...............43, 63
Green, Willis..........17, 36, 90, 91
Greenup, Christopher (Christ.)
                  39, 63, 83, 90, 91
Greer, Samuel...................60
Greeton, John [Grayson?]........27
Gregg, John (Gregs).......33, 36, 56

[204]

List of Names

Gregg, Joseph (Jos.).............. 77
Gregg, Matthew................ 82
Gregory, Samuel (Saml.).......... 52
Gridler, James.................... 34
Griffey, Gorden................... 65
Griffey, Ralph.................... 51
Griffey, Thomas (Tho.)............ 51
Griffing, Ebenezer................ 84
Griffing, Thomas.................. 84
Griffith, Thomas (Griffeth)....... 40
Griffith, William (Wm.).....23, 48, 55
Grisby, Nathaniel................. 60
Grimes, Benjamin..........58, 63, 65
Grimes, Carlos (Carlis)........... 65
Grimes, David..................... 87
Grimes, Esther.................... 54
Grimes, Harris.................... 65
Grimes, James..................... 60
Grimes, John (Jno.).........53, 54, 65
Grimes, Noble..................... 54
Grimes, Philip.............53, 60, 65
Grimes, Stephen............65, 67, 88
Grimes, Thomas.................48, 54
Grimsley, James................... 52
Grissum, William.................. 74
Groom, Zachariah (Zach.)......52, 60
Grubbs, Higgas.............27, 42, 46
Grundy, George.................... 60
Guffey, Alexander................. 74
Guil, James [?]................... 56
Guilliam, Benjamin (Gulliam) .52, 60
Guilliam, Edward.................. 60
Guilliam, Jeremiah (Gullian)...... 60
Guilliam, Robert (Robart)......... 60
Guilliam, John (Gullian).......46, 60
Guilliam, Starke.................. 58
Guilliam, William................. 58
Guiltner, Abraham................. 57
Gullen, Jeremiah (Jeremh.)........ 52
Gullen, John...................... 52
Gutridge, James................... 48
Gutridge, John (Jno.)....32, 34, 48, 54
Guttrey, Benjamin (Benj.).....43, 52
Gwinn, John (Gwenn.).............. 62
Gwinn, Thomas..................... 17

Hackett, Peter.................8, 27
Haff, Peter [Hoff?].............. 84
Haggard, Bartholemew (Barthw.) 60
Haggard, Bartlett.............65, 72
Haggard, James................60, 65
Haggard, Martin.................. 58
Haggard, Nathaniel (Hagard)
  (Nathl.)....................... 65
Haggin, John ....[—?]
Hakens, Samuel ....[—?]

Halbert, Isaac................... 60
Halbert, Isaih................... 65
Hale, Job........................ 58
Hale, John....................58, 60
Hall, Aaron...................60, 63
Hall, Alexander (Alexr.)....43, 53, 93
Hall, Caleb...............56, 63, 78
Hall, Case....................... 47
Hall, Clifton.................... 63
Hall, Edward..................... 45
Hall, Edward Senr................ 47
Hall, Horatio.............62, 66, 84
Hall, James............77, 78, 84, 88
Hall, John......27, 40, 47, 52, 58, 78, 84
Hall, Henry (Henery).......28, 33, 55
Hall, Leonard.................... 58
Hall, Moses...................... 63
Hall, Palmer (Parmer)......26, 27, 58
Hall, Richard.................... 47
Hall, Thomas (T.)..........63, 78, 84
Hall, William (Wm.) (W.)..27, 51,
        52, 57, 60, 68, 84, 88
Halleck, Benjamin (Hallack) ..57, 84
Halleck, Thomas (Hallack)....... 57
Halsey, Benjamin................. 51
Halsey, Joseph................... 54
Halsey, William...............60, 65
Ham, William..................... 27
Haman, Charles (Chas.)........... 63
Hamilton, Archibald (Archd.).... 93
Hamilton, Benjamin............... 93
Hamilton, David 93
Hamilton, Elias.................. 54
Hamilton, Galbreath (Gelbroath)
  (Gilbreath)..................77, 84
Hamilton, James..........36, 54, 78
Hamilton, John....26, 48, 55, 62, 66, 77
Hamilton, Joseph................. 77
Hamilton, Robert..............56, 84
Hamilton, Samuel (Hamelton)... 52
Hamilton, Thomas (Thom.) .55, 66, 84
Hamilton, William................ 93
Hammon, Edmund................26, 58
Hammon, James.................... 58
Hammon, John..................... 58
Hammon, Martin................... 6
Hampton, Andrew.................. 60
Hampton, David (Hamton)........ 72
Hampton, Michael................. 58
Hamson, William [Hanson?]....... 26
Hancock, George.................. 27
Hancock, Samuel (Saml.)......... 93
Hancock, Stephen (Hencock) 8, 27, 64
Hancock, William (Hankock)
  (Hanckok) (Hencock)....8, 9,
                    9 (List) 64
Hand, Edward (Edwd.)..........5, 8

List of Names

Hanks, Absalom............47, 60, 65
Hanks, B.........................47
Hanks, George............52, 60, 65
Hanks, John.....................55
Hanks, Peter....................47
Hanks, William.............60, 65
Hanley, George..................47
Hanley, John....................47
Hannan, James...................46
Hanningston, Bartholemew.......56
Harbeston, John................58
Hardage, William............60, 65
Hardesty, Benjamin (Hardisty)
  ....49, 78, 84
Hardesty, Henry (Hardisty)...78, 84
Hardin, Benjamin...............74
Hardin, John...................60
Hardin, Samuel.................74
Harding, John..................60
Hardwick, John............40, 72
Hardwick, John, Jr. (Jno.)......65
Hargis, John (Harges)......26, 27
Hargrove, Robert (Haregrove)...74
Harlan, Silas (Harland).......3, 16
Harlow, Claiborn (Clabon)......58
Harlow, Michael................58
Harlow, Samuel.................58
Harmon, Israel.................64
Harmon, Robert (Robt.).........52
Harmon, Sol....................23
Harmon, Thomas (Thos.).........52
Harp, Joseph................32, 34
Harper, Alexander..............60
Harper, James..................24
Harper, John..........27, 47, 58, 60
Harper, Peter (Harpar, Petar) 9,
  ....24, 47, 65
Harper, Samuel.................68
Harrard, Samuel................11
Harris, Andrew (Andw.) (Harriss) 64
Harris, Archibald (Harriss)....65
Harris, Christopher.........27, 64
Harris, James (Harriss)......11, 63
Harris, John...................46
Harris, Joshua.................72
Harris, Robert.................27
Harris, Sherwood...............43
Harris, Thomas (Harriss).......65
Harris, William (Wm.).....49, 65, 66
Harrison, Benjamin (Benj.).28, 55, 66
Harrison, Cuthbert.............60
Harrison, Garret (Harsin)......84
Harrison, George (Geo.)........60
Harrison, Hezekiah (Hez.)..51, 53, 93
Harrison, Hiram............40, 45
Harrison, John.................54
Harrison, Joseph (Jos.)........52

Harrison, Law..................56
Harrison, Nicholas (Nicolas)...28
Harrison, Robert...............78
Harrison, William..............74
Harrod, Edward (Herod)....9, 27, 47
Harrod, James..............3, 40, 63
Harrold, Moses.................60
Hart, George (Hartt) (Geo.)11, 58, 60
Hart, James....................60
Hart, John.....................78
Hart, Nicholas.................77
Hartford, Adam.................47
Harthis, Robert [Hargis?]......52
Hartman, Adam..............60, 65
Hartman, Peter.................26
Harvester, John................ 8
Harwood, Joseph (Jos.).........45
Hastings, William..............52
Hastlerigg, Charles
  (Hazelrigg)........12, 45, 47, 48, 65
Hastlerigg, James (Haselrigg)
  (Jas.) (Hazelrigg).........47, 65
Hastlerigg, James, Jr. (Hazelrigg) 65
Hastlerigg, John (Hazelrigg)...12
Hastlerigg, Joshua (Hazelrigg)
  (Jossway)...................12
Hastlerigg, William (Hazelrigg) 12, 65
Hathaway, David.............32, 34
Hathaway, Jonathan.............60
Hatton, Adam (Hatten)..........65
Hatton, John M.............51, 65
Hatton, Robert.............54, 60
Haughn, Jonas [Vaughn?]........65
Havens, Michael (Havns)........88
Hawkins, Gregory (Hewkins).....78
Hawkins, James..............52, 60
Hawkins, John (Jno.)....52, 60, 90, 91
Hawkins, John, Jr..............11
Hawkins, Philemon..............52
Hawkins, Samuel................56
Hawkes, Nicholas...............64
Hawle, Henry [Hall?]...........58
Hay, James.....................60
Hay, William (Will.)...........69
Hayden, Nehemiah...............78
Haydon, Abner..............43, 58
Haydon, Benjamin.........14, 24, 52
Haydon, Enoch (Hayden).........58
Haydon, James............24, 52, 60
Haydon, John.............40, 43, 51
Haydon, Noel (Hayden)..........58
Haydon, Samuel (Hadon)
  (Headon)..................27, 51
Haydon, Thomas (Thos.)......52, 60
Haydon, William (Wm.)
  (Haden)...........24, 51, 52, 60
Haydon, William, Jr..........52, 60

[206]

List of Names

Haynes, Richard (Rich.) 52
Hays, Hugh 36
Hays, James 36
Hays, John 36
Hays, Patrick 36
Hays, Richard (Hayse) 27
Hays, Robert 68
Hays, William (Wm.) 6, 12, 24, 40, 60, 63
Hazard, James (Hazyard) 47
Hazard, John (Jno.) 52
Hazard, Martin 43, 93
Hazard, Thomas (Thos.) 52
Hazard, William 52
Hazel, Daniel 26, 27, 58
Head, Benjamin (Benj.) 69
Headen, Samuel 51
Headdy, Thomas 54
Headley, George 54
Heath, Charles 53
Hedger, William (Wm.) 78
Heldridge, John 56
Helm, John 11
Helm, Meredith (M.) . 23, 32, 34, 48, 54
Helm, William 11, 12
Help, Henry 77
Henbine, Henry 6
Henderson, Alexander 93
Henderson, David 24
Henderson, James 60, 63, 64
Henderson, Joseph 58
Henderson, Nathaniel 7
Henderson, Robert 54, 64
Henderson, Samuel 6, 43, 49, 60
Henderson, William 12, 24
Hendrick, James 47
Hendricks, Absalom 28
Hendricks, George ...... 9 (List), 46
Hendricks, Peter [Henricks] 46
Hendricks, William (Hendrick) (Hendreck) 60, 65
Hendrickson, John 63
Heney, William (Wm.) 17
Henry, John 65, 78 84
Henry, Moses 60, 65
Henry, Robert (Henery) 64
Henry, Thomas (Thos.) 58
Henry, William (W.) (Wm.) 46, 52, 60, 66, 84
Hensley, William (Wm) 51, 52
Henson, Iran 6
Herndon, David 24
Herndon, Henry 24, 60
Herndon, Thomas (Thos). 23, 24, 52, 60
Herren, William (Wm.) 60
Herring, Langford 65
Herrinton, Abijah 74

Herrington, Bartholemew (Berthemelu) 28
Herrington, Charles 74
Herrington, Elisha 74
Herrington, William 74
Hestor, Jacob 84
Hiatt, Abner 58
Hiatt, Frederick 69
Hiatt, John 69
Hiatt, William (Haiet) 58, 69
Hicklin, Hugh 43
Hicklin, John 84
Hickman, Francis 60
Hickman, James 60, 65
Hickman, Joel 60, 65
Hickman, Prescott (Phascott) ... 52
Hickman, Richard (R.) 47, 60, 65
Hickman, Thomas 60
Hickman, Trammell 60
Hickman William (Wm.) . 40, 43, 52, 60
Hickman, William Jr 52
Hicks, Daniel (Hix) 58
Hicks, Harris 45
Hicks, John (Hikes) 49
Higbee, John 60
Higbee, Joseph (Higby) 53
Higbee, Peter (Higby) 53
Higgins, Gideon (Giddron.) (Gidn.) 26, 27, 58
Higgins, Henry (Hnry) (Higgin) 6, 16, 26, 27, 78
Higgins, Jesse (Higgin) 67
Higgins, Joel (Higgin) 60, 67
Higgins, John (Higgin) . 60, 65, 67, 84
Higgins, Richard (Richd.) . 60, 63, 65
Higgins, William (Willm.) (Higgin) (Heggen) 26, 67, 78
Hildreth, John (Hildridg) . 55, 66, 84
Hildreth, Joseph (Jos.) 78
Hildreth, Squier 56
Hill, Clemuel 58
Hill, Humphrey 84
Hill, Joseph 65
Hill, Joshua 24
Hill, Robert 15, 27, 64, 77
Hill, Russell (Russle) 55
Hill, Samuel 52
Hill, William (Wm.) 43, 58, 78
Hilman, Benjamin 77
Hilts, Frederick 58
Himans, Samuel (Saml.) 43
Hinck, Samuel 28
Hind, Samuel 55, 66
Hindman, Samuel 49, 66, 84
Hines, Richard .... 9 (List)
Hinkson, John 28

List of Names

Hinkson, Robert (Robt.)....27, 33, 48
Hinkson, Thomas..............33, 54
Hinkson, William............33, 84
Hitchcock, Obadiah (Hichcock),
   (Obediah)..................... 36
Hite, Abraham, Jr 2
Hite, Charles (Hites)............ 52
Hite, F......................... 16
Hite, Isaac..................... 3
Hite, J. (James) (Hites)...16, 17,
                    42, 52, 93
Hite, Martin.................... 27
Hite, Thomas (Hiet)............. 27
Hitt, Joel...................60, 93
Hitt, Joseph (Josef)............. 69
Hizer, Christopher (Hiser)
   (Christ)....................... 60
Hobbs, John..................... 60
Hoden, Thomas (Thos.)........... 27
Hodges, Jesse (Hodgis) .8, 9, 27, 60, 65
Hoff, Paul...................... 40
Hoffman, Valentine (Hofman)
   (Valintine)..................... 60
Hogan, James.................... 29
Hogan, John..............55, 56, 66
Hogan, Philip (hogan) 27
Hogan, Richard (Hoagans)....... 6
Hogan, Thomas (Hogans)........ 65
Hogan, William (Hogon).......... 6
Hoge, David..................... 28
Hoge, Michael (Michl.).....28, 56, 78
Hogg, Aaron (Aron).............. 26
Holbert, Thomas................. 60
Holder, Francis..........47, 60, 65, 72
Holder, John..........6, 8, 24, 47, 51
Holder, Luke.................... 47
Hole, John...................... 53
Holland, Alexander............... 27
Holland, Henry (Henery) (Hol-
   and)........................... 46
Holley, Francis (Frans.).27, 47, 60, 65
Holley, John (Hollay)..9 (List) 27, 47
Holliday, Stephen (Holladay)..60, 65
Holliday, William................ 56
Holloway, James........35, 51, 60, 63
Holman, Daniel (Holeman)...... 52
Holman, Edward (Holeman)..... 52
Holman, Edward Jr. (Holeman)
   (Edwd.)....................43, 52
Holman, George (Holeman)...... 52
Holman, Henry (Holeman)....... 52
Holman, Nicholas (Holeman).... 52
Holms, John..................60, 65
Holsdon, Jacob.................. 16
Holway, Clayton (Halway) (Cla-
   ton).......................... 58
Homan, Ebenezer.........57, 58, 84
Hone, Jonah..................... 65

Honey, George................... 58
Honey, John..................56, 77
Honsley, William................ 60
Hood, Andrew Sr. (Andw.)....... 78
Hood, Luppin.................... 78
Hood, William................... 74
Hooge, John [Hoge?]............. 77
Hook, John...................... 84
Hope, Richard................... 27
Hopkins, Eldridge (Eldrege)..... 58
Hopkins, Francis................ 58
Horn, Aaron..................... 27
Horn, Christopher............27, 65
Horn, Elizabeth................. 8
Horn, Matthias.................. 27
Hornback, Abraham..........78, 84
Hornback, Jacob................. 78
Hornback, James................. 78
Hornback, John...............78, 84
Hornback, Samuel................ 84
Hornback, Simon.............78, 84
Horne, William (Willm.)......... 27
Hoskins, William................ 27
Hostitler, John.................. 74
Hougham, Moses.............48, 54
Houghton, Aaron................. 54
House, Adam.................78, 84
House, John..................... 58
Houston, John [Huston?]...66, 78, 88
Howard, Charles................. 26
Howard, Clement................. 54
Howard, Elihu................... 74
Howard, John.................... 74
Howard, Joshua.................. 77
Howard, Leroy................... 52
Howard, Philip...............77, 84
Howard, Samuel.................. 60
Howard, William (Wm.).......... 64
Howe, Thomas (Hoo)............. 54
Howes, Aaron (Hoes)............. 27
Hoy, Tm........................ 84
Huckstoft, John (Jno.).......... 53
Hudgens, Daniel................. 36
Huffman, John (Hufman)......... 58
Huffstudler, John................ 74
Hughes, David (Huse)...55, 65, 78, 84
Hughes, James................... 93
Hughes, G....................... 58
Hughes, John (Jno.)32, 34, 56, 63, 83, 93
Hughes, Ralph (Hughs).......... 56
Hughes, Spencer (Hewes)........ 32
Hughes, Thomas (Hughs)..11, 56,
                    60, 62, 66
Hughes, William (Wm.)..32, 34, 60, 82
Hulse, Daniel................... 60
Humble, Michael (Michl.).....26, 58
Humble, Noah................... 84
Hume, George (Geo.)..........53, 60

List of Names

Hume, Joel.................. 63
Hummer, Robert............. 63
Humphrey, Merry............ 52
Humphrey, William.......... 60
Hunt, John.................. 67
Hunt, Thomas............... 26
Hunter, Charles..........12, 52
Hunter, Henry............12, 24
Hunter, Jacob............12, 24
Hunter, John (Huntor).....46, 74
Hunter, Peter............... 12
Hurst, Henry (Henery)...... 93
Hurst, John................. 93
Hurst, Michael.............. 93
Hurt, James................. 82
Huston, Archibald (Archd.) (A.)58, 76
Huston, James............27, 65
Huston, John................ 12
Huston, Samuel.............. 27
Huston, Stephen............103
Huston, William (Wm.)....... 53
Hutcheson, James (Hutchison)... 56
Hutcheson, John..........52, 78
Hutcheson, Peter (Hutchison).28, 33, 49, 55, 56
Hutcheson, John Jr.......... 52
Hutcheson, Robert (Robard)..... 87
Hutcheson, William........55, 88
Hutson, Rawley [Hudson?]...... 52
Hutson, Skinner............. 58
Hutton, Hendrick..........58, 60
Hutton, James.............58, 60
Hutton, Joseph............58, 60
Hutton, Samuel.............. 58
Hynes, Andrew (Andw.) [Hines?]. 12
Hynes, William R. (Wm.)...... 60

Ignew, James [Agnew?]....... 82
Indicut, Aaron [Endicott?].... 52
Indicut, Joseph............. 52
Indicut, Moses.............. 52
Iles, Nicholas.............. 84
Iles, Thomas................ 78
Ingles, James (Ingeles)....78, 84
Ingram, Samuel.............. 6
Ingram, Uria................ 63
Innes, Henry (Harry) 25, 42, 50, 59, 83
Ireland, David...........78, 84
Ireland, James........66, 77, 84
Irvine, Abraham (Irvin)..... 69
Irvine, Christopher....17, 23, 24, 27
Irvine, James (J) (Irvin) (Erwin) 83, 93
Irvine, William (Irwin) (Will.).42, 62, 64, 66
Isrig, Michael.............. 84

Jacks, John................. 52
Jackman, John............58, 69
Jackson, Burwell............ 23
Jackson, Congreve (Congrave).47, 72
Jackson, Ephraim (Ephrim)..... 58
Jackson, John.........27, 43, 60
Jackson, Joseph.........9 (List)
Jackson, Josiah............. 47
Jackson, William............ 62
Jacoby, Henry (Jecoby) (Henery) 78
Jacoby, Ralph (Jecoby)...... 84
James, Daniel.............52, 60
James, Abraham.............. 11
Jameson, Andrew (Andw.)..16, 26, 58
Jameson, George............. 60
Jameson, James (Jas.).....45, 93
Jameson, John..........16, 54, 93
Jameson, Robert............. 26
Jameson, Samuel............. 26
Jameson, Thomas............. 15
Jamison, David............43, 63
Jamison, John.............53, 84
Jamison, William (Wm.)...... 43
January, Ephraim............ 46
January, James.......14, 22, 43, 46
January, John.............46, 52
January, Peter (Petter)..... 14
January, Samuel............. 46
January, Thomas (Thos.)...46, 63
Jarvis, Edward.............. 74
Jefferies, Moses............ 60
Jefferies, Thomas (Jefferys).... 58
Jefferies, William (Wm.).... 58
Jefferson, George (Geffison).... 74
Jenkins, Richard............ 65
Jenkins, Samuel (Jinkins) (Saml.) 57
Jenkins, William........52, 60, 65
Jenners, John............... 27
Jennings, Jonathan.......... 58
Jockars, Charles............ 8
John, Thomas................ 54
Johnson, Andrew.9 (List) 24, 43, 51, 52
Johnson, Cave.........24, 51, 52
Johnson, Isaac.............. 52
Johnson, James.............. 66
Johnson, John (Jonson)....27, 47, 49, 52, 54, 72, 77
Johnson, Jonathan........... 82
Johnson, Joseph (Jos.)...... 52
Johnson, Randolph........... 84
Johnson, Robert 24, 45, 51, 52, 55, 60, 66
Johnson, Samuel (Saml.)...24, 23, 43
Johnson, Thomas............. 84
Johnson, William.........32, 34, 69
Johnston, Alexander......... 60
Johnston, Benjamin [B]...... 68
Johnston, Ga. J............. 68

List of Names

Johnston, Jacob............9 (List)
Johnston, James................. 63
Johnston, John........45, 56, 84
Johnston, Martin (Jonston)....60, 65
Johnston, Robert (Robt.)..12, 60, 67, 84, 90, 91
Johnston, Samuel (Sam)......... 40
Johnston, Thomas............... 78
Johnston, William (Wm.) (Will.)60, 68
Jolly, David.................... 52
Jolly, Jared.................... 77
Jones, Aaron....................104
Jones, Benjamin Sr. (Benj.)...52, 58
Jones, Benjamin Jr. (Benj.)...... 52
Jones, Charles................. 64
Jones, Daniel...................104
Jones, David.................6, 58
Jones, Francis (Fras.).........65, 76
Jones, Frederick (Frd.).......... 60
Jones, James (Jas.).........52, 58, 65
Jones, John.....27, 52, 58, 60, 65, 74, 84
Jones, John Gabriel............. 3
Jones, John Jr..................104
Jones, Josua.................60, 104
Jones, Roger................... 65
Jones, Samuel Paul............. 60
Jones, Stephen................. 74
Jones, Thomas.....52, 60, 62, 66, 88
Jones, Thomas Jr............... 88
Jones, Uriah................... 82
Jones, William (Wm.).....23, 27, 49, 60, 67, 77
Jordan, Patrick................. 26
Joyes, Patrick................68, 83
Judy, John..................... 60

Kage, August................... 68
Kamper, Henry.................. 67
Kamper, John................... 58
Kamper, Reuben..............60, 67
Kamper, William.............60, 67
Kautzman, Michael............78, 84
Kavanaugh, Charles........17, 27, 64
Kavanaugh, Charles Jr.......... 27
Kavanaugh, William..........27, 36
Kay, James..................... 54
Kay, John..................52, 60, 93
Keen, Jonathan................. 93
Keenan, Patrick (Pattk.)......58, 78
Kegans, John................... 60
Kellar, Isaac................... 52
Kellar, John....................104
Kelly, Beal (Kelley)............. 72
Kelly, Benjamin............9 (List)
Kelly, Emanuel................. 24
Kelly, James................... 55
Kelly, John (Kelley) (Kellie).8, 9, 27, 47
Kelly, Joseph (Kelley)..9 (List) 60
Kelly, Samuel................24, 51
Kelly, Stephen (Kelley)......... 47
Kelly, William................. 52
Kelsoe, Andrew................. 58
Kelsoe, Robert (Robt.).......... 58
Kendall, Joseph.........28, 32, 55, 77
Kendall, William............... 60
Kennedy, Andrew.............27, 64
Kennedy, James (Caneday) (Kaneddy)................77, 78
Kennedy, John...........6, 27, 77
Kennedy, Joseph............6, 27
Kennedy, Peter (Kanaday)...... 77
Kennedy, Thomas (Thos.).24, 27, 49, 62, 64, 78
Kennedy, William (Wm.).......23, 25
Kenton, Eran [Aaron?]......... 6
Kenton, John..............32, 34, 48
Kenton, Simon (Kinton) (Centon)................17, 32, 34, 48
Kerlin, Thomas................. 87
Kerns, John.................... 33
Kerns, William..............28, 33
Kerr, David.................... 6
Kersey, John (Jno.) [Searcy?].. 60
Ketcham, Jonathan......6, 9 (List)
Kibbey, Ephraim (Ephm.)....... 54
Kidwell, Jonathan (Kidwel)..... 27
Kilgore, John.................. 56
Killogh, Allan.................. 84
Kilpatrick, Thomas (Thos.)...... 62
Kimbrough, Samuel (Sammel) (Sam)....................55, 56
Kimbrough, William (Wm.)..... 82
Kindred, Edward.............65, 72
Kindred, William............... 72
King, Aaron (Aron)...........[—?]
King, John (Jno. E)......6, 26, 36, 43
King, George (Geo.)..........6, 60
King, Valentine (Vale.).......12, 26
Kinkead, Andrew (Andw.).17, 27, 36, 56, 62, 66, 84
Kinkead, David..............43, 77
Kinkead, Hopson................ 58
Kinkead, James (Kinkiad)....... 27
Kinkead, John..............53, 58, 60
Kinkead, Samuel (Kinkade)..... 56
Kinkead, William (Kinkaid) (Wm.)....................... 27
Kinnett, Chester............... 60
Kinney, Clement (Kiney) (Clemment.)..................... 60
Kinney, James (Jas.).......11, 49, 53, 60, 62, 84

[210]

List of Names

Kinney, John M............53, 65
Kirby, Samuel (Saml.)............68
Kirchevall, John.................63
Kirke, Vincent..........57, 58, 78, 84
Kirkham, Samuel.........43, 51, 52
Kirkman, Robert.................36
Kirkpatrick, Elijah..............66
Kirkpatrick, George..............28
Kirkpatrick, Hugh................64
Kirkpatrick, John............66, 84
Kirkpatrick, Joseph..........77, 88
Kirkpatrick, Thomas......66, 77, 78
Kiser, Christopher (Keiser)....53, 93
Kiser, Jacob (Kieser).......28, 53, 60
Kiser, John.................28, 53
Kiser, Phillip (Ciser)..........78, 84
Kisley, Joseph...................78
Knight, James....................40
Knightley, John..............60, 65
Knox, David (Davd.) (D.)....43, 46, 53, 60
Knox, James..................17, 40
Knox, John......................84
Knox, William (Willem).......60, 65
Kringle, James..................93
Kyle, Joseph....................53

Lacassange, Nl...................68
Lacfaild, Excell (Execell).......58
Lamar, Benjamin..................74
Lamar, Samuel....................74
Lamb, William (Wm.) (Lamm) 32, 34, 48, 54, 58
Lamwalt, Jacob...................88
Lancaster, John (Jno.)...........60
Lance, George....................63
Lander, Charles..............60, 65
Lander, Jacob....................65
Lane, Ellis (Elis)...............84
Lane, Samuel (Sammel)............77
Lane, Edmund (Lanes) (Edmond) 52
Lang, Thomas.....................60
Langford, Stephen................15
Langstone, Jacob..........56, 77, 78
Langstone, John..................77
Lanier, Henry................62, 66
Lanier, Isham................55, 66
Lanier, James (Jas.)..66, 77, 78, 79, 88
Langwait, Thomas (Thos.).........84
Lapsley, Samuel (Sam).........26, 27
Larsh, Charles (Chas.)...........60
Laughlin, William............62, 66
Lause, Jeremiah..................64
Lawrence, John (Larrance).......26
Lawrence, James..................58
Lawson, Aaron....................58

Lawson, Nicholas (Lason).........63
Lawson, Ro.......................83
Lawson, William (Wm.)............58
Layson, John...28, 49, 55, 62, 66, 78, 88
Layson, Robert..........28, 49, 66, 78
Layson, William..................78
Lea, Francis W.............24, 52, 60
Leach, David (Leitch)............63
Leach, James (Leatch)............58
Leary, Daniel (Lary)..........78, 84
Leary, Dennis....................78
Leary, William (Willm.)..........76
Lease, James.....................52
Lease, William...................52
Le Cont, Charles (Lacount).......52
Lecky, Nathaniel (Nathl.)........78
Ledgerwood, James........12, 27, 65
Ledgerwood, William Sr.......65, 78
Lee, Conrad (Lea) (Coonrad)..51, 52
Lee, Henry...........32, 34, 42, 46, 48
Lee, James (Jas.)................52
Lee, Peter...............32, 48, 54
Lee, William..............58, 60, 65
Leforge, Abraham....32, 34, 48, 54, 56
Legget, James (Ligget).......43, 52
Legget, John.....................36
Legon, Charles...................52
Lemare, Gally....................74
Lemasters, Richard...............77
Letcher, Joseph..................78
Levie, Isaac.....................60
Lewis, Alexander.................58
Lewis, Francis...................40
Lewis, George (Geo.).34, 45, 46, 62, 67
Lewis, John (Jno.)............54, 58
Lewis, Joseph....................42
Lewis, Nicholas..................53
Lewis, Samuel (Sammel)...........77
Lewis, Thomas (Thos.)...40, 45, 58, 60
Lewis, William..........16, 32, 34, 40, 52, 53, 58, 63, 93
Lighter, John (Jno.).............57
Lighter, John Jr.................57
Lilly, Anniger...................65
Lincoln, George (Lincn)....9 (List)
Lincoln, Hananiah................24
Lindsay, Anthony.................52
Lindsay, Arthur..................16
Lindsay, David...................56
Lindsay, John (Lindsey)..........52
Lindsay, Joseph (Jos.).......14, 15
Lindsay, Michael (Linsey) (Michel)................60
Lindsay, Nicholas.........43, 52, 60
Lindsay, Vachl. (Lindzey)........52
Lindsay, William (Wm.).......51, 63
Linet, John 53

List of Names

Linkhorn, Mordecai (Mordica)... 60
Linn, John (Lyn)..........58, 85, 93
Linn, Joseph.................... 36
Linn, Patrick................... 54
Linn, William................... 11
Linville, Morgan................ 78
Lips, Jacob..................... 52
Lisle, Henry............60, 65, 72
Lisle, John (Lyle).........60, 65, 72
Liter, John..................... 84
Liter, John Jr.................. 60
Liter, Lewis (Lues)............. 84
Little, James (Jas.) (Littel) (Littell).....24, 27, 49, 55, 56, 78, 79, 88
Little, John (Litle)..........43, 93
Little, William [Lytle?]........ 53
Livingston, Thomas.............. 58
Lizenby, William (Wm.).......43, 52
Lloyd, Richard.................. 54
Lock, Joseph.................... 58
Lockett, James.................. 60
Logan, Archibald (Archibal)..... 63
Logan, Benjamin...6, 16, 17, 18, 25, 42
Logan, David................60, 93
Logan, George................... 52
Logan, John......17, 32, 34, 36, 42, 54
Logan, Nathaniel (Nathl.)....... 53
Logan, Samuel (Saml.).........52, 54
Logan, William (Wm.).....28, 32, 33, 34, 36, 52
Loggins, Samuel................. 74
Long, George.............26, 27, 78
Long, Jacob..................... 27
Long, John........24, 26, 27, 43, 60
Longley, Thomas................. 54
Longstreet, Jonas............... 64
Loper, Jacob.................... 74
Lorin, John..................... 27
Lott, John...................51, 52
Lott, William (Wm.)............. 52
Loughead, David................. 93
Love, Isaac..................... 60
Love, John...................49, 77
Love, Thomas.................... 77
Love, William (Wm.).....6, 52, 78, 84
Loveless, John (Lovlis).......54, 87
Low, Aquilla (Aquilliah)........ 74
Lowe, Edward.................... 43
Lowry, James.................49, 53
Lowry, John..................40, 58
Lowry, Samuel................... 49
Lowry, Stephen.................. 52
Luckie, John.................60, 84
Luckie, Robert.................. 84
Luless, John.................... 48
Luper, George................... 36
Luper, Hugh..................... 36

Lusk, Hugh...................... 58
Lusk, Samuel.................40, 63
Luttrell, Thomas................. 6
Lynam, Andrew...............26, 58
Lynch, David (Lintch)........... 27
Lynch, William.................. 58
Lyne, Edmund.............32, 48, 54
Lyne, James..................... 54
Lyne, Henry..................... 78
Lyon, Hezekiah (Essekiah)....... 55
Lyon, Humphrey...............49, 66
Lyon, John........27, 28, 32, 33, 49, 55, 56, 66, 78, 84
Lyon, John Jr................... 55
Lyon, Joseph.................... 27
Lyon, Peter Jr.................. 58
Lyon, Samuel......27, 28, 33, 49, 55, 56, 62, 66, 84, 88
Lytle, William...............22, 93

Machan, Thomas.................. 56
Machir, John.................... 54
Mack, Daniel.................... 27
Mack, John (Jno.)............... 52
Mack, Randall................... 60
Mack, Thomas (Meck)............. 93
Mack, William................... 33
Mackey, Robert.............. [—?]
Maddox, Wilson (Madox)......32, 34
Madison, Gabriel..........16, 17, 42
Madison, George................. 63
Magill, Alexander............... 78
Magill, David................65, 78
Magill, James................60, 65
Magill, John (Jno.)..........63, 78
Magill, William................. 78
Mahan, Arthur................... 60
Major, Francis (Frans.)......... 84
Major, James.................... 52
Major, John.............52, 78, 84
Major, Thomas (Thos.)........... 52
Mallory, William................ 67
Malon, Michael (Micheal)........ 78
Malster, John................... 28
Man, William (Mand)............. 69
Manian, Thomas J................ 27
Mankins, James............9 (List)
Manley, James................... 54
Mann, Francis (Frances)......... 82
Manuel, George.................. 60
Marble, Earl.............32, 34, 48
Marble, Abner............32, 34, 48
Marble, Ezra.............32, 34, 48
Marks, Thomas (Thos.)........... 77
Marks, William.................. 60
Marksberry, John................ 58

List of Names

Marksberry, Samuel Jr.......... 58
Marsh, John................28, 49
Marsh, William (Willim)......... 28
Marshall, Alexander..........78, 93
Marshall, Archibald...........78, 84
Marshall, George (Marshel)....48, 54
Marshall, Henry.....45, 46, 53, 60, 76
Marshal, James................. 63
Marshall, John (J.) (Marshal).32, 34, 43, 48, 52, 54, 61
Marshall, Joseph............... 47
Marshall, Robert (Marshel)...48, 54, 60, 65
Marshall, Thomas Sr. (Thos.) (T.) 17, 52, 61
Marshall, Thomas Jr. (Thos.)..45, 46, 52
Marshall, William..........11, 58, 63
Martin, Abner.............36, 58
Martin, Benjamin (Benj.)......36, 58
Martin, David..............26, 27, 33
Martin, Henry.............43, 47
Martin, Hugh..............14, 24, 78
Martin, James (Marton)...27, 32, 51, 52, 63, 93
Martin, James Jr............... 47
Martin, John (Martain) (Mearten)..8, 12, 14, 17, 47, 52, 54, 60, 63, 65, 72, 84
Martin, Joseph (Jos.)..........17, 97
Martin, Lindsay (Lindza)........ 58
Martin, Orson.................. 72
Martin, Reuben (Rubin).......... 58
Martin, Richard................ 43
Martin, Samuel..............14, 51
Martin, William (Wm.) (Martan) (Marton)...14, 27, 47, 52, 65, 72, 93
Martzgar, Nicholas.............. 6
Mason, Dorsey.................. 74
Mason, Isaac................... 74
Mason, James.............27, 60, 67
Mason, John (Meson).40, 60, 67, 74, 76
Mason, Michiah (Micijah)....... 60
Mason, Peter................... 51
Mason, Samuel.................. 74
Mason, Thomas...............74, 93
Massie, David.................. 27
Massie, Harris................. 27
Massie, Nathaniel Jr. (Nathl.) 45, 60, 63
Masten, John................... 43
Masten, Peter (Mastin).......51, 63
Masterson, James (Jas.).......24, 53
Masterson, John..............32, 34
Masterson, Moses............... 32
Masterson, Richard...........45, 51
Masterson, Zachariah......32, 34, 52

Matan, John.................... 6
Matan, Lewis [Meytin].......... 43
Mathers, Samuel (Meathers)..... 84
Mathers, Thomas (Tomas)....... 78
Mathers, William (Mcathers)..66, 78
Matland, John.................. 36
Matson, Henry.................. 78
Matson, James...............78, 84
Matson, James Jr............78, 84
Mattox, Rolf (Mattex).......... 58
Matthews, William (Mathews)... 56
Mattingly, Basil (Basel)......... 60
Mattingly, John................ 60
Mauldin, Ambrose............... 74
Mauldin, James................. 74
Mauldin, West.................. 74
Maupin, G...................... 63
Maupin, James (Moppin)........ 62
Maurice, Maurice............... 77
Mavrots, Thomas................ 56
Maxwell, George...........40, 43, 51
Maxwell, John............3, 14, 27, 60
Maxwell, Thomas (Thos.)......40, 62
Maxwell, William............... 40
May, Jesse..................... 15
May, John...................... 18
May, William................... 60
Mayfield, Isaac................ 58
Mayfield, John................. 60
Mayhall, Timothy............... 54
Meeker, Abner.................. 78
Meeker, Joseph................. 54
Meekins, John (Mekins) (Mikkins).................17, 46, 53
Mefford, George..............32, 48
Megg, Rolistin................. 60
Menefee, Jarret (Jarrot)........ 56
Menefee, Jonas................. 6
Menefee, William............... 6
Meriwether, Nicholas..........11, 12
Merritt, Joseph (Merit)......... 27
Merritt, Stephen (Merit)........ 27
Merry, Thomas (Thos.).....65, 67, 72
Mershom, Titus................. 60
Metcalfe, John................. 52
Mickey, Daniel..............28, 33
Middleton, John (Midlton).....40, 60
Migbee, John [Higbee?].......... 76
Mikel, George.................. 23
Miles, Henry................... 60
Miles, Isaac................52, 60
Miles, John............24, 26, 58, 60
Milholland, John (Jno.).......... 33
Millar, Charles................ 27
Millar, Jacob.................. 27
Millar, John Conrad (Miller) (Coonrad)................60, 65

[213]

List of Names

Miller, Abraham.................. 69
Miller, Andrew............... 27, 74
Miller, Charles.................. 60
Miller, Ebenezer.............. 26, 27
Miller, George............... 60, 65
Miller, Henry (Henery).......... 27
Miller, James................... 93
Miller, John................ 66, 84
Miller, Thomas (Thos.).......... 54
Miller, William (Wm.)........... 27
Million, John................... 27
Mills, Aaron.................... 78
Mills, Edward............ 32, 34, 48
Mills, Jacob.................... 54
Mills, James (Milles)........ 74, 78
Mills, Jesse (Jessy)............ 52
Mills, Moses.................... 78
Mills, Thomas............ 32, 34, 54
Milner, Isaac................... 93
Miner, John............... 58, 60, 65
Miner, Thomas............... 60, 65
Minter, Joseph.................. 60
Mira, Michael............... 9 (List)
Miranda, Samuel (Meranda)...... 78
Misbeth, James................[—?]
Mitcham, Dudley[Meatcham?] 43, 52
Mitchell, Alexander (Mitchel)
   (Alex.)...................... 78
Mitchell, David.............. 14, 84
Mitchell, Edward................ 52
Mitchell, Elijah............. 66, 84
Mitchell, Ignatius.............. 41
Mitchell, Isaac.......... 55, 66, 84
Mitchell, James (Jas.) (Mitchel). 84
Mitchell, John (Jno.) (Mitchel). 52, 77
Mitchell, Joseph (Jos.)...... 49, 84
Mitchell, Moses (Mitchel) .. 33, 60, 65
Mitchell, Thomas (Thos.) (Mitch-
   el)............. 40, 43, 52, 60, 77, 84
Mitchell, Wilson (Mitchel)....... 84
Mitchell, William (Willm.). 49, 51,
                              55, 66, 84
Mitchell, William Jr. (Mitchel).. 78
Moat, Alexander More........... 88
Moberley, Edward............ 58, 69
Moberley, John.................. 64
Moffett, George (Moffet.)....... 52
Moffett, John................... 52
Moffett, Robert (Robt.).... 51, 52, 60
Moffett, Thomas................. 72
Moffett, William (Wm.) (Moffot)
                              60, 65, 72
Monroe, Alexander (Alexr.)...... 60
Montgomery, James............... 36
Montgomery, John............ 43, 69
Montgomery, Joseph (Jos.)...... 60
Montgomery, Robert.............. 36
Montgomery, Thomas.............. 60
Montgomery, William (Wm.)..17,
                          36, 42, 60, 62, 93
Montgomery, William Jr. (Wm.)17, 36
Moody, Henry.................... 69
Moon, Thomas.................... 78
Mooney, Samuel.................. 54
Moore, Arthur................... 64
Moore, Benjamin (Benj.)......... 52
Moore, Charles............... 60, 65
Moore, David.................... 78
Moore, Edward (More)............ 36
Moore, Elias.................... 60
Moore, George................... 65
Moore, Henry................. 60, 65
Moore, James (More)...... 53, 60, 65
Moore, John (Moor) (Jno.)...6, 27,
                              52, 58, 78
Moore, Joseph (Jos.)...... 6, 43, 58, 93
Moore, Joseph, Sr............... 15
Moore, Luke (Look).............. 64
Moore, Martin................... 15
Moore, Moses.................... 60
Moore, Peter...... 43, 55, 56, 66, 78, 84
Moore, Philip (More).......... 78, 84
Moore, Quintin.................. 51
Moore, Robert (Moor) 27, 43, 60, 65, 78
Moore, Samuel (Saml.) (Moor)... 60
Moore, Shadrach.............. 52, 58
Moore, Thomas (Thos.)..26, 57,
                              58, 60, 78
Moore, Simeon................... 58
Moore, William Sr........... 15, 17, 43
                          53, 60, 64, 65, 66, 88
Moore, William Jr............ 15, 88
Morehead, John.................. 60
Morehead, Samuel (Morehed).. 66, 84
Morel, Basil (Bazel)............ 27
Morey, James.................... 60
Morgan, Charles (Chas.) 58, 60, 65, 72
Morgan, David................... 68
Morgan, Evan.................... 60
Morgan, Jeremiah................ 65
Morgan, John........ 12, 47, 60, 65, 78
Morgan, John Sr................. 47
Morgan, Mordecai (Mordeceia)
   (Mordachey)............ 12, 47, 65
Morgan, Morgan.................. 43
Morgan, Samuel (Morgen) (Sam-
   mel)......................... 60
Morgan, William................. 65
Morin, James (Morir)...... 56, 62, 66
Morin, John..................... 84
Morrell, Joseph (Yoseph)........ 54
Morris, David................... 54

[214]

List of Names

Morris, Kellis 47
Morris, John [Moris] 33, 48, 77, 78
Morris, James 74
Morris, Robert (Morriss) 54
Morris, Thomas (Thos.) 49, 56, 66, 84
Morris, William (Wm.) 55, 66, 84
Morrison, Hugh 24
Morrison, John (Morrason) .. 12, 14, 23, 40, 43, 45, 51, 53
Morrow, James 14, 24, 47, 60
Morton, Andrew (Andw.) (Mortens) 60
Morton, Benjamin 24
Morton, David 60, 65
Morton, Jeremiah 52
Morton, John (Mortin) .. 9 (List) 20, 27, 47, 51, 52
Morton, Jonathan 47, 60, 65
Morton, Thomas (Thos.) .. 24, 52, 63
Morton, William (Will.) (Wm.) .. 27, 32, 34, 52, 67, 68
Mosely, Jacob (Moely) (Jacop) .. 58
Mosely, Thomas (Thos.) (Moseley) 60, 74
Moseby, Abraham (Abram.) ... 52, 58
Moseby, Daniel (Mosby) ... 49, 57, 78
Mosby, David 45
Mosby, Isaac 52
Mosby, John 17
Mosby, Robert (Robt.) 42
Moss, Frederick (Fredk.) 40
Moss, John 40, 51, 58
Moss, William (Wm.) 40, 51, 58
Moulson, John 24
Moulson, Thomas 55
Mouncy, Matthias [Muncey?] ... 58
Mount, Absalom 15
Mount, John (Mounce) 58
Mount, Smith (Mounce) 58
Mount, Thomas (Mounts) 55
Mountjoy, Alvin 32, 48, 66, 77
Mountjoy, Edmund 55, 88
Mountjoy, George 77
Muir, Samuel 46, 65
Mulberry, Jacob 52, 60
Mullikin, James 60
Muloch, Richard Taylor (Mauloch) 74
Mulvan, John 82
Muncey, John 27
Munday, Edward 27
Munday, Edmund (Edmd.) 58
Munson, Isaac 52
Munter, Patrick (Muntere) (Patk.) 53
Murphy, Andrew 60

Murphy, Dennis 54
Murphey, John (Jno.) 58, 60
Murray, James (Murrey) 27, 52
Murray, William (Murry) 27
Murray, William, Jr. 53
Musselman, Christian 104
Musselman, John 104
Muter, George 25, 42, 45, 59, 83
Mutson, James 33
Myers, George (Mier) 82
Myers, Jacob 17
Myers, Melcher 76
Myers, Phillip (Myars) 74
Myers, William (Miars) 58
McAdams, Samuel 60
McAfee, George 26, 27
McAfee, James 16, 26, 27, 98
McAfee, James, Jr 26
McAfee, Jesse 27
McAfee, John 26, 27
McAfee, Samuel 16, 27
McAfee, Robert 16, 26, 43
McAllister, Joseph 27, 58
McBrayers, James (McBriers) . 16, 27
McBrayers, William (Wm.) 16, 26
McBride, James (McBrids) (Jas.) .. 14, 53
McBride, John 69
McBride, Robert (Robt.) (McBridg) 78
McBride, William 11
McCafferty, John 78
McCaffrey, William 65
McCall, David (McAwl) 33
McCall, James 49
McCall, William 46
McCandlars, James 58
McCann, David (McCame) 28
McCann, John (McCane) 52
McCann, Joseph 60, 93
McCann, Neal 93
McCann, Pleasant 60
McCann, William 88
McCard, David, Jr 60
McCarge, Radford (R) 43, 65, 93
McCarver, Archibald 6
McChandless, John 84
McChord, John (Jno.) 60
McClanahan, Elijah (McClenahan) 88
McClanahan, Thomas (Thos.) ... 84
McCleland, William (Wm.) . 48, 49, 64, 84, 88
McClintock, Joseph 33, 66, 82
McClintock, William (Wm.) 82
McClung, Matthew 93
McClung, William Jr. (Wm.) 42

List of Names

McClure, Alexander (McCluer) (Alexr.)............26, 27, 58, 63
McClure, James................53, 58
McClure, Andrew................ 86
McClure, John (McLure) (McCluere)........23, 36, 53, 58, 62, 84
McClure, Moses (McCle.).9 (List) 26, 27, 60
McClure, Nathan................ 27
McClure, Samuel (McCluer) (Saml.)...........55, 58, 64, 78, 84
McClure, Thomas........26, 27, 58, 60
McClure, William (McCluere).36, 53, 60, 69, 78
McComb, James (Macomb)...... 27
McComb, William (Macomb) ..27, 33
McComsey, John................ 52
McConey, John................ 63
McConnell, Adam............58, 60
McConnell, Alexander (McConall) (Alexr.)............46, 51, 53, 60
McConnell, Andrew 3
McConnell, Francis............12, 60
McConnell, James (Jas.)...22, 24, 43, 45, 53, 60, 63
McConnell, John..............60, 93
McConnell, William (Willm.) (Wm.)........3, 14, 22, 23, 26, 45, 46, 49, 52, 55, 58, 62, 84
McCormick, Daniel (McCormack) 36
McCoun, Andrew (McCune)..... 62
McCoun, David (McCune)...... 33
McCoun, James............16, 26, 66
McCoun, James, Jr............. 16
McCoun, John..............16, 33, 62
McCoun, Joseph.............24, 78
McCoy, William (Wm.)........33, 53
McCracken, Cyrus (McCrakin).12, 60
McCracken, John............77, 78
McCray, Robert (Robt.).......46, 53
McCreery, Andrew............ 77
McCreery, James...........77, 78, 88
McCreery, John...........60, 78, 84
McCulloch, James (McCoollouch) (Coullouch)............16, 26, 93
McCulloch, John (McCollough) (McCullough)............26, 76
McCullom, Samuel.............. 54
McDaniel, Alexander............ 55
McDaniel, Francis (McDannel) 33, 49, 55
McDaniel, James................ 27
McDaniel, John (McDancl)...55, 56, 60, 77
McDaniel, Joseph 77
McDaniel, Mack................ 52
McDaniel, Robert.............. 55
McDaniel, Samuel (Mack Daniel) 77
McDaniel, Rowland............. 55
McDermed, Francis (Frcs.)..14, 23, 43, 47, 53, 76
McDermed, Hugh.............53, 76
McDonald, Alexander (McDonal) 33
McDonald, Eneas (McDoneld) (Enes)................33, 49, 55
McDonald, Francis (McDonnal)14, 78
McDonald, Henry (McDonnal).. 14
McDonald, Hugh (McDonnal)... 14
McDonald, James (McDonnal).14, 78
McDonald, Jeremiah (McDonel). 78
McDonald, John (McDonnal) (McDonnald).....14, 49, 66, 78, 87
McDonald, William............40, 51
McDougall, Robert............. 46
McDowell, Daniel.........55, 56, 66
McDowell, James (Jas.)..26, 43, 63, 93
McDowell, John (Jno.)...17, 40, 45, 54, 60, 63
McDowell, Josias (McDowl)..... 55
McDowell, Samuel (Saml.)....17, 25, 42, 59, 73, 83
McDowell, William (Wm.)...55, 66, 84, 93
McDuff, Daniel................ 74
McElheany, John (Jno.)......... 68
McFaden, Andrew............. 74
McFaden, William (McFadin).... 74
McFarland, Robert (McFadland) (Robt.)..................... 60
McFawl, John................ 58
McFawl, Joseph................ 60
McGary, Daniel (Magary) (Megary)....................26, 27
McGarry, Hugh (McGary)....3, 5, 6, 26
McGarry, Robert (Magary)...... 27
McGee, David................. 8
McGee, James................. 26
McGee, John (Magee) (Megee).16, 26
McGee, Samuel (McGehee)...... 45
McGee, William..........6, 8, 60, 65
McGentery, James.............. 14
McGill, David................. 36
McGill, James................. 74
McGinnis, John (McGinis)..32, 34, 78
McGinnis, John Jr............32, 34
McGinnis, Thomas............. 54
McGinnis, William (Wm.)...32, 34, 64
McGowan, Robert (Megowan) ... 60
McGuire, Alexander (Alr.)....... 60
McGuire, Cornelius............. 60
McGuire, James (Meguire)..24, 43, 52
McGuire, John (McGire) (Jno.).. 47, 60, 62, 63, 65
McHatton, John................ 60
McHuron, Silas................ 52

[216]

List of Names

McIlvain, Hugh..............43, 76
McIlvain, James.............43, 53
McIlvain, John.................. 53
McIlvain, Moses................. 53
McIntyre, Alexander (McEntire) (Alexndr.).................... 48
McIntyre, James (McEntire)..... 78
McIntyre, John (McIntire).24, 56, 60
McKay, Alexander (McCay)..... 82
McKay, James.................48, 54
McKee, David.................... 63
McKee, William (Wm.) (McCee).. 69
McKenzie, Archibald (McKenzey) (Arch)...................... 36
McKenzie, Daniel (McKensy) (Danl.)..................... 27
McKenzie, James (Jas.) (McKinsey)....................... 27
McKenzie, William.............. 70
McKeough, Dennis.............. 74
McKibbins, John................ 93
McKinley, James (Jas.).......... 54
McKinney, Alexander............ 78
McKinney, David................ 51
McKinney, Daniel............... 87
McKinney, James (Jas.)......... 66
McKinney, John.........12, 60, 62, 84
McKinney, Joseph (Jos.)......... 64
McKinney, Robert............... 78
McKinney, Wilson............... 6
McKittrick, Robert...........66, 78
McLaughlin, Thomas (Thos.)..66, 77
McLean, Alexander (McClain)... 14
McLean, Daniel (McClain) (Danniel)....................... 14
McLean, James (McClain)....... 74
McLean, John M................. 27
McLean, Nathaniel (McClane)... 53
McLean, Robert................. 27
McLean, Thomas................. 27
McLeary, John.................. 27
McMillan, David (McMillin)..... 45
McMillan, James (McMillion)..12, 65
McMillan, Jonathan............. 12
McMillan, J. M. (McMillin)...... 24
McMillan, Robert (McMillion).. 12, 60, 65, 72
McMillan, Samuel (McMillion).. 9 (List) 12, 14
McMillan, William (McMillion).. 65
McMoney, William (Willm.)...... 58
McMordie, Tres................. 93
McMullen, Charles.............. 58
McMullen, John (McMullin)..... 58
McMullen, Samuel (Saml.)....... 46
McMullen, Thomas (Thos.)...... 74
McMullen, William.............. 60

McMurry, John.................. 74
McMurtry, James................ 43
McMurtry, John................. 53
McMurtry, Joseph............... 26
McMurtry, William (McMirtry)60, 62
McNab, John..............54, 60, 77
McNeely, Michael............... 64
McNeely, Hugh.................. 48
McNelly, John (McNeely)........ 69
McNickel, Arthur.........77, 84, 88
McNiel, Allen (McNele).......... 47
McNeil, Arthur (McNeile)....... 55
McNeil, Jonathan............... 45
McNiel, Joseph.................. 77
McNiel, Thomas (McNeal) (Thos.)....................45, 52
McNulty, Joseph.............78, 88
McPayne, Daniel (Danl.)..........
McPherson, Adam (McFarson).. 48, 49, 55
McQuady, John.................. 60
McQuady, William (McQuiddy) 43, 52
McQueen, John (Jo.)............. 47
McQuid, Arthur (McWhidd)..... 66
McWhinney, William.......9 (List)
McWilliams, William............ 27

Nagle, W....................... 65
Napier, John (Napper).......... 14
Naylor, John................... 17
Naylor, Nathaniel (Nat.)........ 93
Neal, Allan (Neil) (Allen).....65, 72
Neal, Benjamin (Neale)....12, 78, 84
Neal, Daniel (Neel) (Dannel) (Dan)....................52, 60
Neal, Daniel, Jr................. 52
Neal, John................52, 56, 66
Neal, Spence 52, 60
Neal, William (Wm.) (Neel)...... 36
Neely, Alexander............9 (List)
Neely, Isaac (Niely)............. 58
Neely, Matthew (Mathew).....66, 84
Neely, William (Niely).........58, 60
Nelan, Benjamin (Nelson)....... 6
Nelson, Edward.......8, 9, 12, 24, 51
Nelson, Joseph.................. 78
Nelson, Moses.................8, 65
Nelson, Thomas (Thos.).......... 65
Nelson, William................ 11
Nesbit, Jeremiah................ 56
Nesbit, Nathan (Nesbet)........ 56
Nesbit, Robert (Nesbet) (Neisbeit)....................33, 56, 93
Nesbit, William (Nesbet.)....... 56
Netherland, B................14, 17
Newby, John.................... 9

[217]

List of Names

Newell, Hugh.................. 78
Newell, William (Wm.)........... 40
Newland, George............... 78
Newland, Horeb (Nuland) (Hored).................... 84
Newman, Nathaniel (Nathannel). 93
Newton, Peter................. 58
Niblack, John..............24, 60, 65
Niblack, William...............14, 24
Nichol, Arthur (Nickle).......... 55
Nicholas, G................... 82
Nichols, John (Nickols)..32, 34, 48, 54
Nichols, Thomas (Nicolls) (Thos.) (Nickols)...............32, 34, 48
Nicholson, John (Nichosen)...... 68
Nicholson, Thomas (Nichelson) (Thos.)............40, 55, 56, 60
Nicholson, William (Nickleson).. 27
Nickell, Joseph................ 63
Nicklin, Thomas................ 60
Noble, James................78, 84
Noe, Randall (Randal).......... 65
Noel, Barnard................. 27
Noel, Benjamin (Noahels) (Benj.) 15, 58
Noel, Garret (Noell)............ 58
Noel, George (Noahels).......... 15
Noel, Musco (Noell)............ 58
Noel, John (Noell)............. 58
Noel, Thomas (Noell)...........8, 9
Noland, Henry (Nowland)....... 27
Noland, Matthew (Nowlon) (Nowlen)...................60, 65
Noland, William............... 27
North, Abijah................. 28
Norton, John................60, 63
Nott, John.................... 14
Nourse, James................. 42
Nourse, James, Jr.............. 12
Nudigate, William (Wm.)........ 78
Nutt, Matthew................. 52

Ocoler, Nicholas (Oyler) [?]...78, 88
Ockly, William (Okly).......... 64
Oden, Thomas (Thos.).......... 47
Odom, Michael (Micall)......... 74
Odor, Joseph.................. 63
Ogg, Joshua................... 78
Old, John..................65, 72
Oldfield, Joseph................ 12
Oldham, Richard (Richd.).....65, 72
Oldover, George............... 52
Oldridge, William.............. 57
Oliver, Andrew (Andw.)......... 27
Oliver, John.................6, 78
Olley, Cripley................. 69
O'Neal, John.................. 74

O'Neal, Jonathan............... 74
O'Neal, Robert................ 43
Orchard, Isaac............62, 78, 84
Orchard, John................. 47
Ormsby, John Jr. (Jno.)......... 46
Ormsby, Stephen (Stepn.)....... 68
Orr, Alexander D. (Alexr.)..42, 45, 46
Orr, Samuel (Our.)............. 60
Orr, Thomas (Thos.)............ 60
Osborn, James (Osburn)........ 78
Osborn, Samuel (Osburn)....... 60
Oscar, William...............27, 47
Overfield, Abner..............32, 34
Overstreet, Thomas (Thos.)...... 60
Overton, I. Jr................. 53
Overton, Richard (Rd.).....26, 27, 45
Overton, Samuel............... 58
Overton, Walter.............11, 51
Owen, John................... 52
Owens, Owen.................. 26
Owens, Patrick................ 14
Owings, John Cockey (Jno.) (John C.)...................23, 83
Owings, Joshua................ 78
Owsley, John.................. 48
Owsley, Thomas (Thos.)......... 18
Owsley, William............... 65

Paddock, Jonathan............. 65
Paddock, William............65, 78
Palmer, Ellis (Palmore).......32, 48
Palmer, Gideon (Giddion)....... 32
Palmer, John................28, 33
Palmer, Parmenus (Parmar) (Parmoinus).................... 74
Parberry, James..............44, 46
Pardinez, James................ 6
Paris, David.................. 63
Paris, Moses................65, 78
Park, Robert.................. 57
Parker, Alexander (Alexr.)...45, 46, 53, 60, 93
Parker, Barry................. 60
Parker, Henry (Harry)....53, 62, 63, 67, 76
Parker, James..........46, 53, 60, 63
Parker, John (Jno.)......27, 45, 46, 53
Parker, Richard (Richd.)......52, 60
Parker, Robert (Robt.)......... 46
Parker, Thomas (Thos.)....15, 60, 67, 74, 84
Parker, William (Wm.).........46, 60
Parkison, William (Wm.)........ 54
Parks, John................... 82
Parks, Richard................ 46
Parrish, Robert..............65, 72
Parrish, Timothy.............. 65

List of Names

Parsons, John.................... 77
Partchment, Jacob.............. 54
Partchment, John............... 54
Parton, Uriah.................... 24
Patterson, Arthur................ 53
Patterson, Francis............... 53
Patterson, John.................. 52
Patterson, J............25, 43, 45,
                46, 51, 53, 63, 76, 93
Patterson, Joseph (Jos.).......23, 52
Patterson, Matthew (Mat.)....46, 63
Patterson, Moses........46, 53, 60, 93
Patterson, R...................14, 51
Patterson, Robert (Robt.)....... 42
Patterson, William..............8, 9
Pattie, John..................... 60
Patton, Benjamin (Ben.)......... 17
Patton, James (Patten.)....11, 54, 87
Patton, John (Patten).......... 49
Patton, Roger.................16, 43
Patton, Thomas (Patten)......66, 87
Patton, William (Wm.) (Patten).
                            17, 36, 49
Paul, Andrew (Paull)............ 60
Paul, James..................... 58
Paulding, Benjamin (Benj.)...... 6
Paxton, Thomas................. 93
Payne, Edward (Edwd.).......53, 60
Payne, Edward, Jr. (Edwd.)..53,
                            60, 63, 65
Payne, George................... 11
Payne, Henry..................63, 84
Payne, Jilson...............53, 60, 63
Payne, John..............43, 51, 52
Payne, William (Wm.) (W.)
                            43, 51, 68
Peak, Daniel.................... 52
Peak, Jesse (Peek)............40, 60
Peak, John (Pleak)......40, 52, 60, 72
Peak, Presley................... 60
Peak, Thomas (Thos.)..........52, 60
Peally, Peter.................... 27
Pearce, Thomas................17, 78
Pearl, William.................. 16
Peary, Robert (Robt.)......33, 48, 66
Peary, Thomas (Thos.)......... 78
Peebles, Robert (Robt.)......... 49
Pelham, Charles (Chas.)....51, 60, 61
Pemberton, Charles............. 69
Pendleton, Curtis.............66, 78
Pendleton, Rice................. 77
Penick, Charles................. 58
Penick, Jeremiah (Penck)........ 63
Penick, William...............53, 63
Penington, Isaac (Pennington)..
                            32, 49, 54
Penix, Joshua..................8, 9

Penland, Alexander (Elexander)47, 65
Perkins, James (Purkins)........ 77
Perkins, William................ 52
Perry, John..................... 52
Perry, Lewis.................... 52
Perry, Ted...................... 32
Persons, Edward................ 60
Peters, John (Jno.)...........12, 58
Peters, William (Willm.) (Petters) 58
Pettill, Benjamin................ 6
Petty, Ebenezer................. 58
Petty, John (Pettey)..........58, 78
Peyton, Lewis (Payton).......... 36
Peyton, Timothy (Timoy.)....... 32
Pharis, Elijah [Faris?].......... 58
Phelps, Josiah.................. 11
Phillip, Edmund (Edmond)....48, 66
Phillips, Elijah................. 78
Phillips, Jenkins................ 68
Phillips, John................... 54
Phillips, Moses...............32, 34
Phillips, Phillip (Philips)....... 60
Phillips, William................ 52
Piatt, John..................... 88
Pickens, Aaron.................. 14
Picque, William (Willm.)........ 68
Piels, Conredus................. 58
Pierce, Jeremiah (Jeremia)...... 60
Piettens, Jonathan.............. 69
Pim, John (J.)................58, 60
Pim, John, Jr................... 43
Pitman, Joseph (Jos.).......... 16
Pittey, Henry................... 54
Pitts, Josiah..................51, 52
Pittlen, Frederick............... 54
Platt, Ebenezer S............... 32
Playle, Richard................. 52
Pleak, John..................... 51
Pleak, John, Jr................. 47
Plugh, Elias.................... 52
Plummer, Benjamin (Benj.) 32, 34, 48
Plummer, George..............32, 34
Plummer, Samuel..........32, 34, 54
Plummer, William............... 48
Poage, Elijah................... 51
Poage, Thomas.................. 40
Poage, William.................. 6
Poage, Phillip (Pogue).......... 65
Poe, Benjamin (Benj.).......... 52
Poe, William.................... 69
Poff, George..................17, 32
Polke, Charles.................. 60
Pollard, Absalom................ 58
Pollard, Braxton................ 93
Polley, Edward (Edwd.)......... 58
Pollock, James.................. 56
Pon, John...................... 52

[219]

List of Names

Pope, William.................11, 12
Port, Francis..................... 77
Porter, Andrew.................. 57
Porter, H. J...................... 60
Porter, Joseph................... 57
Portwood, Lloyd (Loyd)......... 27
Portwood, Page.............27, 46
Portwood, Ludy................. 27
Portwood, Thomas...........27, 47
Portwood, Samuel............... 27
Potter, Samuel................... 54
Powell Ambros (Powell) (Ambrous)..................47, 60, 65
Powell, John..................... 52
Powell, Joshua................... 74
Powell, William.................. 52
Power, J. W...................... 78
Power, James.................... 43
Prather, Alexander (Preator).... 27
Prather, Edward (Preator).....26, 27
Prather, Henry (Prater).....6, 26, 58
Prather, John (Prater)........... 26
Prather, Thomas (Preator) (Thommes)..................26, 27
Preston, John.................... 6
Prewitt, Joseph.................. 40
Pribble, James [Prebble?]........ 84
Price, Alexander................. 78
Price, Benjamin.................. 69
Price, Bird............40, 51, 53, 63
Price, David..................... 24
Price, John (J.) 15, 17, 40, 43, 51, 60, 63
Price, John, Jr................... 51
Price, Moses.................11, 27
Price, Pugh............40, 45, 63
Price, Robert.................... 51
Price, Samuel................58, 65
Price, Vinson.................... 15
Price, William (Wm.).17, 40, 51, 58, 93
Proctor, Benjamin................ 27
Proctor, Hezekiah................ 63
Proctor, John (Jno.)............. 52
Proctor, Joseph............9, 24, 27
Proctor, Little Pag............... 24
Proctor, Nicholas (Procter)..8, 9, 24, 27, 64
Proctor, Nicholas, Jr. (Nickles).. 8
Proctor, Reuben (Ruben)....8, 24, 27
Proctor, Thomas................. 60
Protzman, Lawrence............. 55
Provin, John..................... 69
Pryland, Nicholas............32, 34
Pryor, Samuel (Sam.)............ 42
Puckett, Allen................... 63
Puckett, William................. 63
Pullen, Jedediah (Pulen) (Jedyah)..................58, 78, 84
Pullen, John................58, 78, 84
Puntiney, Nelson................. 74
Puppey, Samuel.................. 54
Purcel, Thomas (Tho.).......... 68
Purviance, John (Jno.).......42, 84
Pyburn, Lewis................... 60
Pyburn, Richard................. 60

Qualey, Patrick.................. 78
Quigley, Michael (Michal).....77, 78
Quinn, Benjamin (Benj.)......... 52
Quisenbury see Cusenberry

Raburn, James (Reburn).......33, 46
Raburn, John (Reborn).......... 74
Raburn, John, Sr. (Reburn)...... 74
Raburn, Robert............27, 60, 65
Raburn, William................. 65
Radcliff, Benjamin............... 58
Radcliff, Edward.............78, 84
Ragland, Edmund.......47, 60, 65, 72
Ragland, James..............60, 65
Rains, Cornelius (Reins)...34, 48, 54
Rains, James (Reins)..........32, 34
Rains, John (Reins).....32, 34, 48, 54
Rains, William..........32, 34, 48, 54
Ralls, Horeb..................... 84
Ralph, Morris (Moris)........... 68
Ralston, James.................. 63
Ralston, John (Rolston)......... 63
Ralston, Joseph................. 63
Ramdell, John (Jno.).........63, 93
Ramey, Daniel [Remy?]....47, 60, 65
Ramsey, Alexander.............. 58
Ramsey, George................. 58
Ramsey, John.................... 58
Ramsey, Larkin...............58, 69
Ramsey, William................ 78
Randolph, Malachi (Malachiah). 43
Rankin, Adam................... 83
Rankin, Benjamin (Benj.) (Rankins)..............27, 60, 65, 84
Rankin, David............40, 52, 78
Rankin, Reuben (Rankins) (Ruben)............27, 48, 56, 57, 78
Rankins, Robert (Robart) (Robt.) 27, 32, 34, 54
Rankin, William (Wm.)....43, 46, 51, 53, 63
Ratcliffe, Richard............... 58
Ravenscraft, Thomas (Thos.).33, 49, 55
Rawlings, Aaron................. 93
Rawlings, Pemberton............6, 8
Ray, James...................26, 84
Ray, John (Ree)...........26, 27, 69

[220]

List of Names

Ray, Joseph...................... 27	Rice, William (Wm.)............52, 67
Ray, Stephen..................... 27	Richards, Robert (Robt.)27, 60, 65, 72
Ray, William..................... 27	Richards, William............... 40
Read, Andrew.................... 77	Richardson, James (Jas.)........ 51
Read, William [Reed?]........... 16	Richardson, Jesse................ 15
Reading, Robert, M.............. 66	Richardson, Laudie............... 93
Reager, Barket................... 68	Richardson, Turner.............. 52
Reager, Jacob.................... 68	Richardson, William............. 15
Record, Josiah (Records).32, 34, 48, 54	Richey, Edward................. 52
Record, Laban.................48, 54	Richey, John (Ritchey).......... 60
Reding, George................... 28	Richey, Samuel.................. 60
Reding, Isaac (Redding)......... 52	Ridmer, Gabriel................. 78
Reding, John..................... 28	Riggs, John...........32, 34, 48, 54
Redmon, Daniel.................. 48	Riley, James.................... 74
Redmon, Gabriel................. 48	Ringbolt, Jacob................. 46
Redmon, Thomas................. 48	Ringo, Cornelius..............60, 65
Reed, Alexander.................. 64	Rippey, Samuel................. 54
Reed, James..................... 78	Roach, Henry................... 63
Reed, John.......53, 58, 64, 65, 72, 78	Roach, Little Berry............. 58
Reed, Joseph (Jos.).............. 60	Roach, William (Rosh).......... 67
Reed, Matthew................... 69	Robbins, Aaron................. 60
Reed, Robert..................... 54	Robenit, John................... 77
Reed, Thomas (Thos.).......58, 66, 84	Robert, Benjamin, Jr............ 11
Reed, William (Wm.).......46, 53, 55	Roberts, Edward (Robards)....27, 58
Rees, Azor...................33, 48, 66	Roberts, John (Robers)...6, 52, 58, 60
Rees, David.................45, 46, 77	Roberts, Joseph...........11, 12, 27
Rees, Isaac (Reas)............... 77	Roberts, Nathan................ 27
Reemer, David................... 60	Roberts, Nealey................ 52
Reeves, Elijah...........32, 34, 48, 54	Roberts, Nimrod................ 52
Reeves, George................... 68	Roberts, Thomas (Robartes) 52, 60, 64
Reeves, Matthias (Mathias)...... 57	Roberts, William (Roberds)
Reeves, Michael (Michel)........ 57	(Willm.) (Wm.)............52, 68
Reeves, Spencer...............33, 48	Robertson, Absalom (Absm.)
Reid, Alexander (Alexr.) [Reed?]. 64	(Robinson)................65, 78
Reid, John [Reed]............... 69	Robertson, Alexander........... 27
Remy, Archibald (Archebauld)	Robertson, Benjamin (Robinson)
(Artchy)..............56, 77, 88	12, 43
Remy, Ferdinand (Ferd.)......33, 49	Robertson, Hosea............... 58
Remy, Jeremiah (Jerh.) (Ramy)	Robertson, James (Roberson)..27, 46
(Jerry)................56, 78, 88	Robertson, James Jr............. 27
Remy, Joel...................... 84	Robertson, Jesse (Ropertson).... 65
Remy, Linnet (Ramey) (Reimy)	Robertson, John...............27, 60
(Raimy)...........56, 66, 77, 84	Robertson, Jonathan............ 52
Reno, Teky...................... 56	Robertson, Matthew............ 27
Rentfro, James................... 52	Robertson, Mills................ 54
Rew, Richard (Rue)..........43, 52	Robertson, Samuel.............. 60
Rew, Raleigh (Rews) (Rawleigh)	Robertson, William........27, 60, 64
32, 34	Robeson, John (Jno.)..........26, 58
Reynolds, Aaron................. 24	Robinson, Jeremiah.........53, 63, 78
Reynolds, Thomas (Thos.)..40, 58, 60	Robinson, James................ 64
Rhea, Alexander (Alexr.)........ 55	Robinson, Joseph............... 28
Rhodes, Clifton (Rodes)......... 63	Robinson, William (Wm.)......40, 51
Rhodes, John (Rodes)........... 77	Robison, Alexander............. 58
Rhodes, Frederick (Roads)...... 53	Robison, George................ 60
Rhodes, Robert (Rodes)......... 27	Robison, James................. 58
Rice, David..................46, 58	Robson, Samuel............9 (List)
Rice, John...................24, 65	Rock, John...................57, 78

List of Names

Rock, Patrick..................... 78
Rodgers, Andrew (Andw.)....... 17
Rodgers, Joseph [Rogers?]....... 28
Rodgers, William................. 63
Rodney, Martin (Roddeney) (Marten).................... 55
Roe, Charles..................... 54
Roe, William (Wm.)............. 54
Rogers, Anthony................. 15
Rogers, Barnard.................. 24
Rogers, Edward................... 52
Rogers, James (Jas.).....25, 52, 60, 77
Rogers, Jeremiah (Jereh.)40, 60, 65, 67
Rogers, John..........52, 60, 67, 84
Rogers, Joseph....40, 45, 60, 65, 67, 93
Rogers, Thomas (Thos.).......... 75
Rogers, William........60, 67, 84, 104
Rooney, Patrick (Pattk.) (Runey) 57
Rooney, William (Roney)........ 84
Rorison, Basil.................... 46
Rose, Enoch (Enock)....32, 34, 48, 54
Rose, Jonathan................... 54
Rose, Obezar..................... 27
Rosett, George................... 47
Ross, Ambrose (Ambriss)......27, 46
Ross, Ignatius (Ignatious)....... 54
Ross, Samuel.............57, 78, 84
Ross, Thomas (Thos.)............ 27
Routt, Byram (Buram)..55, 56, 66, 77
Routt, George.................... 65
Routt, Hardy (H.) (Rowts).15, 33, 56
Routt, William................60, 62
Row, Adam....................... 60
Row, William..................... 84
Rowl, Thomas (Rowles).......... 45
Rowl, William.................... 78
Rowan, W........................ 60
Rowland, David.............51, 52
Rowland, John.................... 60
Roy, James, Jr................... 84
Royston, Elijah.................. 65
Ruble, Jacob..................... 60
Ruby, David...................... 60
Rucker, James.................... 52
Rucker, John (Roocker) (Jno.).. 32, 34, 52
Ruddle, Isaac.................... 95
Ruffner, Reuben.................. 58
Rule, Andrew..................... 24
Rule, Samuel..................... 84
Runyan, Henry (Runnen.).....60, 67
Runyan, Joseph................... 58
Rupert, George (Georg).......... 78
Russell, Charles................. 60
Russell, Edward (Edwd.)......... 47
Russell, H....................... 45
Russell, James................... 6
Russell, Joseph.................. 54
Russell, Obediah................. 74
Russell, William (W).......23, 60, 93
Russellhill, Robert.............. 78
Ruth, Davis..................32, 34
Rutherford, John (Reatherford) (J).......................36, 58
Rybolt, Daniel................... 49
Rybolt, Jacob.................... 53
Rybolt, Michael (Mickal)......33, 49
Rylands, Nicholas................ 46
Ryman, Jacob.................40, 47

Sacry, James..................60, 63
Sage, Alexander (Alex.).......... 58
Sage, Jeremiah (Jerrimiah)...... 58
Sage, Jesse...................... 58
Sage, John....................... 58
Sage, William.................... 58
Sage, William, Sr................ 58
Said, Edmund.................... 60
Said, William.................60, 65
Salley, Abraham.................. 60
Salley, Jezreel (Jessril)........ 45
Salley, John..................... 58
Salter, William.................. 56
Sammuel, Anthony................. 67
Samples, Benjamin.............52, 60
Samples, David (Sample)......... 52
Samples, John.................52, 60
Samples, Samuel (Sample)........ 52
Samples, Samuel, Jr.............. 52
Sanders, Elisha.................. 57
Sanders, Gunnell................. 93
Sanders, James................... 53
Sanders, Hezekiah.............60, 65
Sanders, Julius.................. 6
Sanders, John............12, 17, 46, 58, 60, 69, 78, 84
Sanders, Nathaniel (Nath.)....40, 52
Sanders, Robert.................. 24
Sanders, Samuel.............9 (List)
Sanders, Thomas.................. 60
Sandidge, David.................. 67
Sandidge, Larkin................. 67
Sandusky, James.................. 43
Sandusky, John (Sanduske)....... 77
Sapleton, Jobe [Saptleton]...... 26
Sapp, George (Georg.)............ 47
Sappington, Hartley.............. 46
Sappington, John, Sr............. 47
Satterly, Samuel (Saml.)........ 52
Scheibeler, George............... 78
Scholl, Joseph.....12, 24, 51, 52, 60, 65
Scholl, Peter......12, 24, 53, 60, 63, 65
Scholl (Wm.)...........12, 24, 60, 65

[222]

List of Names

Schwartzmer, Nicholas............ 6
Scofield, Thomas................. 78
Sconce, James................49, 84
Sconce, Robert (Robart).......49, 84
Sconce, Thomas...............49, 84
Scooler, William (Wm.) (Schooler)
                          28, 48, 56
Scott, Arthur.................... 84
Scott, Charles (Chs.).......51, 61, 83
Scott, David..................... 43
Scott, Elijah.................... 60
Scott, Elisha.................... 60
Scott, Gabriel................52, 60
Scott, George...23, 49, 52, 55, 58, 60, 66
Scott, Henry (Henery)............ 84
Scott, James (Jas.)...23, 28, 33, 52, 55
Scott, John............33, 49, 58, 77, 78
Scott, Joseph................47, 58
Scott, Levi...................... 60
Scott, Robert..........28, 33, 52, 58
Scott, Samuel (Saml.)............ 58
Scott, Thomas (Thos.).........43, 48
Scott, William (Wm.)..........53, 60
Seal, John....................... 60
Seaman, Charles (Charls)......... 14
Searcy, Bartlett.6, 9 (List) 12, 43, 51, 52
Searcy, Berry.................... 51
Searcy, Edmund (Searcey) (Edmond)........................ 52
Searcy, David.................... 66
Searcy, Reuben (Sercey) (Cercy)
  (Reubin).....6, 8, 43, 51, 60, 64, 93
Searcy, Richard................6, 43
Sebastian, Benjamin (Ben.)....42, 83
Self, Charnt..................... 53
Sellers, James................... 58
Sellers, John.................... 58
Sellers, Joseph.................. 58
Sellers, Nathaniel (Nathan).28, 33, 58
Sellers, Samuel.................. 58
Sellers, William................. 58
Settle, Thomas................... 60
Sevier, Valentine (Val.)......... 74
Sewell, Hugh..................... 84
Sewell, John..................... 11
Shad, George..................... 58
Shanklin, Robert................. 60
Shannon, Nathaniel (Nath)........ 52
Shannon, Hugh.................... 52
Shannon, William................. 89
Sharp, Abraham................27, 58
Sharp, David..................... 49
Sharp, John (Sharpe)..........24, 67
Sharp, Moses..................... 63
Sharp, Solomon................... 77
Shaw, William.................... 54
Shawhan, Daniel.................. 57
Shawhan, Daniel, Jr.............. 57
Shawhan, John [Sheehan?]......... 57
Sheehan, John.................... 60
Sheetz, Henry....................104
Shelby, Evan..................54, 87
Shelby, Isaac.................17, 45
Shelton, Samuel (Saml.).......... 17
Shelton, Thomas (Thos.).......27, 64
Shepard, George.................. 46
Shepard, Samuel (Sam).........52, 60
Shepherd, Adam................17, 26
Shepherd, David.................. 60
Shepherd, John................... 69
Shepherd, William (Wm.).......... 26
Sheridan, Martin................. 60
Sherratt, Tudor (Sherrask)....... 73
Sherry, Bernard (Bernerd)........ 46
Shids, Samuel.................... 84
Shields, Patrick (Shiells)....... 58
Shipp, Colby (Coly.).23, 52, 60, 62, 67
Shipp, Laban...........51, 52, 62, 66, 81
Shipp, Richard W. (Richd.)....... 52
Shoots, John..................... 43
Short, John...................... 52
Short, Peyton.................90, 91
Shortridge, George............... 12
Shortridge, George, Jr........58, 84
Shortridge, Lewis................ 52
Shortridge, William.............. 24
Shortridge, Samuel..........12, 60, 65
Shotwell, John................... 54
Shrope, Adam..................... 57
Shrope, Sebastian................ 57
Shropshire, Benjamin (Shopshare)
                      56, 58, 60, 63, 78, 84
Shropshire, James.............33, 55
Shropshire, John..............78, 84
Shropshire, Joseph............... 67
Shropshire, Edward............... 78
Shubling, William................ 65
Shumaker, Daniel (Shewmaker).. 54
Shut, John....................... 60
Sibley, John..................... 12
Sidwell, Elisha.................. 77
Sidwell, Hugh......32, 34, 48, 55, 56, 84
Silvers, Samuel.................. 60
Simbrell, Francis................ 60
Simons, Robert................... 78
Simons, Sebre.................... 60
Simpson, Allan................48, 54
Simpson, Gilbert (Gilbt.)........ 32
Simpson, James (Sinson).......... 60
Simpson, John.........32, 34, 51, 58
Simpson, Samuel..............32, 34
Sims, John (Jno.) (Simms)52, 55, 77, 84
Singleton, Edmund (Edmd.) (Edmond).............46, 52, 60, 63

[223]

List of Names

Singleton, Jechonias........43, 52, 60
Skiner, Joseph................... 27
Slack, Randolph................ 26
Slagle, Jacob....................104
Slater, John, Toms........46, 53, 63
Slaughter, Cad.................... 68
Slaughter, George, Col........26, 68
Slaughter, James R.............. 68
Slaughter, Thomas............... 4
Sledd, William.................... 58
Sleet, Weden...................... 69
Sleet, John........................ 69
Slott, John........................ 28
Sly, George....................... 27
Smallwood, John................. 65
Smart, James..................... 78
Smart, Jose....................... 84
Smart, Richard (Richd.)......... 78
Smeathers, James................ 74
Smiley, John..............49, 55, 66
Smith, Alexander (Alexr.).....60, 93
Smith, Benjamin (Benj.)...27, 40, 45, 52, 60, 67
Smith, Charles, Sr.............40, 78
Smith, Charles, Jr. (Chas.)...28, 33, 62, 63, 79, 84
Smith, Christian (Smit).......... 54
Smith, Christopher............48, 58
Smith, Daniel (Danl.)..........78, 84
Smith, Ebenezer...............32, 34
Smith, Edmund................... 58
Smith, Elijah............40, 45, 53, 67
Smith, Eleazer.................60, 63
Smith, Francis.................... 60
Smith, Garland (Garld.).......60, 67
Smith, George..................60, 67
Smith, George Stovall (S)..15, 17, 60
Smith, Hawkins.........60, 67, 78, 84
Smith, Henry..................53, 58
Smith, Hugh...................... 27
Smith, Jacob...................... 60
Smith, James, Sr...............60, 86
Smith, James (Jas.).....17, 23, 26, 27, 33, 48, 49, 60, 66, 67, 84
Smith, Jesse...................32, 34
Smith, John (Jno.)......17, 27, 33, 40, 60, 65, 82, 83, 84, 88
Smith, Joseph..........60, 65, 78, 84
Smith, Josiah..................... 52
Smith, Lucas (Lucous)........32, 34
Smith, Michael (Micael)......... 78
Smith, Peter...................... 78
Smith, Rhodus (Rodes).......... 67
Smith, Samuel (Saml.)...51, 52, 54, 60
Smith, Thomas (Ts.).....27, 52, 58, 67
Smith, Trevance.................. 84
Smith, William (Wm.)...23, 53, 60, 93

Smith, Walter.................60, 65
Smith, Zacharias................. 17
Smock, Henry.................... 60
Smock, Joseph (Smott).......... 84
Smyth, Jacob..................... 78
Snell, Charles (Chas.).........78, 84
Snell, John....................... 52
Snell, William.................... 78
Snoddy, John.............15, 17, 27
Snowber, Christopher........... 33
Sodowsky, Jacob [Sadowsky?]... 60
Solomon, Andrew (Andw.)....... 52
Solomon, Jacob (Solsman).....52, 60
Solomon, William (Wm.)........ 52
Sorenency, David..........56, 78, 84
South, John, Sr......8, 9, 23, 27, 40, 46
South, John, Jr.........8, 9, 63, 64
South, Samuel..................8, 27
South, Thomas.............9 (List)
South, Zedikiah (Zediakah)...... 27
South, William................... 27
Southard, Edmund (Edmond)....109
Southern, William................ 58
Sovarnts, Briant.................. 74
Spangler, William................ 12
Sparkle, Andrew.................. 63
Sparks, Elijah.................... 65
Sparks, George................... 48
Sparks, Isaac.................... 65
Sparks, William (Wm.), Sr..32, 34, 48, 49
Sparks, William, Jr............32, 34
Spaulding, William (Wm.) (Spawldin)............................ 52
Spaur, Matthias (Matts.)........ 24
Speaks, Hezekiah (Hesekiah)...28, 49
Speed, James (Jas.)...........17, 42
Spence, William (Wm.).......... 78
Spencer, Michael (Spenser)...... 60
Spencer, William................. 78
Spiers, William (Spirs).........60, 65
Spiller, Craven................... 62
Spillman, Henry (Spilman) (Spelman)..........................26, 27
Spillman, Jacob (Spilman)....... 26
Sportman, William P..........43, 52
Springer, John................... 12
Springkel, Michael (Michel)...... 68
Spurgin, Ezekiel.................. 77
Spurgin, George.................. 78
Spurgin, Isaac.................... 77
Spurgin, James................77, 84
Spurgin, Jeremiah, Sr............ 77
Spurgin, Jeremiah, Jr............ 77
Spurgin, John.................... 77
Spurgin, Samuel.................. 77
Spurgin, Zephaniah (Spurin)..... 77

List of Names

Spurr, Richard (Richd.).........65
Stafford, Henry (Staford)
   (Henery)..................45, 93
Stagge, William.............9 (List)
Stagner, Barnabas...............26
Stamper, Joshua.............24, 46
Standford, Aquilla (Standeford)
                              48, 49, 62, 84
Standford, George..........55, 78, 88
Standford, Nathan (Standeford)
                              49, 55, 56
Stanhope, Robert (Stanhop.) 14,
                              46, 53
Stapleton, John..................60
Stapp, Achilles (Achihles).......60
Stapp, Paul.....................63
Stark, James.................28, 57
Stark, Thomas...................49
Starns, Edward................
Starns, Frederick............9 (List)
Starns, Jacob............8, 9, 27, 47
Starns, Joseph...................9
Station, B......................74
Station, Charles (Staton)........74
Station, John, Curtis............54
Station, John (Staton)...........74
Station, Thomas (Stayton).......60
Steel, Adam....................63
Steel, Andrew (Andw.).........24, 51
Steel, David...................58
Steel, Hugh....................82
Steel, John.................42, 53
Steel, Joseph..........46, 60, 77, 78
Steel, Richard.................60
Steel, Robert................60, 65
Steel, William (Wm.) (Steele)..22,
      23, 24, 31, 46, 52, 53, 58, 60
Stephens, Andrew...............27
Stephens, John (Stevens)...27, 51, 52
Stephens, Joseph (Stevenze)...47, 72
Stephens, Thomas L. (Stevens)
   (Ts.)...............46, 56, 64, 66
Stephens, William (Wm.)........93
Stephenson, Abraham (Abram.)..58
Stephenson, Benjamin (B.)
   (Stevenson)................53, 61
Stephenson, David (Stevenson)..77
Stephenson, James (Stevenson)..
                27, 61, 64, 77, 84
Stephenson, John (Stevenson).12,
     24, 43, 45, 51, 53, 61, 63, 93
Stephenson, Jonathan..........78, 84
Stephenson, Marcus.............54
Stephenson, Robert (Robt.)
   (Stevenson)................24, 45
Stephenson, Samuel (Stevenson)
   (Saml.) (Stevenston) 12, 51, 53, 60

Stephenson, Thomas (Thos.)
   (Stevenson) ...17, 24, 43, 53, 60, 93
Stephenson, William (Wm.)
   (Stevenson)....23, 45, 53, 60, 61, 93
Sterett, James................52, 60
Sterett, John (Starrete) (Jno.)..52, 60
Stewart, Abraham...............74
Stewart, Alexander (Alexr.)....60, 65
Stewart, Ezekiel.................65
Stewart, James (Jas.) (Stuart).26,
                43, 52, 53, 74
Stewart, John.......67, 74, 82, 102, 93
Stewart, Levi..................65, 82
Stewart, Richard................40
Stewart, William..............60, 74
Stidger, Peter................53, 60
Stivers, Edward..............60, 65
Stivers, Reuben..............60, 65
Stocker, Edward................84
Stocker, Hezekiah...............40
Stockton, Dorsey...............54
Stockton, Robert...............54
Stockwell, Samuel..............54
Stokes, Edward...............77, 78
Stone, Obadiah, Jr..............32
Stone, Valentine (Ston) (Volen-
   tine)................27, 47, 60, 65
Stone, William (Steon)..........58
Stoner, Michael (Stonar) (Mical)
                       8, 46, 52
Story, James...................84
Story, William (Wm.).........23, 34
Stott, Rawley...................52
Stotton, George (Geo.)..........54
Stout, Benjamin, Jr..........60, 76
Stout, Jonathan................54
Stout, Obadiah, Sr...........32, 54
Stout, Obadiah, Jr. (Obediah) ...33
Stout, Josiah...................54
Stout, Thomas.............32, 34, 54
Strange, Philip (Phelep).........60
Strange, Stephen (Stepen).......64
Strekes, Allen..................17
Stricklin, Elihu (Elihugh)........74
Stringer, Edmund (Edmond).....63
Striplin, William (Wm.)(Stribling) 72
Strode, James.....32, 55, 60, 65, 66, 78
Strode, John................60, 65, 78
Strode, John, Sr................60
Strode, Samuel..........12, 23, 34, 54
Strode, Stephen.................78
Strong, Walter E................58
Strother, Thomas...............54
Strother, William...............52
Stubblefield, Robert..........60, 67
Stubblefield, William (Wm.).....60
Stucker, Jacob..................24

[225]

List of Names

Stucker, Michael (Mical) ...24, 52, 60
Stuphelbun, John (Stofelbeen)
   (Stopelbeen)............28, 55, 66
Stutville, Charles............60, 65
Sublette, Allen (Sublett.)........ 58
Sublette, Lewis (Sublett.)......43, 52
Sudduth, William............65, 78
Sudland, Angus................ 66
Suggett, John..........52, 55, 60
Sullivan, Daniel, Jr. (Dan)....... 26
Sumalt, Andrew (Zomault).....49, 55
Sumalt, Christopher (Cimmolt)
   (Christerfer) (Zumbalt)
   (Christifer)............49, 55, 56
Sumalt, Jacob (Zumalt) (Jackob)
                       49, 55
Summers, Edward (Edwd.)....27, 65
Summers, Elijah (Summars)..... 54
Summers, John (Summars)..54, 60, 65, 69, 72
Summers, John, Jr.............. 58
Summers, Robert............... 58
Summers, Thomas.............. 69
Summit, Christian.............. 82
Summers, Edward...........60, 65
Summers, Elijah............60, 65
Summers, John......27, 58, 60, 62, 65
Summers, Thomas (Thos.)....... 58
Suter, Jesse................... 52
Sutherland, David............. 65
Sutherland, Frederick (Sutherling)...................60, 65
Sutherland, Thomas (Sutherling). 47
Sutherland, William............ 60
Sutton, Benjamin (Benj.)......54, 87
Sutton, James..............55, 78
Sutton, Nathaniel.............. 55
Sutton, Robert................ 23
Swaine, Thomas (Thos.)......... 60
Swearingen, Thomas (Thos.)..... 23
Swearingen, Van (Swearengen)...45, 56, 62
Sweet, Benjamin (Benj.).32, 34, 48, 54
Sweet, Joseph..............32, 48
Sweet, Joshua..............33, 48
Sweet, Thomas..........32, 34, 48
Swindler, Henry............... 60
Swope, Jacob.................. 27

Tabb, William [Taub?]........60, 65
Talbot, Edmund................ 62
Talbot, Haile.................. 64
Talbot, Isham..............23, 62
Talbot, Isham, Jr.............. 58
Talbot, James, S.............. 62

Talbot, Samuel (Saml.) (Talbert)
                         60, 65
Talifer, Richard............... 82
Tandy, Achilles (Ach.)......51, 63, 93
Tandy, John (Tanday).........52, 67
Tandy, Moses.................. 93
Tandy, William................ 63
Tandy, William, Jr............. 63
Tanner, Archelaus.............. 63
Tanner, John...............27, 52
Tanner, William............... 60
Tarbel, Conrad (Torbell)........ 27
Tardiveau, P.................. 42
Tatman, Joseph................ 57
Taub, Arthur Thomas (Thos.)..60, 63
Taylor, Abraham............... 16
Taylor, Benjamin (Benj.)........ 63
Taylor, Chapman............... 52
Taylor, Elkin.................. 74
Taylor, George (Geo.).......52, 93
Taylor, Griffen.............27, 33
Taylor, Henry (H)...........17, 93
Taylor, Isaac............32, 33, 48
Taylor, John........27, 48, 52, 54, 62
Taylor, John, Jr........27, 32, 34, 62
Taylor, Philip, W.............. 40
Taylor, Richard (Richd.)......52, 60
Taylor, Robert......27, 32, 34, 48, 54
Taylor, Samuel................ 27
Taylor, Thomas................ 60
Taylor, William (Wm.).......58, 78
Taylor, Zachary.............60, 63
Tegarden, George............46, 76
Telford, Alexander (Alexr.)...63, 93
Telford, James (Tillford)......... 27
Telford, William (Wm.).......63, 93
Templin, James................ 48
Templin, John (Templen)....... 27
Tenant, John.................. 54
Terry, Enes................... 27
Terrill, Henry (Terrell).......... 65
Terrill, James (Tarrell).......... 74
Terrill, Joseph (Terrel).......... 15
Terrill, Robert.......28, 33, 49, 56, 66
Teters, George (Teter) (Geo.) .16, 58
Teters, Jonathan.............. 58
Teters, Samuel................ 58
Thanks, Michael (Mical)........ 67
Thatcher, Amos (Thetcher)...32, 34, 46, 57
Thatcher, Daniel (Danl.)......57, 78
Thatcher, Joseph.............. 78
Theobalds, Clement.........55, 78, 84
Theobalds, Thomas.........55, 66, 88
Thoebalds, Sam........55, 56, 84, 88
Theobalds, William............ 78
Theron, Hugh................. 60

[226]

List of Names

Thomas, Absalom 54
Thomas, Charles (Chas.) 60, 67
Thomas, Eli 62
Thomas, Enos 60
Thomas, Ephraim (Ephram) 65
Thomas, Henry 26
Thomas, John 26, 27, 32, 34, 43, 52, 54, 60, 65
Thomas, Levi 54
Thomas, Philip 52
Thomas, Plummer 60, 67
Thomas, M 49
Thomas, Richard 43
Thomas, Rowland 60, 67, 84
Thomas, William (Wm.) ... 40, 52, 56, 60, 65, 79, 84
Thompson, Andrew 32, 34, 48, 74
Thompson, Charles 69
Thompson, Clifton (Thomson) ... 93
Thompson, Even 26
Thompson, Gloss 52
Thompson, Henry 49
Thompson, Hugh 17, 53
Thompson, Isaac 12
Thompson, James 17, 52, 58, 65
Thompson, John (Jno.) 26, 54, 58
Thompson, Joseph (Tomson)58, 63, 78
Thompson, Lawrence (L.) ... 26, 27, 52
Thompson, Robert (Rober.) (Robt.) 14, 53, 56
Thompson, Rhodus (Thomson) (Rodes) 52, 60
Thompson, Samuel (Saml.) .58, 77, 78
Thompson, Thomas 104
Thompson, William (Wm.) .. 17, 43, 63
Thompson, Zacharias 54
Thorp, David 28, 55
Thorp, Dodson 27, 64
Thorp, Henry (Henre) 28, 55
Thorp, John 24
Threlkeld, John 26
Threlkeld, Moses 26
Threlkeld, Thomas (Thos.) 26
Threlkeld, Thomas, Jr 26
Threlkeld, William (Willam.) 58
Tichenor, Elijah 54
Tilley, John 74
Tilley, Thomas 74
Tillery, William 52
Tilton, Robert 43, 46, 53
Tilton, William (Tulton) 65
Timberlake, John 64
Timberlake, Richard 64
Timberlake, Samuel 62
Tindall, William (Tindul) 56
Timmons, Stephen 58
Tingley, Levi 78
Tinsley, William (Wm.) 52
Tipton, Thomas 58
Tired, Joseph 58
Titus, Joseph 64
Todd, Jane 37, 75
Todd, John (Tode) 45, 61
Todd, John, Jr. (Jno.) 14
Todd, Levi 6, 14, 17, 18, 22, 25, 42, 45, 46, 51, 53, 63, 90, 91, 96
Todd, Owen 40, 46, 53, 60, 62, 67
Todd, Robert (Robt.) 41, 43, 45, 46, 52, 63, 75, 90, 91
Todd, Robert, Jr. (Robt.) .. 43, 46, 51
Todd, Thomas 83
Tolbert, Isham 27
Tollen, Robert 69
Tomlin, Nicholas (Nicklis) 60
Tomlin, William 24
Tomlinson, Ambrose (Ambrus) ... 93
Tomlinson, Elijah 93
Tompkins, George R (G. R.) .60, 67, 93
Tompkins, Giles 64
Tompkins, Ham 60
Tompkins, John (Tompskin) 27
Toole, William 11
Tonines, David 93
Torbit, James 52
Torrans, John 14, 24
Torry, Keeble 24
Toul, Benjamin I (Benj.) 60
Townsend, Garret (Townsen) (Townson) (Garrett) 47, 60, 65
Townsend, James (Jas.) (Townsen) 47, 65
Townsend, John 11, 69
Townsend, Oswald (Townsin) (Ozwel) (Towns) 6, 27, 29
Trabue, Daniel 52
Trabue, Edward (Edwd.) 43, 52
Tracy, Samuel (Saml.) (Trasey) .. 52
Tracy, William (Trasey) ..9 (List) 52
Trible, Andrew (A) (Tribble) ..47, 60, 65, 78
Trible, Samuel 65, 72
Trimble, George (Trimbal) (Trimbell) 60, 78
Trimble, Isaac 78
Trimble, James 45
Trimble, John (Jon) (Trimbel) .. 28, 40, 48
Trimble, Thomas (Thos.) 77
Trimble, Walter 84
Trimble, William (Wm.) (Will) .17, 47
Triplett, William 65
Trop, Martin 15
Trotter, David 51, 53, 60
Trotter, James 42, 45, 60

List of Names

Trotter, Richard	77
Trotter, William	40
Troutman, Jacob	57, 60, 84
Troutman, John (Jno.)	62, 66, 78, 84
True, Charles (Chas.)	32, 34
Trumbo, Andrew	78, 84
Trumbo, George (Trumbow.)	84
Trumbo, Jacob	78
Trumbo, John	78
Trumbo, William	78
Tucker, Edward	28, 49
Tucker, George	60
Tucker, Jacob	58
Tucker, John	49, 54, 56
Tucker, Leonard (Lenord)	49
Tucker, William	28
Tull, William	60
Tully, Israel (Isarel)	43, 51
Turner, Daniel	58
Turner, Edward	27, 64
Turner, George	58
Turner, James	27, 34, 77
Turner, John	77
Turner, Joseph	14, 63
Turner, Lewis C	53
Turner, Philip	64
Turner, Thomas	27
Turner, William (Willm.)	63
Turner, Z. E.	63
Turney, Michael	58
Turnham, Thomas (Thos.)	60
Turpin, William (Wm.) (Terpin)	53, 58
Tuttle, David	54
Twetty, William	9 (List)
Twyman, James (Jas.)	24, 51, 63
Twyman, Reuben (Twiman) (Reub.)	51, 52, 60
Twyman, Thomas (Twieman)	60
Twyman, William (Twiman)	52, 60
Tyler, John (Tylor)	74
Tyler, Peter (Tylor)	74
Tyler, William (Wm.)	32
Ulery, Henry	78
Umphreys, William (Umphress)	9 (List)
Underwood, Nathaniel	28, 49, 55, 56, 84
Underwood, Reuben	28, 49, 55
Uria, Robert	32, 34
Usselton, George	52
Utman, Patrick	69
Utterback, Benjamin (Benj.)	52
Valandigham, James (Vanlandingham) (Jas.)	52, 60, 65
Valandigham, George	65
Valandigham, Lewis (Valandagham) (Valladigham)	52, 60
Vance, Andrew (Andw.)	56, 84
Vance, David	14, 24
Vance, John (Jno.)	53
Vance, Joseph	36
Vance, Webb	74
Van Cleve, John	69
Van Cleave, William	6
Vanderen, Barnard	84
Van Hook, Samuel (Samm.)	6, 26, 28, 48, 49, 77
Van Hook, Samuel, Jr	28, 33
Vaniman, Garrett	66
Vanmatre, Jacob [Van Meter?]	12
Vanzant, John (Jno.)	32, 52
Vardiman, Peter (Vardeman) (Peater)	15, 32, 56
Vart, Jacob (Vert)	57, 58, 84
Vaughn, John	52
Velley, Benjamin (Bengiman)	66
Venable, A.	23, 40, 43, 51, 53, 63
Verble, Philip (Phillip)	52
Verzadt, John	48
Vice, John	54
Vinson, P.	15
Violet, Henson	60, 65
Virgin, Price	32, 33
Vivian, John, Sr. (Vivion)	47
Vivian, John (Vivion)	47, 65
Vivian, Thachet	65
Vokes, George (Geo.)	58
Voorhies, Christopher (Vorris)	74
Voorhies, Garrett (Voorheese)	46, 53
Waddle, James	78, 88
Wade, John	47, 60
Wade, Dawson (Dorson)	47, 65
Wade, Dawson, Jr	47
Wade, James	60, 65
Wade, John	65
Wade, Josiah	54
Wade, Richard	9 (List)
Waggoner, John	46
Walden, John	69
Walker, Archibald	52
Walker, David	58
Walker, Henry	52, 58
Walker, James	93
Walker, John	6, 52, 74
Walker, Joseph (J)	58, 64
Walker, Matthew (Mat.)	24, 46
Walker, Nathaniel	55
Walker, Randall (Randel)	52
Walker, Richard	64
Walker, Robert	53

List of Names

Walker, Samuel.................. 93
Walker, William............... 43, 52
Wallace, Andrew................ 78
Wallace, Caleb......... 42, 59, 63, 83
Wallace, James................. 60
Wallace, John (Jno.)..... 43, 60, 78, 93
Wallace, Joseph................ 78
Wallace, Robert........ 43, 51, 53, 58
Wallace, William................ 64
Waller, Benjamin, Jr............ 60
Waller, Edward (Edwd.).55, 62, 66, 79
Waller, James (Wallers)........27, 51
Waller, John............28, 32, 55, 60
Waller, Joseph................. 52
Waller, Patrick................. 69
Waller, Stephen................ 67
Waller, William (Wm.) (Williem) 60, 67
Wallis, David.................. 74
Wallis, John................... 53
Wallis, W. E................... 53
Wallis, William (Walles)........ 74
Wallingfitch, Daniel (Dan) (Daniel)................32, 34, 62
Wallingford, Benjamin (Wollingford) (Wallingsford).......32, 34
Walter, Barnet................. 54
Walter, John...................104
Walton, Matthew.............17, 83
Wann, John (Jno.).............. 48
Ward, George................... 74
Ward, Isaac.................... 43
Ward, Jacob.................... 52
Ward, James....45, 51, 53, 60, 62, 63, 65
Ward, James, Sr. (Jas.)........60, 93
Ward, John....................51, 63
Ward, Joseph................... 78
Ward, Richard.................. 64
Ward, Thomas (Thos.)............ 77
Ward, W.......43, 46, 51, 53, 63, 90, 91
Warden, Philip................. 52
Ware, Daniel (Wer.)............ 27
Ware, Dudley.................58, 69
Ware, Marcum (Markim)........ 47
Ware, Thomas................... 15
Ware, William (Wm.).........52, 60
Warford, John.................. 68
Waring, Thomas (Thos.) (T.)48, 54, 56
Warnock, Michael..........14, 23, 93
Warren, John................... 26
Warren, Thomas................. 27
Warren, William (Warran).....60, 65
Wasson, Charles................ 78
Wasson, James (Jas.) (Wason)..46, 53
Waters, James.................. 6
Waters, R. J................... 68
Watkins, Evan.................. 60
Watkins, John..............45, 52, 60
Watkins, Samuel................ 68
Watkins, Thomas................ 74
Watkins, William............... 69
Watson, Jesse.................. 27
Watson, Michael (Michel)........ 54
Watson, Robert................. 63
Watts, David.................60, 65
Watts, John (Wats.)........27, 52, 62
Watts, Julius.................. 52
Watts, William (Wats)......15, 60, 67
Webb, Augustine (Augustin)...65, 72
Webb, Charles.................. 52
Webb, Forest.................43, 60
Webb, James.................... 78
Webb, John (Web).............63, 65
Webb, William E................ 88
Weddle, George [Waddle?].....32, 34
Weekley, Thomas (Thos.)........ 52
Weiser, Jacob (Wesirr)......... 60
Welch, John (Joh.) [Welsh?] ..31, 55
Welch, Walter (Wilch)..........8, 9
Wells, Abraham................. 60
Wells, Barnet................60, 65
Wells, Basil (Basel) (Bazel).31, 55, 66
Wells, Benjamin..............33, 55
Wells, James................... 78
Wells, John................60, 65, 82
Wells, Jonas (Jones)............ 84
Wells, Peter................... 27
Wells, Thomas (Thos.).......... 93
Welsh, John.................... 28
Welton, John [Walton?].......... 26
Wentzell, Daniel............... 68
West, Charles.................. 40
West, Jonathan................. 46
West, Joseph................... 58
West, Nathaniel (Nethennell)... 47
West, Rezin..................56, 88
West, Thomas (Thos.)....46, 47, 53, 55, 62, 66, 84, 88
West, William (Wm.)............ 67
Westerman, Charles............. 52
Whaley, James.................. 65
Whaley, John................... 54
Wheeler, Benjamin (Benj.)...... 72
Whitaker, Joel................. 60
Whitaker, Mark (Whitacer)...... 52
Whitaker, Thomas (Thos.)....... 52
White, Abraham (Abrm.)......... 43
White, Ambrose................9 (List)
White, Aquila (Aqulla)......27, 46
White, Aquilla, Jr............. 27
White, Benjamin................ 9
White, James..............27, 47, 60
White, Jeremiah..............60, 65
White, Joel..................40, 43

[229]

List of Names

White, John................60, 74
White, John, Sr................27
White, John, Jr..........27, 82
White, Stephen (Steven).........63
White, Thomas................49
White, William................52
Whiteman, Benjamin (Benj.)....48
Whitesett, John................60
Whiteside, John (Jno.).........62, 78
Whiteside, Robert................60
Whiteside, Samuel................60
Whiteside, William................60
Whitledge, Robert........33, 53, 56
Whitledge, Thomas (Thos.).48, 58, 84
Whitley, James (Whittley).....15, 32
Whitley, Solomon (Whittley)..32, 48
Whitley, Thomas (Thos.)........15
Whitley, William..........6, 15
Whitsel, Lewis [Whitsett?].....32, 34
Whitsett, William................78
Whitson, George.............47, 65
Whiwitt, Joseph [—?]............88
Whorl, Samuel................56
Wick, Moses................54
Wickliff, Charles (Wichliff) (Chars.)......................[?]
Wightman, Shardless.............58
Wiginton, Henry................58
Wilburn, Zachariah (Zach.)......64
Wilcox, Aaron................52
Wilcox, Daniel (Willcox) (Wilcocks).....................24, 52
Wilcox, John (Willcocks).32, 33, 34, 43
Wildres, John [Hildreth?].......49
Wiley, John................82
Wilkerson, James..............52, 78
Wilkerson, John................47
Wilkerson, John, Jr................60
Wilkerson, Moses........27, 47, 65, 72
Wilkerson, William................47
Wilkinson, Daniel (Wilconson)..6, 43
Wilkinson, James..............25, 99
Willcockson, Daniel................8
Willcockson, David................63
Willcockson, Edward..........[—?]
Willey, James................93
Wilkin, John................24
Williams, Andrew (Andw.).......58
Williams, Alfred (Alferd).........60
Williams, Barnett................17
Williams, Basil (Bazal).....54, 77, 78
Williams, Beverley (Beaverly)...58
Williams, Charles.............46, 77
Williams, Daniel..............27, 65
Williams, David......14, 48, 51, 52, 58
Williams, Edward........27, 47, 60, 65
Williams, Evan................68
Williams, Isaac................27, 64
Williams, James..........33, 40, 78
Williams, Jesse................49, 56
Williams, Joel................54
Williams, John...12, 14, 24, 27, 32, 34, 43, 45, 48, 51, 52, 54, 56, 60, 66, 74, 77, 78
Williams, John, Jr..........32, 34, 48
Williams, J................23
Williams, Joseph............43, 49, 54
Williams, Lawrence................54
Williams, Peter................24
Williams, Pleasant................54
William, Shadrach (Shadrack)...27
Williams, Thomas....17, 32, 34, 48, 54
Williams, William (Wm.) (W.).27, 43, 58, 64
Williams, William, Jr. (Wm.).....53
Williams, Zadock................54
Williamson, Alden (All.).........72
Williamson, Henry................48
Willmore, Jacob................27
Willmott, Robert................78, 84
Wills, Andrew (Andw.).........60, 65
Wills, Barnet................65
Wills, Matthew..........60, 65, 72
Wills, Oscar................65
Wills, Robert (Will)................27
Wills, Samuel................82
Wills, Thomas (Thos.).........60, 65
Wills, William..........60, 63, 65, 66
Wills, William, Jr................60
Wilson, Amos (Willson)..32, 34, 48, 54
Wilson, Andrew (Willson)........78
Wilson, Daniel................65, 77
Wilson, David................28, 33
Wilson, Edward................49, 78
Wilson, George.............25, 26, 68
Wilson, Henry, Sr................26
Wilson, Henry, Jr................26
Wilson, Isaac................52
Wilson, James........26, 40, 60, 77, 78
Wilson, Jeremiah................60
Wilson, John (Willson).....15, 26, 33, 48, 54, 58, 65, 77, 78, 84
Wilson, John, Jr................58
Wilson, Joseph (Willson).........52
Wilson, Moses................27
Wilson, Nathaniel (Nathl.)....46, 63
Wilson, Peter................77, 78
Wilson, Samuel..........28, 33, 60, 63
Wilson, Thomas (Thos.)51, 52, 65, 84, 93
Wilson, William (Willson)........78
Wiman, Lewis (Lues)............60
Wimore, Frederick (Wimour)....40
Wimore, John (Wymore)...14, 24, 40, 51, 63, 93

List of Names

Windsor, Christopher.........26, 27
Winemiller, Jacob.............48, 55
Winlock, Joseph................ 68
Winn, Adam..............60, 63, 65
Winn, Daniel................... 65
Winn, George................... 65
Winn, Jesse.................... 67
Winn, Owen (Oen).............. 65
Winn, Thomas...............53, 65
Winn, Thomas M. (Thos.)....... 68
Winn, William...............60, 65
Winters, Elisha............53, 60, 63
Winters, William............... 27
Wisdom, John................... 58
Wise, Adam..................... 60
Withers, Berry................. 52
Withers, James............12, 60, 62
Withers, James, Jr............11, 60
Withers, John, Sr.............. 62
Withers, John................60, 62
Withers, Peter (Petter)........ 62
Withers, Stephen (Witters)
  (Steven).................... 60
Wolts, Christopher............. 65
Wood, Abraham.............32, 34, 48
Wood, Ahijah................... 52
Wood, Amos..................... 54
Wood, Andrew (Hood)...32, 34, 48, 65
Wood, Archibald (Archd.)....... 64
Wood, Benjamin (Benj.)....32, 34, 48
Wood, Christopher.............. 54
Wood, George (Geo.)..........48, 54
Wood, Henry.................... 60
Wood, James.................60, 67
Wood, John (Jno.).15, 27, 32, 34, 48, 52
Wood, Joseph................... 33
Wood, Nathaniel (Nathl.)....... 76
Wood, Nicholas (Nichs.)........ 52
Wood, Richard.............32, 34, 48
Wood, Robert (Robt.)........... 68
Wood, Samuel (Sammel) (Saml.)28, 62
Wood, Samuel, Jr. (Sammel).... 28
Wood, William, Sr.............. 34
Wood, William (Wm.)....32, 33, 48, 54
Woodcock, Joseph............... 58
Woodfolk, Augustin............. 40
Woodfolk, Loyal (Lowyell).....52, 60
Woodfolk, Saul (Soyl).......... 51
Woodfolk, Richard.............. 40
Woodlay, William............... 78
Woods, Adam.................27, 64
Woods, Ahijah...............24, 43
Woods, Andrew.................. 27
Woods, Archibald (Archd.)...... 27
Woods, David................... 27
Woods, John.................27, 78
Woods, Michael (Mical)......... 58
Woods, Peter................... 27
Woods, Samuel, Jr.............. 62
Woods, Thomas.................. 58
Woods, William................. 58
Woodruff, David (Woodroff).... 27
Woodruff, John (Woodroof)....24, 27
Woodward, Chesley.........60, 72, 84
Woodward, John (Woodard)...65, 72
Woodward, Levi................. 54
Wooldridge, Edmund (Woodridge)
  (Edmond)..................40, 45
Wooldridge, Edward (Edwd.).... 52
Wooldridge, Elisha............. 52
Wooldridge, John (Wooldreg)..15, 77
Wooldridge, Josiah...........43, 52
Wooldridge, Robert............. 52
Wooldridge, William..........77, 84
Worel, Apewell................. 55
Workman, Daniel..............55, 77
Workman, Morris (Moris)......77, 78
Worley, Caleb (C.)............. 60
Worley, Caleb, Jr.............. 52
Worrel, William................ 40
Worrindon, Owen (Ohen)........ 27
Worthington, B................. 17
Worthington, Edward (Edwd.).43, 58
Wothershead, Christopher
  (Chris.).................... 63
Wrayley, James................. 60
Wright, James.................. 78
Wright, John...............65, 66, 72
Wright, Samuel (Saml.)......... 66
Wright, Thomas................. 60
Writedge, Thomas............... 11

Yager, Cornelius............... 6
Yager, Jacob (Yauger)...32, 34, 48, 78
Yager, Peter (Yawger)......49, 57, 78
Yager, Philip (Yeiger)......... 60
Yarbrough, John.........60, 67, 78, 84
Yarnell, Jesse................. 84
Yates, John (Yets)............. 84
Yeatman, John.................. 28
Yoacom, George (Yoocom)....... 58
Yoacom, Jacob (Yoocom)........ 58
Yoacom, John (Yocam).......26, 27
Yoacom, Matthew (Yocam) (Mat-
  thias)..................26, 27, 58
Yoacam, Samuel (Yoaham)...... 26
York, Elijah................... 54
York, Isaac.................... 78
York, Jeremiah (Jarama)......54, 78
York, Jesse (Yeork)............ 84
Young, Abner................... 63

List of Names

Young, Ambrose................. 63
Young, Henry................... 58
Young, James............58, 60, 67, 69
Young, John.......40, 53, 54, 63, 65, 87
Young, John, Jr................. 52
Young, Joseph.................. 65
Young, Lawrence................ 52
Young, Leonard (Leo.).....40, 52, 67
Young, Lewis................... 52
Young, M....................... 63
Young, Reuben.................. 52
Young, Reuben, Jr.............. 52

Young, Richard (Richd.)..43, 45, 52, 61, 93
Young, Thomas (Thos.)....32, 34, 53, 90, 91
Young, William (Wm.)....40, 51, 52, 60, 63, 65, 67
Younger, Joshua................ 57

Zechledge, William............. 58
Zimmerman, Frederick (Zimerman) (Fredk.)............... 65

Names in Petition No. 1, are not included in this Index, unless they appear on later Petitions.

The word "List" following the number 9, refers to list of persons killed and wounded at Boonesfort, according to Petition No. 9.

INDEX

	PAGE
Alleghany Mountains	1, 7, 9, 80
Askins, John	96

Augusta, West:
    Model for procedure in West Fincastle 38

Bardstown:
    Proposed site for sitting of Supreme Court 124

Baylor, Walker:
    Trustee of Stanford 94

Beach Knobs 56
Beal, Tavener 35
Beallsborough, Nelson County 16

Bedinger, Michael:
    His lands 128

Big Sandy 90, 110, 118

Bird, Captain:
    Invasion of Kentucky 168

Blair, Alexander:
    Trustee of Stanford 94

Blue Lick 73, 117
Bogg's Fork (of Boone's Creek) 130
Boone, Daniel 8, 49
    Capture at Blue Lick 73
    Request for treasury warrant for land 178
    Trustee of Washington and Maysville 92, 156

Boone, Jacob:
    Trustee of Maysville 156

Boone, Squire 61
Boone's Creek 118, 130

Boonesborough:
    Request for a town at 48
    Act to establish 52
    Proposed county seat 107

Boonsfort:
    Seige of 44, 45
    Request from inhabitants of 48
    Slaves at 44, 49

Botetourt, Baron de:
    Petition addressed to 35

Bounty land 49

Bourbon County:
    Act establishing 86
    Requests for division 89, 107, 108, 117, 130
    Protests against division 91, 110, 119, 131
    Acts for division 119
    Requests for towns 91, 121, 127, 147
    Requests for gristmills 144, 148, 150
    Protests against gristmills 145, 146
    Tobacco inspection 120, 152
    Recording deeds 156

Index

	PAGE
Bourbon Courthouse:	
Request for town at	121
Bowman, John	157
County Lieutenant in Lincoln County	168
Bradley, Edward:	
Trustee of Boonesborough	52
Bramlett's Lick	118, 146
Brashiers, Marshem:	
Trustee of Louisville	55
Brooke, G.	186
Brown, J.:	
Of Staunton, Virginia, a letter of	168
Brown, John:	
Trustee of Harrodsburg	83
Buchanan, James	35
Buchanan, William	104
A deposition	45
Bullitt, Alexander Scott:	
Trustee of Louisville	134
Burks, Samuel	35
Bush, William:	
His land	139
Cabell, Frederick	35
Cabell, Hector	35
Cabell, John, Jr	35
Cabell, Joseph, Jr	35
Cabell, Nicholas	35
Cabell, Sanders	35
Cabell, William, Jr	35
Calendar of State Papers	2
Calloway, Richard:	
Trustee at Boonesborough	51, 52
Campbell, John:	
Request to repeal act establishing Louisville	72
Tobacco inspection in Jefferson County	174
Campbellstown, Jefferson County	16
Cartright, Robert	50
Casey, Peter:	
Trustee of Harrodsburg	83
Caveats	76, 77, 124
Chaplaine, Abraham:	
Trustee of Harrodsburg	83
Charlestown:	
Request for town at	100
Act to establish	100
Charlton, Edward:	
Notary at Williamsburg	45
Cherokees	36, 37, 48
Christian, Turner:	
Party to law suit	163
Christian, William:	
Trustee of Harrodsburg	83
Claims, law for settling	171

Index

	PAGE
Clark, George Rogers:	
References to	39, 40, 43, 100, 157, 159, 168, 186, 187, 188
Requests for pay for services	57, 178
A memorial	172
His papers	174
Lands for his soldiers	60
Clark's Run	84
Cleveland, Eli:	
His lands	132
Collins, Henry:	
Tory landholder	70
Colonial Governor, petition addressed to	35
Commissions, military	42
Commissioners:	
For Western accounts	159, 171
Court of	74
To settle claims	100
Act to create	102
Act to extend powers of	102
Congress, Continental	38, 64
Conn, Notley:	
Trustee of Hopewell	128
Connolly, John:	
Tory land-owner	54, 72
Constitution	62, 64
Continental Congress	38, 68
Convention, petitions addressed to	36, 38
Conway, Miles W.:	
Trustee of Washington and Charlestown	92, 100
Counties, division of:	
Request for, in Fincastle County	36, 38
Request for, in Kentucky County	55
Request for, in Bourbon County	89, 107, 108, 117, 130
Request for, in Fayette County	85, 107, 114, 130
Request for, in Lincoln County	84, 141
Court, General, of Virginia	12
Courts:	
Request for Supreme Court	65, 66, 67
Act to establish	66
Acts to amend	98, 136
Request for removal	124
Protest against removal	135
Docket of	124
Courts, county	41, 57
Cowan, John:	
Trustee of Harrodsburg	83
Craig's Creek	105
Crow's Sinking Spring	84
Crow's Station	159
Cumberland, Falls of:	
Request for sixty thousand acres of land at	35
Currency, paper, depreciation of	64, 154
Danville, seat of Supreme Court	121, 124
Davis, John	35

Index

Deeds:
    Request to extend time for recording...... 156
    Act to extend time........................ 157
Dick's River................................. 84
Delawares.................................... 40
Detroit:
    Kentucky captives in................... 46, 169
District of Kentucky:
    Act to establish.......................... 66
Douglass, James.............................. 138
Dry Run...................................... 75
Dumfries..................................... 185
Duncan, James:
    Trustee of Hopewell....................... 128
Dunmore, Lord:
    His land policy......................... 7, 36
Dutch Station, near Louisville............... 157

Eagle Creek.................................. 86
Edmund, John, Clerk of Bourbon County........ 105
Education:
    Lands for public....................... 69, 137
    Interest in............................... 70
    Transylvania Seminary........ 72, 112, 160, 161, 162
Edwards, John:
    Clerk of Bourbon County......... 118, 120, 145
    Trustee of Hopewell....................... 128
Elections:
    Difficulty of attendance.................. 109
    Method at Boonesborough................... 50
Elkhorn Creek................................ 61
Emerson, Ash:
    Employe of Lytle....................... 74, 75
Emigrants on Ohio River...................... 153
Ervin, Mary:
    Request to waive escheat.................. 96
    Act to waive.............................. 97
Escheat:
    Of lands.............................. 69, 70, 72
    Location of lands......................... 138
    Act for............................... 71, 137
Estill, James:
    Trustee of Boonesborough.................. 51
Express to Pittsburgh........................ 42

Falls of the Ohio:
    Requests of inhabitants at (see Louisville, Jefferson County)............................... 53, 54, 56
Fayette County:
    Requests for division........... 85, 107, 114, 130
    Protest against division.................. 116
    Acts to divide......................... 86, 116
    Tobacco inspection...... 98, 102, 105, 113, 132, 139
    For town at Lexington................... 60, 106
    Complaints about land..................... 66
    Concerning clerks......................... 169

Index

	PAGE

Ferries:
    Requests to establish:
        Across Kentucky River 53, 87, 88, 89
        Across Cumberland River 170
    Acts to establish 53, 88
Fincastle County:
    Its extent 39
Fincastle, West:
    Request of inhabitants for jurisdiction of Virginia and establishing of county 36, 38
Floyd, John:
    His survey 61
    Trustee of Louisville 55
Fox, Arthur:
    Trustee of Washington and Maysville 92, 156
Frankfort:
    Tobacco inspection by James Wilkinson 171

Garnett, Thomas 185
Garrard, James:
    Surveyor of Bourbon County 104
    Trustee of Hopewell 128
Gass, David 51
Georgetown, Woodford County 16
Gilmore, John:
    Trustee of Harrodsburg 83
Gloster Town 174
Grant, John:
    Trustee of Charlestown 100
Green, Willis:
    Clerk of Lincoln County 85, 88, 94
Greenup, Christopher:
    Clerk of Supreme Court 97
Gristmills:
    Requests for 144, 148, 150
    Protests against 145, 146
Gutridge, John:
    Trustee of Washington 92

Hains, Benjamin 35
Hains, Joseph 35
Hamilton, Lieutenant Governor:
    Instigation of Indians 45
    His capture 186
Hammond's Creek 56
Hancock, Stephen 51
Hand, Edward:
    Brigadier General 43
Harman, Thomas 35
Harmon's Lick 84
Harris, Edward 35
Harris, John 35
Harris, Thomas 35

Index

	PAGE
Harrod, James:	
Trustee of Harrodsburg	83
Harrodsburg:	
Request of inhabitants for jurisdiction of Virginia	36, 38
Request for town at	82
Act to create (see Lincoln County)	83
Hart, Nathaniel:	
Complaints against	49, 50
Hay, William	164
Henderson, David	89
Henderson, Richard:	
Complaints against	49
Reference to petition from	35
Henderson, William:	
Trustee of Lexington	62
Hening, Statutes:	
Authority for acts quoted in this book	2
Henry, Patrick	3
Herod's Station:	
Place of Hamilton's captivity	187
Hickman's Creek	87, 99
Hines, Andrew:	
Trustee of Louisville	55
Hinkson's Fork of Licking River	144, 145, 150, 176
Hite, Abraham	35
Hite, Abraham, Jr	35
Hite, Isaac	35
Hite, Isaac, Jr	35
Hite, Joseph	35
Holder, John	51
Holder's Landing	139
Holloway, James:	
Services in Revolution	92
Holston River	104
Company raised on	168
Hopewell:	
Request for town at	127
Act to establish	128
Changed to Paris	148
Hopkins, James	35
Hopkins, William	35
Hopson, Henry	35
Hord, William:	
His lands	170
Hornsby, Joseph	35
Horsley, John	35
Horsley, Robert	35
Horsley, William	35
Howard's Creek	86, 139
Hudson, William	188
Hughs, John	35
Illinois:	
Request of claimant to land in	151
Indians:	
Depredations	41, 62, 85, 93, 109, 153
Prisoners	165

Index

	PAGE
Innes, Harry:	35
To present request for separation from Virginia	81
Innes, Hugh	35
Innes, James	35
Attorney-General	163
Innes, Robert	35
Irwin, Will:	
Clerk of Mason County	119
Irwin, Joseph	176

Jack's Creek	88
Jefferson, Thomas:	
Committee in House of Delegates	3
Jefferson County:	
Complaint about land	66
Request for separation from Virginia	79
For division of Kentucky County (seeLouisville and Falls of the Ohio)	55
Shipments of tobacco from	175
Johnston, William:	
Clerk of Jefferson County	134
Johnson, Robert, Surveyor (see facsimile map)	62, 72, 115
Jones, John Gabriel	37, 39, 40
Journal:	
Of House of Burgesses	1
Of Convention	1
Of House of Delegates	2

Kanawha:	
Battle of the Great	37
Kaskaskia	57
Kennedy, John:	
Trustee of Boonesborough	52
Kennedy, William:	
Trustee of Harrodsburg	83
Kentucky:	
Separation from Virginia	27, 62, 66, 78, 79, 82, 91, 121, 122, 141, 165
Kentucky County:	
Request of inhabitants for defense, Act creating	41
Development of salt springs	43
Relief in land troubles	45, 62
Request for division of county	55
Tobacco inspection	128
Act for division of county	57
Kentucky District:	
Act creating	66
Request of inhabitants for circuit courts	76
For settlement of claims by county courts	100
To increase places for Supreme Court	124
Protest against removal of Supreme Court	134
To give Supreme Courts power to establish tobacco inspection	129
To amend act for separation from Virginia	140
To extend time for registration of survey	164

Index

	PAGE
Kiccapoos	40

Kimburlin, John:
    His lands 177

Kirkham, Captain Samuel:
    Indian scout 177

Lamb, William:
    Trustee of Washington 92

Land laws:
    References to 7, 8, 36, 51, 59, 60, 63
    Acts 47, 48, 52
    Amendments 48, 77

Land office 36, 46, 47, 60, 63

Lanier, James:
    Trustee of Hopewell 128

Lapsley, Samuel:
    Trustee of Harrodsburg 83

Lawrence's Creek 100

Lee, Henry:
    Trustee of Washington, Charlestown, and Maysville. 92, 100, 156

Leestown 61

Lee's Town Bottom 171

Lexington Station 56

Lexington:
    Request for town at 60, 106
    Act to establish town 62
    Request for corporate body 106
    Request for added powers 143
    Act to grant added powers 144

Licking River 61
    Navigation of 144, 145, 146, 148, 150

Limestone Settlement 62, 89, 92, 108, 110, 117

Lincoln County:
    Complaint of inhabitants over land troubles 66
    Request for laws on marriage, etc. 68
    Request for towns at Harrodsburg and Stanford 82, 93
    Request for division of county 84, 141
    Act to divide 85

Litigation, extent of 64, 76, 77

Little, James:
    Trustee of Hopewell 128

Logan, Benjamin:
    Trustee of Harrodsburg 83
    Lands in Lincoln County 93
    Trustee of Stanford 94
    Regarding Indian prisoners 167

Logan, John:
    Trustee of Stanford 94

Long knives 40

Louisa River (Kentucky) 38

Louisville:
    Request for town at 53
    Act to establish town 55
    Request to repeal act creating town 72
    Act to repeal 73
    Request for trustees living in town 133
    Act to add trustees 134
    (See Falls of the Ohio and Jefferson County.)

Index

	PAGE
Luttrell, John:	
Complaint against	49
Lyne, Edmund	101
Trustee of Washington	92

Machir, John:
    Trustee of Charlestown..................................... 100
Madin, George... 50
Madison, James:
    Committee in House of Delegates........................ 3
Madison County:
    Act to create... 85
    Request for division..................................... 107
Marriage:
    Request for civil.. 69
    Act for civil.. 69
Martin, Captain John, Indian scout........................51, 177
Mason County:
    Act to establish... 119
Maxwell, John:
    A deposition.. 61
Maysville:
    Request for town at..................................... 155
    Act to establish town................................... 156
McAfee, James:
    Claim for supplies...................................... 171
McConnell's Station... 56
McCowwald, William:
    Trustee of Lexington.................................... 62
McCraw, Samuel... 168
McDonel, John.. 35
McDowell, Samuel:
    President of Convention for Separation.................. 141
McKee, Alexander.. 70
McKenzie, Robert:
    Tory landholder... 70
Megginson, William.. 35
Mercer County:
    Act to create.. 85
Meriwether, George:
    Trustee of Louisville................................... 55
Milford, George:
    Trustee of Maysville.................................... 156
Milford:
    Act to create town in Madison County.................... 128
Militia..42, 55, 56, 68
    Enumerations.......................................91, 111, 114
Mississippi River...6, 46, 176
Mitchell, Ignatius:
    Site of Charlestown..................................... 100
Mitchell, William:
    Trustee of Lexington.................................... 62
Monongahala.. 176
Moore, James F.:
    Affidavit... 159
Morrison, Major.. 176
Morris, Richard:
    Party to law suit....................................... 163

Index

	PAGE
Mosby, Robert:	
Trustee of Harrodsburg	83
Moyers:	
Settlement on State Creek	132
Muster, general	56
Muter, George:	
To present request for separation from Virginia	81
Navigation of Licking River	144, 145, 146, 148, 150
Nelson County:	
Request for separation from Virginia	79
New Market:	
Mercer County	16
Noe, John:	
Justice of Peace in Harlan County	188
Norborne, Baron de Botetourt	35
Obache (Wabash)	57
Opost	40
Orphans, request for law to care for	68
Paint Lick	84
Pamphlet on "Public Good"	64
Parberry, James	103
Paris:	
Act to change from Hopewell	148
Patterson, R.	61
Patterson, Robert:	
Trustee of Lexington	62
Pauling, Henry:	
Trustee of Stanford	94
Payne, Edward	115
Pendleton, John:	
Auditor Public Accounts	163, 171, 178
Petitioning, the process	2
Petitions, references to some not in this book	16, 35
Pittsburgh	42, 43
Pope, William:	
Trustee of Louisville	55
Powell, Levin:	
Trustee of Boonesborough	52
Powell's Valley	36
Quartermaster of Illinois Department	157
Quit rents, attitude of settlers to	6
Randle, Abel	35
Randell, Chilton	185
Rankin, Robert:	
Trustee of Washington	92, 100
Rations:	
Bill for and price	167
Ravin Creek	86

Index

	PAGE
Rawlings, Pemberton	51, 52
Religion, prevailing forms	69
Reserve lands for soldiers in Lincoln County	141

Richmond:
    Capital of Virginia 2, 123, 164

Roads:
    Great Kanawha to Lexington 19
    Limestone to Lexington 103
    Winchester to Fort Pitt 177

Robinson's Fork of Boone's Creek 130
Rockcastle River 84
Ross, Philip 35
Ruddle's Mill 120
Russell, William 115, 176

Saint Asaph's 179

Salt:
    Development of springs 43
    Acts for conservation of 44
    Claim for sale of 162

Salt Spring of Licking 61
Sandy Creek 86

School, public:
    Escheated lands for 69
    Interest in 70
    Law for escheated lands 137

Scott, General Charles 105
Scouts, claims for service 177

Separation of Kentucky from Virginia:
    Account of 27
    Suggested 62, 66, 78, 91
    Requested 79
    Protest against 121
    Acts for 82, 122, 141
    Titles after separation 165

Severn, Ebenezer 35
Seymour, Felix 35

Shannon, William:
    Claim as Quartermaster to Illinois Department ... 157
    Act to settle claim 160

Shelby, Isaac:
    Trustee of Stanford 94, 101

Silver Creek 118

Simon, Joseph:
    Partner of John Campbell 72

Sinclair, M. P 186

Slaughter, George:
    Trustee of Louisville 55

Slaves:
    At Boonsfort 44, 49
    Brought to Kentucky without notice 126
    Act regarding 127
    Provisions concerning in will 183

Smith, Charles, Jr.:
    Trustee of Charlestown 100, 128

Smith, James:
    Early explorations, 1767-1773 154

Smith, John:
    Trustee of Harrodsburg 83

Index

	PAGE
South, John	51

Stanford:
- Request for town at 93
- Act to create town 94

Stanwix, Treaty of Fort 37
State Creek 132
Staunton, Virginia 167

Steel, Andrew:
- Trustee of Lexington 62

Steel, William:
- Trustee of Lexington 62

Stone, William 185
Stone Lick Creek 113
Stoner's Fork of Licking River 108, 110, 144, 145, 148, 150
Strays, request for laws 69
Stuart, Henry, journey down Ohio 176

Sullivan, James:
- Trustee of Louisville 55

Supreme Court:
- Request to remove 12, 124
- Protest against removal 135
- (See Courts.)

Surveys:
- Request for extension of time to record 162, 164
- Act to extend time 164, 165, 176

Tate's Creek 128

Taxes:
- Tobacco used for 102, 105
- Payable in specie only 123
- Tax on clerks of court 170
- Act regarding 170

Taylor, Edmund:
- Trustee of Boonesborough 52

Taylor, Emanuel 35
Taylor, Richard 101

Taylor, Samuel:
- Trustee of Harrodsburg 83

Thomas, Cornelius 35
Thomas, James, Jr 35
Thomas, John 35

Thornton, Thomas, of Fredericksburg:
- His will 182

Thruston, Buckner:
- Trustee of Louisville 134

Thruston, Charles:
- Trustee of Boonesborough 52

Thurston, John 174

Tobacco:
- Requests for inspection:
  - In Fayette County 98, 102, 105, 113, 132, 139
  - In Bourbon County 120, 152
  - At Tate's Creek 128
  - At Frankfort 171
- Protest against inspection 129
- Acts to establish inspection 99, 120
- Use for taxes 102, 105
- Use for currency 103, 172
- Shipments from Jefferson County 175

Index

	PAGE
Todd estate	95, 142
Act to create trustees for	96
Amendment	143
Todd, J. N.	61
Todd, Jane, widow of John Todd	95, 142
Todd, John:	
Trustee of Lexington	62
Todd, John, Jr.:	
Trustee of Louisville	55
Todd, Levi:	
Clerk of Fayette County	86, 87, 169, 170
Todd, Mary Owen	95
Todd, Robert	139
Executor of estate	95, 142
Tories:	
Law to escheat lands	137
Cases of men	54, 69, 70, 72
Towns, request for establishment of, at:	
Boonesborough	48
Louisville	53
Lexington	60, 106
Harrodsburg	82
Stanford	93
Washington	91
Charlestown	100
Bourbon Courthouse	121
Hopewell	127
Paris	148
Maysville	155
(See respective towns.)	
Towns:	
Lists of trustees	50, 51, 52, 55, 62, 83, 92, 94, 100, 128, 134, 156
Transylvania Company	8
Characterization of policy	36
Transylvania Seminary:	
List of trustees	72
Act to grant escheated lands	72
Request for surveyor's fees	112
To secure fund by lottery	160
Act to grant lottery right	161
Request for reduction of trustees	161
Act to grant reduction	162
Trigg, Stephen:	
Trustee of Louisville	55
Trustees:	
Of escheated lands for school	69
For towns	50, 51, 52, 54, 62, 71, 83, 92, 94, 100, 128, 137, 156
Turner, Joseph	35
Unity Station	56
Vincennes (Saint Vincents)	57
Van Meter, Garret	35

Index

	PAGE
Waller, Edward	92
Trustee of Washington and Hopewell	128
Wallace, Caleb	160
Warberton, Benjamin	35
Warberton, John	35

Warren, Thomas:
- Trustee of Charlestown ... 100

Warwick, Lincoln County ... 16
Washington County line ... 56

Washington:
- Request for town ... 91
- Act to create ... 92

Welch's Fork of Boone's Creek ... 130

West, Thomas:
- Trustee of Hopewell ... 128

West Indies ... 171
Wilkinson, Gary ... 35

Wilkinson, James:
- Trustee of Louisville ... 134
- Request for tobacco inspection ... 171

Williams, Captain John ... 186
Williamsburg, capital of Virginia ... 2
William and Mary College, too distant from Kentucky ... 23, 112
Wilson's Station ... 84

Woodford County:
- Act to establish ... 116

Young, Richard:
- Justice of Fayette County ... 115, 116

PETITIONS FROM KENTUCKY

TO THE

VIRGINIA LEGISLATURE

1776 to 1791

A Supplement

to

Petitions of the Early

Inhabitants of

Kentucky

to the

General Assembly of Virginia

1769 to 1792

Compiled by
John Frederick Dorman

This volume was reproduced from
Personal copies located in the
Publisher's private Library

All rights reserved. No part of this publication may be reproduced,
stored in a retrieval system, transmitted in any form, posted
on to the web in any form or by any means without
the prior written permission of the publisher.

Please direct all correspondence and orders to:

www.southernhistoricalpress.com
or
SOUTHERN HISTORICAL PRESS, Inc.
PO Box 1267
375 West Broad Street
Greenville, SC   29601
southernhistoricalpress@gmail.com

Originally published: Frankfort, KY 1914
New Material Copyright 1981
By: The Rev. Silas Emmett Lucas, Jr.
ISBN #0-89308-228-7
All rights Reserved.
Printed in the United States of America

PETITIONS FROM KENTUCKIANS

TO THE VIRGINIA LEGISLATURE

There are preserved at the Virginia State Library, Richmond, Virginia, four boxes of petitions to the General Assembly which originated in the area which became Kentucky in 1792. They are a part of an extensive collection of petitions from all of the counties of Virginia.

Some of these petitions have been printed in James Rood Robertson, Petitions of the Early Inhabitants of Kentucky to the General Assembly of Virginia, 1769 to 1792 (Filson Club Publications, no. 27; Louisville, 1914) but many others have not been printed previously.

The abstracts which follow are intended to give the full details of the petitions in the language used but are not verbatim copies. Those printed by Robertson are omitted here but all others will appear below.

Box 1
Jefferson County, 1783-91; Kentucky County, 1776-80

1776, Oct. 19 - Petition of John Gabriel Jones and George Rodgers Clark on behalf of the inhabitants of Kentucky County to acquaint the House of Delegates with the defenseless state of their constituants and imploring their immediate protection by sending such forces as they think necessary. It is to the interest of Virginia to prevent the inhabitants from abandoning that settlement and will be advantageous in case of an Indian war, an event much to be feared with the Kiccapoos, Victs [?] and other nations of Indians lying west of the River Ohio. In this service they can save the public at least half of what an army must cost to be levied anywhere else on the frontier counties.

1777, Nov. 6 - Petition of sundry inhabitants of Kentucky that were employed by their country to come out of the lower parts of Virginia and North Carolina to serve as soldiers in defending the country and protecting the inhabitants of Kentucky against the depredations and cruelties of the savages, in which service they were wounded and rendered incapable of getting their living and maintaining themselves for the future. They ask help to render their life supportable and to prevent their becoming wretched and ending their days in misery and want.

Richard Epperson
Catlit Jones

Certified by Daniel Boone, Capt.
[Endorsed: Ł10 present relief and Ł5 per annum for life allowed Richd. Epperson; Ł20 present and Ł10 per annum during life to Catlit Jones; (Ł10 present and Ł5 per annum for a/c to R. Epperson [?])]

1783, Nov. 28 - Petition of divers inhabitants of Jefferson, Fayette and Lincoln counties and of sundry others that during the existence of paper money several acts of Assembly were passed to guard against the evil arising from its depreciation and particularly that surveyors and others entitled to tobacco fees might not suffer thereby, but finding every preceeding effort ineffectual, the Legislature passed an Act [for regulating] the Registers' and Surveyors' Fees in Tobacco, which by

Act passed November Session 1781 was limited to 12 sh. 6 d. per hundred specie. Under the law the surveyors kept and accepted their offices and although the deputies were allowed but one-half of 5/6 of the full fees, deputies in abundance were easily procured. The Act of October session 1782 revised the Act but the petitioners conceive it was intended for clerks and sheriffs and the surveyors' fees were never intended to be altered. The principals and deputies of these counties conceive themselves entitled to the fees allowed by the law, with this additional circumstance of oppression that instead of 10 sh. per hundred the tobacco is now settled at 12/6. They refuse to survey or deliver plots and certificates of survey out of the office without receiving their fees, a circumstance that if allowed will be the means of losing to many poor and honest men their just claims for want of money to clear them out. By Act of October 1782 the principals are allowed to act by deputy and two of them reside at great distance. By default of their deputy, the sufferer must travel 600 miles to commence prosecution in a strange place without the benefit of the testimony or a jury of the vicinage, so that the principal has a sinecure worth thousands a year and is hardly accountable for his conduct. They pray a remedy of the evils and that the fees remain as they were settled by the Act for Regulating the Fees of the Land Office except that deputies be allowed half of the full fees, and as the principal has no other trouble but recording the certificate after it is made out by the deputy that the sixth payable to the University of William and Mary should be paid from his own share and that the Act giving the principal power to act by deputy be repealed, and also that until the resources of the state will admit that more adequate salaries can be given to the officers of the Supreme Court, that a tax of 5 sh. a hundred for every 100 acres of land above 1400 contained in one survey or contiquous to other land belonging to the same person should be paid, and that the salaries of the judges be made equal.

David Gwinn	John Bentley
Geo. Davidson	Philip Bush
James Clide	Gabr. Madison
Geo. S. Smith	Cyrus McCrakin
James Neill	James Forbis
Peter Ford	Wm. Bush
James Magill	Wm. Dryden
Edmund Powell	James Feland
Isiam [?] Farris	John Haydon
Thomas Davis	Andrew Kennedy
William Moore	Thos. Kennedy
Jacob Starns	John Clary
James Paxton	John Crawford
Davi Briggs	William Moore
Jacob Myers	Alexander Blane
William Thomson	Wm. Montgomery
James Gilman	John Hall
William Calmes Smith	James Renick
Samuel Westerfield	John Warford
Patrick Doran	James Knox
Walter Baker	William Pitman
John Bisscoe Junr.	Benjamin Logan
Samuel Bridgs	William Logan
Wm. Meriwether	Ebenr. Brooks
Wm. Montgomery	Ja. Speed
Lewis Craig	Joseph Craig
Hugh Ross	Isaac Shelby
Samuel Davis	John Sloan
Reasonable.	

1784, Nov. 23 - Petition of inhabitants of the County of
    Jefferson. From considerations of safety and an order of
Court to have a petition preferred to the Assembly for a
division of the county, the public buildings were erected at the
Falls of Ohio. This petition for some reasons has laid dormant
but is now ordered to be presented by the delegates of the county.
From the very great expense of time and money they are subjected
to in attending courts at the distance of from forty to seventy
miles, they beg leave to concur. A very considerable number of
late immigrants are settling on the south side of Salt River.
There are upwards of 800 tithables now in the county, more than
500 of which are on the south side of said river. They ask for
an Act for the division of the county, making Salt River the
dividing line and also directing the public buildings of the
present county to be sold and the money arising to be divided
between the two counties according to the list of tithables that
contributed to the building of them. Dated 5 May 1784.

Will. Pope
David Hawkins
Peter Lord [?]
John Hawkins
Josiah Phelps
Marsham Brashears
George Phelps
William Chapman
Peter Barthmess
Anthony Phelps
Gerrett Williams
Willim Kendall
Richard Morton
Joseph Harris
James Huse
Danil Boys
James McDonald
Thos. Whitledge
John Keith
John McElhose [?]
Mathew Rodgers
Samuel Vitertow
William Rodgers
Daniel Vittertow
William Keith
John Conway
William Chiseton [?]
Samuell Parttrick
Archibald Allison
Willam Brigs
Jorge Crist
Proctor Ballard
Samuel Duncan

John Uncile [?]
Nick Kell
William Case
Adam Wible
John Wible
Wm. Luce
Solloman Stevens
Joseph Conway
John Cunningham
Dennis Pursel
Willm. Casbeur
Enoch Comes
gnbean[?] Coms [Carns?]
Zacharia Wade
Thomas Morton
Richd. Chenowith
Nicolas McCarty
Robert Tyler
Jas. Samuels
Charles Polk
Richard Simmons
Thomas Hynes
Edwd. Truman
William Simmons
Francis Shain
Levi Simmons
Uriah Thompson
Benj. Jones
William Snelling
John [?]
John Whitacre
Isaac Cox

    Referred to Committee on Propositions
    The Court of Jefferson County represents that in 1782 the
Court had the matter of a division of the County under
consideration and entered an order for a petition praying that
the south side of Salt River should be separated from the
County of Jefferson. We wish that the public buildings which
had been erected at the joint expense of the county be disposed
of and the money arising be applied proportionally to the
number of tithables when the levy for the same was made.

    1785, Dec. 9 - Petition of John Campbell stating that he has
        laid out a piece of land opposite the lower falls of the

River Ohio into 150 lots with convenient streets, several of which lots he has sold to persons who mean to settle there. It will be an encouragement to others to have the town established and that a public ferry from his landing below the Falls to the mouth of Silver Creek and Mill Run on the opposite side of the Ohio River be established also. He prays that the lands may be established as a town by the name of Bithrow or Bethhoron and that the owners of lots within the same or those that may be laid off adjoining thereto so soon as they have built a dwelling house twenty feet square with a brick or stone chimney may be entitled to all the privileges other lot holders within other towns in this state are entitled to, and that no wooden chimneys be allowed to be built or hogs belonging to the inhabitants be suffered to run at large and that a public ferry be established.
 Reasonable and bills drawn.

1785, Dec. 9 - Petition of Peter Rezard de Wouves Darges stating
 that on 10 Aug. 178[4?] a Negro man slave named Peter the
property of Francis Vigo, was tried at a Court of Oyer and Terminer held for the County of Jefferson, on which trial he was found guilty of burglary and felony and sentence of death passed on him. The Court valued the slave to Ŀ80 current money. Previous to the day appointed for the execution the slave made his escape, crossed the Ohio River and was killed by the savages. He had purchased the certificate of Monsr. Vigo but the Auditors of Public Accounts refused to pay because he could produce no certificate of the execution.
 Reasonable.
 Certificate of Will: Johnston, Clerk, of the valuation of Negro Peter, condemned to be hanged.

1786, Dec. 7 - Petition of Joseph Dixon stating that he was
 engaged in the public service in the fall of 1776 in guarding
a quantity of public powder from Fort Pitt to Harrodsburg. On 25 Dec. 1776 while on duty he was taken prisoner by the Shawnee Indians in which captivity he suffered incredible hardships and underwent a variety of cruelties. He was not released until 13 March last. He prays such redress or other recompence as may seem meet. Dated 10 Oct. 1785.
 Allowed soldiers [pay?] from the time made a prisoner until 13 March 1785.

1786, Dec. 7 - Petition of William Pope, executor of Leonard
 Helm, that Leonard Helm performed various services in the
Illinois Country by special appointments of General Clark. He was killed in 1782 without an opportunity of settling his claims, having previous to his death made a will and appointed the petitioner executor. Many claims have appeared against the decedent's estate and have been paid by the petitioner, relying principally in his demand against the State for reimbursement.
 Referred to Committee on Claims.

1787, Nov. 6 - Petition of sundry inhabitants of the County of
 Jefferson that it would be necessary and convenient to
  establish a ferry from the lands of Thomas Hynes in the County of Jefferson over Salt River to the lands of Benjamin Pope on the opposite side in the County of Nelson.
  Will: Johnston   John R. Gaither
  Stepn. Ormsby   James Standiford
  Ga. J. Johnston   Anthony Phelps
  Ben. Sebastian   George Phelps
  Patr. Joyes   robird Pottenger

Robt. Elliott	William Hynes
Danl. McCluer	William R. Hynes
James Scott	William Peyton
Thos. Whitledge	Elias Neeld
C. Broughton	Mical Jurnhart [?]
J. Davis [?]	Alexr. Breckinridge
Richd. Taylor	G. R. Clark
Rich: Kaster [?]	Joseph Case
James Patten	Robert Gray
Jas. Sullivan	Ruben Case
Aquila Whitaker	Robert Crawford
John Clark	Joseph Case
W. Croghan	David Case
Peter Cummins	John Nelson

Reasonable.

4 Sept. 1787. William Johnston, Clerk of the Court of Jefferson County, certifies that Thomas Hynes advertised on two Court days his intention of preferring this petition to the General Assembly.

1787, Nov. 20 - Petition of William and Richard Taylors and Charles Mynn Thruston stating that Edmund Taylor, late of Jefferson County, made his last will and testament on 15 Sept. 1783 at which time the testator was resident in the County of Frederick. The witnesses to the will are all inhabitants of said county. The testator in 1784 emigrated to the County of Jefferson and there in June 1785 departed this life without making any alteration in his will. The petitioners were nominated executors but in consequence of Edmund's removal to Kentucky they are prevented from either taking upon themselves the execution of the trust reposed in them or relinquishing their right of executorship under the present laws. Great inconvenience and real injuries arise not only to the relict and children but to his creditors.
William Taylor
C. M. Thruston

Reasonable.

1787, Nov. 22 - Petition of Richard Chinowith that in Jan. 1781 he was employed by Col. George Slaughter and Capt. William Shannon to build one square of Fort Nelson (the stipulated sum being ₤1200). He employed workmen and perfected the same. Public credit being at a low ebb, no person could be induced to undertake the remainder of the work. He was then applied to and every possible argument made use of to induce him to undertake it. He undertook it on the condition that six men mutually chosen, Col. John Todd, Col. William Pope, Capt. William Oldham, Capt. James Patton, Henry Floyd and Benjamin Pope should as soon as perfected estimate the same. He finished the fort on 11 March. The work was valued at ₤30,725 to be equal to the first cost in value, which was forty for one, the notorious custom of exchange in this District at that time. He was never an opulent man and having employed a great number of workmen to complete his engagement and paying them off while able, the rest of them bringing suits, have rendered him almost to beggary together with a small helpless family. He asks for relief.

3 Nov. 1784. The Jefferson County Court certified that the petition was just and reasonable.
Reasonable; 7 Dec. 1787 allowed ₤768 specie with interest.

1788, Nov. 22 - Petition of Martha Donne and Joseph Hunter, administrators of John Donne, that John Donne furnished provisions and other articles for the use of the troops under the

command of General Clark in the Western Department. Being absent from Kentucky in the public service when the Commissioners for settling accounts were in that country, he had no opportunity of laying his account before them. He afterward sent his account to Richmond in order for settlement, which was again prevented by various causes. On hearing that the County Courts were again authorized to liquidate claims he made application to the Court of Jefferson who thought the account reasonable. Application being made to the Auditor of Public Accounts, he gave for answer that the law had expired prior to the date of the certificate and he could not issue the usual warrant. They ask relief.
    10 Dec. 1789. Postponed to next session.

1788, Nov. 22 - Petition of William Pope, executor of Leonard Helm, stating that an account for supplies furnished by Helm for the use of troops in the western Department has been certified just by the Court of Claims in Jefferson County but the Auditor of Public Accounts refuses to issue a warrant because the Act authorizing the Court had expired previous to their granting the same. He prays relief.
    10 Dec. 1789. Postponed to next session.

1788, Nov. 22 - Petition of Andrew Clark stating the Court of Claims for Jefferson County granted him a certificate for his services as an artificer but the Auditor of Public Accounts refuses to issue the usual warrant thereon because the Act authorizing County Courts to issue such certificates expired prior to their granting the certificate.
    Rejected.

1788, Nov. 22 - Petition of Valentine Thos. Dalton that he obtained a certificate from the Court of Claims of Jefferson County for certain furnishes and disbursements by him made for the use of the troops in the Western Department. The Auditor of Public Accounts refuses to grant the usual warrant because the Law which authorized the Court expired prior to their granting his certificate.
    10 Dec. 1789. Postponed to next session.

1788, Nov. 22 - Petition of John Harris that he served the public as an armourer and also had his tools lost in the public service and has yet received no compensation. He applied to the Court of Jefferson County who granted him a certificate. The Auditor refuses to issue the usual warrant because the Act allowing County Courts to liquidate such claims expired prior to the granting the certificate.
    Rejected.

1789, Oct. 22 - Memorial of John Campbell that he was a candidate in the last election of Jefferson County for delegates to the General Assembly. Several causes combined to make the election illegal. He thinks it unnecessary to be particular on any other of the proceedings except those of Peter Smith possessing himself of the Poll Books and of the Sheriff not making a special return when demanded. If a practice so new as in the former should be established, then any candidate may employ a man of bodily strength, rough uncultivated manner and lawless disposition who with a few others like himself might easily be bribed with a cask of spirits to favor his election it would be a most certain mode of gaining it. ... He asks that the House provide against the Commission of such enormities in the future.

    In obediance to order of the County Court of Jefferson 2 June last, Richard C. Anderson, William Croghan, Alexr. Breckinridge, William Taylor and Robert Breckinridge, commissioners, met in Louisville at the house of Capt. John Harrison on 24 Aug. 1789 to take the depositions of witnesses respecting the late election of Abner Field and Buckner Thruston Esqrs., returned as representatives for the said county to serve in the next General Assembly.

[The recording of the evidence is extensive and somewhat repetitious. The items which follow are representative.]

Richard Woolfolk said he was appointed one of the Clerks of the Poll and Peter Smith violently possessed himself of Woolfolk's poll book and kept the same, which was acknowledged by Mr. Field. Mr. Field also acknowledged that Smith by violence seized the poll book kept by Mr. Gabl. Johnston, and possessed himself thereof, which occasioned an adjournment of the election until the next day.

James Sullivan said he heard Mr. Laccasagne say that the election should be a free one, that every person was entitled to vote, and that he heard Peter Smith say on the second day of the election that if the two young men were not elected he would do as he had done before.

Mr. John Clark said that on the first day of the election he saw Peter Smith standing in the Court house door with some papers in his hand, swearing that no man should vote unless the election was free, which threats appeared to stop several men from entering the door, but that Smith attempted no violence to him on his going into the Court house.

Mr. Clark deposes that in consequence of the confusion and disorder he went home without giving his suffrace that day and did not return.

Mr. Thruston took the notice given him by Col. Campbell off the Commissioners' table and tore it in pieces in their presence.- This inserted at the instance of Col. Campbell.

James Standiford said that on Wednesday, the second day of the election, he intended to go to the Court house to give his vote but hearing from James Quartermous one of his neighbors of the disturbance and confusion occasioned by Peter Smith, he determined not to go.

James Sullivan deposed it rained on the second day of the election, moderately, but with intervals between the showers, until about twelve o'clock.

Mr. Cadwallader Slaughter deposed it rained enough so that he would not have ridden 15 or 16 miles.

In consequence of both the returned members being objected to, the Commissioners determined to take up the business of enquiry separately. Mr. Thruston was denied the privilege of asking the witnesses questions relative to Peter Smith but conceived himself at liberty to put to the witnesses any interrogatories which might tend to set the business in its proper point of view.

William Roberts deposed it rained moderately on the second day of the election about one hour near eleven o'clock and earlier in the day the rain would scarcely have wet a man in his shirt. Roberts rode to town in the morning, distant about nine miles.

Col. Campbell acknowledged to have had in his possession the late Act of Assembly of 1788 respecting the election of Delegates and that he did not show it to Mr. Field until about an hour before sun set on the first day of the election.

Mr. Roberts, who was one of the candidates, deposed the Act did not come to his knowledge until about the adjournment of the election on the first day.

Mr. Richard Terrell, who was one of the candidates, said he

believed he had seen the Act before the election, but not in Jefferson County.

Col. Campbell and Mr. Terrell say they demanded as a right to keep the poll open another day, at least, which the sheriff acknowledged.

By consent of the parties Mr. Thruston declared that on the first day from the great confusion excited by Peter Smith, Col. Campbell passively assented to the mode of free or general suffraces being admitted in order to pacify the people until several voters were recorded by the poll clerks, but conceiving some inaccuracy would arise in adjusting the poll of ascertaining the legal votes, Campbell withdrew his assent .

James Francis Moore deposed that on the first day he happened in company with Jacob Mooney together with seven or eight other men. Mooney told him he was come to vote for Col. Campbell and Mr. Cadwallader Slaughter and also the company with him but were prevented by the turbulence of Peter Smith and on seeing it continue Mooney and his party went home without giving their votes. His brother John Gay Moore, on hearing of the irregular proceedings of Peter Smith, prevented him from coming to town the second day. Jno. G. Moore intended to give his vote to Col. Campbell. Question whether Jacob Mooney is a freeholder: I heard Mooney say he had a deed for the land he lives on and Mr. Wilson confessed to me he had acknowledged one. Question whether the company with Mooney were freeholders: I rather incline to think some of them were not.

Mr. Richard Terrell deposed that since he had been in Kentucky it had been customary for all persons aged 21 years to be admitted their suffrages by consent of the candidates. Question whether he believed a great majority of the electors of Jefferson County gave their votes at the last election: I do not believe they did. Question whether he believed the majority of the resident freeholders of Jefferson gave their votes: I do.

Mr. Field acknowledged that at the election when he and Col. Campbell were elected representatives for the County of Jefferson in 1787 the election was conducted agreeable to law and none but freeholders polled. Question whether he knew of any other candidate except Col. Campbell who confined elections to the suffrages of freeholders only: I do not know of any other person in the District of Kentucky.

Mr. Will. Johnston, Clerk of Jefferson County, stated a majority of the resident freeholders gave their suffrages on the day of the last election and that a majority of those who had their deeds recorded voted.

[The remainder of the proceedings concern the manner of taking the testimony, a controversy over the placing of the inquiry about Mr. Field's election before Buckner Thruston's complaint, and the question whether challenged votes and those of nonjurors were expunged before the election closed. The proceedings continued through 26 Aug. 1789.]

Deposition of Richard Jones Waters, taken 25 Aug. 1789 at Louisville: Some time last month the deposition of Peter Smith was taken before him as a justice of the peace at the request of Mr. Abner Field, in the presence of Col. More and sundry other gentlemen at the house of Mr. Jno. Harrison in the town of Louisville. The purport of Smith's deposition was that any riotous behavior of his at the election was not at the instance or encouragement of Mr. Field but contrary to Mr. Field's advice.

The Register of the Land Office on 29 Oct. 1789 certified that grants for upwards of 4000 acres in Jefferson County were issued to Charles M. Thruston previous to 1788.

[John Campbell's letters to Thruston and Field list the votes he disputed and object to both of them as candidates for want of freehold in the county.]

The Commission decided that the violence was not sufficient to invalidate the election.

The Poll taker for Jefferson Election April 7th 1789:
[The numbers beside the names refer to the seven candidates:
1 Cad. Slaughter, 2 Abner Field, 3 Wm. Roberts, 4 B. Thruston, 5 Richd. Terrell, 6 Jno. Campbell, 7 Thos. Styles. An asterisk indicates refused swearing; an x indicates a disputed vote.

Martin Daniel 3 4
Hardi Hill 2 4
John Murphy x 4 5
John Finley x 2 4
John Metcalf x 1 4
James Dunbar x 2 4
Jno. McClintic x 1 2
Jno. Applegate x 2 5
Campl. Ferguson x 2 5
Danl. Wintzell 2 4
Robert Spears * 4 5
Elias Neald x 1 6
Thos. Aplegate 1 7
William Neald x 1 4
Jas. Meriwether 1 6
William Taylor 4 6
Samuel Wells 2 3
John Hughes 1 6
Ga. J. Johnston 1 7

Adjourned till Wednesday 8th of April in the evening being interrupted by a certain Peter Smith & at the request of the Candidates. Wednesday 8th of April the election & poll was again opened. [W. Roberts declined]

Basil Prather x 6 7
Joseph Hunter 2 6
Richd. Woolfolk 4 6
Joseph Sanders 2 4
Peter Smith * 2 4
Henry Smith * 2 4
Mark Thomas 1 6
David Morgan 2 4
Luke Foster * 2 4
Edward Tyler 1 6
Jacob Reager 2 4
John Felty 2 4
William Lyun 2 4
Henry Ditto 2 6
Nicholas Buckner 2 4
Burkt. Reager 1 4
Patrick Joyes 1 4
John Warford 1 2
Mos. Warford (sworn) 1 2
Will Kennady * 1 2
David W. Meriwether 1 6
Samuel Oldham 2 6
Moses Kuykendall 4 6
Richd. C. Anderson 4 6
Peyton Short 4 6
Jacob Coleman x 2 5
Thomas Curry 2 4
Robert Tyler 4 5
John Bartlett 2 4
Robert Daniel 4 7
Ths. Standsbury x 2 4
Benjamin Pope 2 4
Edward Goodin 2 6
Saml. Watkins 1 4
James Sullivan 4 6
Fredk. Edwards 4 5
Richard Finlay 4 5
William Pope 2 4
Richd. J. Waters 2 4
William Roberts 2 4
Jas. Asturgus 4 6
Geo. Crevinsten[?] 1 2
Richard Eastin 2 4
John Bailey 2 6
Marsham Brashear 2 4
John Davis * 4 6
Michael Springle 2 4
William Croghan 4 6
Geo. Slaughter 2 4
James F. Moore 6
Jno. Armstrong 4 6
John McGerson 2 4
John Brown 4 6
Micl. Lacassagne 2 4
Ben Earechson [?] 4 5
Samuel Kirby 2 4
William Peyton 6 7
David Ferguson 4 6
Charles Thruston 6
Joseph Brooks 2 6
William Johnston 2
John Kennison 2 5
Hugh Grymes 2 5
Richard Terrell 4 6
Cad. Slaughter x 4 6

	1)	2)	3)	4)	5)	6)	7)
Whole number of votes	18	45		54	11	30	5
Objected to &c	5	11		12	5	4	1
	13	34		42	6	26	4

1789, Nov. 4 - Petition of James Meriwether that in July 1781 he, being a lieutenant in the corps of cavalry raised for the western frontier, had a horse pressed into the public service for the purpose of carrying an express to Harrodsburg by order of Maj. George Slaughter, commandant at Louisville. The horse was taken by Indians and has never been returned. He never had power to secure documents for the support of his claim until the period fixed by law for the reception and settlement of such claim was expired.

    4 June 1781. Robt. Todd, William Gillaspy and Thos. Quirk appraise a horse of Lieut. James Meriwether, who is now in service, to 11,250 pounds.

    3 June 1788. George Slaughter, formerly Commandant at the Fall of Ohio, certifies at Louisville that a horse of Mr. James Meriwether was taken by the savages when on express from Fort Nelson to Harrodsburg. Witness: James Blackwell, Magistrate of Jefferson County.

1789, Nov. 9 - Petition of Alexr. S. Bullitt that as commanding officer of Jefferson County, finding the frontier inhabitants greatly distressed by the depredation of the Indians and conceiving it to be his duty to adopt those measures for the common defense which were likely to prove most effectual, did in 1788 order a troop of militia cavalry to range on the frontiers of said county. He was induced to prefer cavalry to a company of foot from a conviction of their superior usefullness. Foot rangers though ever so alert were altogether inadequate to the prevention of incursions or to the pursuit of savage fugitives. He prays that the expences incurred by the forage for the troop of cavalry, the hire of horses and the difference in pay between cavalry and foot be paid out of the Treasury.

    Reasonable.

1789, Nov. 14 - Memorial of Alexander Breckinridge that as surveyor of Jefferson County he conceives it his duty to represent a state of the books in which are contained all the entries for land made in this District previous to a division thereof into counties. A considerable part of these entries are recorded in very indifferent books, some of which were formed of sheets of paper stitched loosely together and covered with coarse linen, which have become so mutilated as to endanger the loss of some entries and others so defaced it is with difficulty they can be read. He asks that they be transcribed as soon as possible. The transcript already ordered by Act of 1787 is to be lodged with the Clerk of the Supreme Court of this District.

    No revenues having been collected in this District, in consequence of which the certificates issued by certain commissions for defraying the expence of carrying on two expeditions against the Indians have fallen so much in value that the sum allowed for each copy of an entry is no compensation if paid in these certificates, he asks for relief.

    Books to be provided at the public expense; funds rejected.

1791, Oct. 21 - Petition of William Cooper and Mary his wife that in July 1785 Philip Lutz, the former husband of Mary, died intestate seized on 800 acres in Jefferson County, part of a preemption of 1000 acres. Philip Lutz left no heirs known to the petitioners who can by law inherit the lands. Since the death of Philip Lutz they have continued to improve the lands at a considerable expense and risk from hostile savages. They ask an act to vest the lands in Mary Cooper and her heirs.

    Reasonable.

    Philip Lutz was killed by the Indians on 31 July 1785.

14 Sept. 1791. Jefferson Co., Ky. Elizabeth Karr made oath that in 1785 she lived in Philip Lutes' family. He was former husband of Mary Cooper, wife of William Cooper of Jefferson County. She was present on the last day of July in the same year when the Indians killed Philip Lutes about 100 yards from his own house on Bullskin Creek in Jefferson County.

14 Sept. 1791. Jefferson Co., Ky. Katharine Fullenwider made oath that she lived in Philip Lutes' family and made a similar statement.

10 Sept. 1791. Jefferson Co., Ky. Squire Boone states he heard Philip Lutes say at the time he took out his certificate for his preemption that he did not care much about his lands as he had not any relations in America to give it to. Lutes was some time afterward killed by the Indians and William Cooper married his widow.

10 Sept. 1791. Jefferson Co., Ky. Jacob Fullenwider declares his sister Mary Fulinwider married Philip Lutes and he was killed by the Indians. She married William Cooper. He frequently heard Lutes say he had no heirs or relations in America as he knew of.

1791, Nov. 11 - Petition of Samuel Haycraft that he served as a soldier in the 13th Virginia Regiment for two years and six months. He sent his discharge to Col. Prestley Neville which miscarried and was lost. His remote situation in the western country has prevented him from applying for a settlement of his claim.
    Reasonable.
    6 Sept. 1791. Jno. Harrison, late lieutenant, 13th Virginia Regiment, and Jas. Sullivan, captain, 13th Virginia Regiment, certify that Samuel Haycraft was enlisted as a private in the 13th Virginia Regiment commanded by Col. William Russell in the company of Capt. James Hook for two years and six months and was then discharged.
    Richd. Taylor, major, 9th Virginia Regiment, certifies that Samuel Haycraft was a soldier in the 9th Virginia Regiment commanded by Col. John Gibson (being first the 13th commanded by Col. William Russell) and he served out the time for which he was enlisted and was discharges by Col. John Gibson.

Box 2 District of Kentucky

1782, June 3 - Petition of inhabitants of the frontiers on the western waters that by reason of the present war they have been obliged to make their settlements at considerable distance from each other. For want of ministers of the Gospel among them some of the Magistrates and principal inhabitants of the country have (after the custom of Pennsylvania and other states) at divers times undertaken to celebrate marriages in different parts of the country, which marriages as the law now stands are declared to be illegal. They pray that such marriages as have been celebrated in the aforesaid form may be declared valid in law. Dated Louisville, Jefferson County, 2 April 1782.

W. Pope	Edward Tyler
Merth. Price	John Clin
Daniel Sullivan	John Hume
Ben Pope	John Williamson
Leond. Helm	John McManus
Isaac Keller	James Quartermous
Jos. Archer	James Hougland
John Helm	John Handley
John Tuell	George Pomeroy
Samuel Wells	George Creavenson
Aquilla Whitaker	James Vorhies

         Thos. McCarty   James Galloway
         Richd. Chinoweth   Arthur Park
         Thos. Curry   John Vorhees
         Robert Tyler   Samuel Westerfield
         William Galloway   John Harris
         Jas. McKeag   Morias Hansbrough
    9 June 1782. Reasonable.

    [1784-5?] Petition of inhabitants of Kentucky County that a
         memorial was presented in December last to the Assembly then
         sitting for a Court of Assize for their better government.
    The very great distance from the seat of government renders it
    impossible for those in poorer circumstances to maintain their
    just rights to lands and next to impossible for civilists to
    punish offences of the most criminal nature.
         Congress has not only refused the cession offered them by a
    former Assembly but a committee of that body resolved that
    Virginia has not any just right to the lands northwest of the
    Allegheny Mountains.
              They wish Virginia protection to them as part of the state.
         G. R. Clark   William Pritchett
         Will: Shannon   Charles Morgan
         John Crittenden   John Moore
         Jno. Baley   William Crump
         Robt. George   Jas. Baxter
         Rd. Brashear   Willm. Smith
         [H?   ] Clark   Fras. Maccdormet
         Moses Kenny   John Oakley [Ockley?]
         Jas. Finn   Patk. Maras [?]
         Jno. Dodge   Charles Evanes
         George Wilson   Wm. Purssell
         John Handley   Isack[?] Yeater
         Henry Floyd   Joshua Pruitt
         James A. Sturgus   William Elms
         Will. Oldham   George Leffesten
         Isaac McCrakry [?]   Nace Creys [?]
         Jas. Graham   Thomas Hopert
         Clough Overton   Rannel Weit
         Wm. Mratin [sic?]   Thos. Gaskin
         Wm. Harris   John Mongomery
         Benjamin Anderson   John Chrisp. Horn
         Wm. Johnston   Wm. McKinzey
         William Stewart   Johan donran X
         James Berwick   Edward Parker
         Leod. Helm   X Josep Ros
         J. Girault   Samewil Watkins
         Garret Williams   Alex Dinnis
         Ben: Pope   [?]
         J. Donne   James Sherley
         Jas. Patten   Page Portwood
         Moses Kuykindall   John Janston
         Marsham Brashear   Buarey Bush
         Joseph Saunders   Robbert Weet
         Bland Ballard   James Breyen
         Mark Thomas   Thomas Mc donat [?]
         William Pritchett   Mathy Jons
         Abrm. Chapline   Abraham Meller
         Jos. Calvit   Lewis Mcghee [?]
         Michl. Miles   Wm. Krosley
         Jno. Vaughan   Wm. Elleyre
         Abrm. Frazer

    1783, June 18 - Memorial of George Rogers Clark and John Crittenden

that being impressed with the most zealous dispositions to further the interests of Virginia they did in October 1782 furnish at their costs a supply of provisions for the garrison at Fort Nelson at the falls of Ohio amounting to ₤1175.10.11½ as will appear by vouchers in possession of the Western Commissioners. They pray for the discharge of their claim.
    24 June 1783. Claims discharged and referred to the Committee on Claims.

1784, May 26 - Petition of John Lee that in 1775 he improved
    lands in the western frontier of this state which entitled him
    to the preemption of 1000 acres. Being an officer in the
State Line and on duty in the defense of his country at the time of establishing the Land Office and during the sitting of the Commissioners he was prevented from laying his claim before them. He left the southern army in the fall of 1781 and upon enquiry finds that a preemption right had been proved in his name and a warrant obtained and located, but by whom he knows not, nor was it done by his desire. The warrant was laid on another person's improvement with the intention of depriving him, as he conceives, of his just right. He has obtained from the County Court of Fayette a certificate of his title to the preemption of 1000 acres and has applied to the Register of the Land Office for a warrant to survey, which he refused to grant as being contrary to an Act of Assembly.
    Reasonable.

1786, Nov. 9 - Petition of John Curd that having land in Mercer
    County at the conflux of Kentucky and Dicks rivers where it is
    proposed to erect warehouses for the inspection of tobacco, he
prays that a town may be established thereon called New Market, the situation being most beautiful and healthy, and that a ferry may be established across the River Kentucky from his land on the south side to the opposite side.
    Reasonable.

1787, Oct. 19 - Petition of Rebecca McAfee and George McAfee,
    executors, that William McAfee of Mercer County was killed by
    the Indians in 1780. Dying intestate he left a widow and
three small children, all females. The moveables of his estate were sold for paper currency which before payment depreciated to little value, from which circumstance it appears necessary that a part of the land be sold to defray the expense of surveying and clearing the same out of the Register's office, besides discharging of debts and for the support of the widow and children. He left an estate in lands of one settlement and preemption and 1200 acres located by virtue of a Treasury Warrant. They pray an Act enabling the executors to dispose of 800 acres of the Treasury Warrant land.
    Reasonalbe.
    The advertisement of their intention to petition, dated 27 Aug. 1787, was set up at the door of the Court house of Mercer County at the August and September Courts 1787.

1787, Nov. 19 - Petition of Thomas Welch that he has been a very
    considerable expense in building boats and setting himself at
    the Kentucky River on a public road from Madison County Court
House to Fayette County where a public ferry will be of service to the public. He prays a ferry may be established across the Kentucky at the mouth of Jacks Creek.

Squire Boone	John Collier
James Martin	William Turpin
Jno. Miller	John Pitman

       Thos. Shelton   Jesse Naler
       Haile Talbot   Harly [?]
       Will Irvine   Robert Esher [Roder?]
          Reasonable.

1787, Nov. 19 - Petition of William Turpin that he has been at
   very considerable expense in building boats and settling himself at the Kentucky River on a public road from Madison County
Court House to Fayette County where a public ferry will be of service to the public. He prays a ferry may be established across
the Kentucky at the mouth of Silver Creek.
       Charles Dibrell   Hizk. Grubb [?]
       John Phelps Jr.   Shadrack Barns
       Cary Phelps   James Turner
       Abraham Burton   Edward Turner
       Stephen Salle   Matthew Sims
       John Sanders   Ben Presly
       Phil Williams   Thomas Gileson
       William Harvey Jr.   Henry Wells
       Wm. Holland   John Addams
       Stout Brunson   Edward Williams
       John Goggin   John Bartlett
       Thos. Stalker   Nathan Bartlett
       Jno. Phelps   Willm. Jones
       Wm. Harvey Senr.   John Tudor
       Jno. Harvey   Anze Townzin
          Reasonable.

1787, Nov. 22 - Petition of Jane Todd, widow of John Todd, that
   by virtue of a petition to the last Assembly in the names of
   her and Robert Todd, executor of the said John Todd, certain
lands were to be sold but the lands whereon John Todd resided at
his death (with others) were particularly reserved. The reservation of the land whereon John Todd resided was contrary to her
desire as it is a small tract and probably will be less valuable
at a future period than others directed to be sold. She prays an
Act to amend the aforesaid and to reserve the lands on which she
resides and prays James Overton may be added to the Trustees.
          Reasonable.

1790, Nov. 13 - Petition of John Stuart of Bourbon County that he
   is brother and heir at law to Charles Stuart, deceased.
   Charles improved land and raised corn in that part of the district of Kentucky now called Bourbon County in 1776. Early in
1777 he enlisted in the 9th Virginia Regiment in which he continued till his death towards the close of that year. Persons
acquainted with his brother's right to a settlement and preemption
agreeable to the land law of 1779 sued out his certificate. The
petitioner until lately living in a remote part of Pennsylvania
and being too young to attend to business of consequence did not
hear of the provision made for persons in his situation till the
time for entering his warrant was nearly expired. Immediately on
his arrival in Kentucky he sent the necessary papers to the
Auditors of the Land Office but while he was absent and unexpect-
edly detained in removing his aged parents to the Kentucky District
the time elapsed. As he has paid his money into the Treasury he
prays further time to enter his warrant of preemption and certificate of settlement.
          Dated 20 Sept. 1790.
          Referred to Courts of Justice.

1791, Nov. 7 - Petition of John Shelby that James Shelby his
   brother was commissioned a captain in the Illinois Regiment

and served until 1 May 1780. James Shelby was entitled to the pay and emoluments of a captain but was killed by the Indians some short time after he was discharged without having obtained a certificate. He is the elder brother and heir at law of James. Court of Washington Co., Va., 17 Oct. 1786, ordered that the Clerk give a certificate to John Shelby that he is elder brother and heir at law to Capt. James Shelby, deceased.

G. R. Clark certifies, 2 May 1791 in Mercer Co., Ky., that Capt. James Shelby, deceased, enlisted a company and served as a captain in the Illinois Regiment from 18 Dec. 1778 until 1 May 1780 and is entitled to the pay and emoluments of a captain.

Box 3 State of Kentucky, Miscellaneous - 1792-1825, 1864

1780, June 8 - Petition of inhabitants at and near the falls of the Ohio that they are situated generally near 100 miles from the Court house of this county in a compact, rich settlement. So great a distance from holding court and general musters, renders all civil and military regulations altogether ineffectual. The number of settlers at present amount to at least 800. They pray that all that part of the south side of Kentucky River which lies below Hammond's Creek and the Beach Knobs be erected into a separate County.

William Pope
Wilhelm [?]
Andw. Hynes
William Helm
Cyrus McCrakin
Jacob Vanmatre
Joseph Roberts
John McKinney
James Withers
Robt. Johnston
   Reasonable.

Wm. Bryan
John Edwards
Benjamin Neale
Nicholas Meriwether
Valentine King
Samuel Strode
Sanford Edwards
John Peters
Cuthbert Combs
Edward Bulger

[1780, June 8] - Letter of John Grant at Grant's Station, Head of Liken, to Col. John Todd, Delegate, at Harrodsburg, dated 24 April 1780. He is pleased to sign the petition for a division of the county, as also the whole station is. "We are mostly strangers in Virginia to the Law Civil of Military." "... my wife, her father & Brother Viz Oald Capt. Saml. Mosby and young Sam." The Court has been pleased to appoint me captain of the militia at the request of the people; the people have pointed out Manoah Singleton lieutenant. I intend to go myself to the town against the Shawnees and expect you have influence to procure me some advantageous post. List of names:

Jno. Tamplin
Jno. Jackson
Samson Culpeper
Stufel Stucker
Philip Drake
Christopher Harras
Wm. Vancleave
Manoah Singleton
Thos. Gilbert
Wm. Liley
Wm. Loving
Robert Harris
Jas. Rowland
Josiah Underwood

John Vancleave
George Stucker
Frederick Hunter
Wm. Morrason
James Gray
Henry Millar
Stephin Murphey
Michel Stucker
Edmond Lilley
George Stucker Ser.
Jacob Stucker
John Vancleave Senr.
Samson Hough
Wm. Ellis

There are six more at this station that I can't properly call effective and near ten I daily expect.

1780, June 8 - Memorial of inhabitants of the Kentucky country.

A memorial was presented in December last praying for a court of assize &c for their better government, but was not attended to. They have lately been alarmed at finding that Congress has not only refused the cession offered them by a former Assembly but a Committee resolved that Virginia has not any just right to land northwest of the Allegany Mountains. They conceive that if the country they possess does not belong to Virginia, the property must be vested in themselves and that Congress has no right to any part thereof. But they have ever considered themselves a part of Virginia.

John Helder
John Craig
Robt. Johnson
Hugh Morrison
Jeremiah Craig
Robert Sanders
John Long
Aaron Reynolds
John H. Craig
Cave Johnson
Thos. Ficklin
Francis W. Lea
John Gatewood
John Ficklin
John Childress
John Arnold
Andrew Johnson
James Arnold
John Suggett
David Herndon
Thos. Herndon
William Tomlin
Barnard Rogers
Uriah Garton
Joshua Stamper
John McIntire
Keeble Terry
John Rice
John Douglass
Matt^s. Spaur
John Woodroof
William Clinkinbeard
Isaac Clinkinbeard
John Constant
James Meguire
Emanuel Kelley
Nicolas Procter
Jams. Dulan
Beallia Skely
Reubin Procter
Joseph Procter
Absolom Crook
James Littel
little pag Procter
Roger Clements
Danil Boone
Tho. Boone
Hananiah Lincoln
Thos. Brooks
Squire Boone
Saml. Boone
Samuel Boone Junr.

Jacob Stucker
Mical Stucker
Thos. Bell
Peter Williams
John Miles
Henry Herndon
Fredrick Mitchel [? blot]
Daniel Wilcocks
Philip Drake
John Williams
William Shortridge
Lewis Flannagan
Mathew Gale
Andrew Bonn [?]
Abijah Woods
James Twyman
Jo. Fleming
Benjamin Couchman
Frederick Couchman
Thos. Kennedy
James Harper
Peter Harper
Joshua Bennett
Presley Anderson
[?]
[?]
Wm. McConnell [?]
John [?] Dickerson [?]
[Four names too dim to be read]
John Stevenson
James Morrow
Jos. McConnell
Joseph McCown [?]
Hugh Martin
John Moulson
William Dickerson
Wm. Stull
Robt. Stevenson
Thos. Stevenson
Thomas Davis
Henry Green
John Wigmore
Andw. Steele
Saml. Johnson
Jas. Masterson
John Williams
S. M. McMillin
David Vance
Josiah Collins
Elisha Collins
Wm. Henderson

Joshua Hill	John Torrans [?]
Oswald Towns	Valintine Dicerson
William Hays	Wm. Hayden
Samuel [?]	Benjamin Haydon
[?]	James Haydon
Henry Hunter [?]	John Sharpe
Jacob Hunter	John Mikkin [?]
Andrew Rose [?]	John Niblack
Willm. Scholl	Samuel Kelly
Peter Scholl	William Niblack
Hugh Thompson	Matthew Walker

1792, Oct. 15 - Memorial of George Rogers Clark that being at the head of the military department on the western frontiers of Virginia during the course of the late war, he found in 1782 that the funds of the state were so exhausted that no supplies could possibly be procured on its credit. A cargo of flour, the property of Mr. Holker of Philadelphia, amounting to 70,000 pounds, on its passage to New Orleans, was purchased by him at $5 per hundred for which he gave his own bond and Sands as security, for which flour he has since paid and has received therefor but little compensation from the public. This flour being flung into the public stores, he prays he may be allowed redress.

Having served in the army and not discharged until 2 July 1783, he conceives himself under the spirit and words of the several laws to half pay and prays satisfaction for his claim for half pay.

Reasonable.

1792, Oct. 15 - Petition of Margaret Lapsley that her late husband Captain Samuel Lapsley died possessed of a tract of land in Greenbrier County. She, the mother and next friend of the infant heir (a daughter) of Samuel Lapsley, is a resident of Kentucky in which the residue of the real estate of Lapsley lies. Samuel Lapsley in securing the bounty lands allowed him by the Commonwealth of Virginia contracted debts which his personal estate is unable to discharge and to maintain and educate the heir. She prays an Act to authorize the sale of the tract in Greenbrier County.

4 Dec. 1792. Reasonable.

Petition of Margaret Lapsley, widow and administratrix of Samual Lapsley and guardian to Sally Lapsley, only child and heir at law to the deceased, that Samuel Lapsley was possessed of a tract of land in Greenbrier and did in Sept. 1787 execute a letter of attorney authorizing his brother Joseph Lapsley of Rockbridge County to sell the same. In November in the same year and before Joseph had acted, Samuel on his return to Kentucky in the neighborhood of Fort Pitt departed this life. In 1786 he made a purchase of lands near Harrodsburg for which he executed bonds, payable at different periods, to Richard Overton. He executed a bond to Abram Chaplin who undertook the locating, surveying &c of the lands granted to him for his services in the late army. He also executed a bond to Samuel Greenlee payable when his land in Greenbrier should be sold and out of the monies arising from the sale thereof. She has made every exertion in her power toward discharging the debts and other imcumbrances which lay on the estate, insomuch that she is left without a competency for her own subsistance and the education of her child and some of the debts still remain unpaid. It would be of advantage to sell the tract in Greenbrier County. Signed by Margaret Lapsley, James Lapsley and Jno. Lapsley.

Letter from Saml. McDowell to Mr. Joseph Lapsley at Rockbridge (by Wm. McDowell), dated Mercer County, 23 Sept. 1787;

addressed to "Dear Uncle." His son dying on a journey prevented him from making a will and his moveable estate not being sufficient to clear out the lands he had located, it is necessary to apply for an Act of Assembly to sell some of the lands to pay the debts and support his dear little daughter. You and cousin Jospeh ought to sign as well as cousin James and John Lapsley.

6 Sept. 1786. Samual Lapsley of Mercer County have appointed my brother Joseph Lapsley of Rockbridge County my attorney to sell tract in Greenbrier County containing 363 acres. Witnesses: Wm. McDowell, A. Reid, Saml. Greenlee.

1805, Dec. 18 - Petition of Lewis Rouse that in 1792 he was by law placed on the list of pensioners of the State of Virginia.

Having lately removed to Kentucky, the expense and trouble necessarily attendant on an application for his annual allowance constrain him to solicit the Legislature to commute his pension by granting him a sum in lieu thereof.

Reasonable, 24 Dec. 1805.

Lewis Rouse is a pensioner with an allowance of $26.67 per annum. He has drawn his pension to Jan. 1805.

1811, Dec. 18 - Petition of Jonas McDonald and Edwd. Bean, executors of Bryant McDonald and guardians to the minor legatees of the estate, that they are entitled to a tract of land in Kentucky which is claimed and in the possession of Robert Didlack who has held and improved the same for many years. They are not prepared to enter into a long and uncertain law suit and are desirous to sell the land to David McGee who is disposed to purchase on condition that they are able to transfer the claim legally. They pray the Legislature to pass a legal conveyance to said land. Those of the legatees who are of age that have seen the land are very desirous to sell.

Referred to Committee on Courts of Justice.

1821, Dec. 14 - Petition of Hannah Russell, widow and executrix of John Russell, and of James L. Russell, Gervas E. Russell,

Joshua Russell and John B. Russell sons and executors of John Russell, that John Russell at the last session presented a petition that he joined the minute company of Capt. Samuel Hawes of Caroline County in 1775 and in May 1776 enlisted with Capt. Thomas Meriweather for two years and while in service enlisted on board the Brig Liberty commanded by Capt. Thomas Liller and continued on board until January following. While at sea they took a fine ship and cargo which was sold as a prize at the town of York in Virginia. He again enlisted with Capt. Meriwether for three years and in Dec. 1778 was appointed a lieutenant in the First Virginia State Regiment and continued to serve until Oct. 1780 when he was sent home as supernumerary. He with many other officers in 1791 presented their claim for half pay for life or for full pay for five years. The Auditor rejected their claims. They appealed to the District Court, where they obtained a judgment which was reversed by an appeal to the Court of Appeals in 1792. He is now a resident of Kentucky and is old and very infirm. He served in the same regiment and at the same time with Capt. Wm. Campbell. An Act of Assembly allowed to Capt. Wm. Campbell full pay for five years. This petition was withdrawn on account of the death of the petitioner. He left a widow and eleven children, a part of whom are still with their mother.

9 Jan. 1822. Reasonable.

Letter of Wm. Campbell, dated Orange 25 Nov. 1820, to Mr. James Russell, requesting that he represent him at a meeting of Revolutionary state officers and soldiers in Richmond next month.

Of the four tracts of 1000 acres each to which he was entitled as captain, three were entered in the lands in Kentucky lately ceded by the Chickasaw Indians but were withdrawn and entered on the waters of Green River. One of the tracts he gave the locator. The other three by recent survey held only 2316 acres, one 1065, 905 and 246 by interferences with prior surveys. Every acre has been sold for the direct taxes of 1815 and he is asked $2000 to redeem it. He received commutation of five years' pay in lieu of half pay for life, but no interest.

Letter of Wm. Campbell at Orange, 28 Dec. 1821, to Reuben Burton at Richmond. His letter should have been directed to Barboursville P. O. Letters directed to the County are lodged at the Court House and never forwarded. His residence is near fifteen miles above. Lt. John Russell served in the 1st Virginia State Regiment with him from the spring of 1777 to the summer of 1780 when several officers were supplied with money to recruit. Whether Russell left as recruiting officer or as supernumerary he cannot say. He had been several months before the regiment was organized in the marine service, as that regiment was composed of some companies raised for the U. States service and others for the service of the state infantry and marines.

The Virginia Auditor certified that on 12 May 1783 a certificate was issued to Lt. John Russell for ╚203.1.5 which was received by Lt. Vaughter.

J. R. [sic] at Mount Superior, Henry Co., Ky., 12 July 1820, to Col. Richard M. Johnson at Scott Co. [Ky.] states that he joined the minute company under Capt. Saml. Haws, Caroline County, in 1775, but never was called on. In May 1776 he enlisted with Capt. Ths. Meriweather for two years on board the Brig Liberty commanded by Capt. Ths. Liller, continued to January, went to sea and was fortunate enough to take a ship which ship and cargo was sold at Yorktown in Jan. 1777. He enlisted with Meriweather for three years in the 1st Virginia State Regiment, was lucky enough to be appointed 1st Lieutenant in Dec. 1778, and continued until Oct. 1780 when he was sent home as supernumerary for want of command. At the District Court held in Richmond in Sept. 1791 he obtained judgment for half pay for life or five years' full pay in commutation. [Copy of the judgment appended.]

Anthony New, at City of Washington, 4 April 1812, to John Smith at Henry Co., Ky., states he made inquiry respecting the estate of Joseph Elam, deceased, and inquired at the War Department about something due Maj. Russell for his services during the Revolution.

Anthony New at Washington City, 8 March 1813, to Maj. John Russell, Henry Co., Ky., states he incloses a note signed by P. Hagner, Pr. Clk., 29 Nov. 1812, stating that since John Russell belonged to a Virginia State Regiment he is not entitled to land or allowances from the United States.

Richard M. Johnson at Blue Spring, 4 Aug. 1820, to John Russell at New Castle, writes concerning the action of Congress on the Revolutionary claims.

1823, Dec. 13 - Petition of Caroline H. Preston, widow of Maj. William Preston of Louisville, Ky., executrix of his last will and testament, and James McDowel, James Pearce and Garnett Peyton, executors, that at the time of his death he was indebted in a large amount and for payment directed that lots in part of the town of Louisville called Preston's Enlargement should be sold. The debts amount to about $14,711.90. Property in the neighborhood of Louisville has sunk in value. Much of the personalty has already been sold to pay the interest on the debts. They ask to sell tracts in Wythe and Giles cos., Va., the first called Robinson's tract and the second lying on Cole River. Also signed by Henrietta Preston, Maria Preston, Caroline Preston, Josephine Preston.

8 Jan. 1824. Reasonable.

Copy of the will of William Preston, Jefferson Co., Ky., 1821 [See The Filson Club History Quarterly, v. 6, p. 177, for an abstract].

Edwd. Shippen, Cashier of the Bank of the United States at Louisville, 12 July 1823, certifies that William Preston owed $2842.14 which is still owing.

John D. Colmisnil at Louisville 16 Dec. 1823 states he sold an undivided one-half of five acres a few years ago for $6000. It would not produce $1000 now. He has lived in Louisville and actively engaged in business for twelve years.

John Bustard stated 16 Dec. 1823 he has lived in Louisville twenty-six years. He owns seven lots for which he could have gotten $15,000 or $20,000 five years ago and could not now effect a sale for $3500.

Frans. Preston states 18 Dec. 1823 he came to Louisville four weeks ago to collect money due him and sell some lots in Preston's Enlargement. In both objects he has been totally disappointed.

Cuthbert Bullitt states 15 Dec. 1823 he has lived in Louisville about twenty years. Property continued to rise in value until about four or five years ago. Forced sales of real estate would be attended with a ruinous sacrifice.

Worden Pope states 17 Dec. 1823 he has lived in Kentucky upwards of forty-four years and in Louisville since Aug. 1795.

Richd. A. Maupin states 18 Dec. 1823 he has been a resident of Louisville nineteen years.

Ro. Breckinridge, Edwd. Shippen, Wm. H. Neilson and Jno. P. Oldham also make statements about the value of land.

1825, Dec. 20 - Petition of Hannah Russell, widow and executrix of John Russell, and of James L. Russell, Gervas E. Russell,
Joshua Russell and John B. Russell, sons and executors. Their previous petition was not acted on and papers were mislaid. John Russell left a widow and eleven children, a part of whom are still living with their mother.

Letter of Chs. Ewell at Dumfries [Va.] 14 Sept. 1825 to James B. Russell.

Copy of will of John Russell, dated 15 Dec. 1821 and proved in Henry Co., Ky., March 1821, naming wife Hannah, sons James B., Gervas, Joshua and John B. Russell, daughter Mary Russell wife of Jno. Smith, daughter Elizabeth J. Smith wife of Thos. Smith, and daughter Susan P. Russell wife of James Hollingsworth.

Copy of Judgment in suits at the Court of Appeals [of Virginia] 29 Oct. 1792 of the Commonwealth against Thomas Carter late surgeon of the Cavalry under Col. Dabney; James Minson Galt, late Senior field surgeon; Thomas Quarles, late lieutenant in Col. Dabney's Legion; William Vawter, late a lieutenant in the First Virginia; John Williams, late a captain in the State Artillery; Frederick Woodson, late a captain in the State Service; William Armistead, late a captain of cavalry in the legion commanded by Col. Dabney; Christopher Roane, late a captain in the State Artillery; William Campbell, late a captain in the first State Regiment; Nathanial L. Savage, late lieutenant of cavalry in the legion commanded by Col. Dabney; Samuel Tinsley, late a cornet in the legion commanded by Col. Dabney; John Russell, late a lieutenant in the first Virginia State regiment; William

Hoffler, late a captain in the first Virginia State regiment; Robert Brough, administrator of James Bradley, deceased, late a captain in the State Regiment of Artillery. Decision of the District Court, which granted them five years' pay or half pay for life, reversed.

1864, Jan. 14 - C. J. Boyd for himself and as attorney for James Layne and Christiana Hacker presents a claim for property taken in Dec. 1862 by state line troops. [There is much information on the details of the property and on attempts to recover it.]

Statement of John N. Clarkson, late colonel in the military forces of the State line of Virginia under the command of Maj. Gen. John B. Floyd in the matter of the petition of Layne and others: In Dec. 1862 when the forces of the State line were in Western Virginia and on the borders of Kentucky, he was ordered by Gen. Floyd to take command of the cavalry and proceed to the border counties of Kentucky, Floyd County among them, to harrass the enemy and particularly to break up the Home Guards who were under the orders of the commanding officers of the enemy and had been committing depredations upon the loyal citizens of both Virginia and Kentucky. These Home Guards had been making raids in the border counties of Virginia and carrying off large numbers of Negroes, horses and cattle, destroying other property, killing and arresting and otherwise annoying the loyal citizens. In Floyd County he found that nearly the whole people were Union men. His troops were bushwhacked and fired upon by irregular bands on every occasion where the nature of the country permitted it to be done. He punished the organized bands to the extent he could and seized Negroes and a portion of the cattle mentioned in the petition. He had no personal knowledge of the people except from information furnished by the friends of [the Confederate] cause. He brought the Negroes, cattle and horses out with him and turned them over to the Quartermaster in command. While they were in camp after this expedition, Mrs. Honaker, accompanied by Mr. Elliott, M[ember of] C[ongress] from Kentucky, came to Gen. Floyd to demand the Negroes taken from her. Gen. Floyd after investigation returned the Negroes to her. At the same time Gen. Floyd was informed by Mr. Elliott that Layne was a notorious Union man, that he had a son in the Federal army, and Elliott agreed in the justice of taking his property. One little Negro girl was given by Gen. Floyd to Capt. Hunt as some remuneration to him for bringing out the other Negroes. The weather was very bad, the streams swollen, and the risk, expense and danger of bringing them to Virginia was great. The price charged for the property is altogether unreasonable. The best yokes of oxen could at that time have been purchased in Logan Co. [W.] Va., or Floyd Co., Ky., for $50, the horses and other cattle for one-third the prices charged.

Bourbon County - 1786-1790

1789, Oct. 28 - Petition of John Waller of the County of Bourbon that Mr. Charles Smith, Mr. Notley Conn, Mr. Henry Lee and he were candidates for the present General Assembly. At Bourbon April Court previous to opening the polls Mr. Smith, Mr. Conn and he entered into an agreement that no non-resident unless he was possessed of a deed or patent should vote but that all free male inhabitants of the county above the age of 21 years should have that liberty. No sooner was the poll opened than the agreement was violated by the agent of Mr. Conn or some other persons. The neighboring part of Fayette was industriously searched and all that could be prevailed on were brought, traveling men were

persuaded from the road and boys were prevailed on to vote.
   Rejected.

Cumberland County - 1811

1811, Dec. 9 - Petition of George Wills of Cumberland Co., Ky., that in the winter of 1808 he removed from Henry Co., Va., to Kentucky and carried with him certain Negroes, natives of Virginia, David, Easter, Silvia, Cretia and Fanny. Being anxious to return with all his family to his native state he prays authority to bring with him into Virginia the Negroes mentioned.
   Rejected.

Box 4
Fayette County - 1781-1791, 1824

1789, Nov. 14 - Petition of inhabitants of Fayette County that a lot of land in Lexington measuring 24 poles in front and 13 back was by the Act of Assembly for establishing the town reserved for a Court house, prison, etc. The Court house is erected on one end. The other end is cut by a hollow and drain. The lot is bounded on every side by wide streets which leaves a large vacancy of ground. They pray the lot may be divided and the part which will be northwest of the line may be vested in commissioners for the special purpose of erecting thereon a house for public worship for the Lexington Presbyterian Society.

Aron Redmon	David Henderson
Matthias Mount	James McCullough
Gilbt. Simpson	John McKinsey
Beverley Longdon	William Millroy
James Alexander	George Feares
John McClelen	Jas. McDowell
Joseph Waker	Edwd. Cavins
Samuel Walker	Robert Craig
Jas. McCrosby	William Armstrong
John Mikemson	Samuel Clinton
Sanford Gorham	Charles Mansfield
Andrew Mikemson	John Archer
John Carnahan	William Carnahan
James Renglad [?]	Andw. Christy
Saml. Moor	Francis Dill
James Will	

[Another petition with the same text:]

Robert Parker	Saml. Blair
John Parker	Peter January
James Parker	Jno. January
Robt. McFarland	John Goudy
Thos. Marshal	Alexr. Parker
Jas. Davidson	[?]
Hiram Harrison	Henry Marshal
John Vance	James Trotter
John Hamilton	Wm. Campbell
John McCrahen	Robert Megowan
John Toms. Slater	James Ward
Saml. Meredith Junr.	Wm. Ward
John Bigger	Robt. Joud [?]
William Trimble	Thos. Arnold
William Byrne	William Bush
Aron Griffin	Bartlet Collins
William Henry	Edw. Hall
John Stewart	Owen Todd
John Greassem	Saml. McMillin
Henry Brock	Bryant Ferguson

William Garrard junior   Lewis Marshall jr.
John Watkins junr.   Stephen Bunnel
Lewis Craig   Moses Patterson
Levi Todd   Jonas Davenport
Jas. McDowell   Jacob Cthunted [?]
Will: McConnell   Thomas Bodley Junr.

Plat of the public square certified 11 Sept. 1789 by Robert Parker, Clerk, Trustee, and Surveyor of Lexington.

1824, Dec. 10 - Petition of Leonard (X) Moseley that on 6 Dec. 1785 he was inscribed on the pension list of Virginia on account of wounds received while in the service of the U.S. The small sum of L6 per annum seemed but an indifferent remuneration, yet when he reflected it was a reward measured not by the feelings but by the poverty of the state, he was satisfied. He moved to the District of Kentucky soon after he recovered from his wounds. He asks payment in his age for what he suffered in his youth.
Rejected.

W. H. Richardson, practicing physician at Lexington, 18 July 1818, certifies that he examined Leonard Moseley, a private in Col. Abm. Buford's regiment of horse, and finds on his body the following scars which he says he received in Buford's defeat: A scar on the right side of his head extending through the ear, several inches long, with a depression of the skull produced by a broad sword; a musket shot passing immediately under his left collar bone and out through the shoulder blade; the forefinger off from his right hand by the broad sword; a sword wound on his left wrist which disables his thumb of the same hand; a musket shot in his left leg; a musket ball in his left knee just above the knee pan[?]. The degree of disability is of the first grade.

The Virginia Auditor reports that Leonard Moseley, a wounded soldier, was placed on the pension list by order of Council 1 Dec. 1785 at the rate of L6 per annum.

Leonard (X) Moseley states in Fayette Co., Ky., 18 July 1818, that having moved to this state many years ago and not knowing in what manner to proceed, he never received his pension.

W. Foushee states 6 Dec. 1786 that on examination of Leonard Moseley he finds he has received much injury by a number of wounds, particularly two, one on the right side of the head. He says his brain at certain times is much disordered. The other is by the passage of a ball from the fore part of the sternum through the spine of the left scapula.

Thomas Davis in Fayette Co., Ky., 13 July 1818 states he is acquainted with Leonard Moseley, now resident in Woodford Co., Ky., formerly of Hanover Co., Va., and knows he was in service about eighteen months and was wounded in many places in Col. Abraham Buford's defeat, his right fore finger cut off, a large sword cut in his right ear, and on the right side of his head and a ball in his shoulder.

Jefferson County - 1826

1826, Dec. 20 - Petition of Richard Taylor Robertson of Jefferson County that Richard Taylor, formerly of Virginia, entered
service as a captain and commander of the schooner Hornet soon after the beginning of the Revolutionary War and about the latter part of 1777 he took command of the ship Tartar and continued to command on board until 1779 when he was wounded in an engagement between the ship Tartar and a British schooner near the capes of Chesapeake Bay. He then for a short time was not in active service but had the command of various boats in the rivers emptying into the Chesapeake until the siege of York by Gen. Washington at

which time he was employed in supplying the French fleet and American vessels with provisions. He continued in service until about Nov. or Dec. 1783. He was commissioned by his Excellency Beverley Randolph in 1786 to command the public boat Patriot which he did until the vessels of the State line were transferred to the federal government or otherwise disposed of in 1787. Richard Taylor moved to Kentucky about 1796 or 1797. He was at that time in independent circumstances and would not ask for Half Pay. Soon after from unavoidable accidents and inability on account of his wounds to attend to his business, he sustained great losses. He died in Aug. 1825 leaving the memorialist (his grandson) all moneys granted according to the Act of May 1779.

[Documents accompanying the petition, including a certificate of Benjamin Taylor Sr., Jefferson Co., Ky., 19 March 1826, and Wm. Taylor Sr., Oldham Co., Ky., 6 March 1826, and his commission, 2 Aug. 1786, are listed but are not in the file.]

24 Jan. 1827. Reported.

Madison County - 1788-1789

1788, Oct. 22 - Petition of James Barnet that at the late election of delegates to represent the County of Madison in the present General Assembly he with Green Clay and Thomas Kennedy were candidates. The poll was conducted in a manner illegal and unfair and although he polled the greatest number of legal votes, Thomas Kennedy was returned with Green Clay duly elected. During the election a number of persons were admitted to poll who had before polled and others under age. He prays the election of Thomas Kennedy be set aside.

1789, Oct. 24 - Petition of inhabitants of Madison that Samuel Estill and the heirs of John Estill, deceased, proprietors of the land at Madison Courthouse are about to lay off fifty acres into lots and streets for the purposes of a town. They ask that the fifty acres be vested in trustees with power to lay off the same into lots and sell and convey the same to the highest bidder, allowing to Samuel Estill the privilege of reserving to himself any number of lots not exceeding five.

John Reid	Samuel Estill
James Adams	Will Irvine
Robert Kirkpatrick	Sum [?] South
Hugh Campbell	Alexander Reid
Thomas Campbell	John Gass
Reuben Searcy	Peter Woods
William McGinniss	Isaac Anderson
Gabriel Dunkin	John Aevson [?Awson?]
Cornelus Daugherty	John Hopkins
Jo Kennedy [?]	William Bucher
James Stephenson	Archibald Woods
Andw. Harris	Richard Dunn
Jas. Barnett	Haile Talbot
Alexr. Reid	Elias Barns
James Price	Wm. Powell
David Gass	Benjamin Morton
Richd. Davis	John Wilson
Wm. South	Ben Okley
John Snoddy	Thos. Okley
Richard Christmas	Edwd. Parker
William Christmass	John Briselton [?]
Jacob Sneed	Jacob Williams
Michel Ferres	Thos. Robarts
Wm. Wood [?]	Dan Williams [?]
John South	Jesse Hodges

John Pitman
Richard Walker
Ben South
William Boone
John Adams
John Campbell
Nich. Hawkin
Benj. Proctor
Wm. Gass
Andw. Kennedy
Robt. Branck
Adam [?]
Elisha Estis
Richd. Callaway
Benj. Campbell
Richd. Batcher
George Finley
Wm. Moore
Henry Boyer

Daniel Williams
Peter Evans
Wm. Roy
David Walker
John Mitchel
Wm. M. Williams
Richard Gordon
Philip Turner
David Lynch
Saml. Black
Jas. Young
Thos. Mc guire
John Rush
Peter Rush
Charles Colley
James French
Wm. Jones
Isaac Williams

Mercer County - 1786-1789

1786, Oct. 26 - Petition of the freemen of the County of Mercer that the progress of agriculture and flattering prospect of a considerable crop of tobacco make it absolutely necessary public warehouses should be provided at some convenient landing on the Kentucky River for the inspection of their products. They recommend the landing at the conflux of Kentucky and Dicks rivers and ask for establishment of an inspection on the land of John Curd.

George Muter
Saml. McDowell
Caleb Wallace
Harry Innes
Ben: Sebastian
Richd. Terrell
Stepn. Ormsby
J. Marshall
G. R. Clark
J. Brown
Ja. Speed
Peyton Short
Thos. Allen
Matt. Flournoy
George Caldwell
Robt. Mosby
Nicho: Meriwether
James Hackley
Wm. T. Caldwell
James Curd
John Berry
John Coock
John Jouitt
John Curd
Constant Perkins
William Trigg
John Gill
Nathl. Massie Jr.
Gabl. Madison
John Smith
David Lawrance
W. Bradshaw
Jno. Cowan

Benja. Bradshaw
Ro. Craddock
Richd. E. Beale
Edwd. Willis
Henry Chiles
M. Nagle
Bu 1. Jackson
Andrew McCalla
Joshua Barbee
W. Henry
Saml. Lapsley
W. Gaines
Vivion Goodloe
Jno. Summers
Philip Caldwell
John Sleet
Wm. Stafford
Micl. Humble
Noah Humble
Saml. Pryor
John Haris
Willm. Agun [?]
John Byrne [? Syme?]
Richd. Woolfolk
John Clarke
James Moody
James Moore
Martin Daniels
Newton Curd
Barnet Fisher
Hum Nelson
John Dicken
John Vandewall

Joseph [?]
James Prichard
Tho. West
John Rodgers
John Lillard
John Lawrnce
John Harbor [?]
John A. Buston
John McLauglen
Mark Lee
Stephen Fisher
John Irvine
Edmund Singleton
Rane McKinney
George Mayfield
Thos. Hopkins
Henry Thomas
Wm. C. Wakeland
James Hord
Jesse Robards
John Taylor
David Woods
Robert Caldwell
Benj. Bennet
John Mosby
Wm. Rice
Litty. Mosby Jr.
John Fowler
Robt. Bowmer
George Smith
James Connyers
John McGuire
Job Hale

Thomas Tutt
Wm. Barbee
Joseph Robards
Jonathan Jennings
Hopson Kinkade
John McKee
James Hatton
Anthony Crockett
Joseph Crockett
H. Marshall
J. McDowell Jur.
Ebenr. Brooks
K. Marshall
Chas. Ballard
David Wright Jur.
Samuel McGehee
John Downing
Jas. Moore
Elias Fisher
Moses Threlkeld
John Threlkeld
Jas. Crutcher
Lewis Robards
Wilm. Griffin
Dominick Flanigan
Joshua[?] Mosby
John Haggin
John Davis
Edmd. Ware
W. Smith
Hugh Smith
Isaac Shelby

[Another petition with same text:]

William McMurtry
Benjamin Davis
John Brown
Charles Davis
John Watts
Henry Spilman
Benj. Field
P. Tardiveau
Abraham Thomas
James Feland
Robert Cox
James Cocke
Xr. Dickey
T.[S?] Taylor
Isaac Coffman [?]
John McFall
Parman Hall
Jo. Fleming
Wm. Murray
Jno. Kincaid
Saml. Woods
George Shad
Josiah McKinney
[Monetisor?] Sherridon
Fisher Rice
Martin Nall
Adam Fisher
Richard Foley
Eward[?] Polly

Jacob Lee
Georg Wilson
William Griffy
James Brumfield
Wm. Adams
Joseph Brumfield
Thos. Onens
John Shackelford
John Wilson
Wm. Kenton
Vincent Wren
Henry Pushikon [?]
Jacob Froman
Thos. Henry
Paul Humble
John Thomas
Alexr. Robertson
Isham Talbot jr.
Edmund Talbot
George Caldwell Jur.
Christopher Lillard
Peter Keeny
James Davis
William Bassett
Patrick Doran
John Milner
Joseph Davis
Ambrose Gordon
Thomas Hambilton

Lewis Willhide
Peter Watts [?]
Elisha Pruett
William Connor
Robert McKee
Isham Prewitt
Thomas Lewis
  Reasonable.

Henry Wilson
John Summers
Zachariah Bunch
Charles McKinney
Stephen McKinney
William McKinney
Rane McKinney

1787, Nov. 19 - Petition of inhabitants of Danville and others, proprietors of the lots therein, that Walker Daniel, late deceased, in his lifetime pruchased of John Crow 76 acres for the purpose of erecting a town. Walker proceeded to lay off a part of the land into lots and streets and disposed of some of the lots. Since his death Robert Daniel the elder brother and heir at law of Walker Daniel laid the remainder of the land off into lots and disposed of them. For the safety of purchasers Robert has conveyed in fee simple the streets and springs within the tract of George Muter, Harry Innes, Peter Tardiveau, Thomas Perkins, and Andrew McCalla in trust for the benefit of the inhabitants. There is a public square containing one acre laid off for the purpose of erecting the Courthouse of the district and other public buildings which is conveyed to Harry Innes and Christopher Greenup in trust for the benefit of the District, and on which the Courthouse and prison are now erected. They pray for an Act to establish the land into a town called Danville.

Harry Innes
P. Tardiveau
Robert Daniel
David Furguson
Jno. Belli
John Crow
Thos. Barbee
Samuel Irwin
Ben Grayson
George Muter
Jas. Dunlap
Willis Green
  Reasonable.

Martin Daniel
Robert Corbin
James Lawrence
J. Brown
Stepn. Ormsby
Andw. McCalla
M. Nagle
Christo. Greenup
John Irvine
Ro: Craddock
Thomas Lodg [?]

1789, Oct. 21 - Petition of Edmond Munday and Bernard Noel that they (being ignorant of the laws) were induced to accept appointment as inspectors in the County of Mercer at Curd's Warehouse for the moderate salary of Ł30 per annum, which services they have performed with the utmost attention. Not being served with the inspection laws on the opening of the inspection they could not ascertain the lawful tax per hogshead on tobacco exported. They took bonds on sundry exporters for what should be lawful when ascertained. They experience the horrid imposition of certificates for militia services in lieu of cash, which are currently selling at three shillings in the pound, which though sanctioned by laws could never be the intent of the legislature. They pray such relief as may seem just and right.
  Reasonable.

Nelson County - 1787-89

1787, Oct. 20 - Petition that advantage would accrue to the public from the establishment of a town and a tobacco inspection on a tract of land the property of Walter Beall in Nelson County and at the mouth of the Beach Fork of Salt River. They ask a law establishing a town lately laid off at the place with a tobacco inspection and warehouses.

Walter Beall	Bryan Young
James Morrison	David Cox
Israel Dodge	James Dozer [?]
Charles Stevenson	John Ray
Zach [Oza?]	Charles Read
Ben [Penc?]	Benjamin Cleaver
Adam Shepherd	Frederick Rizer
Anthony Foster	Martin Curts
William Briggs	Saml. Ewing
Richard Parker	Jno. Dozer
James Tayton	William King
Charles Ewing	Thomas Elliott
Thomas Howard	Jas. Dozer
Samuel Ray	Danl. McClure
John Grundy	John McClure
John Floyd	Tho. Baird
Joshua Ferguson	Ignatius Cartin [Carter?]
John Vertrees	Michl. Campbell
John Young	Richard Jas. Rapier
Cain Withers	John Helm
John Husbands	Jno. Coppedge
Augustine Cumpton	Isaac Cox
Elijah Payton	Peter Kern
Charles Pierpoint	Andrew White
William Pile	James Brown
Proctor Ballard	Thomas Merrifield
William Cleaver	Joseph Ferguson
Anthony Roberts	Alexander Leshly
Peter Cummins	Jacob Yoder
John King	William Taylor
Saml. Pottenger	John Fenwick
John Lancaster	James Adams
Thos. Cunningham	Geo: Harrison
Jacob Diem[?]	Gabriel Cox
James Wims	Hugh Crawford
Thos. Liddel	John Read
W. McGill [?]	P. Philips
Laurence Protzman	Graves Wapshott
William Kincheloe	Thos. Hall [?]
James Beard	John Filson
Cuthbert Harrison	Jacob Dyeatt
David Glen	Geo: Hartt
John Botsel	William Combs
John Stewart	Thomas L. Lansdale
John Henderson	Robt. Housley
Richd. Beall	John Steele
William Adams	Henry Kisnard
Thos. Bullett	Alexr. McCann
Will. May	Joseph Small
Wm. McClurg	Benjn. Beall

1 May 1787. I intend petitioning the next General Assembly for the establishment of a town and a tobacco inspection on the south side of the Rolling Fork, opposite the mouth of Beech Fork.
                                                    Walter Beall
     Plat of Beallsborough, surveyed 10 July 1786 by John E. King for Walter Beall, Esq.

1788, Nov. 3 - Petition of inhabitants of Bairdstown and Nelson
    County that early in 1781 the outlines of a town were laid
  off upon a preemption of 1000 acres centrally situated in said county and held by David Baird and John C. Owing in joint tenancy. In February in the same year an advertisement was set up under the signature of William Baird for the proprietors encouraging

the settlement of the town and specifying the terms and conditions under which lots were to be obtained and held. Several of the petitioners settled upon lots in said town and made considerable improvements. On 10 March 1784 another advertisement was set up by William Baird notifying that he had disposed of all the out-lots he intended and that those who wished to possess in-lots must purchase them from him. Although a number of the petitioners have settled upon lots, they cannot obtain any titles to them. They have reason to believe the proprietors cannot agree upon the division of the preemption or any plan for assuring the petitioners titles to the lots. They pray an Act for the condemnation of 300 acres including the present town, that commissioners may be appointed to appraise the value of the land, that trustees be appointed, that those lots that have been built or improved upon may not be sold at public auction but that they may have titles made to them.

E. Miller	Dennis Pursel
Isaac Morrison	James Terry
Thos. Morton	Robert Gillavies [?]
John Handley	Hugh Crawford
James Morrison	Peter Panebaker
James Adams	Chrisr. Kauffman
Saml. Ewing	Wm. Hynes
Henry Hart	Ben Hook
Moses Jefferis	James Pursel
George Stroop	Samuel Crawford
Christian Hibnor	Jno. Ray
William Adams	George Tucker
Joseph Rane	John Harbison
Thomas Cunningham	John Kincad [?]
James Raman [?]	William Rowan
Denis Nevil	John Peter Lausbery
John Adams	Jacob Vader [?]
Elijah Adams	Michl. Campbell
Chas. Broughton	Robert Forsythe
Samuel Horine	Edmund Price

Reasonable in part; rejected in part.

1788, Nov. 5 - Petition of inhabitants of the County of Nelson that a number of people of the county, desirous of encouraging literature in this infant country, have by voluntary subscription erected a stone edifice at Bairdstown for the purpose of a seminary of learning and have appointed the petitioners to superintend the seminary. It now consists of twenty-five students in the learned languages though it is not yet six months since it was first opened, to which numbers are frequently adding. They pray for the incorporation of the institution under the style of Salem Seminary. Dated 15 Aug. 1788.

John Caldwell	Geo. Harrison
Andw. Hynes	James Baird
Isaac Morrison	Joseph Barnett
Terrah Templin	James Morrison
Mat. Walter absent	James Allen
John Steele absent	Cuthbert Harrison
Philips Philips	William Taylor
Walter Beall	

Reasonable.

1789, Oct. 23 - Petition of Matthew Walton and other inhabitants of the County of Nelson that it would greatly increase the interest and promote the happiness of the petitioners by establishing a warehouse and inspection on the lands of Matthew Walton on the south side of Salt River at the first Yellow Bank below the mouth of Long Lick Creek, the situation being between the two principal salt works in the District of Kentucky about three miles from the Long lick and about three miles from Bullitt's Lick. The river at all seasons of th year is navigable. It is contiguous to many public roads. They pray an Act establishing a warehouse and inspection.

Moses Moore
Jno. Moore
William Overall
Thoms. Foreman
Joseph Foreman
Ephraim Stanford
Isham Burn
Weiant [?] Esting
Thomas Morcarta
Wm. Rogers
Jno. Williams
Jacob Williams
David Nottingburg
Wm. Mabry
Hugh Snilling [?]
Charles Lainn
Joshua Ferguson
George Robertson
Wm. Roberts
Brackill Owins
Lo. Lewis [?]
Jno. Richey
Jesse Clark
James Johnson
Lai iff Coxor
Arther Hall
George Wilson
Saml. Smith
Wm. McClung
John Essery
David Clarke
Philip Wise
Rubin Case
Josep Case
David Case
Daniel Case
John Bell
Nathaniel Wallace
Andrew Criswell
Abraham Neal
Robert Brian
Ben Hawberry
Nicholas Crist
Nicholas Crist
Jacob Crist
Peter Halm Senr.
Peter Shephard
James Morrison
Thompson Averall
Jeremiah Anderson
Peter Young
John Liman
Edmd. Able
    Reasonable.

Wm. Pannabaker
Cornelius Voisst
Wm. Simmons
Loyd Miles
Joseph Ridgeway
Saml. Ridgeway
Christo. Marias [?]
Nathan Robinson
Jno. Win
John Carpenter
Wm. Hopkins
Francis Shain
David Shay
Abner Hill [?]
James McMannas
George Heeth
Wm. Marcus
Jno. Armstrong
Peter Pannebaker
Saml. Martan
Thompson Briggs
Jacob Williams
Richard Lowe
Wm. Briggs
Thoms. Shain
Thoms. Gotewell [?]
Amos Atkins
Ignatius Brashears
Robt. Brashears
Atkinson Hill
Wm. Kendell
Jno. K. Gaither
James Caldwell
Edwd. Truman
Geo. Hart
Jonathan Irons
Joshua Hoffs
Jno. Willson
Weeant Pannaber
Peter Fraugh [Traugh?]
Henry Brady
Wm. Shepherd
Christo. Hann
Michael Shepherd
Adam Shepherd
Aron Arlvin [?]
Michael Rench [?]
Jonathan Cox
Jacob Yoder
Coleman Denbar
Anthony Hundly
William Wright

1789, Oct. 24 - Petition of inhabitants of Nelson County that they are very inconvenient to an inspection and from the badness of the roads labor under many inconveniences in carrying their produce to market. They ask an Act to establish a warehouse and inspection on the Beech fork at the mouth of Cartwright's creek on the land of Richd. Parker.

Thomas Pitman	John Robertson
Joshua Harrison	John Batsel
Benjamin Marks	Peter Peters
Isaac Blackburn	Robert Johnston
Daniel Crume	Eliazer Birket
Thomas Hutchison	G. Wapshatt
William Harreld	Robert Alvey
Joseph Hobbs	Joseph Alvey
Henry Cotton	William Smith
William Humphrey	Jams. [?] [?]
Richard Parker	John Long
John Nalle	George Robison
Thomas Hatsall	Isaac Davis
John Overlin	Wm. Kincheloe
William Overlin	Thos. Kincheloe
Coleman Brown	Benjamin Purcel
William Dotson	

[another petition, same text]

Thomas Lewis	James Hughs
Jeremiah Fletcher	Nathaniel Hughs
Wm. Lent	John Cooksey
Samuel Williams	Ralph Crume
Wm. Hughs Jr.	George Jeboe
John Moore	Moses Harrell
Jesse Crume	Moses Daily
Samuel Bland	John Lewis
Wm. Hughs Sr.	Isaac Marks
James Williams	Charles Crume
John Hughs	Benjamin Marks

[another petition, same text]

John Robertson	Joseph Stillwell
Wm. Kindrick	Henry Watson
William Allin	James Underhill
William Robertson	William Watson
George Marks	John Maginniss
James Watson	Nathaniel Hughs
James Allan	Samuel Brown
William Butler	John McDonald
Daniel Friley	Joshua Ferguson
John Tucker	Joseph James

[another petition, same text]

Philemon Waters	Archy Paton
Isaac Forman	Bijah Pelham
John Neighbours	Frances Pelham
John Mulkelmorney	William Coppage
Henry Hines	George Coppage
Lewis Piburn	William Wilson
Benjamin Deen	Mosis Man
Thomas Harrison	Charles Phillips
Benjamin Harrison	Antony Sandusky
Samuel Wilson	John Silvers
Allen Wilson	John Sandusky
John Wilson	Samuel Silvers
Moses Draper	William Nappier Senr.
Jones Phillips	William Nappier Juner.
William Galloway	Richard Nappier
Nathaniel Ray	Moses Gill
William Ray	Zacariah Ricket Sener
John Galloway	Zacariah Ricket Juner

Robert Galloway
Nathaniel Martin
Phillip Walker
Elliekzander Bags
Georg Robbison
Danniel Neves
John Lians
Peter Dicson
Peter Brunt
William Cooly
Joseph Grey
Henry Young
Boston Damewood
Makus Followay[?]

Samuel Sandusky
William Ridge
Edward Robinson
Benjamin Fickle
Christopher Stretch
Joseph Richison
James Hambleton
John Miller
Thomas Heirs
Robert Heirs
Joseph Heirs
Jeans Harall
Wm. McElwee

[another petition, same text]
John Alvey
John Nalle Junr
John Nalle son of Francis
Robert Parker
James Nalle
David Glen [?]
Joseph Barr [?]
James Harrell
Isaac McCarty
Jos. Lewis
Edmund Callons
Joseph Ferguson
Henry Stephen [s?]
Josep McCollum
Wm. T. Caldwell
Thomas Bayne
Wm. Young [? torn]
Nath. Grigsby
Jesse Moore
John Redman
Nimrod Shumate [?]
John Young
Thomas Redmon

Thomas Halbert
Alexander Johnstone
John Naidin
Thomas Tayler
[   ] [torn]
Charles Polk
Bryan Young
Sam: Pryor
Jesse Davis
Elijah Milton
Ben Pope
James McCullum
Moses Milton Junr.
Greenbery Dorsey
Moses Milton
David Smith
John [Bu?]rns
[   ]blon Collings
[   ]ly Hobbs
Thomas Collings
John Redmon Jur.
Le[wis] Kincheloe
[   ] Davis [torn]

1789, Oct. 24 - Petition of inhabitants of Nelson County that
    they are subjected to many inconveniences for want of a warehouse and inspection of tobacco at or near the mouth of
Stewart's Creek on the North side of the Beech Fork. There is
a large and extensive settlement around the place. The Beech
Fork is navigable for large boats as high up as this place and
it is within a mile of Bairdstown. They ask an Act to establish
a warehouse and inspection at the aforesaid place.

Will McClung
Alexr. McCown
Benjn. Frye
Fras. Shain
Stepn. Ormsby
Thos. Morton
James Adams
John Crawford [?]
Hugh Crawford
Saml. Paul Jones
G. Calhoon
Trammell Hickman
James Murphy
W. Rowan
Thos. Spencer
George Robison

James Herrald
William Milligan
John Kelley
Edmund Price
Peter Kerr
Samuel Greene
Moses Harrell
John Read
John Freman
Isac McCarty
Henry Stevens
Danl. Furry [Feerry?]
Richd. Sutton
John McCollum
J. Lewis
Joseph Bane

Moses Jefferis
Geo. Hartt
J. Gillon [?]
Jno. Floyd
Thoms. Halbert
Thos. Wood
Joseph Jefferis
Atkinson Hill
Jacob Ruble
Rubin Case
Wm. Gill
John Thompson
John Marshall
Cain Withers
John Mills
Joshua Ferguson
Edmund Atwell [?]
David Glen
Adam Wible
Michl. Campbell
Laurence Green
Thomas Tayler
Joseph Blackford
Allepher [?] Rowin
Josey [? Topey?] HeyCraft
Wm. McBride
Uriah Blue
Richd. Pile
Caleb Cash
James Abbot
George King
Peter Panebaker
Samuel Morton
Elias Moore
Thos. Lowry [?]
Thomas Hurley
Samuel Steglan
Job Eldridge
Laurence Smith
Samuel Brown
William Kelley
William Combs
James Baird
John Gallway
Andrew Rowan
James Pursel
Jacob [?]
Arthur Hall
Daniel Scott
Chrisr. Kauffman
Abraham Reamer Sr.
Abraham Reamer Jr.
Charles Miller
James Winn
Joseph Reid
Cornelias Gater
John Batsel
John Gilkey
James Brown
Job Eldridge
John William
Henry Heant [?]

Mathis Ambrose [?]
Joseph Connaway
Israel Jennings
Valentine King
Isaac Maslin
Dennis Pursel
Jas. Duncan
Jacob Yoder
Thos. M: Winn
Wm. Kincheloe
Thompson Briggs
Jas. Priestley
John Esrey
John Kelley
Benjamin Lasly
Hananiah Lincoln
William Hammill
Chas. Lynch Jur.
Jams. Hackley
Saml. Smyth
Michael Runner
John Mothaol [?]
Raphael Lancaster
Sam. Pryor
Hugh Orafam
Anthony Thomson
James Raine
Benjamin Seaul [?]
John Paul
Philip Read
Henry [Humphrey?]
Eliehizer Miller
Joshua Scott
Edward [?] E[?]
James Leacon
James Brady [?]
James White
Walter Beall
Philip Caldwell
Mark Hardin
Ben Grayson
Robert Housley
Jacob Derry [?]
Gervis Hammond
Daniel Folsan [?]
Martin Curts
Henry Funk
Jacob [?]
Andrew Rowan
Michael Ryan
Proctor Ballard
Christn. Pringle
David Blackburn
Archabel Pike
Isaac Sollers
Gilman Moores
Elias Payton
Elijah Payton
[?] Ferry
Chester Howell
Samuel Cox
Thomas Hargis

Chas. Lynch Sr.
Samll. Steegeler
Jas. Ross
Laurence Haff
David Evans
John Hedges
William Berry
John McDaniel
Thomas Montgomery
William Marshal
John Allen
Andrew Allen
Jno. Lancaster
Jno. Depur [?]
Edmd. Collan
Benja. Cox
Daniel Conner
John Pickins
Hallsworth Thornhill
Joseph Forman
John Boyl
David Cox
Jacob Dicker
Johathan Cox
James Cox
James Allen
Robert Jeffers
James Woods
Nicolas McCarty
Ch: Knight
John Briggs
William King
Henry Wise
Robert Marshal
Thomas Spenser
William Briggs
Abraham Dale
Halesworth Valintine
   Thornhill
Moses Person
William Niel
Zacchariah Leaton
Thomas Piety
Jerimiah Anderson
John Bye [?]
Will Magee [?]
David McFauk [?]
Geo. Prerry [?]
Samuel Osburn
Presley Gray
Wm. Case Jr.
Willm. Bruce
James White
Hugh Rodman
Henry Floyd
[?]
David Smith
Isaac Marks
John Handley
   Reasonable.

Temple Cotton
John Hobbs
Joshua McDonald
John Cotton
Zacharrahs Wor [?]
James Hady
Tho. Smyth
John Ritchie
Msheek Cart[er]
Anthony Foster
Benjam. Cle[ ]
Jos. Baird
Hensley Pres[ ]
John Read
William Jones
William Gray
Isaac Malins
Joshua Hobbs
William Gilb[ert?]
Thomas Burn [ ]
James Deacon
Bryon Onsel
John Unsel
Niskils King
Thos. Langley
Sam McAdams
Moses Kerl [?]
Soloman Fos[ter?]
Olover Havin [?]
Geo. Harrison
George Marks
John Grundy
Richard Uerel [?]
Cutht. Harrison
Gabriel Cox
D[?] Mulins [?]
Ben Pope
Robert Wilson
Robt. Baird
James Allen
Garret[?] Suttle
Zach. Pearl
Henry Cotton
Thomas Baird
David Smith
James Sheddes
Geo. Muse
David Clever
Peter Springsone
Ignatius MedCalf
Geo. Blair
Jon[?] Briant [?]
James Cleaver
Hananiah Lincoln
John Bye
Isaac Blackburn
Andrew Vaughan
David Conner
Peter Cissell

Pike County - 1849

1849, Jan. 31 - Petition of residents of Kentucky that they

intend petitioning the next Legislature of Kentucky for a law ceding to Virginia that portion of the county of Pike included within the following boundaries:...at the mouth of Big Creek on the west side of the Tug Fork of Sandy River... to the top of the main dividing ridge between the waters of the Tug and Lavica ... to the line between Kentucky and Virginia. They suffer many inconveniencies in consequence of the present dividing line between the states. Violators of the law can in a moment of time pass from one state to the other and thus elude officers of the law. The present line divides neighborhoods, friends and relations.

John Ferrell	Ferrell Hatfield
John McCoy	Mitchel Rumspsy [?]
Wm. Tiller	Asa Harmon Rumby [?]
Joseph Murphey	Richard Hatfield
John Coy	John Hatfield
Aly Hatfield	Thos. Hatfield
Daniel McCoy	Joseph Hatfield Jur.
Richard Fuerrell [?]	Joseph Hatfield
John Murphy	Ulysses McCoy
Benjamin White	Nathan Pabnett [?]
Aandrew Varney	John Walford
Jacob Webb	Canly Blankenship
John McCoy	Ezekiel Blankenship
M. G. B. Davis	Federick Walford
Asa McCoy	Isaac McNew
James Vace	William Blackburn
Richard Maynard	Henry G. Davis
David Maerds	Peter M. Alley
Andy Murphy	William T. Cline
Cummens Musick	Randolph McCoy
John Sanson	Samuel Canada
Samuelale[?] Mounts	William Davis
Herndon Murkey	Madison Hatfield
George Hatfield	Samuel Farley
Valentine Hatfield	

Referred to Courts of Justice.

Shelby County - 1825

1825, Dec. 17 - Petition of Elliot Rucker of Shelby Co., Ky., that in 1775 he enlisted as a private in the first regular company raised in Virginia and marched to Williamsburg where he remained until his term expired. In Jan. 1777 he was appointed ensign in the 1st Virginia State Regiment commanded by Col. George Gibson. They marched to the north and joined Washington's army where he continued for three years. He was promoted to lieutenant. In 1780 he returned to Virginia with the regiment and among other officers became supernumerary. He held his commission to the end of the war and acted as major by brevet in several engagements. He was at the capture of Lord Cornwallis at the siege of York and marched with the prisoners to the north. He asks commutation pay as lieutenant for five years.

30 Aug. 1825. Shelby Co., Ky. John Shipman certifies he served in the campaign of 1781 under Maj. Elliott Rucker. He commanded a battalion styled the White Squad. They were drafts for nine months. He fought under him at the battles of Hot Water, Jamestown and at the siege of York. He was attached to Gen. Wayne's brigade.

Nov. 1825. Angus Rucker in Madison Co., Va., certifies that in May 1775 a full company met at Culpeper Court House and pledged themselves to each other and composed a company that should equip and hold themselves at all times ready to act under the authority of the Committee of Safety. They chose Col. William Champ as their captain. Maj. Elliot Rucker served as a minute man. The company was trained at or near Culpeper Court House. When Col. Henry moved towards Williamsburg to meet the enemy, the company was moved and Rucker marched until they met a messenger to stop them for further orders. They remained about ten days and were remanded back. At their August Term John Green was appointed captain and authorized to raise a company to serve twelve months. Rucker enlisted and served his time out. In Jan. 1777 Elliot Rucker was appointed ensign in the 1st Virginia State Regiment and marched to Williamsburg and joined the regiment. The regiment was ordered north and Rucker rose to the command of lieutenant. When the British troops marched to York he accepted a brevet as major.

4 Nov. 1825. Churchill Gibbs in Madison Co., Va., certifies that Maj. Elliot Rucker enlisted under Capt. John Green of Culpeper County about 20 Sept. 1775, the first regular company raised in Virginia, for twelve months and marched to Williamsburg as a guard to the seat of government and remained until his term of service expired. He was in Jan. 1777 appointed ensign in the 1st Virginia State Regiment commanded by Col. George Gibson and as soon as they were organized marched to the north and joined Washington's army. He returned to Virginia in the winter of 1780. In May of the same year they were ordered to Williamsburg and were furnished money for the purpose of enlisting soldiers. He afterward commanded as a major and was in the action of Hot Water or Green Spring and at the capture of Wallis [Cornwallis] at York and marched to the north with the prisoners. He was in the same regiment with Maj. Charles Ewell and Maj. Broaddus. At the north under the command of Gen. Washington he was promoted to lieutenant.

17 Nov. 1825. Charles Ewell in Prince William Co., Va., certifies that Elliott Rucker was a lieutenant in the 1st Virginia State Regiment and marched in 1777 from Williamsburg to the north where he continued until 1779 or 1780 when the regiment marched to the south and in Virginia in 1781 at the siege of York. He with other officers of the 1st and 2nd regiments was made supernumerary.

23 Nov. 1825. Joseph Carpenter in Madison Co., Va., certifies he served under Maj. Elliot Rucker in the battle of old Jamestown in 1781. He then commanded militiamen as major, but he understood he was lieutenant in Col. George Gibson's regiment. He led his men on well and encouraged them to fight for their country. He was beloved by his men.

Woodford County - 1789-1791

1789, Nov. 6 - Petition of inhabitants of Woodford County that the settled and more fertile part of their county is near forty miles in length and only about one-third that distance in width. This and the county's extending across two main forks of Elkhorn make it impossible to fix any place for holding courts which will not be extremely inconvenient to many of the inhabitants. They pray the county of Woodford may be divided into two by a line beginning where a line of Fayette County crosses the town fork of Elkhorn, down to the South Fork and to its junction with the North Fork, thence down main Elkhorn to the Kentucky.

Joseph Willson	Benja. Craig
Thoms. Graves	Francis W. Lea
Robt. Bradley	Bartlet Peary
Dan Neale	Archd. Campbell
John Peak	Michal Stucker
John Grant	Robt. Blackwell

Robt. Johnson
John Hawkins
Forest Webb
Julius Gibbs
Henry Elley
Toliver Craig
Thos. Herndon
Danl. Neel Junr.
Christor. Fort
Toliver Craig Jr.
Julius Christy
Stephen Archer
James Beatty
Jo. Bepeak [?]
Hugh Shannon
Thos. Dinwiddie

James McAfee
James Craig Myles
John Craig
James Dupuy
Jas. Cochran
John Neck
Michael Dickey
Vernon Goodloe
Thos. Branham
Robert Cautinell [?]
R. Seary
Benjamin Berry
Smyel[?] Woolfolk
Thos. Ficklin
Benjamin Cooper

[Another petition with same text:]
Henry Sanders
William Campbell
Jno. Davis
John Baldwin
John Branham
Aron Reynolds
Robt. Fost Gale
Jesse Threlkeld
Moses Bladwin
Danniel Baldwin
Elijah Craig
John Grayson
Nicolas Bitner
Wm. Wilson
John Cummings
Wm. McGuide
Edward West
Wm. M. West
Jas. West
Lewis West
Saml. McCally
Thomas Barlow
Henry Barlow Senr.
Henry Barlow Junr.
William Barlow
Jas. Barlow
James Bauchyard
John Gibson
William Smith
John Hall [Snr.?]
Henry Herndon
John Hall [Jur.?]
Isham Conn
J. J. Flournoy
Paul Gibson
Wm. Henry
John Gibson
Jonathan Gibson
Ambrose Christy
John Cummings
James Wilson
William Wilson
Jacob Stucker

Jas. Martin
John Vanzant
Thomas Martin
Zenus Sheperd
Saml. Sheperd
Richard Camel
James James
James Davis
Walter Brightman
Joseph Brightman
John Sims
William McCoffrey
Benja. Hamilton
Joseph Wallace
Edward Steel
John Ross
Elijah Davis
Thomas Woolfolk
Isaac E. Gano
Rhodin Coppedge
Henry Cave
James Brown
John Tanner
Saml. Grant
John Garth
David Flournoy
Henry Bellow
Phillip Stucker
David Stucker
[?]
John Porter
Partrick   [?] Contal
Wm. Rogers
Joseph Rogers
John Campbell
George Christy
William Cave
Thomas Wood
James Brown
John Cave
Bartlet Graves
John Scott

[Another petition with same text:]
Robt. Mackey

Richd. Young

283

Jno. Lowny
Thomas Gainey [?]
John Lindsay
Benja. Applegett
Thomas Duley
John McHatton
Robt. Creswell
Jno. McCoy
Wm. McHatton
James Stephenson
Thos. Bradley
William Ficklin
Thomas Mitchell
Thos. Perry
Edmond Perry
Thomas Davis
Daniel Campbell
Allen Campbell
Alexd. Campbell
Henry Field
Jas. Lindsay
John Rogers
Henry Shous
Bartlet Searcy
Jno. Stone [?]
Samuel Sinkhowe [?]

Richd. Fox
E S Bloy [?]
Martin Nall
Thos. Elley
James Meek
William Meek
Geo. Gray
Daniel Branham
Matthew Gale
Thos. Moseley
John Rogers
Saml. Flournoy
Jechonias Singleton
John Finney
John Collins
Hugh Emerson
Adam McConnell
Lewis Nuckolls
Thomas Poindexter
Thomas McQuady
Joel White
Benjamin Quinn
John McComesy [?]
Jos. Collins
Jas. Vanlandingham
Stephen Collins
Thos. Lindreeny [?]

[Another petition with same text:]
Bartlet Collins
James Strett
Christopher Fort
John Suggett
William Shortridge
James Money
Lewis Vallandingham
Reuben Twyman
William Twyman
John Uselton
George Uselton
William McClure
Elijah Craig
William Logan
Anthony Logan
John McClur
Robert Farquher
Matthew Barkley
Edward Rogers
George Cotter
Thomas McCluer
William McKinstree
Ackilis Stepp
Wm. Steele
James Craig
John Watkins
Thos. Blanton
James Blanton
Martin Hazard
William Lizenby
John Lott
George Admire
Thomas Eavens
John Jack

Samuel Shepard
Robert Sanders
Jacob Mullery
James Drake
William Cave
Charles Holleway [?]
William Steel
Larkin Perrey
John Franklin
Hugh Masterson
Joshua Jeinings
John Vaughan
David Williamson
Wm. Lindsay
Archey Stuart
George Campbell
Wilm. Ewing
William Tolber [?]
Henry Lindsay
Joseph Ewing
Jacob Eavins
Edward Dehaven
Joseph Archer
William Allen
John Stewart
John Ewing
Jas. Cochran
Michl. Sheehy [?]
Samuel Deheven
John McGrew
Jacob Dehaven
Andrew Criswell
Jothn. Robinson
Asah Stone

    Benjn. Guttrey   Wm. Turner
    Robert Uppum   Wm. Kelly
    Josiah Collins
      [Map of Woodford County attached]
      Referred to next session.

1790, Oct. 21 - Petition of Elijah Craig of Woodford County that
    he settled on the frontiers on the north fork of Elkhorn in
    1786 and being distressed by the savages was advised by some
of his principal neighbors to lay off a village and sell it out
to induce settlers and strengthen the settlement against the enemy.
In the fall of 1787 he laid off forty town and 37 out lots, the
chief of which are now sold. About 200 inhabitants live in the
village and are desirous it should be established as a town. It
is a convenient seat for mechanics and has considerable natural
advantages. He prays it may be established by law and called
George Town and that Robert Johnson, William Cave, Rodes Thompson,
Toliver Craig, John Grant, Archibald Campbell and William Henry,
Gent., be appointed trustees and be impowered to lay off more
lots and sell them.
    We the inhabitants of Lebanon village are very desirous the
village should be established as a town:

Edward West Senor	William Worrell
Wm. Mills West	William Worrell Jur.
Lewis West	Thos. Moorhead Snr.
James West	Thos. Moorhead Junr.
Wm. McQuady	Thos. Barlow
James Jameson [?]	Henry Barlow Junr.
Josiah Pitts	James Barlow
John Vanzant	Thomas Martin
John Campbell	Jno. Green
Barnet Shanneg	Nathl. Lowrey
Samuel McCall	Nicolas Bitner
Lindsey Osburn	Garnar McNamar
Saml. Shepard	Walter Brightman
Zenas Shepard	Thos. Cain
Henry Barlow Snr.	James Crail.

      Reasonable.

1790, Oct. 25 - Petition of inhabitants of Woodford County that
    they labor under great disadvantages for want of a division of
    the county. They were divided from Fayette County by a line
of fifty degrees variation which rendered it difficult to fix on
a center for holding court. The Court has wisely fixed on a
place for the Court House and other public buildings in the
center of one end of the county with the expectation that a division would soon take place, which causes the other end to
suffer. The number of our militia the first of April was 1047
and the settlement is extended to the Ohio which is ninety miles
in length. They pray the county of Woodford may be divided [as
described in the 1789 petitions].

Benjn. Branham	Saml. Stevenson
Archd. Campbell	Rodes Thomson
George Moore	Thomas Woolfolk
William Craig	Elijah Woolfolk
Toliver Craig	Rhodin Coppedge
William Threlkeld	Moses Bauldwin
Henry Sanders	Daniel Neail
Daniel Munro	Solomon Belew
Landon Key	Isaac Coppedge
Richard Burt	Daniel Deale
Richard Branham	Uriah Edwards

James Harndon	Jacob Mulberry
Martin Herndon	William Davis
James Hawkins	William Rogers Jr.
Elisha Thomas	Robt. Connely
David Herndon	Jas. Connely
Thomas Lucas	Thos. Church
Thos. Elley	Spence Neall
George Hanks	Francis Gholso [sic]
Moses Burt	Wm. Logan
Aaron Reynolds	Joseph Willson
John Meed	Ephraim Baits
William Cave	Nemiah Derozal
James Smith	John Riely
Joshua Orr	Hy. Herndon
William Shortridge	John Eagleton
John Garnett	John Cave
Beverley Bradly	Ambrose Christy
Bartlet Collins	John Christy
Robt. Bradley	Josia Jenings
James Allen	Jeremiah Hase
Aaron Denney	Thomas Johnson
Edward Webb	John Watts
Forest Webb	Lewis Deweese
John Hawkins	Thomas Dewley
Jamison Hawkins	Henry Cave
Philn. Hawkins	Hugh Creswell
James Davis	Robert Criswell
Lewis Shortridge	Henry Hicks
William Barlow	Jacob Holderman
Elijah Davis	Christopher Fort
Wm. Vaden	Josiah Gayle
James Allen	Thomas Bradley
Joshua Orr	John Ficklin
Frederick Burdett	Thos. Ficklin
John Peak	John Torrance
John Pearson	Robt. Johnson
William Tanner	Abraham McGilellon
Chichester Matthews	Samuel Thorngloon [?]
Jacob Counts	James Kelly
Jas. Riding	Matthias Mount
Francis L. Slaughter	Paul Gibson
John Suggett	Julius Gibbs
Henry Elley	Thos. Landrum
Jessey Thrailkill	James Kay
Wm. Campbell Jr.	John Branham
Wm. Campbell Sr.	Andrew Johnson
John Davis	James Drake
Thomas Sanders	Richard Applgitt
William Cave	Benjamin Applgitt
John Rogers Senr.	James Barlow
Larkin Perry	Edmond Wood
Joel White	Manhar Lucus [?]
Richd. Flynt	John Peak
James Johnson	Josiah Pitts
John Brock	Thomas Martin
Rd. Parker	Jas. Martin
Nicolas Burtt	Thos. Moorhead jr.
John Cummings	Lyn West
Daniel O. Cain	James West
James Merritt	Julius Christy
Garnar McNamar	William Love
John Green	William Rogers
Henry Barlow Snr.	James Logan

John Campbell	John Sterett
Robert Hartnass	William Brown
Joseph Rogers	Younger Pitts
William McQuidey	John Rogers
Samuel McCall	Clements Mosley
Thos. Nicklson	David Flournoy
Saml. Thomson	Benjamin Ray
Thos. Cain	John Harwood
Lewes West	Christopher Snewbery
Thos. Barlow	John Grant
James Hurley	George Christey
Stephen Archer	Jacob Holderman
Zacariah Archer	Robert McLaughlin
Jacob Stucker	William Smith
Zenas Shepard	John Gath
Alexr. Craigmiler	John Hall
Jno. Finwick	Andw. Raburn
Joseph Finwick	Nathl. Lowrey
Barney Shery	John Thomson
James Limmons	Philip Stucker
Nicholas Tombolane	Nicolas Bitner
James McAfee	David Stucker
James Crak [?]	Francis Coalman
Thomas Morhead	Moses Ray
William Worrell	John Ray
George Shannon	Edward West
John Boid	William West
Walter Brightman	Philip Rootes
Thomas McCoy	Nathinel Robison
Thomas Beard	William Cave
John Vanzant	Robt. Crichton
Charles Snell	Henry Creighton
Henry Oneal	David Scott
Robert Forman	Thomas Smith
John McCoy	John Craig

    Reasonable.

1791, Oct. 24 - Petition of James Twyman of the County of Woodford
    that he entered service as a volunteer soldier on 27 March
1791 in an expedition from the District of Kentucky to Scioto
against the hostile Indians under Col. Alexander D. Orr and while
in service received a very distressing wound on his leg from the
kick of a horse which confined him three months and twenty-three
days and which also obliged him to employ a surgeon who attended
him nearly every day during that time and extracted several
pieces of fractured bone from his leg, one of which was five
inches and one quarter long and from one half inch to three
quarters wide. The surgeon's account against him amounted to
L15.17.9 which he has paid. He was a considerable distance from
home and was obliged to procure lodgings and other necessary
accomodations and has paid L8.5.-. He conceives it reasonable
that the sums of money be refunded.
    Reasonable.
    23 July 1791. Dr. John Johnston in Mason Co., Ky., certifies
that he attended James Twyman as a surgeon from 31 March 1791
until 23 July following and extracted several pieces of fractured
bone from his leg, one of which was five inches and one quarter
long and from one half inch to three quarters wide. Twyman for
more than two months and one half was not able to get out of the
room.

1791, Oct. 26 - Petition of inhabitants of Woodford County that
    they labor under great inconveniences and disadvantages on

account of not having a division of the county. They ask a
division by a line where the Fayette line crosses the Town Fork
of Elkhorn and down that fork to its junction with the South Fork
and down to a line which will extend to Eight Mile Tree on the
road from Frankfort to Georgetown and then to where the Buflow
[sic] Road crosses the dividing ridge between the head of Lacounts
Run and Ceder Creek, thence to the Ohio at the mouth of the Big
Bone Lick Creek.

Thomas Barlow
Wm. Tannehill
Wm. Barlow
Henry Barlow
John Millikan
David King
Barney Sherry
Joseph Swan
Joseph Crain
John Campbell
James McAfee
Alexr. Craigmyler
James Johnson
John Green
James Barlow
Thos. Wood
Richard Cave
Thos. Martin
Jno. Vanzant
Thomas Moorhead
William McQuadie
Wm. Boyd
James Flanigan
Jno. Michel
Wm. Brent
John Ewing
William Anderson
Ezekiah Wilson
George Shannon
James Lamen [?]
Alexr. McCallister
Edward Cahill
John MCantire
John Vaughan
Jno. Brown
Jas. Martin
Moses Chirry

Edward West
Wm. West
Robt. F. Gale
Jas. West
Thos. Beaty
Danl. Neal
William Brown
Wm. Grayson
Wm. Smith [?]
Henry Nixon
William Cave Senr.
James Pollock
Jas. McClure
Jno. Boyd
Will Turner
Thomas McFarland
Joseph Frakes
Jas. Hamilton
Rodes Thomson
Hy. Herndon
James Steritt
John Garth
Henry Bellis
Danl. Cane
Demes[?] Carrill
Nathaniel Cand [?]
Samuel Scott
John Scott
Thomas Smith
Saml. M. Warigh [?]
Jas. McClean
Thomas McClean
Jno. McCrory
Jno. Mosby
Samuell Dunn [?]
John Henderson
William Henry

[Another petition with same text:]
Y.[?] Pitts [?]
Wm. [?] Johnston
Wm. Steele
Sam. Shepard
William Cave
James Gordon
Matthew Craignigle
[?] Wiett [?]
Wm. Kelley
Thos. Smith
Younger Pitts
Jas. Finly
Wm. Rogers
[?] Hill [?]
Taverner Branham
Jno. McQuid [?]

Samuel Scott
Wm. Smith
Jno. Smith
James West
James Christy
Robart Raney
John Rainey
Robert Raney Jnr.
Achills Stapp
Jas. Morgan
Joseph Anderson
Jameson Hawkins
Philn. Hawkins
Charles Green
S. [?] Grant
Israel Judy

John Thomson	Evan James Mong [?]
Jms. Conneley [?]	Thos. Brent
Lewis Dewese	Henry Vaden
Willia Cero	Wm. Worrel
Thomas Scott	Thos. Elmore [?]
Wm. Worrel	John Cave
Saml. Moor	John Hall
Nathl. Lowrey	Wm. Ewing
Wm. McFarland	Jeto Peak
Thomas Woolfolk	Robt. Holoway
[ ] Rogers	John Inlow
John Waugn	Charles Halloway
John Scott	George Christy
Julius Christy	

[Another petition with same text:]

Jno. McHatton	Zachariah Archer
Jno. McHatton Jur.	Aldr. McHatton
Wm. McHatton Junior	Charles Kilgore
Thos. Townsley	John Carnagey
Jas. Anderson	Alex. Hutchinson
Robt. Stubbs	Wm. Denney
James White	Aldr. Curry
Thos. Cain	Charles Hamilton
James Denney	Wm. Owins
Simon Denney	Daniel Cliffin
Daniel Curry	Picket Finch
Arch. Curry	Tho. Baird
Reasonable.	

1791, Oct. 26 - Petition of inhabitants of Woodford County that the Court of this county made an order in the latter part of 1789 fixing their Court house on the land of Hezekiah Brisco heir to John Brisco at a place known by the name of the Falling Springs, in consequence of which Patrick Doran (attorney for John Brisco who is guardian to Hezekiah Brisco) did lay off 124 lots of half an acre each with proper streets and alleys with two acres in the centre for the purpose of erecting the Court House and other necessary buildings. Doran has sold at public sale to the highest bidder about 100 lots and has given bond to make sufficient deeds. Several of the purchasers have built and are now settled on their lots and the justices wish to build a good Court House. Doubts have arisen whether it is in the power of Doran to make proper deeds of conveyance. They ask an Act to confirm the sales and appoint turstees to make deeds and make sale of the balance of the lots and that the town be established and known by the name of Versailles.

T. Marshall	Robet Sanders
Jno. Watkins	Hugh Ferguson
Robt. Johnson	Lewis Craig
Wm. Steele	Jno. Graves
Richd. Young	William Graves
Patrick Doran	John Williams
Joseph Delaney	Jesse Ellis
Saml. Kirkham	John Jacks
James McAfee	Joshua Whittington
Jordan Harris	John Stevenson
David Blackwell	William Elliott
Poland[?] Hughes	Herman Bownor
George Muter	Ruben Searcy
Thos. McQuady	John Long
John Ellison	Moses Cherry
John Perry	Wm. Murray

George Francisco
Joseph Holt
Armiger Bell
Robert Mahan
James Powers
Tims. [?] Connerlly
John Jones
Elisha Bishop
Lewis Young
Robt. Blackwell
Jacob Hearn
Isaac Hearn
John Butler
Gresham Forrest
H. Marshall
James Farquher
George Cotter
Tho. Arnold
Robt. Moffett
John Allen
Thos. Hamilton
George Brintton [?]
Lewis Subley
Thos. Kinkead
  Rejected.

James Stevenson
John Stevenson Junr.
James Blanton
Saml. Meredith Jr.
Phillip Rootes
J. Roberts
Hezekiah Roberty
Nely Roberts
Joseph Kinkead
Samuel Clark
David Driskell
John Poe
Paul Grugin
George Admires
William McCumshe
Jno. Jackson
Dennis Rearden
John Rearden
Mordecai Read
John Kinkade
Charles L. Francisco
Charles Lecompt
And. Francisco
Henry Rarden Senr.

[After the abstracts of these petitions were made, the Virginia State Library rearranged the Kentucky petitions. They are now in chronological order rather than being divided according to county or other designations. The Box numbers shown at the heading of each installment are no longer applicable.]

INDEX
Petitions from Kentuckians To The Virginia Legislature

———, John 249
Abbot, James 279
Able, Edmd. 276
Adams, Elijah 275
  James/Jas. 270,274,275,278
  John 271,275
  William/Wm. 272,274,275
Addams, John 260
Admire, George 284,290
Aevson (Awson), John 270
Agun, Willm. 271
Alexander, James 268
Allan, ___ 277
Allen, Andrew 280
  James 275,280,286
  William 284
Alley, Peter M. 281
Allin, William 277
Allison, Archibald 249
Alvey, John 278
  Joseph 277
  Robert 277
Ambrose, Maths 279
Anderson, Benjamin 258
  Isaac 270
  James 289
  Jeremiah 276,280
  Joseph 288
  Presley 262
  Richard C. 253,255
  William 288
Aplegate, Thos. 255
Applegate, Jno. 255
Applegett, Benja. 284
Applgitt, Benjamin 286
  Richard 286
Archer, John 268
  Jos. 257
  Joseph 284
  Stephen 283,287
  Zacariah 287,289
Arlvin, Aron 276
Armistead, William 266
Armstrong, Jno. 255,276
  William 268
Arnold, James 262
  John 262
  Thos. 268,290
Asturgus, James 255
Atkins, Amos 276
Atwell, Edmund 279
Averall, Thompson 276

Bags, Elliekzander 278
Bailey, John 255
Baird, David 274
  James 275,279
  Jos. 280
  Robt. 280
  Tho./Thomas 274,280,289
  William 274,275
Baits, Ephraim 286
Baker, Walter 248
Baldwin, Danniel 283
  John 283
  Moses 283,285
  (see Bladwin also)
Baley, Jno. 258
Ballard, Bland 258
  Chas. 272
  Proctor 249,274,279
Bane, Joseph 278
Barbee, Joshua 271
  Thos. 273
  Wm. 272
Barkley, Matthew 284
Barlow, Henry 288
  Henry, Jr. 283,285
  Henry, Sr. 283,285,286

Barlow, cont'd:
  James/Jas. 283,285,286,288
  Thomas/Thos. 283,285,287,288
  William/Wm. 283,286,288
Barnet/Barnett, James 270
  Joseph 275
Barns, Elias 270
  Shadrack 260
Barr, Joseph 278
Barthmess, Peter 249
Bartlett, John 255,260
  Nathan 260
Bassett, William 272
Batcher, Richd. 271
Batsel, John 277,279
Bauchyard, James 283
Baxter, Jas. 258
Bayne, Thomas 278
Beale, Richd. E. 271
Beall, Benjn. 274
  Richard 274
  Walter 273,274,275,279
Bean, Edwd. 264
Beard, James 274
Beatty/Beaty, James 283
  Thos. 288
Belew, Solomon 285
Bell, Arminger 290
  John 276
  Thos. 262
Bellow, Henry 283
Belli, Jno. 273
Bellis, Henry 288
Bennet/Bennett, Benj. 272
  Joshua 262
Bentley, John 248
Bepeak, Jo. 283
Berry, Benj/Benjamin 283
  John 271
  William 279
Berwick, James 258
Bigger, John 268
Birket, Eliazer 277
Bishop, Elisha 290
Bisscoe, John, Jr. 248
Bitner, Nicolas 283,285,287
Black, Saml. 271
Blackburn, David 279
  Isaac 277,280
  William 281
Blackford, Joseph 279
Blackwell, David 289
  James 256
  Robt. 282,290
Bladwin (see Baldwin)
Blair, Geo. 280
  Saml. 268
Bland, Samuel 277
Blane, Alexander 248
Blankenship, Canly 281
  Ezekiel 286
Blanton, James 284,290
  Thos. 284
Bloy, E. S. 284
Blue, Uriah 279
Bodley, Thomas, Jr. 269
Boid, John 287
Bonn, Andrew 262
Boone, Daniel 247,262
  Saml. 256
  Samuel, Jr. 262
  Squire 257,259,262
  Tho. 262
  William 271
Botsel, John 274
Bowmer, Robt. 272
Bownor, Herman 289
Boyd, C. J. 267

Boyd, cont'd:
  John 288
  Wm. 288
Boyer, Henry 271
Boyl, John 280
Boys, Danil 249
Bradley/Bradly, Beverley 286
  James 267
  Robt. 282,286
  Thomas/Thos. 284,286
Bradshaw, Benja. 271
  W. 271
Brady, Henry 276
  James 279
Branck, Robt. 271
Branham, Benjn. 285
  Daniel 284
  John 283,286
  Richard 285
  Taverner 288
  Thos. 282
Brashear, Marsham 255,258
  Rd. 258
Brashears, Ignatius 276
  Marsham 249
  Robt. 276
Breckinridge, Alexander 251,253,256
  Robert 253,266
Brent, Thos. 289
  Wm. 288
Breyen, James 258
Brian, Robert 276
Briant, Jon. 280
Bridas, Samuel 248
Briggs, Davi 248
  John 280
  Thompson 276,278
  William 274,276,280
Brightman, Joseph 283
  Walter 282,285,287
Brigs, William 249
Brintton, George 290
Brisco(e), Hezekiah 289
  John 289
Briselton, John 270
Broadus, ___ 282
Brock, Henry 268
  John 286
Brooks, Ebenr. 248,272
  Joseph 255
  Thomas 262
Brough, Robert 267
Broughton, C. 251
  Chas. 275
Brown, Coleman 277
  J. 271,273
  James 274,279,283
  John 255,272,288
  Samuel 277,279
  William 287,288
Bruce, Willm. 280
Brumfield, James 272
  Joseph 272
Brunson, Stout 260
Brunt, Peter 278
Bryan(t), William 261
Bucher, William 270
Buckner, Nicholas 255
Buford, Abraham 269
Bulger, Edward 261
Bullett/Bullitt, Alexr. S. 256
  Cuthbert 266
  Thos. 274
Bunch, Zachariah 273
Bunnell, Stephen 269
Burdett, Frederick 286
Burn, Isham 276

291

Burn, cont'd:
   Thomas 280
Burns, John 278
Burt, Moses 286
   Richard 285
Burton, Abraham 260
   Reuben 265
Burtt, Nicholas 286
Bush, Buarey 258
   Philip 248
   William 248,268
Bustard, John 266
Buston, John A. 272
Butler, John 290
   William 277
Bye, John 280
Byrne, John 271
   William 268

Cahill, Edward 288
Cain, Daniel O. 286
   Thos. 285,287,289
Caldwell, George 271
   George, Jr. 270
   James 276
   John 275
   Philip 271,279
   Robert 272
   Wm. T. 271,278
Calhoun, G. 278
Callaway/Calloway, Richd. 271
Callons, Edmund 278
Calvit, Jos. 258
Camel, Richard 283
Campbell, ___ 253,254
   Alexd. 284
   Allen 284
   Archd./Archibald 282,285
   Benj. 271
   Daniel 284
   George 284
   Hugh 270
   John 249,252,254,255,271, 283,285,287,288
   Michael 274,275,279
   William/Wm. 264,265,266, 268,283
   Wm., Jr. 286
   Wm., Sr. 286
Canada, Samuel 281
Cand, Nathaniel 288
Cane, Danl. 288
Carnagey, John 289
Carnahan, John 268
   William 268
Carpenter, John 276
   Joseph 282
Carrill, Demes. 288
Carter, Msheek 280
   Thomas 266
Cartin, Ignatius 274
Casbeur, Willm. 249
Case, Daniel 276
   David 251,276
   Joseph 251,276
   Ruben/Rubin 251,276,279
   William 249
   Wm., Jr. 280
Cash, Caleb 279
Cautinell, Robert 283
Cave, Henry 283,286
   John 283,286,289
   Richard 288
   William 283,284,285,286, 287,288
   William, Sr. 288
Cavins, Edwd. 268
Cero, Willia(m) 289
Champ, William 282
Chaplin(e), Abra'm 258,263
Chapman, William 249
Chenowith, Richd. 249,251, 258

Cherry/Chirry, Moses 288, 289
Childress, John 262
Chiles, Henry 271
Chiseton, William 249
Christmas, Richard 270
   William 270
Christey/Christy, Andw. 268
   Ambrose 283,286
   George 283,287,289
   James 288
   John 286
   Julius 283,286,289
Church, Thos. 286
Cissell, Peter 280
Clark, Andrew 252
   George Rogers 247
   G. R. 251,258
   H. 258
   John 251,253
   Samuel 290
Clarke, David 276
   John 271
Clarkson, John N. 267
Clary, John 248
Clay, Green 270
Clea___ (Cleaver?), Benjn. 280
Cleaver, Benjamin 274
   James 280
   William 274
Clements, Roger 262
Clever, David 280
Clide, James 248
Cliffin, Daniel 289
Clin, John 257
Cline, William T. 281
Clinkinbeard, Isaac 262
   William 262
Clinton, Samuel 268
Coalman, Francis 287
Cochran, Jas. 283,284
Cocke, James 272
Coffman, Isaac 272
Coleman, Jacob 255
Collan, Edmd. 280
Colley, Charles 271
Collier, John 259
Collings, ___blon 278
   Thomas 278
Collins, Bartlet 268,284, 286
   Elisha 262
   John 284
   Jos. 284
   Josiah 262,284
   Stephen 284
Colmisnil, John D. 266
Combs, Cuthbert 261
   William 274,279
Comes, Enoch 249
Coms, gnbean(?) 249
Conn, Isham 283
   Notley 267
Connaway, Joseph 279
Conneley/Connely, Jas. 286
   Jms. 289
   Robt. 286
Conner, Daniel 280
   David 280
Connerlly, Tims. 290
Connor, William 273
Connyers, James 272
Constant, John 262
Contal, Patrick 283
Conway, John 249
   Joseph 249
Coock, John 271
Cooksey, John 277
Cooly, William 278
Cooper, Benjamin 283
   Mary 256,257
   William 256,257

Coppage/Coppedge, Geo 277
   Isaac 285
   Jno. 274
   Rhodin 283,285
   William 277
Corbin, Robert 273
Cornwallis, Lord 281
Cotter, George 284,29_
Cotton, Henry 277,280
   John 280
   Temple 280
Couchman, Benjamin 26_
   Frederick 262
Counts, Jacob 286
Cowan, John 271
Cox, Benj. 280
   David 274,280
   Gabriel 274,280
   Isaac 249,274
   James 280
   Jonathan 276,280
   Robert 272
   Samuel 279
Coxor, Lai iff(?) 276
Craddock, R. 271,273
Craig, Benja. 282
   Elijah 283,284,285
   James 284
   Jeremiah 262
   John 261,283,287
   John H. 262
   Joseph 248
   Lewis 248,268,289
   Robert 268
   Toliver 283,285
   Toliver, Jr. 283
   William 285
Craigmiler/Craigmyler
   Alexr. 287,288
Craignigle, Matthew 2_
Crail, James 285
Crain, Joseph 288
Crak, James 287
Crawford, Hugh 274,27_
   John 248,278
   Robert 251
   Samuel 275
Creavenson, George 25_
Creighton, Henry 287
Creswell, Hugh 286
   Robt. 284
Crevinsten, Geo. 255
Creys, Nace 258
Crichton, Robt. 287
Crist, Jacob 276
   Jorge 249
   Nicholas 276
Criswell, Andrew 276,
   Robert 286
Crittendon, John 258
Crockett, Anthony 272
   Joseph 272
Croghan, William (W.) 253,255
Crook, Absalom 262
Crow, John 273
Crume, Charles 277
   Daniel 277
   Jesse 277
   Ralph 277
Crump, William 258
Crutcher, Jas. 272
Cthunter(?), Jacob 26_
Culpeper, Samson 261
Cummings, John 283,28_
Cummins, Peter 251,27_
Cumpton, Augustine 27_
Cunningham, Jno./John
   Thos. 274,275
Curd, James 271
   John 259,271
   Newton 271
Curry, Aldr. 289

Curry, cont'd:
  Arch. 289
  Daniel 289
  Thomas 255,258
Curts, Martin 274,279

Dabney, ___ 266
Daily, Moses 277
Dale, Abraham 280
Dalton, Valentine Thos. 252
Damewood, Boston 278
Daniel/Daniels, Martin 255,
  271,273
  Robert 255,273
  Walker 273
Daugherty, Cornelus 270
Davenport, Jonas 269
Davidson, Geo. 248
  Jas. 268
Davis, Benjamin 272
  Charles 272
  Elijah 283,286
  Henry G. 281
  Isaac 277
  J. 251
  James 272,283,286
  Jesse 278
  Jno./John 255,272,283,
   286.
  Joseph 272
  M. C. B. 281
  Richd. 270
  Samuel 248
  Thomas 248,262,269,284
  William 281,286
Deacon, James 280
Deal/Deale, Daniel 285
Deen, Benjamin 277
Dehaven, Edward 284
  Jacob 284
  Samuel 284
Delaney, Joseph 289
Denbar, Coleman 276
Denney, Aaron 286
  James 289
  Simon 289
  Wm. 289
Depur, Jno. 280
Derozal, Nemiah 286
Derry, Jacob 279
Deweese/Dewese, Lewis 286,
  289
Dewley, Thomas 286
de Wouves Darges, Peter
  Rezard 250
Dibrell, Charles 260
Dicerson, Valentine 263
Dicken, John 271
Dicker, Jacob 280
Dickerson, John 262
  William 262
Dickey, Michael 283
  Xr. 272
Dicson, Peter 278
Diem, Jacob 274
Dill, Francis 268
Dinnie, Alex 258
Dinwiddie, Thos. 283
Ditto, Henry 255
Dixon, Joseph 250
Dodge, Israel 274
  Jno. 258
Donne, J. 258
  John 251
  Martha 251
donran, Johan 258
Doram, Patrick 248,272,289
Dorsey, Greenbery 278
Dotson, William 277
Douglas, John 262
Downing, John 272
Dozer, James 284,286
  Philip 261,262
Draper, Moses 277

Driskell, David 290
Dryden, Wm. 248
Dulan, Jams. 262
Duley, Thomas 284
Dunbar, James 255
Duncan, James 279
  Samuel 249
Dunkin, Gabriel 270
Dunlap, Jas. 273
Dunn, Richard 270
  Samuell 288
Dupuy, James 283
Dyeatt, Jacob 274

E___, Edward 279
Eagleton, John 286
Earechson, Ben. 255
Eastin, Richard 255
Eavens, Thomas 284
Eavins, Jacob 284
Edwards, Fredk. 255
  John 261
  Sanford 261
  Uriah 285
Elam, Joseph 265
Eldridge, Job 279
Elley, Henry 283,286
  Thos. 284,286
Elleyre, Wm. 258
Elliott, ___ 267
  Robt. 251
  Thomas 274
  William 289
Ellis, Jesse 289
  Wm. 261
Ellison, John 289
Elms, William 258
Emerson, Hugh 284
Epperson (Apperson), Richd.
  247
Esher, Robert (Roder) 260
Esrey, John 279
Essery, John 276
Estill, John 270
  Samuel 270
Esting, Weiant 276
Estis, Elisha 271
Evanes, Charles 258
Evans, David 280
  Peter 271
Ewell, Charles 266,282
Ewing, Charles 274
  John 284,288
  Joseph 284
  Saml. 274,275
  Wilm./Wm. 284,289

Farley, Samuel 281
Farquher, James 284
  Robert 284
Farris, Isiam 248
Feares, George 268
Feland, James 248,272
Felty, John 255
Fenwick, John 274
Ferguson, Bryant 268
  Campl. 255
  David 255
  Hugh 289
  Joseph 274,278
  Joshua 274,276,277,279
Ferrell, John 281
Ferres, Michel 270
Ferry, ___ 279
Fickle, Benjamin 278
Ficklin, John 262,286
  Thos. 262,283,286
  William 284
Field, Abner 253,254,255
  Benj. 272
  Henry 284
Filson, John 274
Finch, Picket 289
Finlay, Richard 255

Finley, George 271
  John 255
Finly, Jas. 288
Finn, James 258
Finney, John 284
Finwick, Jno. 287
  Joseph 287
Fisher, Adam 272
  Barnard/Barnet 271
  Elias 272
  Stephen 272
Flanigan, Dominick 272
  James 288
Flannagan, Lewis 262
Fleming, Jo. 262,272
Fletcher, Jeremiah 277
Flournoy, David 283,287
  J. J. 283
  Matt. 271
  Saml. 284
Floyd, Henry 251,258,280
  Jno./John 274,279
  John B. 267
Flynt, Richd. 286
Foley, Richard 272
Followay, Makus 278
Folsan, Daniel 279
Forbis, James 248
Ford, Peter 248
Foreman, Joseph 276
  Thoms. 276
Forman, Isaac 277
  Joseph 280
  Robert 287
Forrest, Gresham 290
Forsythe, Robert 275
Fort, Christopher 283,284,
  286
Foster, Anthony 274,280
  Luke 255
  Solomon 180
Foushee, W. 269
Fowler, John 272
Fox, Richd. 284
Frakes, Joseph 288
Francisco, And. 290
  Charles L. 290
  George 290
Franklin, John 284
Fraugh (Traugh), Peter 276
Frazer, Abrm. 258
Freman, John 278
French, James 271
Friley, Daniel 277
Froman, Jacob 272
Frye, Benjn. 278
Fuertrell, Richard 281
Fulinwider, Mary 257
Fullenwider, Jacob 257
  Katharine 257
Funk, Henry 279
Furguson, David 273
Furry (Feery), Danl. 278

Gaines, W. 271
Gainey, Thomas 284
Gaither, Jno. K. 276
  John R. 250
Gale, Matthew 262,284
  Robt. F. 288
  Robt. Fost 283
Galloway, James 258
  John 277
  Robert 278
  William 258,277
Gallway, John 279
Galt, James Minson 266
Gano, Isaac E. 283
Garnett, John 286
Garrard, William, Jr. 269
Garth, John 283,288
Garton, Uriah 262
Gaskin, Thos. 258
Gass, David 270

Gass, cont'd:
  John 270
  Wm. 271
Gater/Gatter, Cornelias 279
Gatewood, John 262
Gath, John 287
Gayle, Josiah 286
George, Robt. 258
Cholso(n), Francis 286
Gibbs, Churchill 282
  Julius 283,286
Gibson, George 281,282
  John 257,283
  Jonathan 283
  Paul 286
Gilbart, Thos. 261
Gilbert, William 280
Gileson, Thomas 260
Gilkey, John 279
Gill, John 271
  Moses 277
  Wm. 279
Gillaspy, William 256
Gillavies, Robert 275
Gillon, J. 279
Gilman, James 248
Girault, J. 258
Glen, David 274,278,279
Goggin, John 260
Goodin, Edward 255
Goodloe, Vernon 283
  Vivion 271
Gordon, Ambrose 272
  James 288
  Richard 271
Gorham, Sanford 268
Gotewell, Thoms. 276
Goudy, John 268
Graham, Jas. 258
Grant, John 261,282,285,287
  S. 288
  Saml. 283
Graves, Barlet 283
  Jno. 289
  Thoms. 282
  William 289
Gray, George 284
  James 261
  Presley 280
  Robert 251
  William 280
Grayson, Ben 273,279
  John 283
  Wm. 288
Greassem, John 268
Green, Charles 288
  Henry 262
  John 282,285,286,288
  Laurence 279
  Willis 273
Greene, Samuel 278
Greenlee, Samuel 263,264
Greenup, Christopher 273
Grey, Joseph 278
Griffin, Aron 268
  Wilm. 272
Griffy, William 272
Grigsby, Nath. 278
Grubb, Hizk. 260
Grugin, Paul 290
Grundy, John 274,280
Grymes, Hugh 255
Guttrey, Benjn. 285
Gwinn, David 248

Hacker, Christiana 267
Hackley, James 271,279
Hady, James 280
Haff, Laurence 280
Haggen, John 272
Hagner, P. 265
Halbert, Thomas 278,279
Hale, Job 272
Hall, Arthur 276,279

Hall, cont'd:
  Edward 268
  John 248,287,289
  John, Jr. 283
  John, Sr. 283
  Parman 272
  Thomas 274
Halloway, Charles 289
Halm, Peter, Sr. 276
Hambilton, Thomas 272
Hambleton, James 278
Hamilton, Benja. 283
  Charles 289
  Jas. 288
  John 268
  Thos. 290
Hammill, William 279
Hammond, Gervis 279
Handley, John 257,258,275,280
Hanks, George 286
Hann, Christo. 276
Hansbrough, Morias 258
Harall, Jeans 278
Harbeson, John 275
Harbor, John 272
Harden, Mark 279
Hargess/Hargis, Thomas 279
Haris, John 271
Harper, James 262
  Peter 262
Harras, Christopher 261
Harreld, William 277
Harrell, James 278
  Moses 277,278
Harris, Andw. 270
  John 252,258
  Jordan 289
  Joseph 249
  Robert 261
  Wm. 258
Harrison, Benjamin 277
  Cuthbert 274,275,280
  Geo. 274,275,280
  Hiram 268
  John 253,254,257
  Joshua 277
  Thomas 277
Hart, George 276
  Henry 275
Hartness, Robert 287
Hartt, Geo. 274,279
Harvey, Jno. 260
  William, Jr. 260
  Wm., Sr. 260
Harwood, John 287
Hase, Jeremiah 286
Hatfield, Aly 281
  Ferrell 281
  George 281
  John 281
  Joseph 281
  Joseph, Jr. 281
  Madison 281
  Richard 281
  Thos. 281
  Valentine 281
Hazard, Martin 284
Heant, Henry 279
Hearn, Isaac 290
  Jacob 290
Hedges, John 280
Heeth, George 276
Heirs, Joseph 278
  Robert 278
  Thomas 278
Helder, John 262
Helm, John 257,274
  Leonard 250,252,257,258
  William 261
Henderson, David 268
  John 274,288
  William 262
Henry, ___ 282

Henry, cont'd:
  Thos. 272
  William/W./Wm. 268,271,283,285,288
Herndon/Harndon, David 262,286
  Henry 262,283
  Hy. 286,288
  James 286
  Martin 286
  Thos. 262,283
Herrald, James 278
Heycraft, Josey 279
Hibnor, Christian 275
Hickman, Trammell 278
Hicks, Henry 286
Hill, ___ 288
  Abner 262
  Atkinson 276,279
  Hardi 255
  Joshua 263
Hines, Henry 277
Hobbs, ___ly 278
  John 280
  Joseph 277
  Joshua 280
Hodges, Jesse 270
Hoffler, William 266,267
Hoffs, Joshua 276
Holderman, Jacob 286,287
Holker, ___ 263
Holland, Wm. 260
Holleway, Charles 284
Hollingsworth, James 266
  Susan P. 266
Holoway, Robt. 289
Holt, Joseph 290
Honaker, ___ 267
Hook, Ben 275
  James 257
Hopert, Thomas 258
Hopkins, John 270
  Thos. 272
  Wm. 276
Hord, James 272
Horine, Samuel 275
Horn, John Chrisp. 258
Hough, Samson 261
Hougland, James 257
Housley, Robert 274,279
Howard, Thomas 274
Howell, Chester 279
Hughes, John 255
  Poland 289
Hughs, James 277
  John 277
  Nathaniel 277
  Wm., Jr. 277
  Wm., Sr. 277
Humble, Micl. 271
  Noah 271
  Paul 272
Hume, John 257
Humphrey, Henry 279
  William 277
Hundley, Anthony 276
Hunt, ___ 267
Hunter, Frederick 261
  Henry 263
  Jacob 263
  Joseph 251,255
Hurley, James 287
  Thomas 279
Husbands, John 274
Huse, James 249
Hutchinson, Alex 289
Hutchison, Thomas 277
Hynes, Andw. 261,275
  Thomas 249,250,251
  William/Wm. 251,275
  William R. 251

Inlow, John 289
Innes, Harry 271,273

Irons, Harry 271,273
Irvine, John 272,273
  Will 260,270
Irwin, Samuel 273

Jack(s), John 284,289
Jackson, Bu__l. 271
  Jno./John 261,290
James, James 283
  Joseph 277
Jameson, John 285
Janston, John 258
January, Jno. 268
  Peter 268
Jeboe, George 277
Jefferis, Joseph 279
  Moses 275,279
Jeffers, Robert 280
Jeinings, Joshua 284
Jenings, Josia 286
Jennings, Israel 279
  Jonathan 272
Johnson, Andrew 262,286
  Cave 262
  James 276,286,288
  Richard M. 265
  Robert 262,283,285,286, 289
  Saml. 262
  Thomas 286
Johnston, Ga. J. 250,255
  Gabl. 253
  John 287
  Robert/Robt. 261,277
  Will./William 250,251, 255,258,260,288
Johnstone, Alexander 278
Jones, Benj. 249
  Catlit 247
  Jno./John 290
  Jno. Gabriel 247
  Saml. Paul 278
  William/Willm./Wm. 260, 271,280
Jons, Mathy 258
Joud, Robt. 268
Jouitt, John 271
Joyes, Patr./Patrick 250, 255
Judy,__Israel 288
Jurnhart, Mical 251

Karr, Elizabeth 257
Kaster, Rich. 251
Kauffman, Chrisr. 275,279
Kay, James 286
Keeny, Peter 272
Keith, John 249
  William 249
Kell, Nick 249
Keller, Isaac 257
Kelley, Emanuel 262
  John 278,279
  William/Wm. 279,288
Kelly, James 286
  Samuel 263
  William 285
Kendall/Kendell, William/ Wm. 249,276
Kennady, Will 255
Kennedy, Andrew/Andw. 248, 271
  Jo 270
  Thomas/Thos. 248,262, 270
Kennison, John 255
Kenny, Moses 258
Kenton, Wm. 272
Kerl, Moses 280
Kern, Peter 274
Kerr, Peter 278
Key, Landon 285
Kilgore, Charles 289
Kincad, John 275

Kincade, John 290
Kincaid, John 272
Kincheloe, Lewis 278
  Thos. 277
  William/Wm. 274,277,279
Kindrick, Wm. 277
King, David 288
  George 279
  John 274
  Niskils 280
  Valentine 261,279
  William 274,280
Kinkade, Hopson 272
Kinkead, Joseph 290
  Thos. 290
Kirby, Samuel 255
Kirkpatrick, Robert 270
Kisnard, Henry 274
Knight, Ch. 280
Knox, James 248
Krosley, Wm. 258
Kuykendall, Moses 255,258

Lacassagne, Mic'l. 253,255
Lacompt, Charles 290
Lainn, Charles 276
Lamen, James 288
Lancaster, Jno./John 274, 280
  Raphael 279
Landrum, Thos. 286
Langley, Thos. 280
Lansdale, Thomas L. 274
Lapesly/Lapsly, James 263, 264
  Jno./John 263,264
  Joseph 263,264
  Margaret 263
  Sally 263
  Saml./Samuel 263,264,271
Lasly, Beniamin 279
Lausbery, John Peter 275
Lawrence, David 271
  James 273
  Jno./John 272
Layne, James 267
Lea, Francis W. 262,282
Leacon, James 279
Leaton, Zachariah 280
Lee, Henry 267
  Jacob 272
  John 259
  Mark 272
Leffesten, George 258
Lent, Wm. 277
Leshly, Alexander 274
Lewis, J. 278
  John 277
  Jos. 278
  Lo. 276
  Thomas 273,277
Lians, John 278
Liddel, Thos. 274
Liley, Wm. 261
Lillard, Christopher 272
  John 272
Liller, Thomas 264,265
Lilley, Edmond 261
Liman, John 276
Limmons, James 287
Lincoln, Hananiah 262,279, 280
Lincreeny, Thos. 284
Lindsay/Lindsey, Henry 284
  James 284
  John 284
  Wm. 284
Littel, James 262
Lizenby, William 284
Lodg, Thomas 273
Logan, Anthony 284
  Benjamin 248
  James 286
  William 248,284,286

Long, John 262,277,289
Longdon, Beverley 268
Lord, Peter 249
Lott, John 284
Love, William 286
Loving, Wm. 261
Lowe, Richard 276
Lowny, Jno. 284
Lowery, Nathl. 285,287,289
Lowry, Thos. 279
Lucas, Thomas 286
Luce, Wm. 249
Lucus, Manhar 286
Lutts/Lutz/Lutes, Mary 256, 257
  Philip 256,257
Lynch, Chas., Jr. 279
  Chas., Sr. 280
  David 271
Lyum, William 255

McAdams, Sam 280
McAfee, George 259
  James 283,287,288,289
  Rebecca 259
  William 259
McBride, William 279
M'Cantire, John 288
McCall, Samuel 285,287
McCalla, Andrew 271,273
McCallister, Alexr. 288
McCally, Saml. 283
McCann, Alexr. 274
McCarty, Isaac 278
  Nicholas 249,280
  Thomas 258
McClean, Jas. 288
  Thomas 288
McClelan, John 268
McClintic, Jno. 255
McClung, Will./Wm. 276,278
McClure, Dan'l. 251,274
  Jas. 288
  John 274,284
  Thomas 284
  William 284
McClurg, Wm. 274
McCoffrey, William 283
McCollum, John 278
  Josep 278
McComesy, John 284
McConnell, Adam 284
  Jos. 262
  William 262,269
McCown, Alexr. 278
  Joseph 262
McCoy, Asa 281
  Daniel 281
  Jno./John 281,284,287
  Randolph 281
  Thomas 287
  Ulysses 281
McCracken, Cyrus 251,261
McCrahen, John 268
McCrakry, Isaac 258
McCrory, Jno. 288
McCrosby, Jas. 268
McCullough, James 268
McCullum, James 278
McCumshe, William 290
McDaniel, John 280
McDonald, Bryant 264
  James 249
  John 277
  Jonas 264
  Joshua 280
McDonat, Thomas 258
McDowell, James 265,268,269
  J., Jr. 272
  Saml. 263,271
  Wm. 263,264
McElhose, John 249
McElwee, Wm. 278
McFall, John 272

McFarland, Robt. 268
   Thomas 288
   Wm. 289
McFauk, David 280
McGee, David 264
McGehee, Samuel 272
McGerson, John 255
Mcghee, Lewis 258
McGilellon, Abraham 286
McGill, W. 274
McGinniss, William 270
McGrew, John 284
McGuide, Wm. 283
McGuire, John 272
   Thos. 271
McHatton, Aldr. 289
   John 284,289
   John, Jr. 289
   Wm. 284
   Wm., Jr. 289
McIntire, John 262
McKeag, Jas. 258
McKee, John 272
   Robert 273
McKinney, Charles 270
   John 261
   Josiah 272
   Rane 272,273
   Stephen 273
   William 273
McKinsey, John 268
McKinstree, William 284
McKinzey, Wm. 258
McLaughlen, John 263
   Robert 287
McMannas, James 276
McManus, John 257
McMillin, Saml. 268
   S. M. 262
McMurtry, William 272
McNamar/McNamur, Garner 285,286
McNew, Isaac 281
McQuadie/McQuady, Thomas, Thos. 284,289
   William/Wm. 285,288
McQuid, Jno. 288
McQuidy, William 287

Mabry, Wm. 276
Macdormet, Frs. 258
Mackey, Robt. 283
Maddeson/Madison, Gabl./ Gabr. 248,271
Maerds, David 281
Magee, Will 280
Maginniss, John 277
Mahan, Robert 290
Malins, Isaac 280
Man, Mosis 277
Mansfield, Charles 268
Maras, Patk. 258
Marcus, Wm. 276
Marias, Christo. 276
Marks, Benjamin 277
   George 277,280
   Isaac 277,280
Marshal/Marshall, H. 272, 290
   Henry 268
   J. 271
   John 279
   K. 272
   Lewis, Jr. 269
   Robert 280
   T. 289
   Thos. 268
   William/Wm. 280
Martan, Saml. 276
Martin, Hugh 262
   James/Jas. 259,283,286, 288
   Nathaniel 278
   Thomas/Thos. 283,285,

Martin, Thomas cont'd: 286,288
Maslin, Isaac 279
Massie, Nathl., Jr. 271
Masterson, Hugh 284
   James 262
Matthews, Chichester 286
Maupin, Richd. A. 266
May, William 274
Mayfield, George 272
Maynard, Richard 281
Medcalf, Ignatius 280
Meed, John 286
Meek, James 284
   William 284
Megowan, Robert 268
Meguire, James 262
Meller, Abraham 258
Meradith/Meredith, Saml., Jr. 268,290
Meriweather/Meriwether, David W. 255
   James 255,256
   Nich./Nicholas 261,271
   Thomas/Ths. 264,265
   Wm. 248
Merrifield, Thomas 274
Merritt, James 286
Metcalf, John 255
Michel/Michell, Jno. 288
Mikemson, Andrew 268
   John 288
Mikkin, John 263
Miles, John 262
   Loyd 276
   Michl. 258
Millar, Henry 261
Miller, Charles 279
   E. 275
   Eliehizer 279
   Jno./John 259,278
Milligan, William 278
Millikan, John 288
Millroy, William 268
Mills, John 279
Milner, John 272
Milton, Elijah 278
   Moses 278
   Mose, Jr. 278
Mitchel/Mitchell, Fredrick 262
   John 271
   Thomas 284
Moffett, Robt. 290
Money, James 284
Mong, Evan James 289
Montgomery, John 258
Montgomery, Thomas 280
   Wm. 248
Moody, James 271
Mooney, Jacob 254
Moor, Saml. 268,289
Moore, Elias 279
   George 285
   James/Jas. 271,272
   James F. 255
   James Francis 254
   Jesse 278
   Jno./John 276,277
   Moses 276
   William/Wm. 248,271
Moores, Gilman 279
Moorhead, Thomas 288
   Thos., Jr. 285,286
   Thos., Sr. 285
Morcarta, Thomas 276
More, ___ 254
Morgan, Charles 258
   David 255
   Jas. 288
Morhead, Thomas 287
Morrason, Wm. 261
Morrison, Hugh 262
   Isaac 275

Morrison, cont'd:
   James 274,275,276
Morrow, James 262
Morton, Benjamin 270
   Richard 249
   Samuel 279
   Thomas/Thos. 249,275, 278
Mosby, Jno./John 272,288
   Joshua 272
   Litty, Jr. 272
   Robt. 271
   Saml. 261
Moseley, Leonard 269
   Thos. 284
Mosley, Clements 287
Mothaol, John 279
Moulson, John 262
Mount, Matthias 268,286
Mounts, Samuelale 281
Mratin(Martin?), Wm. 258
Mulberry, Jacob 286
Mulins, D___ 280
Mulkelmorney, John 277
Mullery, Jacob 284
Munday, Edmond 273
Munro, Daniel 285
Murkey, Herndon 281
Murphey, Joseph 281
   Stephin 261
Murphy, Andy 281
   James 278
   John 255,281
Murray, Wm. 272,289
Muse, Geo. 280
Musick, Cummens 281
Muter, George 271,273,289
Myers, Jacob 248
Myles, James Craig 283

Nagle, M. 271,273
Naifin, John 278
Naler, Jesse 260
Nall, Martin 272,284
Nalle, Francis 278
   James 278
   John 277,278
   John, Jr. 278
Nappier, Richard 277
   William, Jr. 277
   William, Sr. 277
Neail, Daniel 285
Neal, Abraham 276
   Danl. 288
Neald, Elias 255
   William 255
Neale, Benjamin 261
   Dan 282
Neall, Spence 286
Neck, John 283
Neel, Dan'l. Jr. 283
Neeld, Elias 251
Neighbours, John 277
Neill, James 248
Neilson, Wm. H. 266
Nelson, Hum. 271
Neves, Danniel 278
Nevil, Denis 275
Neville, Prestley 257
New, Anthony 265
Niblack, John 263
   William 263
Nicklson, Thos. 287
Niel, William 280
Nixon, Henry 288
Noel, Bernard 273
Nottingburg, David 276
Nuckolls, Lewis 284

Oakley(Ockley), John 258
Okley, Ben 270
   Thos. 270
Oldham, Jno. P. 266
   Samuel 255

Oldham, cont'd:
  Will./William 251,258
Oneal, Henry 287
Onens, Thos. 272
Onsel, Bryon 280
Orafam, Hugh 279
Ormsby, Stephn. 250,271,
  273,278
Orr, Alexander D. 287
  Joshua 286
Osburn, Lindsey 285
  Samuel 280
Overall, William 276
Overlin, John 277
  William 277
Overton, Clough 258
  James 260
  Richard 263
Owing, John C. 274
Owins, Brackill 276
  Wm. 289
Oza, Zach. 274

Pabnett, Nathan 281
Panebaker/Pannabaker,
  Peter 275,276,279
  Wm. 276
Pannaber, Weeant 276
Park, Arthur 258
Parker, Alexr. 268
  Edwd./Edward 258,271
  James 268
  John 268
  Richard/Rd. 274,277,286
  Robert 268,269,278
Parttrick, Samuell 249
Paton, Archy 277
Patten, James/Jas. 251,258
Patton, James 251
Paul, Jno./John 279
Paxton, James 248
Payton, Elias 279
  Elijah 274,279
Peak, Jeto 289
  John 282,286
Pearce, James 265
Pearl, Zach. 280
Pearson, John 286
Peary, Bartlet 282
Pelham, Bijah 277
  Frances 277
Penc, Ben 274
Perkins, Constant 271
  Thomas 273
Perry/Pery, Edmond 284
  John 289
  Larkin 284,286
  Thos. 284
Person, Moses 280
Peters, Jno./John 261
  Peter 277
Peyton, Garnett 265
  William 251,255
Phelps, Anthony 249,250
  Cary 260
  Jno. 260
  John, Jr. 260
  Josiah 249
Philip/Philips/Phillips,
  Charles 277
  Jones 354
  P./Peter 274,275
Piburn, Lewis 277
Pickins, John 280
Pierpoint, Charles 274
Piety, Thomas 280
Pike, Archabel 279
Pile, Richd. 279
  William 274
Pitman/Pittman, John 259,
  271
  Thomas 277
  William/Wm. 248

Pitts, Josiah 285,286
  Younger 287,288
  Y. (same as above)
Poe, John 290
Poindexter, Thomas 284
Polk/Polke, Charles 249,
  278
Pollock/Polock, James 288
Polly, Eward 272
Pomeroy, George 257
Pope, Ben./Benjamin 250,
  251,255,257,258,278,280
  W./Will./Wm. 250,251,
  252,256,257,261
  Worden 266
Porter, Jno./John 283
Portwood, Page 258
Pottenger, robird 250
  Saml/Samuel 274
Powell, Edmund 248
  Wm. 270
Power/Powers, James/Jas.
  290
Prather/Preather/Prether,
  Basil/Beazel 255
Prerry, Geo. 280
Pres___, Hensley 280
Presly, Ben 260
Preston, Caroline 266
  Caroline H. 265
  Frans. 266
  Henrietta 266
  Josephine 266
  Maria 266
  William 265,266
Prewitt, Isham 273
Price, Edmund 275,278
  James 270
  Merth 257
Prichard, James 272
Priestley, Jas. 279
Pringle, Christn. 279
Pritchett, William 258
Procter/Proctor, Benj. 271
  Joseph 262
  little pag 262
  Nichs./Nicholas 262
  Reuben/Reubin 262
Protzman, Laurence 274
Pruett, Elisha 273
Pruitt, Joshua 258
Pryor, Sam/Saml. 271,278,
  279
Purcel/Pursel/Pursell,
  Benjamin 277
  Dennis 249,275
  James 275,279
  Wm. 258
Pushikon, Henry 272

Quarles, Thomas 266
Quartermous, James 253,257
Quinn, Benjamin 284
Quirk, Thomas/Thos. 256

Raburn, Andw. 287
Raine, James 279
Rainey, John 288
Raman, James 275
Randolph, Beverley 270
Rane, Joseph 275
Raney, Robart 288
  Robert, Jr. 288
Rapier, Richard Jas. 274
Rarden, Henry, Sr. 290
Ray, Benjamin 287
  Jno./John 274,275,287
  Moses 287
  Nathaniel 277
  Samuel 274
  William 277
Read, Charles 274
  John 274,278,280

Read, cont'd:
  Mordecai 290
  Philip 279
Reager, Burkr. 255
  Jacob 255
Reamer, Abraham, Jr. 279
  Abraham, Sr. 279
Rearden, Dennis 290
  John 290
Redmon, Aron 268
Redman/Redmon, John 278
  John, Jr. 278
  Thomas 278
Reid, A. 264
  Alexander 270
  John 270
  Joseph 279
Rench, Michael 276
Renglad, James 268
Renick, James 248
Reynolds, Aaron/Aron 262,
  283,286
Rice, Fisher 272
  John 262
  Wm. 272
Richardson, W. H. 269
Richev, Jno. 276
Richison, Joseph 278
Ricket, Zachariah, Jr. 277
  Zachariah, Sr. 277
Ridge, William 278
Ridgeway, Joseph 276
  Saml. 276
Riding, Jas. 286
Riely, John 286
Ritchie, John 280
Rizer, Frederick 274
Roane, Christopher 266
Robards, Jesse 272
  Joseph 272
  Lewis 277
Robarts, Thos. 268
Robbison, Georg 278
Roberts, Anthony 274,
  J. 290
  Joseph 261
  Nely 290
  William/Wm. 253,255,
  276
Robertson, Alexander 272
  George 276
  John 277
  Richard Taylor 269
  William 277
Roberty, Hezekiah 290
Robinson, Edward 278
  Jothn. 284
  Nathan 276
Robison, George 277,278
  Nathaniel 287
Rodgers, John 272
  Mathew 249
  William 249
Rodman, Hugh 280
Rogers, ___ 289
  Barnard 262
  Edward 284
  John 284,287
  John, Sr. 286
  William/Wm. 276,283,
  286,288
  William, Jr. 286
Rootes, Philip/Phillip
  287,290
Ros, Joseph 256
Rose, Andrew 263
Ross, Hugh 248
  James 280
  John 283
Rouse, Lewis 264
Rowan, Andrew 279
  W. 278
  William 275

Rowin, Allepher 279
Rowland, Jas. 261
Roy, Wm. 271
Ruble, Jacob 279
Rucker, Angus 281
    Elliott 281,282
Rumby, Asa Harmon 281
Rumspsy, Mitchel 281
Runner, Michael 279
Rush, John 271
    Peter 271
Russell, Elizabeth J. 266
    Gervas E. 264,266
    Hannah 264,266
    James B. 266
    James L. 264,266
    John 264,265,266
    John B. 264,266
    Joshua 264,266
    Mary 264
    Susan P. 264
    William 264
Ryan, Michael 279

Salle, Stephen 337
Samuels, Jas. 249
Sanders, Henry 283,285
    John 260
    Joseph 255
    Robet. 289
    Robert 262,284
    Thomas 286
Sandusky, Antony 277
    John 277
    Samuel 278
Sanson, John 281
Saunders, Joseph 258
Savage, Nathaniel L. 266
Scholl, Peter 263
    Willm. 263
Scott, Daniel 279
    David 287
    James 251
    Jno./John 283,288,289
    Joshua 279
    Samuel 288
    Thomas 289
Searcy, Bartlet 284
    Reuben 270,289
Seary, R. 283
Seaul, Benjamin 279
Sebastian, Ben. 250,271
Shackelford, John 272
Shad, George 272
Shain, Francis 276
    Fras. 278
    Thoms. 276
Shanneg, Barnet 285
Shannon, George 287,288
    Hugh 283
    William/Wm. 251,258
Shay, David 276
Sheddes, James 280
Sheehy, Michl. 284
Shelby, Isaac 248,272
    James 260,261
    John 260,261
Shelton, Thos. 260
Shepard/Sheperd, Saml/Samuel 283,284,285,288
    Zenas/Zenus 283,285,287
Shephard, Peter 276
Shepherd, Adam 274,276
    Michael 276
    Wm. 276
Sherley, James 258
Sherridon, (Monetisor) 272
Sherry, Barney 287,288
Shipman, John 281
Shippen, Edwd. 266
Short, Peyton 255,271
Shortridge, Lewis 286
    William 262,284,286
Shous, Henry 284

Shumate, Nimrod 278
Silvers, John 277
    Samuel 277
Simmons, Wm. 276
Simpson, Gilbt. 268
Sims, John 283
    Matthew 260
Singleton, Edmund 272
    Jechonias 284
    Manoah 261
Sinkhowe, Samuel 284
Skely, Beallia 262
Slater, John Toms. 268
Slaughter, Cad./Cadwallader 253,254,255
    Francis (L.) 286
    Geo./George 251,255,256
Sleet, John 271
Sloan, John 248
Small, Joseph 274
Smith, Charles 267
    David 278,280
    Elizabeth J. 266
    George 272
    George Stovel(Stokes) 248
    Henry 255
    Hugh 272
    James 286
    Jno./John 265,266,271,288
    Laurence 279
    Mary 266
    Peter 252,253,254,255
    Saml. 276
    Thomas/Thos. 266,287,288
    W. 272
    William/Wm. 258,277,283,287,288
    William Calmes 248
Smyth, Saml. 279
    Tho. 280
Sneed, Jacob 270
Snell, Charles 287
Snelling, William 249
Snewbery, Christopher 287
Snilling, Hugh 276
Snody/Snoddy, John 270
Sollers, Isaac 279
South, Ben 271
    John 270
    Wm. 270
Spaur, Matts. 262
Spears, Robert 255
Speed, Ja. 248,271
Spencer/Spenser, Thomas/Tho. 278,280
Spillman, Henry 272
Springle, Michael 255
Springsone, Peter 280
Stafford, Wm. 271
Stalker, Thos. 260
Stamper, Joshua 262
Standiford, James 250,253
Standsbury, Ths. 255
Stanford, Ephraim 276
Stapp, Achills 288
Starns, Jacob 248
Steegeier, Saml1. 280
Steel, Edward 283
    William 284
Steele, Andrew 262
    John 274,275
    Wm. 284,288,289
Steglan, Samuel 279
Stephen(s) Henry 278
Stephenson, James 270,284
Stepp, Ackilis 284
Sterett, John 287
Steritt, James 288
Stevens, Henry 278
    Sollomon 249
Stevenson, Charles 274

Stevenson, cont'd:
    James 290
    John 262,289
    John, Jr. 290
    Robt. 262
    Saml. 285
    Thomas 262
Stewart, John 268,274,284
    William 258
Stillwell, Joseph 277
Stone, Asah 284
    Jno. 284
Stretch, Christopher 278
Strett, James 284
Strode, Samuel 261
Stroop, George 275
Stuart, Archey 284
    Charles 260
    John 260
Stubbs, Robt. 289
Stucker, David 283,287
    George 261
    George, Sr. 261
    Jacob 261,262,283,287
    Mical/Michel 261,262,282
    Philip/Phillip 283,287
    Stufel 261
Stull, Wm. 262
Sturgus, James A. 258
Styles, Thos. 255
Subley, Lewis 290
Suggett, John 262,284,286
Sullivan, Daniel 257
    James/Jas. 251,253,255,257
Summers, Jno./John 271,273
Suttle, Garret 280
Sutton, Richd. 278
Swan, Joseph 288

Talbot, Edmund 272
    Haile, 260,270
    Isham, Jr. 272
Tambolane, Nicholas 287
Tamplin, Jno. 261
Tannehill, Wm. 288
Tanner, John 283
    William 286
Tardiveau, P/Peter 272,273
Taylor, Benjamin, Sr. 270
    Edmund 251
    John 272
    Richard 251,257,269,270
    Thomas 278,279
    T. S. 272
    William 251,253,255,274,275
    Wm., Sr. 270
Tayton, James 274
Templin, Terrah 275
Terrell, Richard 253,254,255,271
Terry, James 275
    Keeble 262
Thomas, Abraham 272
    Elisha 286
    Henry 272
    John 272
    Mark 255,258
Thompson, Hugh 263
    John 279
    Rodes 285
    Uriah 249
Thomson, Anthony 279
    John 287,289
    Rodes 285,288
    Saml. 287
    William 248
Thorngloon, Samuel 286
Thornhill, Halesworth Valentine 280
    Hallsworth 280
Thrailkill, Jessey 286

Threlkeld, Jesse 283
  John 272
  Moses 272
  William 285
Thruston, B. 255
  Buckner 253,254
  Charles 255
  Charles M. 254
  Charles Mayn/Mynn 251
Tiller, Wm. 281
Tinsley, Samuel 266
Todd, Jane 260
  Jno./John 251,260,261
  Levi 269
  Owen 268
  Robt/Robert 256,260
Tolber, William 284
Tomlin, William 262
Torrance, John 286
Torrans, John 263
Towns, Oswald 263
Townsley, Thos. 289
Townzin, Anze 260
Trigg, William 271
Trimble, William 268
Trotter, James 268
Truman, Edwd. 249,276
Tucker, George 275
  John 277
Tudor, John 260
Tuel/Tuell, John 257
Turner, Edward 260
  James 260
  Philip 271
  Will 288
  Wm. 285
Turpin, William 259,260
Tutt, Thomas 272
Twyman, James 262,287
  Reuben 284
  William 284
Tyler, Edward 255,257
  Robert 249,255,258

Uerel, Richard 280
Uncile, John 249
Underhill, James 277
Underwood, Josiah 261
Unsel, John 280
Uppum, Robert 285
Uselton, George 284
  John 284

Vace, James 281
Vaden, Henry 289
  Wm. 286
Vader, Jacob 275
Vallandingham, Lewis 284
Vance, David 262
  John 268
Vancleave, John 261
  John, Sr. 261
  Wm. 261
Vandewall, John 271
Vanlandingham, ___ 284
Vanmatre, Jacob 261
Vanzant, John 283,285,287,
  288
Varney, Andrew 281
Vaughan, Andrew 280
  John 258,284,288
  Vaughter, ___ 265
Vawter, William 266
Vigo, Francis 250
  Peter (slave) 250
Vertrees, John 274
Vitertow/Vittertow, Daniel
  249
  Samuel 249
Voisst, Cornelius 276
Vorhees, John 258
Vorhies, James 257

Wade, Zacharia 326

Wakeland, Wm. C. 272
Waker, Joseph 268
Walford, Federick 281
  John 281
Walker, David 271
  Mathew 263
  Phillip 278
  Richard 271
  Samuel 268
Wallace, Caleb 271
  Joseph 283
  Nathaniel 276
Waller, John 267
Walter, Mat. 275
Walton, Matthew 275
Wapshatt, G. 277
Wapshott, Graves 274
Ward, James 268
  Wm. 268
Ware, Edmd. 272
Warford, John 248,255
  Mos. 255
Warigh, Saml. M. 288
Waters, Philemon 277
  Richd. J. 255
  Richard Jones 254
Watkins, John 284,289
  John, Jr. 269
  Saml. 255
  Samewil 258
Watson, Henry 277
  James 277
  William 277
Watts, John 272,286
  Peter 273
Waugn, John 289
Wayne, ___ 281
Webb, Edward 286
  Forest 283,286
  Jacob 281
Weet, Robbert 258
Weit, Rannel 258
Welch, Thomas 259
Wells, Henry 260
  Samuel 255,257
West, Edward 283,287,288
  Edward, Sr. 285
  James 283,285,286,288
  Lewis 283,285,287
  Lyn 286
  Tho. 272
  William/Wm. 287,288
  Wm. M. 283
  Wm. Mills 285
Westerfield, Samuel 248,258
Whilledge, Thos. 249
Whitacre, John 249
Whitaker, Aquilla 251,257
White, Andrew 274
  Benjamin 281
  James 279,280,289
  Joel 284,286
Whitledge, Thomas 251
Whittington, Joshua 289
Wible, Adam 249,279
  John 249
Wiett, ___ 288
Wigmore, John 262
Wilcocks, Daniel 262
Will, James 268
Willhide, Lewis 273
William, John 279
Williams, Dan/Daniel 270,
  271
  Edward/Edwd. 260
  Garret 249,258
  Isaac 271
  Jacob 270,276
  James 277
  Jno./John 262,266,276,
  289
  Peter 262
  Phil 260
  Samuel 277

Williams, cont'd:
  Wm. M. 271
Williamson, David 284
  John 257
Willis, Edwd. 271
Wills, George 268
Willson, Jno. 276
  Joseph 282,286
Wilson, ___ 254
  Allen 277
  Ezekiah 288
  George 258,272,276
  Henry 273
  James 283
  John 270,272,277
  Robert 280
  Samuel 277
  William/Wm. 277,283
Wims, James 274
Win, Jno. 276
Winn, James 279
  Thos. M. 279
Wintzell, Danl. 255
Wise, Henry 280
  Philip 276
Withers, Cain 274,279
  James 261
Wood, Edmond 286
  Thomas 279,283,288
  Wm. 270
Woodruff, John 262
Woods, Abijah 262
  Archibald 270
  David 272
  James 280
  Peter 270
  Saml. 272
Woodson, Frederick 266
Woolfolk, Elijah 285
  Richard 253,255,271
  Smyel 283
  Thomas 283,285,289
Wor, Zacharrahs 280
Worrel/Worrell, William
  285,287,289
  William, Jr. 285
Wren, Vincent 272
Wright, David, Jr. 272
  William 276

Yeater, Isack 258
Yoder, Jacob 274,276,279
Young, Bryan 274,278
  Henry 278
  Jas. 271
  John 274,278
  Lewis 290
  Peter 276
  Richd. 283,289
  Wm. 278

SLAVES:
Wills, Cretia 268
  David 268
  Easter 268
  Fanny 268
  Silvia 268

NO SURNAME:
_____, Adam 271
_____, Harly 260
_____, Jacob 279
_____, Jams 277
_____, Joseph 272
_____, Samuel 263
_____, Wilhelm 261

www.ingramcontent.com/pod-product-compliance
Lightning Source LLC
Chambersburg PA
CBHW020055020526
44112CB00031B/186